READINGS IN
GREEK HISTORY

READINGS IN GREEK HISTORY

Sources and Interpretations

SECOND EDITION

D. Brendan Nagle

Professor Emeritus of History
University of Southern California

Stanley M. Burstein

Professor Emeritus of History
California State University, Los Angeles

New York   Oxford
OXFORD UNIVERSITY PRESS

Oxford University Press is a department of the University of Oxford.
It furthers the University's objective of excellence in research, scholarship,
and education by publishing worldwide.

Oxford   New York
Auckland   Cape Town   Dar es Salaam   Hong Kong   Karachi
Kuala Lumpur   Madrid   Melbourne   Mexico City   Nairobi
New Delhi   Shanghai   Taipei   Toronto

With offices in
Argentina   Austria   Brazil   Chile   Czech Republic   France   Greece
Guatemala   Hungary   Italy   Japan   Poland   Portugal   Singapore
South Korea   Switzerland   Thailand   Turkey   Ukraine   Vietnam

For titles covered by Section 112 of the U.S. Higher Education Opportunity
Act, please visit www.oup.com/us/he for the latest information about
pricing and alternate formats.

Published by Oxford University Press
198 Madison Avenue, New York, NY 10016
www.oup.com

Oxford is a registered trademark of Oxford University Press.

Library of Congress Cataloging-in-Publication Data

Nagle, D. Brendan, 1936–
Readings in Greek history : sources and interpretations / D. Brendan Nagle,
Professor Emeritus of History, University of Southern California;
Stanley M. Burstein, Professor Emeritus of History,
California State University, Los Angeles. —Second Edition.
    pages cm
ISBN 978-0-19-997845-8 (pbk. : alk. paper)
1. Greece—History—To 146 b.c.   2. Greece—History—To 146 b.c.—Sources.
I. Burstein, Stanley Mayer.   II. Title.
DF12.N35 2013
938—dc23   2013005119

Printing number: 9 8 7 6 5 4 3 2 1

Printed in the United States of America
on acid-free paper

To the memory of our parents

Mary and Dermot Nagle

and

Eva and Maxwell Burstein

CONTENTS

LIST OF MAPS AND FIGURES

Maps

Figures

TIMELINE

PERIOD	EVENTS	CULTURAL DEVELOPMENTS
Greek Bronze Age **3000–1200 B.C.**	2300–2000: Indo-European speaking peoples spread throughout Greece and Anatolia. 2200–1400 B.C.: **Minoan Age** in Crete. 1900 B.C.: Proto-states (also called "Palaces") develop in Crete. Trading contacts with mainland Greece and Middle East. 1600–1200 B.C.: **Mycenaean Age** of Greece. Proto-states ("palaces") flourish at Mycenae, Pylos, Athens, and elsewhere. Shaft grave period. 1490–1375 B.C.: Mycenaean dominance of Crete. 1200–1050 B.C.: **Collapse of Mycenaean** proto-states. Widespread destruction throughout Aegean and Levant.	2500 B.C.: Use of bronze spreads throughout the Aegean. 1800 B.C.: **Linear A**, an early form of writing, is developed in Crete. 1450 B.C.: Greek form of writing, **Linear B**, develops. 1200–1050 B.C.: Onset of **Dark Ages** in Greece with loss of writing and arts of high civilization.
Greek Dark Age **1050–750 B.C.**	1050 B.C.: Immigration of Greeks to Ionian coast of Asia Minor. Small chiefdoms emerge throughout Greece.	1050 B.C.: Iron technology spreads in the Aegean. 1050–900 B.C.: Protogeometric pottery.

continued

PERIOD	EVENTS	CULTURAL DEVELOPMENTS
	900 B.C.: Greek **revival** begins with an increase in population and revived contacts with the Middle East.	900–750 B.C.: Geometric pottery styles develop. 800 B.C.: Greeks develop an **alphabet** based on a Phoenician model.
	800 B.C.: Rapid expansion of population and cultivation of new agricultural land.	776 B.C.: Traditional date of first **Olympic Games**.
The Archaic Age	750 B.C.: Rise of small **city-states** (*poleis;* sing. *polis*). Greeks begin to migrate to sites throughout the Mediterranean, Adriatic, and Black Sea areas.	750–720 B.C.: *Iliad* and *Odyssey* ascribed to epic poet **Homer** composed.
	700–650 B.C.: Massed infantry or **hoplite** style warfare develops.	720 B.C.: Borrowing of art motifs from Middle East ("Orientalizing Period").
	670–500 B.C.: Strong men (**"Tyrants"**) rule in many Greek cities.	700 B.C.: Epic poet **Hesiod** composes the *Theogony* and *Works and Days*. Many other poets compose poems continuing or expanding on the work of Homer and Hesiod.
	650 B.C. Lycurgan reforms at Sparta.	650 B.C.: First stone temples built. Corinthian black figure-style pottery.
	620 B.C. **Draco** compiles a law code at Athens.	600–500 B.C.: Minting of coins pioneered by Lydians of Asia Minor. Emergence of philosophical, scientific, and mathematical speculation with such figures as Thales, Anaximander, Anaximenes, **Pythagoras**. Age of Lyric poets: Alcman, **Pindar, Sappho**, Simonides, and others.
		582–573 B.C.: Pythian, Isthmian, and Nemean games initiated. With the Olympic games they become the principal **panhellenic festivals**.
	560–510 B.C.: Peisistratid tyranny at Athens.	530 B.C.: Athenian red figure vases.

continued

PERIOD	EVENTS	CULTURAL DEVELOPMENTS
	545 B.C.: Conquest of Ionian Greeks by Persians. Sparta dominant in Peloponnese. 507–501 B.C.: Reforms of **Cleisthenes** at Athens. 499–494 B.C. Ionian Greek **revolt** against the Persians. 490 B.C.: First Persian invasion of mainland Greece. Athenians fend off Persians at **Marathon.** 480–479 B.C.: Second Persian invasion. Greek victories at **Salamis, Plataea,** and Mycale.	518–446 B.C.: Lyric poet Pindar composes hymns, dance songs, dirges, choral victory songs, and other poems.
The Classical Age **480 B.C.–323 B.C.**	477 B.C.: **Delian League** established for defense of Greece against Persians. Expansion of democracy at Athens.	480–323 B.C.: Classical style of art spreads throughout Greek world. Itinerant teachers, **"sophists"** move from city to city offering courses in natural philosophy, math, science, and especially the techniques of persuasion and oratory. 470–456 B.C.: Temple of Zeus at Olympia constructed. 472–458 B.C.: Tragic playwright **Aeschylus** active. Surviving plays include *The Persians, Seven Against Thebes, Suppliant Women, Oresteia.*
	461 B.C.: Rise of **Pericles** to power at Athens. 460–445 B.C.: First Peloponnesian War between Athens and Sparta and their allies.	450 B.C.: **Herodotus** at work on his *Histories.* 447–409 B.C.: Tragic playwright **Sophocles** composes over 120 plays. Surviving plays include *Ajax, Antigone, Electra, Oedipus the King, Suppliants, Philoctetes.*
	457 B.C.: Athens builds long walls connecting the city and the port of Piraeus.	447–432 B.C.: Temple of Athena (the Parthenon) built at Athens. 438–408 B.C.: Tragic playwright **Euripides** composes some 90 plays, among them *Alcestis, Bacchae, Medea, Hippolytus, Helen, Andromeda, Orestes.* 431 B.C.: **Thucydides** begins his history of the Peloponnesian War.

continued

PERIOD	EVENTS	CULTURAL DEVELOPMENTS
	431–404 B.C. **Peloponnesian War**	
	430 B.C.: Plague at Athens.	
	429 B.C.: Death of Pericles.	425–405 B.C.: Comic playwright **Aristophanes** composes 43 plays of which 11 survive, among them *Archarnians, Knights, Clouds, Wasps, Lysistrata, Frogs,* and *Peace.*
	415–413 B.C.: **Sicilian Expedition**. Major Athenian defeat.	
	411–410 B.C.: Oligarchic coup at Athens.	
	404 B.C.: **Fall of Athens**. Long walls pulled down. Thirty Tyrants rule at Athens.	
	403 B.C.: Fall of the Thirty. Restoration of democracy at Athens.	399–360 B.C.: **Xenophon** composes *Anabasis, Hellenica, Cyropaedia, Apology, Symposium, Socratic Memoirs, Oeconomicus,* and other works.
	401 B.C. Cyrus attempts to unseat his brother, Artaxerxes II, king of Persia, with the help of Greek mercenaries. The expedition fails and Xenophon leads the 10,000 mercenaries back to Asia Minor.	399–345 B.C.: **Plato** composes his dialogues and founds the **Academy**.
	394–391 B.C.: Long walls rebuilt at Athens.	380 B.C. In his *Panegyricus,* the orator and important educator **Isocrates** urges Greece to unite under the leadership of Athens and Sparta.
	399 B.C.: Trial and **Death of Socrates**.	
	377 B.C.: Athens forms a new naval league.	375–330 B.C.: Works of sculptor Praxiteles.
	371 B.C.: Peace between Sparta and Athens. Thebans defeat Spartans at Battle of Leuctra.	
	371–362 B.C.: Preeminence of Thebes.	368–348 B.C. **Aristotle** studies at the Academy.
	359 B.C.: **Philip II** accedes to throne of Macedon.	
	356 B.C.: Birth of **Alexander III** (the Great).	352–340 B.C. **Demosthenes'** orations against Philip (the *Philippics*).

continued

PERIOD	EVENTS	CULTURAL DEVELOPMENTS
		Ca. 350 B.C.: **Aeneas Tacticus** writes the first theoretical work on warfare in Greek.
		347 B.C.: Death of Plato.
		346 B.C.: Isocrates encourages Philip to unite Greece in a crusade against Persia (*Philippus*).
	338 B.C. Defeat of Thebes and Athens by Philip II at **Battle of Chaeronea**. Formation of **Corinthian League**.	338 B.C.: Death of Isocrates.
	337 B.C.: Corinthian League declares war on Persia.	
	336 B.C.: Philip II assassinated; accession of Alexander III.	
	335 B.C.: Thebes revolts and is destroyed by Alexander.	335 B.C.: Aristotle founds his school, the **Lyceum**.
	334 B.C. Alexander launches his campaign against Persia. **Battle of the Granicus**.	
	333 B.C.: **Battle of Issus**.	
	332 B.C.: Alexander's conquest of Egypt.	
	331 B.C.: Alexander founds **Alexandria; battle of Gaugamela**. Alexander occupies Babylon, Susa, and Persepolis.	331 B.C.: Alexander visits the shrine of Zeus Ammon at Siwah in Libya.
	327–325 B.C.: Indian Campaigns.	
	323 B.C.: **Death of Alexander at Babylon**.	324 B.C.: Trial and exile of Demosthenes.
The Hellenistic Age: 323–30 B.C.	323–301 (?)B.C.: Wars among Alexander's successors. Emergence of **Ptolemaic, Seleucid, and Antigonid** kingdoms.	322 B.C.: Death of Aristotle and Demosthenes.
		321–292 B.C.: Career of comic playwright **Menander**.
		306 B.C.: **Epicurus** founds the "Garden," a school of philosophy, at Athens.
		301 B.C.: **Zeno** founds the Stoic School of philosophy at Athens.

continued

PERIOD	EVENTS	CULTURAL DEVELOPMENTS
		307–283 B.C.: Ptolemy I of Egypt founds the **Museum and Library** at Alexandria.
		362 B.C.: **Diogenes**, a major figure in Cynic philosophy, settles in Athens. Death of Zeno.
	274 B.C. First Syrian War: Antiochus I defeats Ptolemy II.	Third century B.C.: Satyrus, Peripatetic scholar, author of biographies.
	260 B.C. Second Syrian War begins. Antiochus II vs. Ptolemy II and Antigonus.	283–222 B.C.: Poets **Theocritus**, Callimachus, and Apollonius of Rhodes.
	280–275 B.C. **Pyrrhus** of Epirus invades Italy and is defeated by Romans.	
	279 B.C.: **Gauls** (Celts) invade Greece and Asia Minor where they are known as "Galatians."	Ca. 340–260 B.C.: Philochorus, son of Cycnus. Athenian priest and historian of Athens.
	241 B.C.: **Attalus** I consolidates his rule of Pergamum; founds Attalid dynasty. Defeats Gauls 230 B.C.	246 B.C. Scientist **Eratosthenes** librarian at Alexandria. Advances in astronomy, mathematics, mechanics, medicine.
	215 B.C.: **Philip V** of Macedon joins Hannibal in war against Romans. First Macedonian War.	212 B.C.: **Archimedes** dies during siege of Syracuse by Romans.
	200–197 B.C.: Second Macedonian War: Philip V defeated by Romans at Cynoscephalae.	200 B.C.: Romans begin to compose histories of Rome in Greek.
	168–164 B.C.: Antiochus IV prohibits the practice of Judaism. Maccabee revolt leading to the reestablishment of Judaism in Judaea.	
	146 B.C.: Achaean War: Corinth sacked by Romans. Rome annexes Macedonia.	Ca. 150 B.C.: Callixeinus of Rhodes, historian of Alexandria.
		167 B.C.: Statesman, soldier, and historian **Polybius** at Rome.

continued

PERIOD	EVENTS	CULTURAL DEVELOPMENTS
		100 B.C.: Latin oratory and literature begins to flourish with such figures as **Cicero, Sallust, Livy, Catullus, Caesar, Vergil.**
		70 B.C.: Composition of 2 *Maccabees.*
		Ca. 60–7 B.C.: Life of Dionysius of Halicarnassus. Literary critic and historian of Rome from the foundation of the city to the First Punic War.
	31 B.C.: **Battle of Actium** and suicide of Antony and Cleopatra. Rome annexes Egypt.	Ca. 64 B.C.–25 A.D.: Life of **Strabo.**
		Ca. 60 B.C.–30 B.C.: **Diodorus of Argyrium** composes his *Library of History.*
	30 B.C.–476 A.D. Roman Empire.	40 A.D.–54 A.D.: **Curitius Rufus** writes his history of Alexander.
		Ca. 45–120 A.D.: Life of **Plutarch.**
		Ca. 86–160 A.D.: Life of **Arrian.**
		162–166 A.D.: Macedonian rhetorician **Polyaenus** dedicates his *Strategemata* to Marcus Aurelius and Lucius Verus.
		180 A.D.: **Aulus Gellius** publishes the *Attic Nights.*
		Ca. 200 A.D.: **Justin** abridges the universal history of the first-century B.C. historian **Pompeius Trogus.**

INTRODUCTION

It has been said that the study of antiquity is like trying to reconstruct the contents of the rooms of the Palace of Versailles by looking through keyholes. Some rooms are in complete darkness, and nothing is visible. Others are full of light, but only a few of the objects in the room can be made out. Yet others are poorly illuminated so that we can only guess at the room's contents. Whole floors are completely unavailable for examination, even if only through keyholes.

The reconstruction of Greek history presents similar challenges. The elite of Greek society and its interests is over-represented in the historical record while ordinary people are woefully under-represented. Even among the elites, however, only a tiny percentage are known to any extent at all. The representation of women's viewpoints—by women—is virtually non-existent, though on occasion males, such as the playwright Euripides, made good-faith efforts to guess what women might have felt about, for instance, marriage or warfare. Then there are geographical under- and over-representations. Some cities, such as Athens and Sparta, are relatively well represented, but the histories of the vast majority of the 1200-odd *poleis* that made up the Greek world are practically blank except for passing references in speeches or histories or other documents (principally originating in Athens), perhaps an inscription or two, or the mute stones of archaeological excavations where these have been undertaken.

The written sources, which constitute the bulk of the evidence for Greek history, have their own built-in biases. Inscriptions, of which there are tens of thousands, tend to be formulaic and repetitive. As for literature, it is estimated that only about 5 percent of all the compositions of ancient Greek writers actually survives. For example, of the 120 plays Sophocles wrote, only seven survive intact. Why this particular 5 percent survived was not purely—or only—a matter of accident but the product of a complicated process of selection. Some choices were made in antiquity. An ancient critic by the name of Dionysius of Halicarnassus said of the historian Polybius (much of whose history has perished), that he was "an author whom no one could bear to read to the end" (*de comparatione verborum*, 4). Most, however, were chosen for their educational value in a curriculum that gave priority to studying the classics of fifth- and fourth-century B.C. Athens. Still other choices were made by medieval intermediaries who were ultimately responsible for passing on this potpourri of antiquity to later generations. The textual evidence for Greek history ranges, as a consequence, from the highly polished literary works of *some* historians, *some* poets, *some* playwrights, and so on, to scraps of papyrus containing lists of purchases and sales. On occasion we know more about days or weeks of some periods than we do about years or whole centuries of other periods.

Then again, ancient sources are not sources in the modern sense. Sometimes our departmental colleagues who work in more recent periods of history are surprised (sometimes shocked) to find that ancient historians deal, largely, with literature, not archives. Outside of Egypt, whose climate has made possible the preservation of a mass of documentary material, there is no equivalent for ancient historians to the archives of presidential libraries or the Library of Congress, the records of institutions such as businesses, churches, and universities, or the diaries, memoirs, and papers of prominent individuals. Although military affairs predominate in Greek historical narratives, there are no minutes of the meetings of generals and their staffs before battles such as we have, for instance, for the deliberations of George Washington during the siege of Boston when his generals restrained him from a frontal (and probably doomed) assault on the city which was then occupied by the British. The closest we come to these kinds of sources are the debates Herodotus reports as having taken place in the Greek councils of war during the days before the decisive battle of Salamis. But these are reports written a generation or more after the events, not the minutes of the actual meetings.

Archaeological excavations and field surveys of large areas of the Greek world provide various kinds of material evidence that illuminate numerous areas of Greek life ignored in the written sources. Some of this evidence consists of artistic objects such as vases, statues, reliefs, and the architectural remains of temples, theaters, and other buildings. Coins produced by the thousand-plus Greek cities scattered throughout the Mediterranean and Black Sea are abundant. From Egypt come thousands of papyrus documents covering public and private affairs for the period after Alexander the Great, but the records of Greek Egypt are exceptions to the general rule.

For the earliest periods of Greek history—the whole of the second millennium (2000–1000 B.C.)—our information is derived almost exclusively from art objects, archaeological data, Middle Eastern records, and a few archives of clay tablets written in a variety of syllabic scripts from destroyed palaces in Greece and Crete. From about 1000–450 B.C. we begin to have somewhat more abundant written materials in the form of poems composed by epic poets (Homer and Hesiod, for example); lyric poets (Sappho, Pindar, and many others); genealogical poems such as the *Catalogue of Women;* and the poems of the politician and lawgiver Solon. From about 450 B.C. onward, Greek cities all over the Mediterranean generated large volumes of written material and inscriptions. With Herodotus and his successors, Thucydides and Xenophon, we get the first true histories of Greece. However, hundreds of poets, philosophers, playwrights, novelists, biographers, historians, and scientists are known only by name. Even the surviving historians are problematic. They were not like modern scholars toiling in the archives to create specialized works intended mainly for other scholars, but admired stylists who wrote mostly about events of their own times for a general public which, for the most part, heard their histories read to them rather than read them themselves.

Despite the shortcomings of our sources they constitute in their totality an amazing assemblage of materials. Pulling them together required the labor of thousands of highly competent scholars from dozens of countries over many centuries. Simply establishing the texts of the surviving documents occupied generations of scholars (palaeographers and philologists) since the Renaissance (not to mention the work done by ancient scholars prior to that time). Epigraphists have labored to gather inscriptions from all over the Greek world, publish them and, where possible, preserve them in specialized museums and institutions. Papyrologists sift through hundreds of thousands of fragments of early forms of paper (mostly papyrus, hence the name) found mainly in Egypt, to reconstruct valuable literary, economic, and social texts. Numismatists labor to catalogue and make sense of the millions of surviving coins from the scattered Greek cities of the Mediterranean and Black Sea. Survey archaeology, a new approach involving the examination of the rural territories of Greek cities, has begun to provide a new understanding of Greek agricultural life, economic, and social life. Perhaps no other period in world history, except possibly Roman history, has had such a long history of investigation, or has had so many resources lavished on it. The work continues to the present as new tools, techniques, and perspectives are brought to bear on the ancient Greek past. Students will find in this book a wide variety of written and physical sources from all periods of Greek history from the Bronze Age to the Roman Era. These sources are not presented in isolation but are grouped around important themes in order to enable students to examine important developments in Greek history from different perspectives.

New to this Edition

- New readings on the Bronze Age, religion in the Archaic and Classical Periods, Athenian democracy, and Roman relations with the Greeks
- New maps
- Revised illustration program
- New introduction on sources
- New timeline

Acknowledgments

What we have done in this book is to cherry-pick from the work of our predecessors, who made the sources of Greek history available to us in such profusion. At times we were overwhelmed by the richness of the material, but more often, time and chance had already limited our choice. Our thanks go particularly to the Oxford University Press reviewers for suggestions on how to improve our book: Lorraine Attreed, The College of the Holy Cross; Nikolaos Lazaridi, Sacramento State University; Giovanni Ruffini, Fairfield University. We continue to be grateful to Robert Miller, executive editor at the press, for encouraging the development of the first edition of this book and to our editor, Charles Cavaliere, his assistant Lauren Aylward, and their capable staff for their invaluable assistance with the second edition. Finally, we would like to thank Dr. Mahmoud Omidsalar of the John F. Kennedy Library at California State University, Los Angeles, for generously translating the Middle Persian material cited in this book. We would also like to thank the publishers, who granted us permission to reprint translations from their publications. Unattributed translations are by the authors.

1

EARLY GREECE

From the Bronze Age to the Origin and Spread of the *Polis* System

Aristotle once observed: "Man is a political animal." This famous quotation is usually invoked as evidence of Aristotle's prescience in recognizing the universality of government in human society, an interpretation he would have indignantly repudiated. A more accurate translation would be: "Man is a *polis* animal," a translation that reflects the absolute centrality of the *polis* to the ancient Greek experience. In the Greek view the *polis* set them apart from all other peoples.

The conventional translation of *polis* (pl. *poleis*) is "city-state." That term captures well one of the central features of the *polis* system—namely, that every *polis* is or ought to be independent and sovereign—but otherwise it is seriously misleading in two ways. First, the word "city" conjures up an image of large, socioeconomically diverse urban centers with imposing architecture. An unusual *polis* such as fifth-century B.C. Athens might fulfill such expectations, but the vast majority of the more than 1500 *poleis* scattered throughout the Mediterranean and Black Sea regions rarely had territories exceeding a hundred square miles and had citizen bodies of a few thousand or less, little in the way of significant public buildings, and overwhelmingly agricultural economies. Second, the word "state" suggests a formal governmental structure responsible for the maintenance of internal order and the conduct of foreign relations, but *poleis* normally had few permanent political institutions. Rather, *poleis* had *politai*, "citizens," who, in Aristotle's phrase, "govern and are governed in turn." A *polis*, therefore, was not so much a state in the modern sense of that term as it was a community of self-governing citizens. Because of the high-risk environment of these small communities, this meant in practice that the core of a *polis* was composed of adult males whose citizenship was validated by fictitious claims of descent, usually father to son, from common ancestors. Theirs and theirs alone were the rights both to own land and to participate in all aspects of public affairs and the obligation to defend the *polis* and its interests, as is well illustrated by the fact that Greek documents regularly identify as the agency responsible for political activity not the *polis*, but its citizens, not Athens or Sparta, but the Athenians or the Spartans.

Less clear is the origin of the *polis* system. Historians often claim that its origin is to be found in the rugged geography of Greece, with its limited water sources, scattered patches of farmland, and difficult communications, all of which, it is said, encouraged the political fragmentation characteristic of classical Greece. Geography, however, is not destiny. More than a century of productive archaeological activity, beginning with Heinrich Schliemann's dramatic discoveries at Troy and Mycenae in the 1870s, has demonstrated that the political landscape of second-millennium B.C. Greece was dominated by a small number of kingdoms ruled from fortified palaces. The few surviving records of these kingdoms, which are written in an early form of Greek called Linear B, reveal that, unlike the later *poleis*, these kingdoms had complex class structures and were governed by scribal bureaucracies similar to those of the states of the Ancient Near East. The Mycenaean Age and its kingdoms ended violently around 1100 B.C. Then ensued a period of severe economic and cultural retrenchment and population decline, which historians call the Dark Ages. During the almost 350 years of the Dark Ages, the basic unit of Greek life was the self-sufficient farming village, and it was from groups of such villages that the new *poleis* emerged in the eighth century B.C. The lack of significant foreign enemies during the critical early centuries of its existence allowed the *polis* system to take root and spread from its Aegean home throughout much of the Mediterranean and Black Sea basins. The result was that until the great crisis of the ancient Western world in the third century A.D., almost a millennium later, the Greeks were, as Aristotle said, "*polis* animals."

A. Greece in the Second Millennium B.C.[1]

1. THE MYCENAEAN KINGDOMS (ca. 1650–1150 B.C.)

Decipherment of Linear B by Michael Ventris

The decipherment of Linear B by Michael Ventris in 1952 revealed that fortresses such as Mycenae and Pylos in Greece and the palace of Knossos on Crete were ruled by Greek speakers during the mid- and late second millennium B.C. Although the Linear B tablets are short and cryptic administrative documents written on clay tablets accidentally baked when the fortresses were destroyed, they reveal a political and socioeconomic system totally unlike later Greece. Characteristic of these states was a centralized redistributive economy marked by large estates held by both political and religious officials (A–D), complex class structure (D), governmental maintenance of the military (E, F), and state support of religion (G).[2]

[1] Throughout this section, comments in parentheses are explanations added by the original translator. Words in brackets are words the translator believes were originally in the text but have for one reason or another been lost because a clay tablet or inscription has been broken at that point.

[2] Texts A and B are from John Chadwick, *The Decipherment of Linear B*, 2nd ed. (Cambridge, 1970), p. 159. Texts C–G are from Michael Ventris and John Chadwick, *Documents in Mycenaean Greek* (Cambridge, 1956), pp. 220, 244–245, 305–306, and 357.

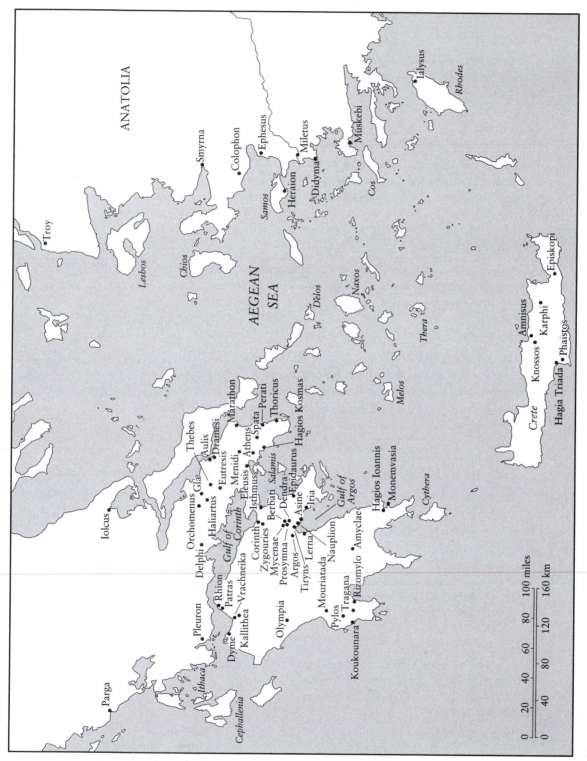

Figure 1.1 Mycenaean sites in the thirteenth century B.C.

3

A. PY Eb 297

The priestess holds (this) and claims that the deity holds the freehold (?), but the plot-owners (claim) that she holds (only) the leases of communal plots: 474 litres of wheat.

B. PY Er312

The estate of the King, seed at so much: 3600 litres of wheat. The estate of the *Lawagetas* [=*Leader of the People, war leader?*]: 1200 litres of wheat. (The lands) of the *teslestai* [=*functionaries*], so much seed: 3600 litres of wheat: so many telestai: 3 men. The deserted (?) (land) of the cult-association: seed at so much: 720 litres of wheat.

C. 96=Un02 [138]

At Pylos: *due* from *Dunios*: 2220 litres of barley, 526 litres of *eating* olives, 468 litres of wine, fifteen rams, eight *yearlings*, one ewe, thirteen he-goats, twelve pigs, one *fat hog*, one cow, two bulls.

D. 116=En659

#6 The *private* (plot) of ?*Qᵘēleqᵘhontās*, so much seed: 276 litres (of) wheat. Now this is how the *tenants* hold plots belonging to ?Qᵘēleqᵘhontās:

R., servant (m.) of the god, holds a *lease*, so much seed: 12 litres (of) wheat,
W. the priest holds a *lease*, so much seed: 12 litres (of) wheat,
Thuriatis, servant (f.) of the god, from P. (!) the old man, so much seed: 108 litres (of) wheat.
T. servant (m.) of the god, holds a *lease*, so much seed: 6 litres (of) wheat.

E. 257=Jn09+[829]

Thus the *mayors* and their wives and the vice-*mayors* and key-bearers and supervisors of *figs* and *hoeing*, will contribute bronze for ships and the points for arrows and spears:

Pi-*82, the *mayor*: 2 kilograms bronze; the vice-*mayor*: 750 grams bronze, etc. (Total: *mayors*: 39 kilograms; vice-*mayors*: 12 kilograms).

F. 267=SD0409+0481

One horse-(chariot without wheels) painted crimson, (fully) assembled inlaid with leather *cheek-straps* (and) bronze *bits*.

G. 200=Fpl (A xix)

In the month of Deukios:

To the Diktaian Zeus:	12 litres (of) oil.
To Daidaleion:	24 litres (of) oil.

To *Pa-de-*:	12 litres (of) oil,
To all the gods:	36 litres (of) oil,
To the *augur*: ?	12 litres (of) oil.
Amnisos, to all the gods:?	24 litres (of) oil,
To ?Erinys:?	6 litres (of) oil.
To **47-da-*:	2 litres (of) oil,
To the priestess of the winds:	8 litres (of) oil.
(total)	136 litres (of) oil.

2. MYCENAEAN RELATIONS WITH THE HITTITES: THE TAWAGALAWAS LETTER (SELECTIONS)

Archaeological evidence has revealed Mycenaean commercial activity throughout the central and eastern Mediterranean basin, while inscriptions and tomb paintings document diplomatic relations between the Aegean and New Kingdom Egypt. More complicated, however, were relations between a kingdom called Ahhiyawa (=Achaea) and the Hittite empire in Central Anatolia over a period of almost a century in the late second millennium B.C. Ahhiyawa is now recognized to be a Greek kingdom located somewhere in the Aegean but with possessions in Western Anatolia. In this selection the Hittite king Hattusili III (ca. 1267–1237 B.C.) writes to the king of Ahhiyawa to apologize for invading the Ahhiyawan city of Millawanda (= Miletus) while in "hot pursuit" of a "freebooter" named

John Garstang and O. R. Gurney, *The Geography of the Hittite Empire*

Figure 1.2 The Walls of Mycenae: fourteenth century B.C. The massive polygonal masonry, which was expensive and time consuming to build, argues against the walls being built to defend against an imminent threat. Photo by Stanley Burstein.

Figure 1.3 This is one of five bases of over-life-size statues of the 18th dynasty Pharaoh Amenhotep III (ca. 1391–1353 B.C.) from his mortuary temple at Thebes. Each statue represented Amenhotep as sovereign over one of the five geographical regions known to the Egyptians. The front face of this base contains cartouches with the king's titles and the names of two Aegean regions in rings surmounted by torsos and heads with arms bound behind their backs: Keftiu (biblical Caphtor) = Crete and Tny (= Tanaia = Land of the Danaoi) = Greece. On the sides of the base are the names of six identifiable locations on Crete: Amnisus, Phaestus, Cydonia, Eleia, Cnossus, and Lyctus; and four on the Greek mainland: Mycenae, possibly Messenia, Nauplion, and Cythera. The source of the Aegean list is unknown, but it proves the existence of diplomatic relations between Egypt and several Mycenaean kingdoms on Crete and the Greek mainland in the fourteenth century B.C. Photograph by J. Strange, courtesy of E. H. Cline.

Piyama-radus. Particularly interesting is the reference to previous tension between Ahhiyawa and Hattusili III, possibly concerning a state in the Troad named Wilusa (= Ilion), of which Troy may have been the capital.[3]

(I, 32–4.) These matters which I have written to you, how they [occurred], I, the Great King, have taken my oath; [let] the Storm-god hear, [and] let [the other gods] hear, how these things [*took place*].

(I, 35–52.) Now when I [had destroyed] the land of Iyalanda, though [I destroyed] the whole land, in loyalty to [*Millawanda*] Atriya as the one remaining fortress I left, and back [to Iyalanda] I came up. [So long as I was up] in Iyalanda and was *annihilating* the whole land, [*I did not go after the*]

---

[3] From John Garstang and O. R. Gurney, *The Geography of the Hittite Empire* (London, 1959), pp. 111–113.

prisoners. When there was no water [I *would have gone after them,*] but my forces were [too small and] I did not go after [the prisoners, but] came up [to rest in *Aba* . . .]. If [*Piyama-radus had not taken them* (i.e. the prisoners), I would have had] nothing against him. Now [while I was up] in *Aba*-[. . .], [I wrote to Piyama-radus] at Millawanda: "Come here to me!" [And to my brother also] before [I *crossed*] the frontier I wrote thus, *and charged him in this matter*: "The fact that Piyama-radus is making repeated attacks on this [land]—[does my] brother [know] this or does he not know it?"

(I, 53–74.) But when [my *brother's messenger*] arrived at my quarters, he brought me no [greeting] and [he brought] me no present, but he spoke [as follows]: "He has written to Atpas (saying) 'Put Piyama-radus at the disposal of the king of Hatti.'" So I went [into] Millawanda. But I went firm [also] in [this] resolution: "The words which I shall speak to Piyama-radus, the subjects of my Brother also shall hear them." But Piyama-radus escaped by ship. Awayanas and Atpas heard the charges which I had against him. Now since he is their father-in-law, why are they concealing the matter? I obtained an oath from them, so they ought to report the matter truthfully to you. . . .

(II, 58–III, 6.) See now, I have sent Dabala-Dattas, the groom. Now Dabala-Dattas is not some man of low rank; from my youth up he used to ride with me as groom on the chariot, also with your brother and with Tawagalawas he used to ride [on the chariot]. To Piyama-radus [*I have already given*] the guarantee. Now in the land of Hatti the guarantee is as follows: if one has given any man bread and *salt*, then he plans no evil against him. But over and above the guarantee I sent this (*message*): "Come, make an *appeal to* me, and I will set you on the road *to promotion*; and how I will set you on that road, that I will write to my Brother. If you are satisfied, let it be so; but if you are not satisfied, then one of my men will bring you back, just as you came, into the land of Ahhiyawa." Otherwise this groom shall stay in his place until he comes (and) until he returns thither again. And who is this groom? Since he has (a wife) of the family of the Queen—in the land of Hatti the family of the Queen is highly respected—is he not actually a brother-in-law of mine? And he shall stay in his place until he comes (and) until he returns. Greet him *kindly*, my Brother. And let [one of] you [*men*] bring him (i.e. Piyama-radus); and, my Brother, convey to him (*my*) guarantee in the following form: "Do not offend against me, the Sun, any more, and I will let [you] go back [into your land]."

(III, 52–62.) Further, behold, it is [*reported that*] he is accustomed to say: "I will go over into the land of Masa (or) the land of Karkiya, but the captives, my wife, children and household I will leave here." Now according to this rumor, during the time when he leaves behind his wife, children and household in my Brother's land, your land is affording him protection. But he is continually raiding my land; but whenever I have *prevented* him in that, he comes back into your territory. Are you now, my Brother, favorably disposed to this conduct?

(Ill, 63–IV, 10.) (If not), now, my Brother, write him at least this: "Rise up, go forth into the land of Hatti, your lord has settled his account with you! Otherwise come into the land of Ahhiyawa, and in whatever place I settle you, [*you must remain there*]. Rise up [with your captives,] your wives and children, [and] settle down in another place! So long as you are at enmity with the king of Hatti, exercise your hostility from (some) other country! From my country you shall not conduct hostilities. If your heart is in the land of Karkiya (or) the land of Masa, then go there! The king of Hatti and I—in that matter of *Wilusa* over which we were at enmity, he has converted me and we have made friends; . . . a war would not be right for us."

3. THE SEA PEOPLES AND THE END OF THE BRONZE AGE

Inscription from Medinet-Habu

The end of the Bronze Age in Greece was marked by the destruction of the Mycenaean palaces and their culture and widespread depopulation during the twelfth century B.C. But these phenomena were not limited to Greece. Archaeological and textual evidence indicate that developments in the Agean were part of a broader series of upheavals throughout the eastern Mediterranean basin. The most important account of these events is this inscription from Medinet-Habu, the mortuary temple of the Egyptian king Ramses III (ca. 1184–1153 B.C.) at Thebes, which records his successful defense of Egypt in the eighth year of his reign against a coalition of peoples historians call the Sea Peoples, which he claims had caused widespread destruction throughout central and southern Anatolia and Syria. Much is still unclear about these events, but two references in Ramses' account indicate that peoples from the Aegean took part in them. The first is the destruction of the kingdom of Alashiya on Cyprus, which archaeology indicates was followed by the settlement of a new population having Mycenaean-style material culture and speaking a form of Greek closely related to that written in the Linear B tablets. The second is the inclusion among the Sea Peoples of the Peleset—the biblical Philistines—who occupied several formerly Canaanite cities on the coast of Palestine at the end of the Bronze Age and whose material culture also was Mycenaean in character. Unlike the Greek immigrants to Cyprus, however, the Philistines ultimately were absorbed by the local Canaanite population. As a result, by the eighth century B.C. all traces of their Aegean origin had disappeared.[4]

The foreign countries conspired in their islands. Lands were disturbed and taken away in the fray at one time. Not one stood before their hands, from Kheta (= Hittites), Kode (= Cilicia), Carchemish, Arzawa (= southwest Anatolia), Alashiya (= Cyprus), they were wasted. They [set up] a camp in one place in Amor. They desolated its people and its land like that which is not. They came with fire prepared before them, forward to Egypt. Their main support was Peleset (= Philistines), Tjekker, Shekelesh, Denyen, and Weshesh. (These) lands were united, and they laid their hands upon the land as far as the Circle of the Earth. Their hearts were confident, full of their plans.

Now, it happened through this god, the lord of gods (= Amon), that I was prepared and armed to [trap] them like wild fowl. He furnished my strength and caused my plans to prosper. I went forth, directing these marvelous things. I

---

[4] Translated by James Henry Breasted, *Ancient Records of Egypt*, vol. 4. (Chicago, 1906), pp. 37–39, with corrections based on Eric H. Cline and David O'Connor, "The Sea Peoples" in: Eric H. Cline and David O'Connor (eds.), *Ramses III: The Life and Times of Egypt's Last Hero* (Ann Arbor, 2012), p. 181.

equipped my frontier in Zahi, prepared before them. The chiefs, the captains of infantry, the nobles, I caused to equip the river-mouths, like a strong wall, with warships, galleys, and barges, [---].* They were manned [completely] from bow to stern with valiant warriors bearing their arms, soldiers of all the choicest of Egypt, being like lions roaring upon the mountain-tops. The charioteers were warriors [---], and all good officers, ready of hand. Their horses were quivering in their every limb, ready to crush the countries under their feet. I was the valiant Montu (= the Theban war god), stationed before them, that they might behold the hand-to-hand fighting of my arms. I, king Ramses III, was made a far-striding hero, conscious of his might, valiant to lead his army in the day of battle.

Those who reached my boundary, their seed is not; their heart and their soul are finished forever and ever. As for those who had assembled before them on the sea, the full flame was in their front, before the river-mouths, and a wall of metal upon the shore surrounded them. They were dragged, overturned, and laid low upon the beach; slain and made heaps from stern to bow of their galleys, while all their things were cast upon the water. (Thus) I turned back the waters to remember Egypt; when they mention my name in their land, may it consume them, while I sit upon the throne of Harakhte, and the serpent-diadem is fixed upon my head, like Re (= the sun god). I permit not the countries to see the boundaries of Egypt to [---] [among] them. As for the Nine Bows (= all of Egypt's traditional enemies), I have taken away their land and their boundaries; they are added to mine. Their chiefs and their people (come) to me with praise. I carried out the plans of the All-Lord, the august, divine father, lord of the gods.

B. Greek Definitions of the *Polis*

The Politics *of Aristotle (384–322 b.c.) is the fullest and most important surviving ancient analysis of the* polis *system. The central feature of all of Aristotle's works is the attempt to base theoretical analysis on an extensive body of empirical data, and especially so in the* Politics. *The content of the* Politics *was derived from data collected for a survey of political behavior unequaled in scope and scale before modern times: the description of the constitutions (*politeiai; *sing.* politeia) *of 158 Greek and selected non-Greek states. Although not a perfectly finished work—the* Politics *seems, in fact, to be composed of the syllabi of several courses Aristotle gave at his school in Athens sometime between 335 and his death in 322 b.c.—the work contains a comprehensive account of the* polis *system, including a description of the full variety of known* polis *constitutions (both real and imaginary) and the strengths and weaknesses of their institutions. This selection from the* Politics *provides a theoretical definition of the* polis *as a natural association of rational human beings and an analysis and evaluation of the relationships between the various categories of individuals that compose the citizen body.*[5]

Aristotle, *Politics*

[5] Aristotle, *Politics*, 1.1252a–1252b, based on translation of B. Jowett, in *The Politics of Aristotle* (Oxford, 1885).

1. THE NATURAL ORIGINS OF THE *POLIS*: "MAN IS BY NATURE A POLITICAL ANIMAL"

Out of the two relationships between man and woman, master and slave, the family first arises, and Hesiod is right when he says—"First a house and wife and an ox for the plough." . . . The family is the association established by nature for the supply of men's every day wants, and the members of it are called by Charondas "companions of the cupboard" and by Epimenides the Cretan, "companions of the manger." But when several families are united, and the association aims at something more than the supply of daily needs, then comes into existence the village. And the most natural form of the village appears to be that of a colony from the family, composed of the children and grandchildren, who are said to be "suckled with the same milk." And this is the reason why Greek states were originally governed by kings; because the Greeks were under royal rule before they came together, as non-Greeks still are today. Every family is ruled by the eldest, and therefore in the colonies of the family the kingly form of government prevailed because they were of the same blood. As Homer says (of the Cyclopes in the *Odyssey*): "Each one gives law to his children and to his wives." For they lived dispersed, as was the manner in ancient times. Wherefore men say that the Gods have a king, because they themselves either are or were in ancient times under the rule of a king. For they imagine, not only the forms of the Gods, but their ways of life to be like their own.

When several villages are united in a single community, perfect and large enough to be nearly or quite self-suffing, the state comes into existence, originating in the bare needs of life, and continuing in existence for the sake of a good life. And therefore, if the earlier forms of society are natural, so is the state, for it is the end of them, and the completed nature is the end. For what each thing is when fully developed, we call its nature, whether we are speaking of a man, a horse, or a family. Besides, the final cause and end of a thing is the best, and to be self-suffing is the end and the best.

Hence it is evident that the state is a creation of nature, and that man is by nature a political animal. And he who by nature and not by mere accident is without a state, is either above humanity, or below it; he is the "Tribeless, lawless, hearthless one," whom Homer denounces—the outcast who is a lover of war; he may be compared to a bird which flies alone.

2. THE NATURE OF CITIZENSHIP: "HE WHO HAS THE RIGHT TO TAKE PART IN DELIBERATIVE OR JUDICIAL ADMINISTRATION IS A CITIZEN"

Aristotle,
Politics

The modern term "constitution" does not do justice to politeia, *the Greek term used to translate it. A constitution or* politeia *in Greek understanding was not just a set of laws or a legal document but an entire cultural, social and economic way of life—a* bios. Poleis *differed among themselves according to their different* politeiai. *A democratic* politeia, *for instance, represented a different* bios *and not merely a different political system than, say, the* politeia *of an oligarchy. The following reading is from the introduction to Book 3 of the* Politics, *which is usually thought to contain some of Aristotle's most penetrating political analysis. Note that his idea of the* polis *is not limited to Greek examples but includes a Semitic language–speaking state, Carthage in north Africa, of which Aristotle had a high opinion.*[6]

He who would inquire into the essence and attributes of various kinds of governments must first of all ask "What is a *polis*?" At present this is a disputed question. Some say that when a *polis* does such-and-such an act it is "an act of a state," while others say no, it is not "an act of the state," but, for instance, "of the oligarchy or the tyrant" that rules the state. Secondly, the legislator or statesman is concerned entirely with the *polis* (*and so we must understand the* polis *in order to understand this activity*). Finally, a constitution (*politeia*) is an ordering of the inhabitants of a state (*according to a particular political arrangement*). Now a state is a composite or compound, and like any other whole it is made up of many parts; in this case, since it is a *polis* we are talking about, these parts are the citizens who compose it. It is evident, therefore, that we must begin by asking, "Who is the citizen, and what is the meaning of the term?"

Here again there may be a difference of opinion. He who is a citizen in a democracy will often not be a citizen in an oligarchy. We may begin by leaving out of consideration those individuals who have been made citizens in some exceptional manner, by naturalization for example. Nor is citizenship constituted by domicile, that is, simply because a person lives in a particular place, for resident aliens (*metics*) and slaves share a domicile (*with citizens but are clearly not citizens*); nor is he a citizen who has no legal right except that of suing and being sued; for this right may be enjoyed under the provisions of a treaty. Thus, metics (*resident aliens*) in many places do not possess even such rights completely, for they are obliged to have a patron, so that they participate in citizenship imperfectly, and we call them citizens only in a qualified sense, as we might apply the term to children who are too young to be on the register of citizens, or to old men who have been relieved from state duties. Of these we do not say quite simply that they are citizens, but add in the one case that they are not of age, and in the other, that they are past the age, or something of that sort; the precise expression is immaterial, for our meaning is clear. Similar difficulties to those which I have mentioned may be raised and answered about disenfranchised or exiled citizens. But the citizen whom we are seeking to define is a citizen in the strictest sense, against whom no such exception can be taken, and his special characteristic is that he shares in the administration of justice, and in public offices or magistracies.

Now of offices some are discontinuous, and the same persons are not allowed to hold them twice, or can only hold them after a fixed interval; others have no limit of time, for example, the office of a juryman or a member of the assembly (*which legislates and makes policy decisions*). It may, indeed, be argued that these are not magistrates at all, and that their functions give them no share in the

[6] Aristotle, *Politics*, 3.1274b32–1275b, based on translation of B. Jowett, in *The Politics of Aristotle* (Oxford, 1885).

government. But surely it is ridiculous to say that those who actually have sovereign power do not govern. Let us not dwell further upon this, which is a purely verbal question; what we want is a common term including both juryman and assemblyman. Let us, for the sake of distinction, call such an office "an indefinite or indeterminate office," and we will assume that those who share in such offices are citizens. This is the most comprehensive definition of a citizen, and best suits all those who are generally so called.

Such, more or less, is the definition of citizen which most satisfactorily fit all those to whom the name is applied . . . (*but this still leaves a number of difficulties*). Now we see that constitutions or *politeiai* differ in kind, and that some of them are superior and others inferior in quality; for those which are faulty or perverted are necessarily inferior to those which are free from defect. (What we mean by faulty will be explained later). It follows then that citizenship of necessity differs under each form of *politeia*. Our definition is best adapted to the citizen of a democracy; but not necessarily to other states. For in some states there is no recognized body of the people (*demos*), nor have they any regular assembly, but only extraordinary ones; and in so far as law suits are concerned, they are delegated to special groups of magistrates. At Sparta, for instance, the Ephors (*annually elected officials*) determine suits about contracts, which they distribute among themselves, while the Gerousia (*Council of Elders*) are judges of homicide, and other causes are decided by other magistrates. A similar principle prevails at Carthage; there certain magistrates decide all causes. We may, indeed, modify our definition of the citizen so as to include these states. In them it is the holder of a definite, not of an indefinite office, who legislates and judges, and to some or all such holders of definite offices is reserved the right of deliberating or judging about some things or about all things. The conception of the citizen now begins to clear up. He who has the right to take part in deliberative or judicial administration is a citizen of that state in which he has such a right. Generally speaking, a state (*polis*) is a body of citizens sufficiently numerous for securing a self-sufficient existence (*autarkeia*).

C. Greek Life in the Eighth Century B.C

1. HOMER: THE SHIELD OF ACHILLES

Homer,
Iliad

The clearest idea of Greek life at the time the polis *system originated is found in the* Iliad. *The* Iliad *and the* Odyssey *are the central texts of Greek culture—the two books familiar to all educated Greeks. Allusions to them abound in Greek literature and art from the seventh century B.C. to the end of antiquity. Two centuries of scholarship have demonstrated that these two remarkable poems are the final products of a tradition of oral poetry stretching back to the second millennium B.C. Like all such poetry—and fortunately for the historian—the Homeric epics are characterized by anachronism. While they claim to tell the story of an event of the late second millennium B.C., the Trojan War, the social and economic background against which that story unfolds is that of the poet's own time. In the case of the* Iliad, *that time is the late eighth century* B.C., *the period in which the basic elements of classical Greek civilization can first clearly be distinguished. It was also the period in which archaeologists find the first clear evidence of renewed urbanization in the Greek world after the collapse of Mycenaean civilization in the late second millennium* B.C. *A vivid picture of Greek life in war and peace at the end of the Dark Ages is found in Book 18 of the* Iliad *in the description of the shield created for the poem's hero, Achilles, by the god Hephaestus.*[7]

When he had so said he left her and went to his bellows, turning them towards the fire and bidding them do their office. Twenty bellows blew upon the melting-pots, and they blew blasts of every kind, some fierce to help him when he had need of them, and others less strong as Hephaestus willed it in the course of his work. He threw tough copper into the fire, and tin, with silver and gold; he set his great anvil on its block, and with one hand grasped his mighty hammer while he took the tongs in the other.

First he shaped the shield so great and strong, adorning it all over and binding it round with a gleaming circuit in three layers; and the baldric was made of silver. He made the shield in five thicknesses, and with many a wonder did his cunning hand enrich it.

He wrought the earth, the heavens, and the sea; the moon also at her full and the untiring sun, with all the signs that glorify the face of heaven—the Pleiades, the Hyades, huge Orion, and the Bear, which men also call the Wain and which turns round ever in one place, facing Orion, and alone never dips into the stream of Oceanus.

He wrought also two cities, fair to see and busy with the hum of men. In the one were weddings and wedding-feasts, and they were going about the city with brides whom they were escorting by torchlight from their chambers. Loud rose the cry of Hymen, and the youths danced to the music of flute and lyre, while the women stood each at her house door to see them.

Meanwhile the people were gathered in assembly, for there was a quarrel, and two men were wrangling about the blood-money for a man who had been killed, the one saying before the people that he had paid damages in full, and the other that he had not been paid. Each was trying to make his own case good, and the people took sides, each man backing the side that he had taken; but the heralds kept them back, and the elders sat on their seats of stone in a solemn circle, holding the staves which the heralds had put into their hands. Then they rose and each in his turn gave judgment, and there were two talents laid down, to be given to him whose judgment should be deemed the fairest.

About the other city there lay encamped two hosts in gleaming armor, and they were divided whether to sack it, or to spare it and accept the half of what it contained. But the men of the city would not yet consent, and armed themselves for a surprise; their wives and little children kept guard upon the walls, and with them were the men who were past fighting through age; but the others sallied

[7] Homer, *Iliad* 12, lines 290–328. From *The Iliad of Homer*, trans. Samuel Butler (London, 1914).

forth with Ares and Pallas Athena at their head—both of them wrought in gold
and clad in golden raiment, great and fair with their armor as befitting gods, while
they that followed were smaller. When they reached the place where they would
lay their ambush, it was on a river-bed to which livestock of all kinds would come
from far and near to water; here, then, they lay concealed, clad in full armor. Some
way off them there were two scouts who were on the look-out for the coming of
sheep or cattle, which presently came, followed by two shepherds who were playing on their pipes, and had not so much as a thought of danger. When those who
were in ambush saw this, they cut off the flocks and herds and killed the shepherds. Meanwhile the besiegers, when they heard much noise among the cattle as
they sat in council, sprang to their horses, and made with all speed towards them;
when they reached them they set battle in array by the banks of the river, and the
hosts aimed their bronze-shod spears at one another. With them were Strife and
Riot, and fell Fate who was dragging three men after her, one with a fresh wound,
and the other unwounded, while the third was dead, and she was dragging him
along by his heel: and her robe was bedrabbled in men's blood. They went in and
out with one another and fought as though they were living people hauling away
one another's dead.

He wrought also a fair fallow field, large and thrice ploughed already. Many
men were working at the plough within it, turning their oxen to and fro, furrow
after furrow. Each time that they turned on reaching the headland a man would
come up to them and give them a cup of wine, and they would go back to their
furrows looking forward to the time when they should again reach the headland.
The part that they had ploughed was dark behind them, so that the field, though
it was of gold, still looked as if it were being ploughed—very curious to behold.

He wrought also a field of harvest wheat, and the reapers were reaping with
sharp sickles in their hands. Swathe after swathe fell to the ground in a straight line
behind them, and the binders bound them in bands of twisted straw. There were
three binders, and behind them there were boys who gathered the cut corn in arm-
fuls and kept on bringing them to be bound: among them all the owner of the land
stood by in silence and was glad. The servants were getting a meal ready under
an oak, for they had sacrificed a great ox, and were busy cutting him up, while the
women were making a porridge of much white barley for the laborers' dinner.

He wrought also a vineyard, golden and fair to see, and the vines were loaded
with grapes. The bunches overhead were black, but the vines were trained on
poles of silver. He ran a ditch of dark metal all round it, and fenced it with a fence
of tin; there was only one path to it, and by this the vintagers went when they
would gather the vintage. Youths and maidens all blithe and full of glee, carried
the luscious fruit in plaited baskets; and with them there went a boy who made
sweet music with his lyre, and sang the Linus-song with his clear boyish voice.

He wrought also a herd of horned cattle. He made the cows of gold and tin,
and they lowed as they came full speed out of the yards to go and feed among the
waving reeds that grow by the banks of the river. Along with the cattle there went
four shepherds, all of them in gold, and their nine fleet dogs went with them. Two
terrible lions had fastened on a bellowing bull that was with the foremost cows, and

bellow as he might they haled him, while the dogs and men gave chase: the lions tore through the bull's thick hide and were gorging on his blood and bowels, but the herdsmen were afraid to do anything, and only hounded on their dogs; the dogs dared not fasten on the lions but stood by barking and keeping out of harm's way.

The god wrought also a pasture in a fair mountain dell, and a large flock of sheep, with a homestead and huts, and sheltered sheepfolds.

Furthermore he wrought a green, like that which Daedalus once made in Cnossus for lovely Ariadne. Hereon there danced youths and maidens whom all would woo, with their hands on one another's wrists. The maidens wore robes of light linen, and the youths well-woven shirts that were slightly oiled. The girls were crowned with garlands, while the young men had daggers of gold that hung by silver baldrics; sometimes they would dance deftly in a ring with merry twinkling feet, as it were a potter sitting at his work and making trial of his wheel to see whether it will run, and sometimes they would go all in line with one another, and much people was gathered joyously about the green. There was a bard also to sing to them and play his lyre, while two tumblers went about performing in the midst of them when the man struck up with his tune.

All round the outermost rim of the shield he set the mighty stream of the river Oceanus.

2. HESIOD'S *WORKS AND DAYS*

Hesiod, *Works and Days*

In The Shield of Achilles, *Homer portrays life at the end of the Dark Ages bathed in a bright light. A different and harsher vision is provided by Homer's Boeotian contemporary, the poet Hesiod. Hesiod uses the occasion of a suit between himself and his brother over the division of their father's property to describe in a manner reminiscent of the contemporary Jewish prophets life in a world in which the gods have ordained that man can prosper only through endless toil in competition with his neighbors.*[8]

(ll. 1–10) Muses of Pieria who give glory through song, come hither, tell of Zeus your father and chant his praise. Through him mortal men are famed or unfamed, sung or unsung alike, as great Zeus wills. For easily he makes strong, and easily he brings the strong man low; easily he humbles the proud and raises the obscure, and easily he straightens the crooked and blasts the proud,—Zeus who thunders aloft and has his dwelling most high. Attend thou with eye and ear, and make judgments straight with righteousness. And I, Perses, would tell of true things.

Hesiod urges his brother to understand that there is no shortcut to prosperity. Life is competition, and the only way to succeed is to work more successfully than others.

[8] Hesiod, *Works and Days* (selections). From *Hesiod, The Homeric Hymns, and Homerica,* trans. G. H. Evelyn-White (Cambridge, 1914).

So, after all, there was not one kind of Strife alone, but all over the earth there are two. As for the one, a man would praise her when he came to understand her; but the other is blameworthy: and they are wholly different in nature. For one fosters evil war and battle, being cruel: her no man loves; but perforce, through the will of the deathless gods, men pay harsh Strife her honor due. But the other is the elder daughter of dark Night, and the son of Cronos who sits above and dwells in the aether, set her in the roots of the earth: and she is far kinder to men. She stirs up even the shiftless to toil; for a man grows eager to work when he considers his neighbor, a rich man who hastens to plough and plant and put his house in good order; and neighbor vies with his neighbor as he hurries after wealth. This Strife is wholesome for men. And potter is angry with potter, and craftsman with crafts-man, and beggar is jealous of beggar, and minstrel of minstrel.

Perses, lay up these things in your heart, and do not let that Strife who delights in mischief hold your heart back from work, while you peep and peer and lis-ten to the wrangles of the court-house. Little concern has he with quarrels and courts who has not a year's victuals laid up betimes, even that which the earth bears, Demeter's grain. When you have got plenty of that, you can raise disputes and strive to get another's goods. But you shall have no second chance to deal so again: nay, let us settle our dispute here with true judgment divided our inherit-ance, but you seized the greater share and carried it off, greatly swelling the glory of our bribe-swallowing lords who love to judge such a cause as this. Fools! They know not how much more the half is than the whole, nor what great advantage there is in mallow and asphodel.

For the gods keep hidden from men the means of life. Else you would easily do work enough in a day to supply you for a full year even without working; soon would you put away your rudder over the smoke, and the fields worked by ox and sturdy mule would run to waste. But Zeus in the anger of his heart hid it, because Prometheus the crafty deceived him; therefore he planned sorrow and mischief against men. He hid fire; but that the noble son of Iapetus stole again for men from Zeus the counselor in a hollow fennel-stalk, so that Zeus who delights in thunder did not see it. But afterwards Zeus who gathers the clouds said to him in anger:

"Son of Iapetus, surpassing all in cunning, you are glad that you have outwit-ted me and stolen fire—a great plague to you yourself and to men that shall be. But I will give men as the price for fire an evil thing in which they may all be glad of heart while they embrace their own destruction."

For ere this the tribes of men lived on earth remote and free from ills and hard toil and heavy sickness which bring the Fates upon men; for in misery men grow old quickly. Or if you will, I will sum you up another tale well and skillfully—and do you lay it up in your heart,—how the gods and mortal men sprang from one source.

Although Zeus did not deprive humanity of the fire stolen by Prometheus, he and the other gods took away the possibility of a life free from suffering. In this section Hesiod describes the "fall of man" from the blessed life of the Golden Age to the harsh conditions of the Iron Age—the late Dark Ages—in which Hesiod lives.

First of all the deathless gods who dwell on Olympus made a golden race of mortal men who lived in the time of Cronos when he was reigning in heaven. And they lived like gods without sorrow of heart, remote and free from toil and grief: miserable age rested not on them; but with legs and arms never failing they made merry with feasting beyond the reach of all evils. When they died, it was as though they were overcome with sleep, and they had all good things; for the fruitful earth unforced bore them fruit abundantly and without stint. They dwelt in ease and peace upon their lands with many good things, rich in flocks and loved by the blessed gods.

But after earth had covered this generation—they are called pure spirits dwelling on the earth, and are kindly, delivering from harm, and guardians of mortal men; for they roam everywhere over the earth, clothed in mist and keep watch on judgments and cruel deeds, givers of wealth; for this royal right also they received;—then they who dwell on Olympus made a second generation which was of silver and less noble by far. It was like the golden race neither in body nor in spirit. A child was brought up at his good mother's side an hundred years, an utter simpleton, playing childishly in his own home. But when they were full grown and were come to the full measure of their prime, they lived only a little time in sorrow because of their foolishness, for they could not keep from sinning and from wronging one another, nor would they serve the immortals, nor sacrifice on the holy altars of the blessed ones as it is right for men to do wherever they dwell. Then Zeus the son of Cronos was angry and put them away, because they would not give honor to the blessed gods who live on Olympus.

But when earth had covered this generation also—they are called blessed spirits of the underworld by men, and, though they are of second order, yet honor attends them also—Zeus the Father made a third generation of mortal men, a brazen race, sprung from ash-trees; and it was in no way equal to the silver age, but was terrible and strong. They loved the lamentable works of Ares and deeds of violence; they ate no bread, but were hard of heart like adamant, fearful men. Great was their strength and unconquerable the arms which grew from their shoulders on their strong limbs. Their armor was of bronze, and their houses of bronze, and of bronze were their implements: there was no black iron. These were destroyed by their own hands and passed to the dank house of chill Hades, and left no name: terrible though they were, black Death seized them, and they left the bright light of the sun.

But when earth had covered this generation also, Zeus the son of Cronos made yet another, the fourth, upon the fruitful earth, which was nobler and more righteous, a god-like race of hero-men who are called demigods, the race before our own, throughout the boundless earth. Grim war and dread battle destroyed a part of them, some in the land of Cadmus at seven-gated Thebes when they fought for the flocks of Oedipus, and some, when it had brought them in ships over the great sea gulf to Troy for rich-haired Helen's sake: there death's end enshrouded a part of them. But to the others father Zeus the son of Cronos gave a living and an abode apart from men, and made them dwell at the ends of earth. And they live untouched by sorrow in the islands of the blessed along the shore of deep swirling Ocean, happy heroes for whom the grain-giving earth bears honey-sweet fruit flourishing thrice a year, far from the deathless gods, and Cronos rules over them; for the father of men and gods released *him* from his bonds. And these last equally have honor and glory.

And again far-seeing Zeus made yet another generation, the fifth, of men who are upon the bounteous earth. Thereafter, would that I were not among the men of the fifth generation, but either had died before or been born afterwards. For now truly is a race of iron, and men never rest from labor and sorrow by day, and from perishing by night; and the gods shall lay sore trouble upon them. But, notwithstanding, even these shall have some good mingled with their evils. And Zeus will destroy this race of mortal men also when they come to have gray hair on the temples at their birth. The father will not agree with his children, nor the children with their father, nor guest with his host, nor comrade with comrade; nor will brother be dear to brother as aforetime. Men will dishonor their parents as they grow quickly old, and will carp at them, chiding them with bitter words, hard-hearted they, not knowing the fear of the gods. They will not repay their aged parents the cost of their nurture, for might shall be their right: and one man will sack another's city. There will be no favor for the man who keeps his oath or for the just or for the good; but rather men will praise the evil-doer and his violent dealing. Strength will be right and reverence will cease to be; and the wicked will hurt the worthy man, speaking false words against him, and will swear an oath upon them. Envy, foul-mouthed, delighting in evil, with scowling face, will go along with wretched men one and all. And then Aidos (*Shame*) and Nemesis (*Retribution*), with their sweet forms wrapped in white robes, will go from the wide-pathed earth and forsake mankind to join the company of the deathless gods: and bitter sorrows will be left for mortal men, and there will be no help against evil.

Hesiod emphasizes that, above all, man should pursue justice through honest toil and not violence.

And now I will tell a fable for princes who themselves understand. Thus said the hawk to the nightingale with speckled neck, while he carried her high up among the clouds, gripped fast in his talons, and she, pierced by his crooked talons, cried pitifully. To her he spoke disdainfully: "Miserable thing, why do you cry out? One far stronger than you now holds you fast, and you must go wherever I take you, songstress as you are. And if I please I will make my meal of you, or let you go. He is a fool who tries to withstand the stronger, for he does not get the mastery and suffers pain besides his shame." So said the swiftly flying hawk, the long-winged bird.

But you, Perses, listen to right and do not foster violence; for violence is bad for a poor man. Even the prosperous cannot easily bear its burden, but is weighed down under it when he has fallen into delusion. The better path is to go by on the other side towards justice; for Justice beats Outrage when she comes at length to the end of the race. But only when he has suffered does the fool learn this. For Oath keeps pace with wrong judgments. There is a noise when Justice is being dragged in the way where those who devour bribes and give sentence with crooked judgments, take her. And she, wrapped in mist, follows to the city and haunts of the people, weeping, and bringing mischief to men, even to such as have driven her forth in that they did not deal straightly with her. But they who give straight judgments to strangers and to the men of the land, and go not aside from what is just, their city flourishes, and the people prosper in it: Peace, the nurse of children, is abroad in their land, and all-seeing Zeus never decrees cruel war against them. Neither famine nor disaster ever haunt men who do true justice; but lightheartedly they tend the fields which are all their care. The earth bears them victual in plenty, and on the mountains the oak bears acorns upon the top and bees in the midst. Their woolly sheep are laden with fleeces; their women bear children like their parents. They flourish continually with good things, and do not travel on ships, for the grain-giving earth bears them fruit. But for those who practice violence and cruel deeds far-seeing Zeus, the son of Cronos, ordains a punishment. Often even a whole city suffers for a bad man who sins and devises presumptuous deeds, and the son of Cronos lays great trouble upon the people, famine and plague together, so that the men perish away, and their women do not bear children, and their houses become few, through the contriving of Olympian Zeus. And again, at another time, the son of Cronos either destroys their wide army, or their walls, or else makes an end of their ships on the sea. . . . That man is altogether best who considers all things himself and marks what will be better afterwards and at the end; and he, again, is good who listens to a good adviser; but whoever neither thinks for himself nor keeps in mind what another tells him, he is an unprofitable man. But do you at any rate, always remembering my charge, work, high-born Perses, that Hunger may hate you, and venerable Demeter richly crowned may love you and fill your barn with food; for Hunger is altogether a meet comrade for the sluggard. Both gods and men are angry with a man who lives idle, for in nature he is like the stingless drones who waste the labor of the bees, eating without working; but let it be your care to order your work properly, that in the right season your barns may be full of victual. Through work men grow rich in flocks and substance, and working they are much better loved by the immortals. Work is no disgrace: it is idleness which is a disgrace. But if you work, the idle will soon envy you as you grow rich, for fame and renown attend on wealth. And whatever be your lot, work is best for you, if you turn your misguided mind away from other men's property to your work and attend to your livelihood as I bid you. An evil shame is the needy man's companion, shame which both greatly harms and prospers men: shame is with poverty, but confidence with wealth. . . .

Call your friend to a feast; but leave your enemy alone; and especially call him who lives near you: for if any mischief happen in the place, neighbors come ungirt, but kinsmen stay to gird themselves. A bad neighbor is as great a plague as a good one is a great blessing; he who enjoys a good neighbor has a precious possession. Not even an ox would die but for a bad neighbor. Take fair measure from your neighbor and pay him back fairly with the same measure, or better, if you can; so that if you are in need afterwards, you may find him sure.

Do not get base gain: base gain is as bad as ruin. Be friends with the friendly, and visit him who visits you. Give to one who gives, but do not give to one who does not give. A man gives to the free-handed, but no one gives to the close-fisted. Give is a good girl, but Take is bad and she brings death. For the man who gives willingly, even though he gives a great thing, rejoices in his gift and is glad in heart; but whoever gives way to shamelessness and takes something himself, even though it be a small thing, it freezes his heart. He who adds to what he has, will keep off bright-eyed hunger; for if you add only a little to a little and do this often, soon that little will become great. What a man has by him at home does not trouble him: it is better to have your stuff at home, for whatever is abroad may mean loss. It is a good thing to draw on what you have; but it grieves your heart to need something and not to have it, and I bid you mark this. Take your fill when the cask is first opened and when it is nearly spent, but midways be sparing: it is poor saving when you come to the lees.

Hesiod emphasizes that hard work, prudence, and planning are the keys to prosperity and the good life for humanity.

Let the wage promised to a friend be fixed; even with your brother smile—and get a witness; for trust and mistrust, alike ruin men. Do not let a flaunting woman coax and cozen and deceive you: she is after your barn. The man who trusts womankind trusts deceivers. There should be an only son, to feed his father's house, for so wealth will increase in the home; but if you leave a second son you should die old. Yet Zeus can easily give great wealth to a greater number. More hands mean more work and more increase. If your heart within you desires wealth, do these things and work with work upon work. . . . First of all, get a house, and a woman and an ox for the plough—a slave woman and not a wife, to follow the oxen as well—and make everything ready at home, so that you may not have to ask of another, and he refuses you, and so, because you are in lack, the season pass by and your work come to nothing. Do not put your work off till to-morrow and the day after; for a sluggish worker does not fill his barn, nor one who puts off his work: industry makes work go well, but a man who puts off work is always at hand-grips with ruin. . . . Get two oxen, bulls of nine years; for their strength is unspent and they are in the prime of their age: they are best for work. They will not fight in the furrow and break the plough and then leave the work undone. Let a brisk fellow of forty years follow them, with a loaf of four quarters and eight slices for his dinner, one who will attend to his work and drive a straight furrow and is past the age for gaping after his fellows, but will keep his mind on his work. No younger man will be better than he at scattering the seed and avoiding doublesowing; for a man less staid gets disturbed, hankering after his fellows. . . . Pass by the smithy and its crowded lounge in winter time when the cold keeps men from field work,—for then an industrious man can greatly prosper his house—lest bitter winter catch you helpless and poor and you chafe a swollen foot with a shrunk hand. The idle man who waits on empty hope, lacking a livelihood, lays to heart mischief-making; it is not an wholesome hope that accompanies a needy man who lolls at ease while he has no sure livelihood.

Farming is the surest way to prosperity, but if a person desires to supplement his income by trade, he must plan carefully to avoid the dangers of seafaring.

But if desire for uncomfortable sea-faring seize you; when the Pleiades plunge into the misty sea to escape Orion's rude strength, then truly gales of all kinds rage. Then keep ships no longer on the sparkling sea, but bethink you to till the land as I bid you. Haul up your ship upon the land and pack it closely with stones all round to keep off the power of the winds which blow damply, and draw out the bilge-plug so that the rain of heaven may not rot it. Put away all the tackle and fittings in your house, and stow the wings of the sea-going ship neatly, and hang up the well-shaped rudder over the smoke. You yourself wait until the season for sailing is come, and then haul your swift ship down to the sea and stow a convenient cargo in it, so that you may bring home profit, even as your father and mine, foolish Perses, used to sail on shipboard because he lacked sufficient livelihood. And one day he came to this very place crossing over a great stretch of sea; he left Aeolian Cyme and fled, not from riches and substance, but from wretched poverty which Zeus lays upon men, and he settled near Helicon in a miserable hamlet, Ascra, which is bad in winter, sultry in summer, and good at no time. But you, Perses, remember all works in their season but sailing especially. Admire a small ship, but put your freight in a large one; for the greater the lading, the greater will be your piled gain, if only the winds will keep back their harmful gales. If ever you turn your misguided heart to trading and wish to escape from debt and joyless hunger, I will show you the measures of the loud-roaring sea, though I have no skill in sea-faring nor in ships; for never yet have I sailed by ship over the wide sea, but only to Euboea from Aulis where the Achaeans once stayed through much storm when they had gathered a great host from divine Hellas for Troy, the land of fair women. Then I crossed over to Chalcis, to the games of wise Amphidamas where the sons of the great-hearted hero proclaimed and appointed prizes. And there I boast that I gained the victory with a song and carried off a handled tripod which I dedicated to the Muses of Helicon, in the place where they first set me in the way of clear song. Such is all my experience of many-pegged ships; nevertheless I will tell you the will of Zeus who holds the aegis; for the Muses have taught me to sing in marvelous song. . . . Another time for men to go sailing is in spring when a man first sees leaves on the topmost shoot of a fig-tree as large as the foot-print that a cow makes; then the sea is passable, and this is the spring sailing time. For my part I do not praise it, for my heart does not like it. Such a sailing is snatched, and you will hardly avoid mischief. Yet in their ignorance men do even this, for wealth means life to poor mortals; but it is fearful to die among the waves. But I bid you consider all these things in your heart as I say. Do not put all your goods in hollow ships; leave the greater part behind, and put the lesser part on board; for it is a bad business to meet with disaster among the waves of the sea, as it is bad if you put too great a load on your wagon and break the axle, and your goods are spoiled. Observe due measure: and proportion is best in all things.

A person should think of marriage and establishing a household only when his prosperity is secure. Even then, prudence in the selection of a wife is essential to success.

Bring home a wife to your house when you are of the right age, while you are not far short of thirty years nor much above; this is the right age for marriage. Let your wife have been grown up four years, and marry her in the fifth. Marry a maiden, so that you can teach her careful ways, and especially marry one who lives near you, but look well about you and see that your marriage will not be a joke to your neighbors. For a man wins nothing better than a good wife, and, again, nothing worse than a bad one, a greedy soul who roasts her man without fire, strong though he may be, and brings him to a raw old age.

D. Colonization and the Expansion of the *Polis* System: The Case of Cyrene

The Histories of Herodotus

Between the mid-eighth century B.C. and the late sixth century B.C., Greeks founded hundreds of new poleis in the Mediterranean and Black Sea basins. Founding a colony was a difficult and dangerous process with a high risk of failure, and failure could mean death for the colonists. Only strong incentives could induce people to take such risks. Dreams of wealth from trade with non-Greeks such as the iron-rich Etruscans of Italy may have attracted some potential colonists, but for most, colonization represented hope for land and a new start—an escape from the socioeconomic and political tensions of archaic Greece. The hopes and fears of those first Greek explorers and colonists are evident in the Odyssey: their fears in the fantastic tales of Odysseus' encounters with savage monsters in his wanderings, and their hopes in Homer's account of Phaeacia, the perfect polis founded in a land of plenty at the ends of the earth. For a concrete idea of the circumstances that resulted in the foundation of a colony, historians turn to the fifth-century B.C. historian Herodotus' account of the founding of the city of Cyrene in modern Libya and to a remarkable fourth-century B.C. Cyrenaean inscription which preserves the original terms under which the colony was organized.[9]

1. HERODOTUS' ACCOUNT

150. Thus far the history is delivered without variation both by the Theraeans and the Lacedaemonians; but from this point we have only the Theraean narrative. Grinus (they say), the son of Aesanius, a descendant of Theras, and king of the island of Thera, went to Delphi to offer a hecatomb on behalf of his native city. He was accompanied by a large number of the citizens,

[9] Herodotus, *The Persian Wars* 4.150–159 (selections). From *The Histories of Herodotus*, vol. 3, trans. George Rawlinson (New York, 1859–1860).

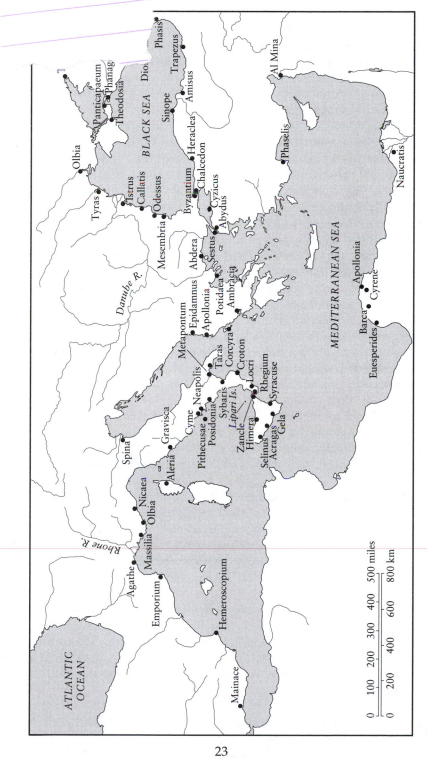

Figure 1.4 Greek colonization: 750–500 B.C.

ATLANTIC
OCEAN

Rhone R.

Danube R.

BLACK SEA

MEDITERRANEAN SEA

Phasis
Trapezus
Dios
Sinope
Amisus
Heraclea
Chalcedon
Cyzicus
Abydus
Byzantium
Sestus
Abdera
Mesembria
Odessus
Callatis
Istrus
Olbia
Tyras
Theodosia
Phanag
Panticapaeum

Al Mina
Phaselis
Naucratis

Apollonia
Cyrene
Barca
Euesperides

Epidamnus
Apollonia
Ambracia
Potidaea
Metapontum
Taras
Corcyra
Croton
Locri
Rhegium
Syracuse
Neapolis
Sybaris
Lipari Is.
Zancle
Himera
Gela
Acragas
Selinus
Cyme
Pithecusae
Posidonia
Gravisca
Spina
Aleria
Nicaea
Olbia
Massilia
Agathe
Emporium
Hemeroscopium
Mainace

0	100	200	300	400	500 miles
0	200	400	600	800 km	

23

and among the rest by Battus, the son of Polymnestus, who belonged to the Minyan family of the Euphemidae. On Grinus consulting the oracle about other matters, the priestess gave him for answer that he should found a city in Libya. Grinus replied to this, "I, O lord, am too far advanced in years, and too inactive, for such a work. Bid one of these youngsters undertake it." As he spoke, he pointed towards Battus; and thus the matter rested for that time. When the embassy returned to Thera, small account was taken of the oracle by the Theraeans, as they were quite ignorant where Libya was, and were not so venturesome as to send out a colony in the dark.

151. Seven years passed from the utterance of the oracle, and not a drop of rain fell in Thera: all the trees in the island, except one, were killed with the drought. The Theraeans upon this sent to Delphi, and were reminded reproachfully, that they had never colonized Libya. So, as there was no help for it, they sent messengers to Crete, to inquire whether any of the Cretans, or of the strangers sojourning among them, had ever traveled as far as Libya: and these messengers of theirs, in their wanderings about the island, among other places visited Itanus, where they fell in with a man, whose name was Corobius, a dealer in purple. In answer to their inquiries, he told them that contrary winds had once carried him to Libya, where he had gone ashore on a certain island, which was named Platea. So they hired this man's services, and took him back with them to Thera. A few persons then sailed from Thera to reconnoiter. Guided by Corobius to the island of Plataea, they left him there with provisions for a certain number of months, and returned home with all speed to give their countrymen an account of the island.

152. During their absence, which was prolonged beyond the time that had been agreed upon, Corobius' provisions failed him. He was relieved, however, after a while, by a Samian vessel, under the command of a man named Colaeus, which, on its way to Egypt, was forced to put in at Plataea. The crew, informed by Corobius of all the circumstances, left him sufficient food for a year. . . .

153. The Theraeans who had left Corobius at Plataea, when they reached Thera, told their countrymen that they had colonized an island on the coast of Libya. They of Thera, upon this, resolved that men should be sent to join the colony from each of their seven districts, and that the brothers in every family should draw lots to determine who were to go. Battus was chosen to be king and leader of the colony. So these men departed for Plataea on board of two fifty-oared ships. . . .

157. In this place they continued two years, but at the end of that time, as their ill luck still followed them, they left the island to the care of one of their number, and went in a body to Delphi, where they made complaint at the shrine, to the effect that, notwithstanding they had colonized Libya, they prospered as poorly as before. Hereon the priestess made them the following answer:

Knowest thou better than I, fair Libya abounding in fleeces? Better the stranger than he who has trod it? O clever Theraeans!

Battus and his friends, when they heard this, sailed back to Plataea: it was plain the god would not hold them acquitted of the colony till they were absolutely in Libya. So, taking with them the man whom they had left upon the island, they made a settlement on the mainland directly opposite Plataea, fixing themselves at a place called Aziris, which is closed in on both sides by the most beautiful hills, and on one side is washed by a river.

158. Here they remained six years, at the end of which time the Libyans induced them to move, promising that they would lead them to a better situation. So the Greeks left Aziris, and were conducted by the Libyans towards the west, their journey being so arranged, by the calculations of their guides, that they passed in the night the most beautiful district of that whole country, which is the region called Irasa. The Libyans brought them to a spring, which goes by the name of Apollo's fountain, and told them, "Here, Grecians, is the proper place for you to settle; for here the sky has a hole in it."

159. During the lifetime of Battus, the founder of the colony, who reigned forty years, and during that of his son Arcesilaus, who reigned sixteen, the Cyrenaeans continued at the same level, neither more nor fewer in number than they were at the first. But in the reign of the third king, Battus, surnamed the Happy, the advice of the Pythian priestess brought Greeks from every quarter into Libya, to join the settlement. The Cyrenaeans had offered to all comers a share in their lands; and the oracle had spoken as follows:

> He that is backward to share in the pleasant Libyan acres, Sooner or later, I warn him, will feel regret at his folly.

Thus a great multitude were collected together to Cyrene, and the Libyans of the neighborhood found themselves stripped of large portions of their lands.

2. THE OATH OF THE COLONISTS[10]

Resolved by the Assembly. Since Apollo spontaneously told Battus and the Theraeans to found a colony in Cyrene, the Theraeans decided to dispatch Battus as the founder of the colony and king. The Theraeans shall sail as his comrades. They shall sail on equal terms; and one son shall be enrolled from each family. Those who sail shall be adults, and any free man from the Theraeans who wishes, may also sail.

Foundation Decree of Cyrene

If the colonists secure the settlement, any colonist who sails later to Libya shall have a share in the citizenship and honors. He also shall receive a lot from the unassigned land. But if they do not make the settlement secure, and the Theraeans cannot come to their aid and they suffer troubles for five years, the colonists may

---

[10] *Supplementum Epigraphicum Graecorum* 9.3. From Sarah B. Pomeroy et al., *Ancient Greece: A Political, Social and Cultural History* (New York, 1999), p. 92. Used by permission.

return without fear to Thera. They may return to their own property and become citizens of Thera.

If anyone is unwilling to sail when sent by the city, let him be subject to the death penalty and let his property be confiscated. Whoever receives or protects such a person—whether a father his son or a brother his brother—shall suffer the same punishment as the person who refused to sail. On these terms oaths were sworn by those remaining at Thera and those sailing to found the colony. They also cursed those who transgressed these conditions and did not abide by them, both those settling in Libya and those staying here.

They formed wax images and burned them while they uttered these curses, all of them together, men and women, boys and girls. The person who does not abide by these oaths, but transgresses, shall melt and flow away just as these images, he and his descendants and his property. But may there be many things and those good ones to those who abide by these oaths, both those sailing to Libya and those remaining in Thera, to themselves and their descendants.

E. Greeks and Non-Greeks in the Greek Colonies: The Foundation of Lampsacus

Plutarch, *Virtues of Women*

Colonization always involves encounters between peoples, and Greek colonization was no exception. Polyphemus, the cannibalistic Cyclops whose people "had no council places and laws" in the Odyssey, *was every colonist's nightmare, but few actually met such savages. Greek settlers sought land to farm and opportunities for trade, and that search brought them into areas already inhabited by settled populations. The results of such encounters varied. Sometimes they were mutually beneficial, as in central Italy or southern France, where the appearance of Greek luxury goods in native settlements attests to profitable trade. More often, unfortunately, the meeting was marked by suspicion and even violence, as is briefly noted at the end of Herodotus' account of the foundation of Cyrene, and as is clearly illustrated in this "cuckoo-in-the-nest" story taken by Plutarch from the history of the city of Lampsacus on the Turkish coast of the Hellespont by the fifth-century B.C. historian, Charon of Lampsacus.*[11]

There were twin brothers named Phobus and Blepsus from Phocaea, members of the family of the Codridae. One of these brothers, Phobus, was the first to throw himself into the sea from the Leucadian rocks, as Charon, the Lampsacenian, records. Possessing royal power and influence, he sailed along the coast to Parium on personal business. Becoming a friend and guest of Mandron, the ruler of the Pityoessenian Bebrycians, he came to their aid and fought as the ally of this people which was being harassed by its neighbors.

Mandron gave many other signs of friendliness to Phobus when he sailed away and promised to give him a portion of the land and city if he should wish to come

[11] Plutarch, *Virtues of Women* 18.

to Pityoessa together with colonists from Phocaea. Phobus, therefore, persuaded his fellow citizens and dispatched his brother, who brought colonists with him. The colonists received from Mandron what they expected. Growing rich from spoils and loot seized from neighboring barbarians, they became first sources of envy and then fear to the Bebrycians. Desiring, therefore, to rid themselves of the settlers, they failed to persuade Mandron, who was a good and just man with regard to the Greeks. When Mandron was away, however, they prepared a plot to kill the Phocaeans.

Lampsace, the daughter of Mandron, an unmarried young woman, who had foreknowledge of the plot, at first tried to deter her friends and relatives and convince them that they were setting their hands to a terrible and unholy deed in killing men who had been benefactors and allies and now were fellow citizens. But as she did not persuade them, she told the Greeks in secret what was being done and urged them to be on their guard. They prepared a sacrifice and feast and invited the Pityoessenians to come outside the city to it. Then they divided themselves into two groups, and one seized the walls and the other slaughtered the Pityoessenians.

After gaining control of the city in this way, they sent after Mandron and urged him to rule jointly with men chosen from themselves. Lampsace, who had died from an illness, they buried in great state in the city and named it Lampsacus after her. And when Mandron begged off living with them in order to escape the suspicion of treachery and asked that he be allowed to take with him the children and wives of the dead, they sent them away gladly without doing them any harm. To Lampsace they first gave heroic honors and later they voted to offer sacrifice to her as a goddess; and they continue doing so.

F. Greeks and Scythians in the Black Sea: Coexistence and Interaction

Not all encounters between Greek colonists and non-Greeks ended in the sort of definitive Greek victory celebrated in the story of Lampsace. On the north coast of the Black Sea, Greek settlers came in contact with the Scythians, Iranian-speaking nomads who dominated the steppe lands of Ukraine. Greek cities such as Olbia, a Milesian colony located on the lower Bug River in western Ukraine, had to find accommodations with the Scythians to survive. The resulting interaction was beneficial for both peoples. The Greek colonies provided trade goods and artisans, who created spectacular art works for the Scythian elite in exchange for the products of their territory such as skins, slaves, and grain. The terms of such accommodation were always precarious and required constant negotiation, as is clearly illustrated by Herodotus' vivid account of the unfortunate fate of the Scythian king Scylas, who tried to live in both worlds.[12]

The History of Herodotus

[12] From *The History of Herodotus*, trans. George Rawlinson (New York, 1859–1860).

76. The Scythians have an extreme hatred of all foreign customs, particularly of those in use among the Greeks. . . .

78. Ariapeithes, the Scythian king, had several sons, among them, this Scylas, who was the child, not of a native Scyth, but of a woman of Istria. Brought up by her, Scylas gained an acquaintance with the Greek language and letters. Some time afterwards, Ariapeithes was treacherously slain by Spargapeithes, king of the Agathyrsi; whereupon Scylas succeeded to the throne, and married one of his father's wives, a woman named Opoea. This Opoea was a Scythian by birth, and had brought Ariapeithes a son called Oricus. Now when Scylas found himself king of Scythia, as he disliked the Scythic mode of life, and was attached, by his upbringing to the manners of the Greeks, he made it his usual practice, whenever he came with his army to the town of the Borysthenites (= *Olbia*), who, according to their own account, are colonists of the Milesians. He made it his practice, I say, to leave the army before the city, and having entered within the walls by himself, and carefully closed the gates, to exchange his Scythian dress for Greek garments, and in this attire to walk about the market-place, without guards or retinue. The Borysthenites kept watch at the gates, so that no Scythian might see the king dressed this way. Scylas, meanwhile, lived exactly as the Greeks, and even offered sacrifices to the gods according to the Greek rites. In this way he would pass a month, or more, with the Borysthenites, after which he would clothe himself again in his Scythian dress, and so take his departure. This he did repeatedly, and even built himself a house in Borysthenes, and married a wife there who was a native of the place.

79. But when the time came, that was ordained to bring him woe, the occasion of his ruin was the following. He wanted to he initiated in the rites of the Bacchic Dionysus, and was on the point of obtaining admission to the rites, when a most strange prodigy occurred to him. The house, which he possessed, as I mentioned a short time back, in the city of the Borysthenites, a building of great extent and erected at a vast cost, round which there stood a number of sphinxes and griffins carved in white marble, was struck by lightning from on high and burnt to the ground. Scylas, nevertheless, went on, and received the initiation. Now the Scythians generally reproach the Greeks with their Bacchanal rage, and say that it is not reasonable to imagine there is a god who impels men to madness. No sooner, therefore, was Scylas initiated in the Bacchic mysteries than one of the Borysthenites went and carried the news to the Scythians. "You Scyths laugh at us," he said, "because we rave when the god seizes us. But now our god has seized upon your king, who raves like us, and is maddened by the influence. If you think I do not tell you true, come with me, and I will show him to you." The chiefs of the Scythians went with the man accordingly, and the Borysthenite, conducting them into the city, placed them secretly on one of the towers. Presently Scylas passed by with the band of revelers, raving like the rest, and was seen by the watchers. Regarding the matter as a very great misfortune, they instantly departed, and came and told the army what they had witnessed.

80. When, therefore, Scylas, after leaving Borysthenes, was about returning home, the Scythians broke out into revolt. They put at their head Octamasadas, grandson (on the mother's side) of Teres. Then Scylas, when he learned the danger with which he was threatened, and the reason of the disturbance, made his escape to Thrace. Octamasadas, discovering whither he had fled, marched after him, and had reached the Ister (= *Danube*), when he was met by the forces of the Thracians. The two armies were about to engage, but before they joined battle, Sitalces sent a message to Octamasadas to this effect, "Why should there be trial of arms between us? You are my own sister's son, and you have in your keeping my brother. Surrender him into my hands, and I will give Scylas back to you. So neither you nor I will risk our armies." Sitalces sent this message to Octamasadas by a herald, and Octamasadas, with whom a brother of Sitalces had formerly taken refuge, accepted the terms. He surrendered his own uncle to Sitalces, and obtained in exchange his brother Scylas. Sitalces took his brother with him and withdrew; but Octamasadas beheaded Scylas upon the spot. Thus rigidly do the Scythians maintain their own customs, and thus severely do they punish those who adopt foreign usages.

G. The Aristocratic Warrior

The close connection between political privilege and military service is evident at the very beginning of classical Greek history and literature in the Iliad. *In this work Homer depicts the societies of both the Greeks and the Trojans as dominated by a warrior elite of great landowners he calls "heroes" and "kings." These aristocratic warriors claimed to be descendants of the gods, and, because of their central role in battle, they alone had the right to take an active role in the governance of their communities. This relationship between military function and socioeconomic and political position is placed in a positive light in this speech, assigned the Lycian hero Sarpedon.*[13]

Homer,
Iliad

1. THE WARRIOR IDEAL

Still the Trojans and brave Hector would not yet have broken down the gates and the great bar, had not Zeus turned his son Sarpedon against the Argives as a lion against a herd of horned cattle. Before him he held his shield of hammered bronze, that the smith had beaten so fair and round, and had lined with ox hides which he had made fast with rivets of gold all round the shield; this he held in front of him, and brandishing his two spears came on like some lion of the wilderness, who has been long famished for want of meat and will dare break even into a well-fenced homestead to try and get at the sheep. He may find the

[13] Homer, *Iliad* 12, lines 290–328. From *The Iliad of Homer*, trans. Samuel Butler (London, 1914).

shepherds keeping watch over their flocks with dogs and spears, but he is in no mind to be driven from the fold till he has had a try for it; he will either spring on a sheep and carry it off, or be hit by a spear from some strong hand—even so was Sarpedon fain to attack the wall and break down its battlements. Then he said to Glaucus son of Hippolochus, "Glaucus, why in Lycia do we receive especial honor as regards our place at table? Why are the choicest portions served us and our cups kept brimming, and why do men look up to us as though we were gods? Moreover we hold a large estate by the banks of the river Xanthus, fair with orchard lawns and wheat-growing land; it becomes us, therefore, to take our stand at the head of all the Lycians and bear the brunt of the fight, that one may say to another, 'Our princes in Lycia eat the fat of the land and drink the best of wine, but they are fine fellows; they fight well and are ever at the front in battle.' My good friend, if, when we were once out of this fight, we could escape old age and death thenceforward and for ever, I should neither press forward myself nor bid you do so, but death in ten thousand shapes hangs ever over our heads, and no man can elude him: therefore let us go forward and either win glory for ourselves, or yield it to another."

Athenaeus, *Deipnosophists*

The real (and sometimes arbitrary) power that the archaic warrior aristocrats could exercise over the rest of their society by virtue of their military preeminence is vividly expressed in the scolion, or drinking song, ascribed to a Cretan warrior named Hybrias.[14]

2. THE WARRIOR AND SOCIETY: THE DRINKING SONG OF HYBRIAS

My great wealth is my spear and sword and fine animal hide shield, the defense of my flesh. For it is with this that I sow, with this that I reap, with this that I tread out the sweet wine from the grape. Because of this I am called lord of slaves. As for those who do not dare to bear spear and sword and fine animal hide shield, the defense of flesh, they all bend their knee in fear and do me reverence, addressing me as lord and great king.

H. The Hoplite Revolution and the Citizen Soldier

Tyrtaeus Fragment 10

The link between community leadership and the achievement of personal glory in battle evident in Sarpedon's speech was severed in the seventh century B.C. with the adoption of the phalanx tactics typical of hoplite warfare by the poleis *of the Greek mainland. Composed of anonymous masses of similarly armed soldiers, the phalanx was the ideal military expression of the communal ideal of the* polis.

The earliest literary evidence for the redefinition of the relationship between the military and the community is provided by the poem of the mid-seventeenth-century B.C. Spartan poet Tyrtaeus.

[14] From Athenaeus, *Deipnosophists* 15.695–696.

Figure 1.5 Departure scenes were common subjects on many Greek vases. Here a hoplite with shield, greaves, helmet, and spear takes his leave of an elderly man, perhaps his father. Warrior departing. Red-figure column crater, ca. 470 B.C. By permission of the Ashmolean Museum.

In this poem Tyrtaeus clearly states for the first time the idea that the willingness to endure the horrid reality of hoplite battle was the primary obligation of a citizen. Tyrtaeus expresses this idea in negative terms by highlighting the scorn of the community for a coward.[15]

1. THE REALITY OF BATTLE

It is a fine thing for a good man to fall in the front line fighting on behalf of his country; but it is a grievous fate for a man to leave his city and rich fields and wander begging with his dear mother, aged father, small children, and wedded wife. For he will be met with hostility by those to whom he comes, humbled by need and awful poverty. He shames his family and ruins his noble beauty, and every form of disgrace and evil follows him. If, therefore, there is no concern or respect

[15] Tyrtaeus Fragment 10. From *Elegy and Iambus*, Vol. 1, ed. J. M. Edmonds (Cambridge, 1931).

or regard or pity for a wandering man, let us fight with all our heart for this land and let us die for our children without ever a thought for our lives. Make the heart in your chests great with courage and do not hesitate to fight with the enemy.

O Young men, stand beside each other and fight. Do not begin shameful flight or fear. Do not leave behind, fallen to the ground, the old men whose knees are no longer agile, for this, indeed, is disgraceful, that an old man, already white haired and gray of beard, lie fallen in the front line, breathing out his brave soul in the dust while holding his bloody genitals in his dear hands. It is a disgraceful sight and one foul to see: his naked flesh. But for a young man all is in order while he has the beautiful bloom of beloved youth. While he is alive, he is admired by men and desired by women and beautiful when he falls in the front line. So let each man set his feet firmly on the earth and wait, biting his lip with his teeth.

The History of | *The positive side of the hoplite ideal is illustrated in this selection, where the Athenian statesman Solon*
Herodotus | *offers the Lydian king Croesus the case of the Athenian Tellus as the exemplar of the idea that a happy life is one that ends well: Tellus died in battle defending Athens, received from his fellow citizens the honor of a civic funeral, and was survived by sons who would fill his place in the citizen body.[16]*

2. A GOOD CITIZEN: TELLUS OF ATHENS

28. Croesus afterwards, in the course of many years, brought under his sway almost all the nations to the west of the Halys. The Lycians and Cilicians alone continued free; all the other tribes he reduced and held in subjection. They were the following: the Lydians, Phrygians, Mysians, Mariandynians, Chalybians, Paphlagonians, Thynians, and Bithynian Thracians, Carians, Ionians, Dorians, Aeolians and Pamphylians.

29. When all these conquests had been added to the Lydian empire, and the prosperity of Sardis was now at its height, there came thither, one after another, all the sages of Greece living at the time, and among them Solon, the Athenian. He was on his travels, having left Athens to be absent ten years, under the pretense of wishing to see the world, but really to avoid being forced to repeal any of the laws which, at the request of the Athenians, he had made for them. Without his sanction the Athenians could not repeal them, as they had bound themselves under a heavy curse to be governed for ten years by the laws, which should be imposed on them by Solon.

30. On this account, as well as to see the world, Solon set out upon his travels, in the course of which he went to Egypt to the court of Amasis, and also came on a visit to Croesus at Sardis. Croesus received him as his guest, and lodged him in the royal palace. On the third or fourth day after, he bade his servants conduct Solon over his treasuries, and show him all their greatness and magnificence. When he had seen them all, and, so far as time allowed,

[16] Herodotus, *The History of the Persian Wars* 1.28–31 (selections). From *The History of Herodotus*, Vol. 1, trans. George Rawlinson (New York, 1859–1860).

inspected them, Croesus addressed this question to him, "Stranger of Athens, we have heard much of your wisdom and of your travels through many lands, from love of knowledge and a wish to see the world. I am curious therefore to inquire of you, whom, of all the men that you have seen, you consider the most happy?" This he asked because he thought himself the happiest of mortals; but Solon answered him without flattery, according to his true sentiments, "Tellus of Athens, sire." Full of astonishment at what he heard, Croesus demanded sharply, "And wherefore do you deem Tellus happiest?" To which the other replied, "First, because his country was flourishing in his days, and he himself had sons both beautiful and good and he lived to see children born to each of them, and these children all grew up; and further because, after a life spent in what our people look upon as comfort, his end was surpassingly glorious. In a battle between the Athenians and their neighbors near Eleusis, he came to the assistance of his countrymen, routed the foe, and died upon the field most gallantly. The Athenians gave him a public funeral on the spot where he fell, and paid him the highest honors."

31. Thus did Solon admonish Croesus by the example of Tellus, enumerating the manifold particulars of his happiness. . . .

32. . . . Croesus broke in angrily, "What, stranger of Athens, is my happiness then, valued so little by you, that you do not even put me on a level with private men?"

"Croesus," replied the other, "you asked a question concerning the condition of man, of one who knows that the power above us is full of jealousy, and fond of troubling our lot. A long life gives one to witness much, and experience much oneself, that one would not choose. . . . For yourself, Croesus, I see that you are wonderfully rich, and the lord of many nations; but with respect to your question, I have no answer to give, until I hear that you have closed your life happily. For assuredly he who possesses great store of riches is no nearer happiness than he who has what suffices for his daily needs, unless luck attend upon him, and so he continue in the enjoyment of all his good things to the end of life.

On the other hand, a man's inability to fulfill the warrior role was always considered grounds for potentially excluding him from the ranks of the full citizens, as can be seen in this selection, where the fourth-century B.C. Athenian historian and essayist Xenophon claims that, unlike farmers, tradesmen cannot be good citizens because the conditions of their work render them unfit for hoplite service.

Xenophon,
Oeconomicus

3. ONLY FARMERS CAN BE GOOD CITIZENS[17]

v.—All this I relate to you (continued Socrates) to show you that quite high and mighty people find it hard to hold aloof from agriculture, devotion to which art

[17] Xenophon, *Oeconomicus* 5–6.10 (selections). From *The Works of Xenophon*, Vol. 3, trans. H. G. Dakyns (London, 1890).

would seem to be thrice blest, combining as it does a certain sense of luxury with the satisfaction of an improved estate, and such a training of physical energies as shall fit a man to play a free man's part. Earth, in the first place, freely offers to those that labor all things necessary to the life of man; and, as if that were not enough, makes further contribution of a thousand luxuries. It is she who supplies with sweetest scent and fairest show all things wherewith to adorn the altars and statues of the gods, or deck man's person. It is to her we owe our many delicacies of flesh or fowl or vegetable growth; since with the tillage of the soil is closely linked the art of breeding sheep and cattle, whereby we mortals may offer sacrifices well pleasing to the gods, and satisfy our personal needs withal.

Earth, too, adds stimulus in war-time to earth's tillers; she pricks them on to aid the country under arms, and this she does by fostering her fruits in open field, the prize of valor for the mightiest. For this also is the art athletic, this of husbandry; as thereby men are fitted to run, and hurl the spear, and leap with the best.

For myself, I marvel greatly if it has ever fallen to the lot of freeborn man to own a choicer possession, or to discover an occupation more seductive, or of wider usefulness in life than this.

But, furthermore, earth of her own will gives lessons in justice and uprightness to all who can understand her meaning, since the nobler the service of devotion rendered, the ampler the riches of her recompense. One day, perchance, these pupils of hers, whose conversation in past times was in husbandry, shall, by reason of the multitude of invading armies, be ousted from their labors. The work of their hands may indeed be snatched from them, but they were brought up in stout and manly fashion. They stand, each one of them, in body and soul equipped; and, save God himself shall hinder them, they will march into the territory of those their human hinderers, and take from them the wherewithal to support their lives. Since often enough in war it is surer and safer to quest for food with sword and buckler than with all the instruments of husbandry.

But there is yet another lesson to be learnt in the public school of husbandry— the lesson of mutual assistance.

"Shoulder to shoulder" must we march to meet the invader; "shoulder to shoulder" stand to compass the tillage of the soil. Therefore it is that the husband-man, who means to win in his avocation, must see that he creates enthusiasm in his workpeople and a spirit of ready obedience; which is just what a general attacking an enemy will scheme to bring about, when he deals out gifts to the brave and castigation to those who are disorderly.

Nor will there be lacking seasons of exhortation, the general haranguing his troops and the husbandman his laborers; nor because they are slaves do they less than free men need the lure of hope and happy expectation, that they may will-ingly stand to their posts.

It was an excellent saying of his who named husbandry "the mother and nurse of all the arts," for while agriculture prospers all other arts alike are vigorous and strong, but where the land is forced to remain desert, the spring that feeds the other arts is dried up; they dwindle, I had almost said, one and all, by land and sea.

Soc. Well, then, we agreed that economy was the proper title of a branch of knowledge, and this branch of knowledge appeared to be that whereby men are enabled to enhance the value of their houses or estates; and by this word "house or estate" we understood the whole of a man's possessions; and "possessions" again we defined to include those things which the possessor should find advantageous for the purposes of his life; and things advantageous finally were discovered to mean all that a man knows how to use and turn to good account. Further, for a man to learn all branches of knowledge not only seemed to us an impossibility, but we thought we might well follow the example of civil communities in rejecting the base mechanic arts so called, on the ground that they destroy the bodies of the artisans, as far as we can see, and crush their spirits.

The clearest proof of this, we said, could be discovered if, on the occasion of a hostile inroad, one were to seat the husbandman and the artisans apart in two divisions, and then proceed to put this question to each group in turn: "Do you think it better to defend our country districts or to retire from the fields and guard the walls?" And we anticipated that those concerned with the soil would vote to defend the soil; while the artisans would vote not to fight, but, in docile obedience to their training, to sit with folded hands, neither expending toil nor venturing their lives.

I. The Hoplite *Polis*: Sparta

Hoplite warfare eventually became the norm for all Greek poleis. The city where the social implications of this form of warfare were most fully realized, however, was Sparta. The masses of enslaved fellow Greeks, called Helots, who were the source of the city's prosperity, also posed an ever-present threat of rebellion. Faced with this danger, the Spartans sought security by remolding their city's institutions to enable every Spartan to serve in the hoplite phalanx. The result was a unique society in which every male Spartan passed through a strictly regimented educational system that was intended to transform him into a hoplite ready to face the rigors of battle described earlier by Tyrtaeus. Paradoxically, this "boot-camp" polis was probably also the earliest Greek democracy, since it was first in Sparta that every male was able to fulfill the citizen's primary obligation of serving his city as a warrior and thereby gained the right to attend the assembly and hold at least some elective offices. For almost three centuries, from the mid-seventh century B.C. until 371 B.C., when the city was massively defeated by Thebes and impoverished as a result of the loss of most of her Helots, the Spartan army seemed invincible. Xenophon's Constitution of the Spartans *gives a vivid picture of Sparta just before her defeat by Thebes, one that is all the more valuable because the author was one of the few Greek authors to write about Sparta from personal experience, having lived there during his exile from Athens in the early fourth century B.C.[18]*

Xenophon,
The Constitution of the Spartans

---

[18] Xenophon, *The Constitution of the Spartans* (selections). From *The Works of Xenophon*, Vol. 2, trans. H. G. Dakyns.

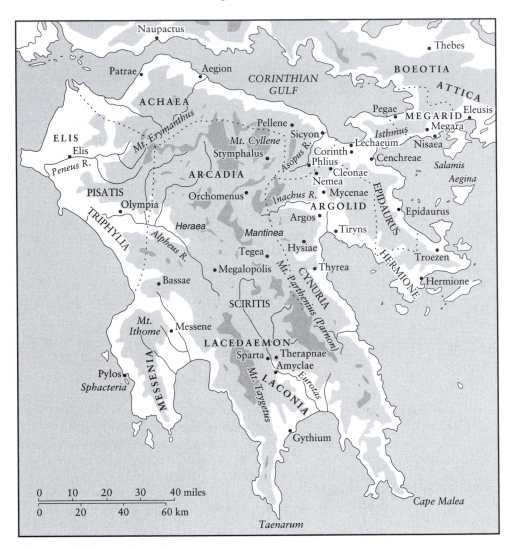

Figure 1.6 Peloponnesus.

1. I recall the astonishment with which I first noted the unique population of Sparta among the states of Hellas, the relatively sparse population, and at the same time the extraordinary power and prestige of the community. I was puzzled to account for the fact. It was only when I came to consider the peculiar institutions of the Spartans that my wonderment ceased. Or rather, it is transferred to the legislator who gave them those laws, obedience to which has been the secret of their prosperity. This legislator, Lycurgus, I admire, and hold him to have been one of the wisest of mankind. Certainly he was no servile imitator of other states. It was by a stroke of invention rather, and on a pattern much in

opposition to the commonly accepted one, that he brought his fatherland to this pinnacle of prosperity.

Marriage and the Rearing of Children

Take for example—and it is well to begin at the beginning—the whole topic of the begetting and rearing of children. Throughout the rest of the world the young girl, who will one day become a mother (and I speak of those who may be held to be well brought up), is nurtured on the plainest food attainable, with the scantiest addition of meat or other condiments; while as to wine they train them either to total abstinence or to take it highly diluted with water. And in imitation, as it were, of the handicraft type, since the majority of artificers are sedentary, we, the rest of the Hellenes, are content that our girls should sit quietly and work wool. That is all we demand of them. But how are we to expect that women nurtured in this fashion should produce a splendid offspring?

Lycurgus pursued a different path. Clothes were things, he held, the furnishing of which might well enough be left to female slaves. And, believing that the highest function of a free woman was the bearing of children, in the first place he insisted on the training of the body as incumbent no less on the female than the male; and in pursuit of the same idea instituted rival contests in running and feats of strength for women as for men. His belief was that where both parents were strong their progeny would be found to be more vigorous.

And so again after marriage. In view of the fact that immoderate intercourse is elsewhere permitted during the earlier period of matrimony, he adopted a principle directly opposite. He laid it down as an ordinance that a man should be ashamed to be seen visiting the chamber of his wife, whether going in or coming out. When they did meet under such restraint the mutual longing of these lovers could not but be increased, and the fruit which might spring from such intercourse would tend to be more robust than theirs whose affections are cloyed by satiety. By a farther step in the same direction he refused to allow marriages to be contracted at any period of life according to the fancy of the parties concerned. Marriage, as he ordained it, must only take place in the prime of bodily vigor, this too being, as he believed, a condition conducive to the production of healthy offspring. Or again, to meet the case which might occur of an old man wedded to a young wife. Considering the jealous watch which such husbands are apt to keep over their wives, he introduced a directly opposite custom; that is to say, he made it incumbent on the aged husband to introduce some one whose qualities, physical and moral, he admired, to beget him children. Or again, in the case of a man who might not desire to live with a wife permanently, but yet might still be anxious to have children of his own worthy of the name, the lawgiver laid down a law in his behalf. Such a one might select some woman, the wife of some man, well born herself and blest with fair offspring, and, the sanction and consent of her husband first obtained, raise up children for himself through her.

The Education of a Boy

2. I wish now to explain the systems of education in fashion here and elsewhere. Throughout the rest of Hellas the custom on the part of those who claim to educate their sons in the best way is as follows. As soon as the children are of an age to understand what is said to them they are immediately placed under the charge of Paidagogoi (*slave tutors*), who are also attendants, and sent off to the school of some teacher to be taught grammar, music, and the concerns of the palaestra (*gymnasium*).

But when we turn to Lycurgus, instead of leaving it to each member of the state privately to appoint a slave to be his son's tutor, he set over the young Spartans a public guardian, the Paidonomos, to give him his proper title, with complete authority over them. This guardian was selected from those who filled the highest magistracies. He had authority to hold musters of the boys, and as their overseer, in case of any misbehavior, to chastise severely. The legislator further provided the guardian with a body of youths in the prime of life, and bearing whips, to inflict punishment when necessary, with this happy result that in Sparta modesty and obedience ever go hand in hand, nor is there lack of either.

3. Coming to the critical period at which a boy ceases to be a boy and becomes a youth, we find that it is just then that the rest of the world proceed to emancipate their children from the private tutor and the schoolmaster, and, without substituting any further ruler, are content to launch them into absolute independence.

Here, again, Lycurgus took an entirely opposite view of the matter. This, if observation might be trusted, was the season when the tide of animal spirits flows fast, and the froth of insolence rises to the surface; when, too, the most violent appetites for pleasures invade the mind. This, then, was the right moment at which to impose constant labors upon the growing youth, and to devise for him a subtle system of absorbing occupation. And by a crowning enactment, which said that he who shrank from the duties imposed on him would forfeit henceforth all claim to the glorious honors of the state, he caused, not only the public authorities, but those personally interested in the youths to take serious pains so that no single individual of them should by an act of cowardice find himself utterly despised within the body politic.

Furthermore, in his desire firmly to implant modesty in them he imposed a special rule. In the streets they were to keep their hands within the folds of the cloak; they were to walk in silence and without turning their heads to gaze, but rather to keep their eyes fixed upon the ground before them. And hereby it would seem to be proved conclusively that, even in the matter of quiet bearing and sobriety, the masculine type may claim greater strength than that which we attribute to the nature of women. At any rate, you might sooner expect a stone image to find voice than one of those Spartan youths; to divert the eyes of some bronze statue were less difficult. And as to quiet bearing, no bride ever stepped in bridal bower with more natural modesty. Note them when they have reached the public table. The plainest answer to the question asked, that is all you need expect to hear from their lips.

Daily Life in Sparta

With regard to those who have already passed the vigor of early manhood, and on whom the highest magistracies henceforth devolve, there is a like contrast. In Greece generally we find that at this age the need of further attention to physical strength is removed, although the imposition of military service continues. But Lycurgus made it customary for that section of his citizens to regard hunting as the highest honor suited to their age; but not to the exclusion of any public duty. And his aim was that they might be equally able to undergo the fatigues of war with those in the prime of early manhood. . . .

5. The above is a fairly exhaustive statement of the institutions traceable to the legislation of Lycurgus in connection with the successive stages of a citizen's life. It remains that I should endeavor to describe the style of living, which he established for the whole body, irrespective of age. It will be understood that, when Lycurgus first came to deal with the question, the Spartans, like the rest of the Greeks, used to mess privately at home. Tracing more than half the current misdemeanors to this custom, he was determined to drag his people out into the daylight, and so he invented the public mess-rooms. Whereby he expected at any rate to minimize the transgression of orders. . . .

This too must be borne in mind, that in other states equals in age, for the most part, associate together, and such an atmosphere is little conducive to modesty. Whereas in Sparta Lycurgus was careful so to blend the ages that the younger men must benefit largely by the experience of the elder—an education in itself, and the more so since by custom of the country, conversation at the common meal has reference to the honorable acts which this man or that man may have performed in relation to the state. The scene, in fact, but little lends itself to the intrusion of violence or drunken riot; ugly speech and ugly deeds alike are out of place. Among other good results obtained through this communal system of meals may be mentioned these: There is the necessity of walking home when the meal is over, and a consequent anxiety not to be caught tripping under the influence of wine, since they all know of course that the supper-table must be presently abandoned, and that they must move as freely in the dark as in the day, even the help of a torch to guide the steps being forbidden to all on active service. . . .

6. There are other points in which this legislator's views run counter to those commonly accepted. Thus: in other states the individual citizen is master over his own children, servants and belongings generally; but Lycurgus, whose aim was to secure to all the citizens a considerable share in one

another's goods without mutual injury, enacted that each one should have an equal power over his neighbor's children as over his own. The principle is this. When a man knows that this, that, and the other person are fathers of children subject to his own authority, he must perforce deal by them even as he desires his own children to be dealt by. And, if a boy chance to have received a whipping, not from his own father but some other, and goes and complains to his own father, it would be thought wrong on the part of that father if he did not inflict a second whipping on his son. A striking proof, in its way, how completely they trust each other not to impose dishonorable commands upon their children.

7. There are yet other customs in Sparta, which Lycurgus instituted in opposition to those of the rest of Greece, and the following among them. We all know that in the generality of states every one devotes his full energy to the business of making money: one man as a tiller of the soil, another as a mariner, a third as a merchant, whilst others depend on various arts to earn a living. But at Sparta Lycurgus forbade his freeborn citizens to have anything whatsoever to do with the concerns of money-making. As freemen, he enjoined upon them to regard as their concern exclusively those activities upon which the foundations of civic liberty are based.

8. But to proceed. We are all aware that there is no state in the world in which greater obedience is shown to magistrates, and to the laws themselves, than Sparta. But, for my part, I am disposed to think that Lycurgus could never have attempted to establish this healthy condition, until he had first secured the unanimity of the most powerful members of the state. I infer this for the following reasons. In other states the leaders in rank and influence do not even desire to be thought to fear the magistrates. Such a thing they would regard as in itself a symbol of servility. In Sparta, on the contrary, the stronger a man is the more readily does he bow before constituted authority. And indeed, they pride themselves on their humility, and on a prompt obedience, running, or at any rate not crawling with laggard step, at the word of command. Such an example of eager discipline, they are persuaded, set by themselves, will not fail to be followed by the rest. And this is precisely what has taken place. It is reasonable to suppose that it was these same noblest members of the state who combined to lay the foundation of the ephorate, after they had come to the conclusion themselves that of all the blessings, which a state, or an army, or a household can enjoy, obedience is the greatest. Since, as they could not but reason, the greater the power with which men fence about authority, the greater the fascination it will exercise upon the mind of the citizen, to the enforcement of obedience.

Accordingly the ephors are competent to punish whomsoever they choose: they have power to exact fines on the spur of the moment; they have power to depose magistrates in mid career, nay, actually to imprison and bring them to trial on the capital charge. Entrusted with these vast powers, they do not, as do the rest of states, allow the magistrates elected to exercise authority as they like, right through the year of office; but, in the style rather of despotic monarchs, or presidents of the games, at the first symptom of an offence against the law they inflict chastisement without warning and without hesitation.

But of all the many beautiful contrivances invented by Lycurgus to kindle a willing obedience to the laws in the hearts of the citizens, none, to my mind, was happier or more excellent than his unwillingness to deliver his code to the people at large, until, attended by the most powerful members of the state, he had betaken himself to Delphi, and there made inquiry of the god whether it were better for Sparta, and conducive to her interests, to obey the laws which he had framed. And not until the divine answer came, "Better will it be in every way," did he deliver them, laying it down as a last ordinance that to refuse obedience to a code which had the sanction of the Pythian god himself was a thing not illegal only, but impious.

9. The following too may well excite our admiration for Lycurgus. I speak of the consummate skill with which he induced the whole state of Sparta to regard an honorable death as preferable to an ignoble life. And indeed if any one will investigate the matter, he will find that by comparison with those who make it a principle to retreat in face of danger, actually fewer of these Spartans die in battle, since, to speak truth, salvation, it would seem, attends on virtue far more frequently than on cowardice—virtue, which is at once easier and sweeter, richer in resource and stronger of arm, than her opposite. And that virtue has another familiar attendant—to wit, glory—needs no showing, since all wish to ally themselves somehow with the good.

Yet the actual means by which he gave currency to these principles is a point which it were well not to overlook. It is clear that the lawgiver set himself deliberately to provide all the blessings of heaven for the good man, and a sorry and ill-starred existence for the coward.

In other states the man who shows himself base and cowardly wins to himself an evil reputation and the nickname of a coward, but that is all. For the rest he buys and sells in the same market-place with the good man; he sits beside him at the play; he exercises with him in the same gymnasium, and all as suits his humor. But at Lacedaemon there is not one man who would not feel ashamed to welcome the coward at the common mess-table, or to try conclusions with such an antagonist in a wrestling bout. Consider the day's round of his existence. The sides are being picked for a game of ball, but he is left out as the odd man: there is no place for him. During the choric dance he is driven away into ignominious quarters. Nay, in the very streets it is he who must step aside for others to pass, or, being seated, he must rise and make room, even for a younger man. At home he will have his maiden relatives to support in their isolation (and they will hold him to blame for their unwedded lives). A hearth with no wife to bless it—that is a condition he must face, and yet he will have to pay damages for incurring it. Let him not roam abroad with a smiling countenance; let him not imitate men whose fame is irreproachable, or he shall feel on his back the blows of his superiors. Such being the weight of infamy which is laid upon all cowards, I, for my part, am not surprised if in Sparta they deem death preferable to a life so steeped in dishonor and reproach. . . .

The Spartan Way of War

11. The above form a common stock of blessings, open to every Spartan to enjoy, alike in peace and in war. But if any one desires to be informed in what way the legislator improved upon the ordinary machinery of warfare and in reference to an army in the field, it is easy to satisfy his curiosity.

In the first instance, the ephors announce by proclamation the limit of age to which the service applies for cavalry and heavy infantry; and in the next place, for the various handicraftsman. So that, even on active service, the Lacedaemonians are well supplied with all the conveniences enjoyed by people living as citizens at home. All implements and instruments whatsoever, which an army may need in common, are ordered to be in readiness, some on wagons and others on baggage animals. In this way anything omitted can hardly escape detection.

For the actual encounter under arms, the following inventions are attributed to him. The soldier has a crimson-colored uniform and a heavy shield of bronze; his theory being that such an equipment has no sort of feminine association, and is altogether most warrior-like. It is most quickly burnished, it is least readily tarnished.

He further permitted those who were above the age of early manhood to wear their hair long. For so, he conceived, they would appear of larger stature, more free and indomitable, and of a more terrible aspect.

So furnished and accoutered, he divided his citizen soldiers into six *morae* (regimental divisions) of cavalry and heavy infantry. Each of these citizen regiments has one polemarch (colonel), four captains of companies, eight lieutenants, each in command of a half company, and sixteen commanders of sections. At the word of command any such regimental division can be formed readily either into single file or into three files abreast, or into six files abreast.

J. The Role of Athletics

1. AN ATHLETIC DYNASTY: THE DIAGORIDS OF RHODES

Pausanias,
Guide to Greece

In the publicly oriented ethics of the Greeks, an athletic victory was not complete if it was not made known to the widest possible audience. One popular way to do so with important implications for the development of Greek art was for the victor to set up a statue of himself in the sanctuary where he won his victory. The result was that the sites of the pan-Hellenic athletic festivals became virtual outdoor museums of the best of Greek sculpture. Pausanias, the second-century A.D. author of a still extant guidebook to ancient Greece, devoted particular attention to recording these monuments of athletic achievement. The selection translated here describes the monuments commemorating the achievements

Figure 1.7 Victories in athletic competitions could be sources of great wealth as well as pride. Victors in the Great Panathenaic games held at Athens every four years, for example, received as many as one hundred vases containing high quality olive oil pressed from trees in Athena's sacred groves. Each vase had a representation of Athena on one side and the event on the other, in this case, the *apobates* competition in which the armed rider jumped on and off the chariot several times during the race. A recent calculation puts the value of the oil in a single Panathenaic vase at approximately $1,356 dollars (David C. Young, *A Brief History of the Olympic Games* [Oxford 2004] 99–100), which the victor could sell together with the vases, which were in high demand as grave goods in Etruria. By the Marsyas Painter (fourth century B.C.). Getty Museum 79.AE. 147. Courtesy of the J. Paul Getty Museum, Malibu.

of the most famous of all Greek athletic families, that of Diagoras of Rhodes and his descendants. The story that one of Diagoras' daughters accompanied her son to the Olympics disguised as a man reflects the fact that it was a capital offense for a married woman to attend the Olympic games.[19]

After viewing these statues, you will come to the statues of the Rhodian athletes Diagoras and his family. They are set up next to each other in the following order. Acusilaus, who took the crown in the men's boxing, and Dorieus, the youngest of the family, who was victorious in all-in-fighting in three straight Olympics. Even before Dorieus, however, Damagetus also defeated those entering the

[19] From Pausanias, *Guide to Greece* 6.7.

all-in-fighting event. These men were brothers and sons of Diagoras. Next to them is set up the statue of Diagoras, who gained the victory in men's boxing. A Megarian sculptor, Callicles, the son of Theocosmus, who also made the statue of Zeus at Megara, sculpted the statue of Diagoras.

The sons of Diagoras' daughters were also boxers and won Olympic victories: Eucles, the son of Callianax and Callipateira, the daughter of Diagoras, in the men's class and Peisirodus in the boys' class. The mother of Peisirodus disguised herself in the clothes of a male trainer and brought her son to the games. The statue of this Peisirodus is also set up on the Altis beside that of his mother's father. People say that Diagoras came to Olympia together with his sons Acusilaus and Damagetus. The young men, after they had won victories in their events, carried him through the throng while he was showered with flowers and called blessed by the Greeks because of his sons.

The family of Diagoras was by origin Messenian in the female line and descended from a daughter of Aristomenes. Dorieus, the son of Diagoras, in addition to his Olympic victories, was victor eight times in the Isthmian games and seven in the Nemean games. He is also said to have won an uncontested victory at the Pythian games. He and Peisirodus were announced as Thurians, since they had been driven out from Rhodes by their political opponents and found refuge at Thurii in Italy. Later, however, Dorieus returned to Rhodes. He was a man who manifested the closest support for Sparta. He even fought a sea battle against the Athenians with his own ships. He was captured by Athenian triremes and brought to Athens as a prisoner. The Athenians, before Dorieus arrived at Athens, had been furious with him and made threats. But when they came together in the assembly and the Athenians saw a man who was so tall and who had achieved such fame in the position of a prisoner of war, they changed their opinion and let him go, although they could have justly punished him. The death of Dorieus is recorded in Androtion's history of Athens. Androtion says that when the Persian king's fleet and his admiral Conon were at Caunus and the Rhodians had been persuaded by Conon to revolt from the Spartans and join the king and the Athenian alliance, Dorieus, who happened to be away from Rhodes in the interior of the Peloponnesus at that time, was arrested by the Spartans. He was brought to Sparta, convicted of doing harm to Sparta, and sentenced to death.

2. ATHLETICS AND THE *POLIS*: A PHILOSOPHICAL CRITIQUE

Xenophanes
Fragment 2

The prominent role of athletics in Greek life was not without its critics. The earliest was Xenophanes (ca. 580–478 B.C.), a philosopher-poet from the Greek city of Colophon on the coast of western Turkey. Unwilling to live under Persian rule, in about the mid-sixth century B.C. he went into voluntary exile in Sicily, where he spent the rest of his life. Xenophanes was not so much an original thinker as a popularizer, who used the new ideas of the early philosophers to criticize traditional Greek attitudes. A good example is the iconoclastic treatment of athletics in the poem translated here.[20]

[20] Xenophanes Fragment 2. From *Elegy and Iambus*, Vol. 1, ed. Edmonds (Cambridge, 1931).

If one should win a victory thanks to the swiftness of his feet or when competing in the pentathlon there in the sanctuary of Zeus by the streams of Pisa at Olympia, or if one should gain the prize in wrestling or painful boxing, or in that fearful contest people call all-in-fighting, to his fellow citizens he would be thought more glorious to look on than ever, and he would win the right to a prominent front row seat at the games and he would gain from his *polis* the right to meals at public expense and a gift which would be his personal treasure. And if his victory were won with horses, he would also gain all these things, even though he is not as worthy as I. For our wisdom is better than the strength of men or horses.

But this custom is completely wrong, nor is it right to prefer strength to good wisdom. For even if there were a good boxer among the citizens or one skilled in the pentathlon or wrestling, or, indeed, even if there were a great sprinter, which holds the front rank among the athletic achievements of men, the *polis* would still not be better governed because of this. A *polis* would gain little joy if someone should win in competition by the banks of the Pisa; for that victory would not fill its storehouses.

2

THE RISE AND FALL OF THE GREEK ARISTOCRACY IN THE ARCHAIC PERIOD

Great changes occurred in every aspect of Greek life during the seventh and sixth centuries B.C. Population increased and new *poleis* appeared throughout the Mediterranean and Black Sea basins. At the same time, vigorous economic growth occurred on a scale unequaled since the second millennium B.C., as can be seen from the proliferation of conspicuous expenditures by the new *polis* governments and their richer citizens: stone temples, city walls, fountain houses, and stone and metal statuary. Finally, the invention and spread of coinage toward the end of the period began to alter the very nature of wealth and economic activity.

These two centuries were also the golden age of the Greek aristocracies. The weak rulers of the Dark Ages were replaced by hereditary aristocracies, who took advantage of the reestablishment of contact with Egypt and the kingdoms of the Near East and were enriched by the new economic opportunities provided by that contact. Typical features of the later Greek aristocratic lifestyle were the great athletic festivals and the drinking party, or *symposium*. The demands of newly rich Greek aristocrats also stimulated the expansion of luxury crafts and new artistic forms such as lyric poetry, sculpture, and the production of fine ceramic and metal tableware and jewelry. The impact on Greek culture of the new aristocratic ideal, with its emphasis on refinement and elegance, can be seen at its best in the celebration of male and female beauty in archaic Greek poetry and the statues of beautiful young men and women that fill the museums of the Western world.

Paradoxically, these two centuries were also the period in which aristocratic domination of Greek social and political life was seriously challenged for the first time. A frequent refrain in the literature of the period is: "Wealth is the man/ no poor man is good or honored." At the same time that the widespread adoption of hoplite warfare undermined aristocratic military primacy, economic growth fostered the appearance of nonaristocratic rich, for whom Greek society offered no status commensurate with their wealth. Whatever the source of their wealth, the attempts of the new rich to penetrate the closed circle of the aristocracies of the Greek cities provoked ridicule and even fear when they found supporters among ambitious but disaffected aristocrats.

46

Thus, the aristocratic Megarian poet Theognis views with foreboding the willingness of some aristocrats in sixth-century B.C. Megara to arrange marriages for their sons with the daughters of men distinguished only by their wealth.

The aspirations of the new rich were an affront to the pride of Greek aristocrats. The sharpening of the division between the rich and the poor during the seventh and sixth centuries B.C., however, directly threatened aristocratic domination of the Greek cities. The causes of the problems are obscure, but the demands for cancellation of debts and redivision of land typical of Greek revolutionary movements suggest that the growing population of the archaic *poleis* led to land shortages, the effects of which could only be aggravated by the Greek laws of debt, which often threatened defaulting debtors with slavery. Sometimes tensions could be eased by colonization, which offered the disaffected hope of land and a fresh start elsewhere. Occasionally, reforms imposed by lawgivers such as the Athenian Solon succeeded in defusing problems before they reached crisis levels. All too often, however, efforts at reform were only partially successful or failed entirely, and the result was revolution, the establishment of tyranny—the Greek term for a military dictatorship—and the violent end of aristocratic rule. Many Greek cities experienced such crises during these two centuries, but the best documented cases are those of Corinth and Athens.

A. Aristocratic Privilege

1. THE GORTYN CODE

The essence of aristocracy is elite status in society based on hereditary privilege. In the Gortyn Code—a fifth-century inscription containing the traditional laws of the city of Gortyn in Crete—this privilege is indicated by the levying of different fines for the same offense according to the social class of the parties involved: highest for a "free" man, lowest for a slave.[1] The Gortyn Code

THE GODS!

I. *Suit for the ownership of a slave or of one so claimed.*—Whoever intends to bring suit in relation to a free man or a slave, shall not take action by seizure before trial; but if he do seize him, let the judge fine him 10 staters for the free man, 5 for the slave, because he seizes him, and let him adjudge that he shall release him within three days. But if he do not release him, let the judge sentence him to a stater for a free man, a drachma for a slave, each day until he shall have released him; and according to the time (of non-payment) the judge shall decide, confirming it by oath. But if he should deny that he made

---

[1] From G. W. Botsford and E. G. Sihler, *Hellenic Civilization* (New York, 1915), pp. 276–277, 278, 282–283.

the seizure, the judge shall render decision with confirmatory oath, unless a witness testify.

But if one party contend that he is a free man, the other that he is a slave, those who testify that he is free shall be preferred. And if they contend about a slave, each declaring that he is his, if a witness testify, the judge shall decide according to the witness; but if they testify either for both parties or for neither of the two, the judge shall render his decision by oath.

II. *Rape and assault.*—If one commit rape on a free man or woman, he shall pay 100 staters, and if on (the son or daughter) of an *apetairos* (=*free persons of inferior status*) 10, and if a slave on a free man or woman he shall pay double, and if a free man on a male or female serf 5 drachmas, and if a serf on a male or female serf, 5 staters. If one debauch a female house-slave by force he shall pay 2 staters, but if one already debauched, in the daytime an obol, but if at night 2 obols; and the slave shall have preference in taking the oath.

If one tries to seduce a free woman, under the tutelage of her relative, he shall pay 10 staters, if a witness testify.

III. *Adultery.*—If one be taken in adultery with a free woman in her father's, or in her brother's, or in her husband's house, he shall pay 100 staters, but if in another's house, 50; and with the wife of an *apetairos*, 10; but if a slave with a free woman, he shall pay double, but if a slave with a slave's wife, 5.

And let (the captor) give notice in the presence of three witnesses to the relatives of the man taken, that they shall ransom him within 5 days, and to the master of the slave in the presence of two witnesses. But if one do not ransom him, it shall be in the power of the captors to do with him as they will. But if he assert that the other has enslaved him, in the case of 50 staters or more, the captor himself with four others shall swear, each calling down curses on himself, and in the case of the *apetairos*, (the captor) himself with two others, and in case of the domestic, the master himself and another, that he took him in adultery, and did not enslave him.

XII. *Miscegenation.*—[If a slave (?)] going to a free woman shall wed her, the children shall be free; but if the free woman to a slave, the children shall be slaves; and if from the same mother free and slave children be born, if the mother die and there be property, the free children shall have it; but if free children should not be born of her, her relatives shall succeed to the property.

2. HOW A BOY BECOMES A MAN IN CRETE

Strabo,
Geography

The life cycle of an aristocratic male consisted of a series of stages, each commemorated publicly by ritual. This fragment from the universal history of the fourth-century B.C. historian Ephorus describes the ritualized abduction that in Crete marked a boy's initiation into the society of adult males.[2]

[2] Quoted in Strabo, *Geography* 10.4.21, C 483. From Strabo, *Geography*, trans. H. L. Jones (Cambridge, 1928).

They have a peculiar custom in regard to love affairs, for they win the objects of their love, not by persuasion, but by abduction; the lover tells the friends of the boy three or four days beforehand that he is going to make the abduction; but for the friends to conceal the boy, or not to let him go forth by the appointed road, is indeed a most disgraceful thing, a confession, as it were, that the boy is unworthy to obtain such a lover; and when they meet, if the abductor is the boy's equal or superior in rank or other respects, the friends pursue him and lay hold of him, though only in a very gentle way, thus satisfying the custom; and after that they cheerfully turn the boy over to him to lead away; if, however, the abductor is unworthy, they take the boy away from him. And the pursuit does not end until the boy is taken to the "Andreium" (*men's club*) of his abductor. They regard as a worthy object of love, not the boy who is exceptionally handsome, but the boy who is exceptionally manly and decorous. After giving the boy presents, the abductor takes him away to any place in the country he wishes; and those who were present at the abduction follow after them. And after feasting and hunting with them for two months (for it is not permitted to detain the boy for a longer time), they return to the city. The boy is released after receiving as presents a military habit, an ox, and a drinking-cup (these are the gifts required by law), and other things so numerous and costly that the friends, on account of the number of the expenses, make contributions thereto. Now the boy sacrifices the ox to Zeus and feasts those who returned with him; and then he makes known the facts about his intimacy with his lover, whether, perchance, it has pleased him or not, the law allowing him this privilege in order that, if any force was applied to him at the time of the abduction, he might be able at this feast to avenge himself and be rid of the lover. It is disgraceful for those who are handsome in appearance or descendants of illustrious ancestors to fail to obtain lovers, the presumption being that their character is responsible for such a fate. But the *parastathentes* (for thus they call those who have been abducted) receive honors; for in both the dances and the races they have the positions of highest honor, and are allowed to dress in better clothes than the rest, that is, in the habit given them by their lovers; and not then only, but even after they have grown to manhood, they wear a distinctive dress, which is intended to make known the fact that each wearer has become "kleinos," for they call the loved one "kleinos": (= noble) and the lover "philetor": (= lover). So much for their customs in regard to love affairs.

B. Religion in Aristocratic Greece

1. RELATIONS BETWEEN MAN AND GODS[3]

Greek ideas about the nature of relations between man and gods appear fully formed at the end of the eighth century B.C. *in the* Iliad *and the* Odyssey. *Unlike the major monotheistic religions, that*

Homer,
Iliad

[3] Homer, *Iliad* 1, lines 17–67. Adapted frrom *The Iliad of Homer*, trans. Samuel Butler (London 1914).

relationship was not based on adherence to specific doctrines but on the performance of rituals or other actions intended to secure positive results such as prosperity, good health, or security through the mutual exchange of favors. So in the Iliad, *when Apollo's priest Chryses' offer to ransom his daughter in order to spare her the normal fate of captive women—a lifetime of drudgery and sexual abuse—is spurned, he invokes Apollo's aid in freeing his daughter in recompense for the services he had rendered the god in the past. And in the epic, at least Apollo responded appropriately and struck the Achaeans with a deadly plague.*

Now Chryses had come to the ships of the Achaeans to free his daughter and had brought with him a great ransom. Moreover, he bore in his hand the scepter of Apollo wreathed with a suppliant's wreath, and he besought the Achaeans, but most of all, the two sons of Atreus, who were their chiefs.

"Sons of Atreus," he cried, "and all other Achaeans, may the gods who dwell in Olympus grant you to sack the city of Priam and to reach your homes in safety; but free my daughter and accept a ransom for her, in reverence to Apollo, son of Zeus."

On this the rest of the Achaeans with one voice were for respecting the priest and taking the ransom that he offered; but not so Agamemnon, who spoke fiercely to him and sent him roughly away. "Old man," said he, "let me not find you tarrying about our ships, nor yet coming hereafter. Your scepter of the god and your wreath shall profit you nothing. I will not free her. She shall grow old in my house at Argos far from her own home, busying herself with her loom and visiting my couch. So go, and do not provoke me or it shall be the worse for you."

The old man feared him and obeyed. Not a word he spoke, but went by the shore of the sounding sea and prayed apart to King Apollo whom lovely Leto had borne. "Hear me," he cried, "O god of the silver bow, that protectest Chryse and holy Cilia and rule Tenedos with your might, hear me, O you of Sminthe! If I have ever decked your temple with garlands, or burned your thighbones in fat of bulls or goats, grant my prayer and let your arrows avenge these my tears upon the Danaans."

Thus did he pray, and Apollo heard his prayer. He came down furious from the summits of Olympus, with his bow and his quiver upon his shoulder, and the arrows rattled on his back with the rage that trembled within him. He sat himself down away from the ships with a face as dark as night, and his silver bow rang death as he shot his arrow in the midst of them. First he struck their mules and their hounds, but presently he aimed his shafts at the people themselves, and all day long the pyres of the dead were burning.

2. ANIMAL SACRIFICE[4]

Homer, *The Odyssey*

Animal sacrifice was the central ritual of Greek religion, a gift that affirmed the shared bond between the members of a community or family and a god through sharing in the meal of the flesh of the

[4] Homer, *Odyssey* 3, lines 418–463. Adapted from *The Odyssey of Homer*, trans. Samuel Butler (London 1900).

sacrificial animal or animals. The earliest and fullest description of an animal sacrifice is found in the following passage of the Odyssey.

Now when the child of morning, rosy-fingered Dawn, appeared, Nestor left his couch and took his seat on the benches of white and polished marble that stood in front of his house. Here aforetime sat Neleus, peer of gods in counsel, but he was now dead, and had gone to the house of Hades; so Nestor sat in his seat, scepter in hand, as guardian of the public good. His sons as they left their rooms gathered round him, Echephron, Stratius, Perseus, Aretus, and Thrasymedes; the sixth son was Pisistratus, and when Telemachus joined them they made him sit with them. Nestor then addressed them.

"My sons," said he, "make haste to do as I shall bid you. I wish first and foremost to propitiate the great goddess Athene, who manifested herself visibly to me during yesterday's festivities. Go, then, one or other of you to the plain, tell the stockman to find a heifer, and come on here with it at once. Another must go to Telemachus' ship, and invite all the crew, leaving two men only in charge of the vessel. Someone else will run and fetch Laerceus the goldsmith to gild the horns of the heifer. The rest, stay all of you where you are; tell the maids in the house to prepare an excellent dinner, and to fetch seats, and logs of wood for a burnt offering. Tell them also to bring me some clear spring water."

On this they hurried off on their several errands. The heifer was brought in from the plain, and Telemachus' crew came from the ship. The goldsmith brought the anvil, hammer, and tongs, with which he worked his gold, and Athene herself came to accept the sacrifice. Nestor gave out the gold, and the smith gilded the horns of the heifer that the goddess might have pleasure in their beauty. Then Stratius and Echephron brought her in by the horns; Aretus fetched water from the house in a ewer that had a flower pattern on it, and in his other hand he held a basket of barley meal; sturdy Thrasymedes stood by with a sharp axe, ready to strike the heifer, while Pesseus held a bucket. Then Nestor began with washing his hands and sprinkling the barley meal, and he offered many a prayer to Athene as he threw a lock from the heifer's head upon the fire.

When they had done praying and sprinkling the barley meal Thrasymedes dealt his blow, and brought the heifer down with a stroke that cut through the tendons at the base of her neck, whereupon the daughters and daughters-in-law of Nestor, and his venerable wife Eurydice (she was eldest daughter to Clymenus) screamed with delight. Then they lifted the heifer's head from off the ground, and Pisistratus cut her throat. When she had done bleeding and was quite dead, they cut her up. They cut out the thighbones all in due course, wrapped them round in two layers of fat, and set some pieces of raw meat on the top of them; then Nestor laid them upon the wood fire and poured wine over them, while the young men stood near him with five-pronged spits in their hands. When the thighs were burned and they had tasted the inward meats, they cut the rest of the meat up small, put the pieces on the spits and toasted them over the fire.

Figure 2.1 Among the earliest public representations of aristocratic life and values are large craters such as this one made in Athens in the late eighth century B.C. (height 42⅝ inches; diameter 28½ inches), which were used as grave markers of aristocratic males. Decorated in the geometric style, its two registers illustrate the familial and public aspects of an aristocratic funeral: the laying out of the body on a bier surrounded by family members and mourners and the procession of horse-drawn wagons and warriors to the burial site. By permission of the Metropolitan Museum of Art, New York, Rogers Fund.

C. Aspects of Aristocratic Life at Its Peak

The four poems in this section illuminate different aspects of Greek aristocratic life from the seventh century B.C. to the end of the sixth century B.C.

1. A FINE SYMPOSIUM: XENOPHANES

Xenophanes, Fragment B1

From the seventh century B.C. onward, the heart of aristocratic culture was the symposium. A male-only drinking party, the symposium offered aristocratic males a rich mixture of music, dance, poetry, games, and sex. New forms of poetry, called lyric because they were sung to accompaniment of the lyre, were created for symposia. Potters and metal workers produced a variety of fine drinking and mixing vessels for symposia, while even house design was adapted to the needs of the symposium. In this poem the sixth-century B.C. philosopher poet Xenophanes of Colophon offers an idealized picture of a fine symposium.[5]

For now the floor is clean and the hands of everyone and the drinking cups also. A slave boy crowns the guests with woven wreathes. Another boy offers them sweet smelling myrrh in a bowl. The mixing bowl stands ready in the center, full

---

[5] Xenophanes, Fragment B1 (Diels).

of good cheer. Other wine, which declares that it will never fail, is ready in the jug, smooth and with a fine bouquet. In the middle frankincense releases its holy odor; and the water is cool and sweet and pure. Yellow loaves of bread and a splendid table loaded with cheese and thick honey stands before us. The altar between us has been decked all round with flowers. The house is full of singing and dancing and feasting.

Merry men must first praise the god with pious stories and pure words. When they have offered libations and prayed that they be able to do what is just—for these are the preliminaries—it is not arrogance to drink as much as would allow a man who is not sunk in old age to come home without a servant to guide him. And that man must also be praised who, while drinking, reveals himself noble with a good memory and striving for excellence. He should not recount the battles of the Titans and the Giants, nor anything about the Centaurs, inventions of our ancestors, or bitter political disputes—there is nothing beneficial in these things—but it is always good to have reverence for the gods.

2. THE LIFE OF AN ARISTOCRAT: ALCAEUS

Athletics, war, and politics were the main themes of aristocratic life. In this poem the Lesbian poet Alcaeus recalls from exile the splendid array of weapons he had kept in his home.[6] | *Alcaeus*

The great house is all agleam with bronze. War has bedecked the whole roof with bright helmets, from which hang waving horse-hair plumes to make adornment for the heads of men; the pegs are hidden with bright brazen greaves to ward off the strong arrow, corselets of new linen cloth and hollow shields are piled upon the floor, and beside them swords of Chalcidian steel, and many a doublet, many a kilt. These we cannot forget, so soon as we undertake this task.

3. WHEN YOU ARE "REPULSIVE TO BOYS AND A LAUGHING STOCK TO WOMEN": MIMNERMUS ON OLD AGE

As Greek art and literature abundantly demonstrate, aristocratic culture was in many ways a youth culture, valuing above all physical beauty, bravery, athletic achievement, and sensuality. In this poem the elegiac poet Mimnermus of Smyrna eloquently voices the despair that comes with old age, which robs men of all those things.[7] | Mimnermus F 1

What is life and what is pleasure without Golden Aphrodite? May I die when secret love, pleasing gifts and bed no longer concern me. Such are the flowers of youth that are dear to men and women. But when grim old age approaches,

[6] Adapted from *Lyra Graeca*, Vol. 1, ed. and trans. J. M. Edmonds (Cambridge, 1928).

[7] From Mimnermus F 1 (Gerber).

Figure 2.2 Probably a majority of painted vases were made for the symposia of the aristocracy. Frequently symposia are themselves represented, although here we see the aftereffects of one. Returning reveler. Red-figure Oinochoe, late fifth century B.C. By permission of the Metropolitan Museum of Art, New York, the Fletcher Fund.

and makes a man completely disgusting and evil, and foul cares always fill his thoughts, and looking on the rays of the sun does not please him, then he is repulsive to boys and a laughing stock to women. So painful has god made old age.

4. A WOMAN'S VIEW OF ARISTOCRATIC LIFE: SAPPHO'S "TO ANACTORIA"

Sappho *Much less is known about the social life and values of aristocratic Greek women than of men. Such evidence as there is, however, indicates that their culture also emphasized music, poetry, and eroticism like that of their male counterparts. In this poem by Alcaeus' contemporary, the poetess Sappho deftly asserts the superiority of female beauty to the military virtues dear to aristocratic males.*[8]

The fairest thing in all the world some say is a host of foot, and some again a navy of ships, but to some it is the heart's beloved. And it is easy to make this understood by any. Helen, who far surpassed all mankind in beauty, chose for the best of men the destroyer of all the honor of Troy, and thought not so much either of child or parent dear, but was led astray by Love to bestow her heart afar, for woman is ever easy to be bent when she thinks lightly of what is near and dear.

[8] Adapted from *Lyra Graeca*, p. 209.

See to it then that you remember us Anactoria, now that we are parted from one of whom I would rather hear the sweet sound of her footfall and see the brightness of her beaming face than all the chariots and armored footmen of Lydia. I know that in this world man cannot have the best; yet to wish that one had share [in what was once shared is better than to forget it].

D. Heroic Athletics: The Chariot Race at Patroclus' Funeral Games

According to a famous American sportsman, "Winning isn't everything, it's the only thing." The Greeks would have agreed, as can be seen from Homer's vivid description of a chariot race, the earliest account of an athletic event in Western literature. Homer's account brilliantly evokes the excitement of the race itself. Equally important, it clearly illustrates the importance the Greeks ascribed not only to winning but also to avoiding the public humiliation that was the inevitable result of defeat.[9]

Homer,
Iliad

When they had thus raised a mound they were going away, but Achilles stayed the people and made them sit in assembly. He brought prizes from the ships—cauldrons, tripods, horses and mules, noble oxen, women with fair girdles, and dark iron.

The first prize he offered was for the chariot races—a woman skilled in all useful arts, and a three-legged cauldron that had ears for handles, and would hold twenty-two measures. This was for the man who came in first. For the second there was a six-year old mare, unbroken, and in foal to a he-ass; the third was to have a goodly cauldron that had never yet been on the fire; it was still bright as when it left the maker, and would hold four measures. The fourth prize was two talents of gold, and the fifth a two-handled urn as yet unsoiled by smoke. Then he stood up and spoke among the Argives saying—

"Son of Atreus, and all other Achaeans, these are the prizes that lie waiting the winners of the chariot races. At any other time I should carry off the first prize and take it to my own tent; you know how far my steeds excel all others—for they are immortal; Poseidon gave them to my father Peleus, who in his turn gave them to myself; but I shall hold aloof, I and my steeds that have lost their brave and kind driver, who many a time has washed them in clear water and anointed their manes with oil. See how they stand weeping here, with their manes trailing on the ground in the extremity of their sorrow. But do you others set yourselves in order throughout the host, whosoever has confidence in his horses and in the strength of his chariot."

---

[9] Homer, *Iliad* 23, lines 262–595 (selections). From *The Iliad of Homer*, trans. S. Butler (London, 1914).

Thus spoke the son of Peleus and the drivers of chariots bestirred themselves. First among them all uprose Eumelus, king of men, son of Admetus, a man excellent in horsemanship. Next to him rose mighty Diomedes son of Tydeus; he yoked the Trojan horses which he had taken from Aeneas, when Apollo bore him out of the fight. Next to him, yellow-haired Menelaus son of Atreus rose and yoked his fleet horses, Agamemnon's mare Aethe, and his own horse Podargus. The mare had been given to Agamemnon by Echepolus son of Anchises, that he might not have to follow him to Ilius, but might stay at home and take his ease; for Zeus had endowed him with great wealth and he lived in spacious Sicyon. This mare, all eager for the race, did Menelaus put under the yoke.

Fourth in order Antilochus, son to noble Nestor son of Neleus, made ready his horses, and fifth in order Meriones got ready his horses. They then all mounted their chariots and cast lots. Achilles shook the helmet, and the lot of Antilochus son of Nestor fell out first; next came that of King Eumelus, and after his, those of Menelaus son of Atreus and of Meriones. The last place fell to the lot of Diomedes son of Tydeus, who was the best man of them all. They took their places in line; Achilles showed them the doubling-post round which they were to turn, some way off upon the plain; here he stationed his father's follower Phoenix as umpire, to note the running, and report truly. . . .

At the same instant they all of them lashed their horses, struck them with the reins, and shouted at them with all their might. They flew full speed over the plain away from the ships, the dust rose from under them as it were a cloud or whirlwind, and their manes were all flying in the wind. At one moment the chariots seemed to touch the ground, and then again they bounded into the air; the drivers stood erect, and their hearts beat fast and furious in their lust of victory. Each kept calling on his horses, and the horses scoured the plain amid the clouds of dust that they raised.

It was when they were doing the last part of the course on their way back towards the sea that their pace was strained to the utmost and it was seen what each could do. The horses of the descendant of Pheres now took the lead, and close behind them came the Trojan stallions of Diomedes. They seemed as if about to mount Eumelus's chariot, and he could feel their warm breath on his back and on his broad shoulders, for their heads were close to him as they flew over the course. Diomedes would have now passed him, or there would have been a dead heat, but Phoebus Apollo to spite him made him drop his whip. Tears of anger fell from his eyes as he saw the mares going on faster than ever, while his own horses lost ground through his having no whip. Athena saw the trick which Apollo had played the son of Tydeus, so she brought him his whip and put spirit into his horses; moreover she went after the son of Admetus in a rage and broke his yoke for him; the mares went one to one side the course, and the other to the other, and the pole was broken against the ground. Eumelus was thrown from his chariot close to the wheel; his elbows, mouth, and nostrils were all torn, and his forehead was bruised above his eyebrows; his eyes filled with tears and he could find no utterance. But the son of Tydeus turned his horses aside and shot far ahead, for Athena put fresh strength into them and covered Diomedes himself with glory.

Menelaus son of Atreus came next behind him, but Antilochus called to his father's horses. "On with you both," he cried, "and do your very utmost. I do not bid you try to beat the steeds of the son of Tydeus, for Athena has put running into them, and has covered Diomedes with glory; but you must overtake the horses of the son of Atreus and not be left behind, or Aethe who is so fleet will taunt you. Why, my good fellows, are you lagging? I tell you, and it shall surely be—Nestor will keep neither of you, but will put both of you to the sword, if we win any the worse a prize through your carelessness. Rush after them at your utmost speed: I will hit on a plan for passing them in a narrow part of the way, and it shall not fail me."

They feared the rebuke of their master, and for a short space went quicker. Presently Antilochus saw a narrow place where the road had sunk. The ground was broken, for the winter's rain had gathered and had worn the road so that the whole place was deepened. Menelaus was making towards it so as to get there first, for fear of a foul, but Antilochus turned his horses out of the way, and followed him a little on one side. The son of Atreus was afraid and shouted out, "Antilochus, you are driving recklessly; rein in your horses; the road is too narrow here, it will be wider soon, and you can pass me then; if you foul my chariot you may bring both of us to a mischief."

But Antilochus plied his whip, and drove faster, as though he had not heard him. They went side by side for about as far as a young man can hurl a disc from his shoulder when he is trying his strength, and then Menelaus's mares drew behind, for he left off driving for fear the horses should foul one another and upset the chariots; thus, while pressing on in quest of victory, they might both come headlong to the ground. Menelaus then upbraided Antilochus and said, "There is no greater trickster living than you are; go, and bad luck go with you: the Achaeans say not well that you have understanding, and come what may you shall not bear away the prize without sworn protest on my part."

Then he called on his horses and said to them, "Keep your pace, and slacken not; the limbs of the other horses will weary sooner than yours, for they are neither of them young."

The horses feared the rebuke of their master, and went faster, so that they were soon nearly up with the others.

Meanwhile the Achaeans from their seats were watching how the horses went, as they scoured the plain amid clouds of their own dust. Idomeneus captain of the Cretans was first to make out the running, for he was not in the thick of the crowd, but stood on the most commanding part of the ground. The driver was a long way off, but Idomeneus could hear him shouting, and could see the foremost horse quite plainly—a chestnut with a round white star, like the moon, on its forehead. He stood up and said among the Argives, "My friends, princes and counsellors of the Argives, can you see the running as well as I can? There seems to be another pair in front now, and another driver; those that led off at the start must have been disabled out on the plain. I saw them at first making their way round the doubling-post, but now, though I search the plain of Troy, I cannot find them. Perhaps the reins fell from the driver's hand so that he lost command of his horses at the doubling-post, and could not turn it. I suppose he must have been thrown out there, and broken his chariot, while his mares have left the course and gone off wildly in a panic. Come up and see for yourselves, I cannot make out for certain, but the driver seems an Aetolian by descent, ruler over the Argives, brave Diomedes the son of Tydeus."

As he was speaking, the son of Tydeus came driving in, plying his whip lustily from his shoulder, and his horses stepping high as they flew over the course. The sand and grit rained thick on the driver, and the chariot inlaid with gold and tin ran close behind his fleet horses. There was little trace of wheelmarks in the fine dust, and the horses came flying in at their utmost speed. Diomedes stayed them in the middle of the crowd, and the sweat from their manes and chests fell in streams on to the ground. Forthwith he sprang from his goodly chariot, and leaned his whip against his horses' yoke; brave Sthenelus now lost no time, but at once brought on the prize, and gave the woman and the ear-handled cauldron to his comrades to take away. Then he unyoked the horses.

Next after him came in Antilochus of the race of Neleus, who had passed Menelaus by a trick and not by the fleetness of his horses; but even so Menelaus came in as close behind him as the wheel is to the horse that draws both the chariot and its master. The end hairs of a horse's tail touch the tire of the wheel, and there is never much space between wheel and horse when the chariot is going; Menelaus was no further than this behind Antilochus, though at first he had been a full disc's throw behind him. He had soon caught him up again, for Agamemnon's mare Aethe kept pulling stronger and stronger, so that if the course had been longer he would have passed him, and there would not even have been a dead heat. Idomeneus's brave squire Meriones was about a spear's cast behind Menelaus. His horses were slowest of all, and he was the worst driver. Last of them all came the son of Admetus, dragging his chariot and driving his horses on in front. When Achilles saw him he was sorry, and stood up among the Argives saying, "The best man is coming in last. Let us give him a prize for it is reasonable. He shall have the second, but the first must go to the son of Tydeus."

Thus did he speak and the others all of them applauded his saying, and were for doing as he had said, but Nestor's son Antilochus stood up and claimed his rights from the son of Peleus. "Achilles," said he, "I shall take it much amiss if you do this thing; you would rob me of my prize, because you think Eumelus's chariot and horses were thrown out, and himself too, good man that he is. He should have prayed duly to the immortals; he would not have come in last if he had done so. If you are sorry for him and so choose, you have much gold in your tents, with bronze, sheep, cattle and horses. Take something from this store if you would have the Achaeans speak well of you, and give him a better prize even than that which you have now offered; but I will not give up the mare, and he that will fight me for her, let him come on."

Achilles smiled as he heard this, and was pleased with Antilochus, who was one of his dearest comrades. So he said—

"Antilochus, if you would have me find Eumelus another prize, I will give him the bronze breastplate with a rim of tin running all round it which I took from Asteropaeus. It will be worth much money to him."

He bade his comrade Automedon bring the breastplate from his tent, and he did so. Achilles then gave it over to Eumelus, who received it gladly.

But Menelaus got up in a rage, furiously angry with Antilochus. An attendant placed his staff in his hands and bade the Argives keep silence: the hero then addressed them. "Antilochus," said he, "what is this—from you who have been so far blameless? You have made me cut a poor figure and baulked my horses by flinging your own in front of them, though yours are much worse than mine are; therefore, O princes and counsellors of the Argives, judge between us and show no favour, lest one of the Achaeans say, 'Menelaus has got the mare through lying and corruption; his horses were far inferior to Antilochus's, but he has greater weight and influence.' Nay, I will determine the matter myself, and no man will blame me, for I shall do what is just. Come here, Antilochus, and stand, as our custom is, whip in hand before your chariot and horses; lay your hand on your steeds, and swear by earth-encircling Poseidon that you did not purposely and guilefully get in the way of my horses."

And Antilochus answered, "Forgive me; I am much younger, King Menelaus, than you are; you stand higher than I do and are the better man of the two; you know how easily young men are betrayed into indiscretion; their tempers are more hasty and they have less judgement; make due allowances therefore, and bear with me; I will of my own accord give up the mare that I have won, and if you claim any further chattel from my own possessions, I would rather yield it to you, at once, than fall from your good graces henceforth, and do wrong in the sight of heaven."

E. The Aristocracy and Its International Connections

The Greek aristocracy were among the most broadly experienced individuals of the archaic period, many serving as soldiers in the armies of the kingdoms of the Near East. The selections that follow illustrate various aspects of their experiences.

1. A GREEK OFFICER IN EGYPTIAN SERVICE

The following text is an inscription on an Egyptian-style statue dedicated at the temple of Athena at Priene by a man named Pedon to commemorate his distinguished career in the service of the Egyptian king Psamtek I (656–610 B.C.).[10]

Inscription at the temple of Athena at Priene

Pedon, the son of Amphinoos, dedicated me, having brought me from Egypt. The Egyptian king Psammetichus gave him a gold arm-band as a reward for bravery and a city because of his excellence.

[10] From Olivier Masson, "Un Inscription Ionienne Mentionnant Psammétique Ier," *Epigraphica Anatolica*, 11 (1988), p. 171.

2. GREEK MERCENARIES IN THE EGYPTIAN ARMY

Inscription from Ramses II's temple at Abou Simbel

Other Greeks chose to make a new life in Egypt. In this inscription from Ramses II's great temple at Abou Simbel Greek soldiers commemorated their role in the Egyptian invasion of Nubia in 593 B.C. Their leader Psammatichos, son of Theokles, bears an Egyptian name, presumably because his father Theokles was born in Egypt to a similarly named Greek soldier who served Psamtek I and chose to settle in Egypt.[11]

When King Psamatichos came to Elephantine, they wrote these things, who sailed with Psammatichos, the son of Theokles, and came above Kerkis as far as the river allowed. Potasimto was in charge of the foreign troops and Amasis of the Egyptian. Archon, son of Amoibichos and Pelekos, son of Eudamos wrote me.

3. THE LIFE OF A SOLDIER: AN ORDER FOR RATIONS AT ARAD IN THE KINGDOM OF JUDAH

Ostracon with military orders

An insight into the life of Greek soldiers in foreign service is provided by this ostracon—a piece of broken pottery used to write brief notes—which records an order to a military officer named Eliashib to provide rations to Kittiyîm (Greeks or Cyprotes), who formed part of the garrison of the fortress of Arad in the Negeb during the reign of King Josiah of Judah (640–609 B.C.).[12]

To Eliashib: And now, give the Kittiyîm, 3 baths of wine, and write the name of the day. And from the rest of the first flour, send one homer of flour in order to make bread for them. Give them the wine from the *aganoth* vessels.

4. ARISTOCRATIC EXILES

Some Greek aristocrats left Greece unwillingly. In the first passage the first century B.C. historian Dionysius of Halicarnassus summarizes the biography of Demaratus of Corinth, whose son Lucomo allegedly became the first Etruscan king of Rome under the name Tarquin the Elder (traditional date 616–579 B.C.).[13] Although more historical fiction than history, this story of the fortunes of a Corinthian refugee in seventh century B.C. Etruria illustrates the close relations between Corinth and Italy and the opportunities made possible by them. Aristocrats were warriors first and foremost. The second passage tells how Antimenides, the brother of the Mitylenian poet Alcaeus, entered Babylonian service after being exiled for participation in a plot against Pittacus, tyrant of Mitylene.

[11] From R. Meiggs and D. Lewis, *A Selection of Greek Historical Inscriptions to the End of the Fifth Century* (Oxford, 1969), no. 7, p. 12.

[12] From Yohanan Aharoni, *Arad Inscriptions* (Jerusalem, 1981), p. 12.

[13] Dionysius of Halicarnassus, *Roman Antiquities* 3.46.3–5.

In this fragment preserved by the early first-century A.D. *geographer Strabo, Alcaeus describes a heroic duel in which his brother defeated a "Goliath"-like giant soldier.*[14]

a. Demaratus of Corinth

There was a certain Corinthian named Demaratus, a member of the Bacchiad family, who chose to engage in commerce. He sailed to Italy with his own goods in his own ship. He sold his cargo in the cities of Etruria, which then were the most prosperous in Italy and acquired great wealth. From then on he no longer wished to visit other ports, but he traveled the same sea continuously, bringing Greek merchandise to the Etruscans and Etruscan to Greece, and became extremely wealthy. But when revolution broke out in Corinth and the tyranny of Cypselus rose up against the Bacchiads, he thought it was not safe for him to live under a tyranny with his great wealth besides belonging to the family that had dominated the oligarchy. Having collected together as much of his wealth as he could, he sailed away from Corinth. As he had many good Etruscan friends because of his frequent dealings with them, particularly in the city of Tarquinia, which was large and prosperous, he built a house there and married a woman from a distinguished family. He had two sons to whom he gave Etruscan names, one Arruns and one Lucumo. He educated them in both Greek and Etruscan learning, and when they reached adulthood, he obtained for them wives from distinguished families.

Dionysius of Halicarnassus on Demaratus of Corinth

b. Antimenides of Mitylene

Mitylene has produced famous men: in early times, Pittacus, one of the Seven Wise Men; and the poet Alcaeus, and his brother Antimenides, who, according to Alcaeus, won a great struggle when fighting on the side of the Babylonians, and rescued them from their toils by killing "a warrior, the royal wrestler" (as he says), "who was but one short of five cubits in height."

Strabo, Geography

5. SAPPHO ON INTERMARRIAGE BETWEEN ARISTOCRATS

Aristocratic women also traveled. In this poem the poet Sappho consoles herself for the absence of a girl, who probably has married into the Lydian aristocracy, with the thought that her beauty outshines that of the women of Sardis, the capital of the kingdom of Lydia.[15]

Sappho F 86

[Atthis, our beloved dwells in far-off] Sardis, but she often sends her thoughts hither, thinking how once we used to live in the days when you were like a glorious Goddess to her and she loved your song the best. And now she shines among

[14] Strabo, *Geography*, 13. 2. 2–3, C 617. From Strabo, *Geography*, trans. H. L. Jones (Cambridge, MA, 1929).

[15] Sappho F 86 (Edmonds). Adapted from J. M. Edmonds, *Lyra Graeca*, Vol. 1, 2nd ed. (Cambridge, MA, 1928).

the dames of Lydia as after sunset the rosy-fingered Moon beside the stars that are about her, when she spreads her light over the briny sea and also over the flowery field, while the dew lies so fair on the ground and the roses revive and the dainty chervil and the melilot with all its blooms. And often time while our beloved wanders abroad, when she calls to mind the love of gentle Atthis, her tender breast, for sure, is weighed down deep with longing; and she cries aloud for us to come thither; and what she says we know full well, you and I, for flower-tressed Night that hath the many ears calls it to us along all that lies between.

F. The Crisis of the Aristocracy

1. THE LAMENT OF THEOGNIS

Theognis,
Elegies

Theognis is the author of two books of short poems. The few facts that are known concerning his life suggest that he was an aristocrat from the city of Megara just west of Athens and that he wrote during the sixth century B.C. *The main theme of his poetry is one common to aristocratic literature worldwide: the transmission of wisdom acquired by an experienced adult during his life to a young male protégé. The topics of his poetry are varied, but one that recurs frequently is the disruption of aristocratic social and political life by new wealth. The translation of the poems has been kept as literal as possible to highlight the simple moral oppositions characteristic of aristocratic morality, in which nobles are "good" and commoners are "bad," and any advancement by the latter is viewed as a threat to a just social order.*[16]

Dangerous Times for Megara

Cyrnus, this city is pregnant, and I fear that it will bring forth a man (= *tyrant*) who will be the chastiser of our evil arrogance. For the citizens are sensible but their leaders have turned straight toward complete evil.

Greed and the Origins of Social Strife

Never, Cyrnus, have good men (= *nobility*) destroyed a city; but whenever it pleases bad men (= *non-nobles*) to act arrogantly and corrupt the people and render judgments in favor of unjust men for their own gain and power, then do not expect that this city will remain unshaken for long, not even if it now lies in great peace, not when these things have become dear to bad men: the gains that accompany public ill. For from these come divisions and communal slaughters and rulers. May such things never please this city.

The End of the Aristocratic Monopoly of Government

Cyrnus, this city is the same city, but its people are different. Those who previously knew neither judgments nor laws, but wore goatskins about their flanks, and grazed like deer outside this city, now even these are good men, O Son of

[16] From Theognis, *Elegies* 1, lines 39–42, 43–52, 53–60, and 183–192.

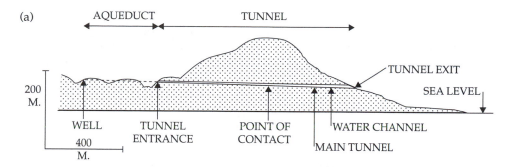

Figure 2.3a One of the most remarkable achievements of the Archaic Period was the almost one-mile-long tunnel dug by Eupalinus of Megara through a mountain on the island of Samos to bring water from a natural spring to the city of Samos. Diagram from K. D. White, *Greek and Roman Technology* (Ithaca 1984), p. 159.

Figure 2.3b Tunnel of Eupalinus. The grating covers the second lower tunnel, which carried the water. Photo by Stanley Burstein.

Polypaus. And they who formerly were nobles are now of no account. Who can endure observing these things? Laughing, they deceive each other, these men who know the stamp of neither bad nor good.

Wealth and the Decline of the Aristocracy

We seek rams and asses, Cyrnus, and horses that are well-bred, and one wishes to breed them from good stock. But to wed the bad daughter of a bad man does not shame a noble man, if one gives him much wealth; nor does a woman refuse to be the bedmate of a rich man, but she wishes a rich man instead of a good man. For they honor riches; and a noble man weds the offspring of a bad man and a bad man that of a noble man. Wealth confuses the stock. So do not wonder, O Son of Polypaus, that the stock of the citizens is obscured. For noble things are mixed with bad things.

2. VULGAR UPSTARTS: ARTEMON AND RHODOPIS

The core of Theognis' complaint is that social status is no longer determined by birth but by wealth. What disturbed him is well illustrated by the sixth-century B.C. poet Anacreon's vivid portrait of the upstart Artemon, who went from slave to rich man,[17] and Herodotus' account of the legendary courtesan Rhodopis, who some Greeks believed built the pyramid of Mycerinus (= Menkaure) and who used her wealth to make a dedication at Delphi just like any aristocrat.[18]

Anacreon

A. Once he went about in the pointed hat of a Cimmerian, with wooden knuckle bones in his ears, and about his ribs a hairy oxhide that had been the unwashed cover of a wretched shield—the scoundrel Artemon who made a fraudulent living by consorting with bread-wenches and whores-for-choice, with his neck often bound to the whipping-stock or else to the wheel, and his back often scarred with the leather scourge and his hair and beard plucked out; but now he goes in a coach, wearing earrings of gold like a mix-with-all, and carries an ivory sunshade as though he were a woman.

The History of Herodotus

B. 134. He (*sc. Mycerinus*) too left a pyramid, but much inferior in size to his father's. It is a square, each side of which is 280 feet, and is built for half its height of the stone of Ethiopia. Some of the Greeks call it the work of Rhodopis the courtesan, but they report falsely. It seems to me that these persons cannot have any real knowledge who Rhodopis was; otherwise they would scarcely have ascribed to her a work on which uncounted treasures, so to speak, must have been expended. Rhodopis also lived during the reign of Amasis, not of Mycerinus, and was thus very many years later than the time of the kings who built the pyramids. She was a Thracian by birth, and was the slave of Iadmon, son of Hephaestopolis, a Samian. Aesop, the fable-writer, was one of her fellow-slaves. That Aesop belonged to Iadmon is proved by many facts—among others, by this. When the Delphians, in obedience to the command of the oracle, made proclamation that if any one claimed compensation for the murder of Aesop he should receive it, the person who at last came forward was Iadmon, grandson of the former Iadmon, and he received

---

[17] Adapted from *Lyra Graeca*, ed. and trans. by J. M. Edmonds (Cambridge, MA, 1927), Vol. 2, pp. 189–191.

[18] *The History of Herodotus* 2.134–135 (New York, 1859–1860), trans. George Rawlinson.

the compensation. Aesop therefore must certainly have been the former Iadmon's slave.

135. Rhodopis really arrived in Egypt under the conduct of Xantheus the Samian; she was brought there to exercise her trade, but was redeemed for a vast sum by Charaxus, a Mytilenaean, the son of Scamandronymus, and brother of Sappho the poetess. After thus obtaining her freedom, she, remained in Egypt, and as she was very beautiful, amassed great wealth, for a courtesan; not, however, enough to enable her to erect such a work as this pyramid. Any one who likes may go and see to what the tenth part of her wealth amounted, and he will thereby learn that her riches must not be imagined to have been very wonderfully great. Wishing to leave a memorial of herself in Greece, she determined to have something made the like of which was not to be found in any temple, and to offer it at the shrine at Delphi. So she set apart a tenth of her possessions, and purchased with the money a quantity of iron spits, such as are fit for roasting oxen whole, whereof she made a present to the oracle. They are still to be seen there, lying of a heap, behind the altar which the Chians dedicated, opposite the sanctuary. Naucratis seems somehow to be the place where such women are most attractive. First there was this Rhodopis of whom we have been speaking, so celebrated a person that her name came to be familiar to all the Greeks; and, afterwards, there was another, called Archidice, notorious throughout Greece, though not so much talked of as her predecessor. Charaxus, after ransoming Rhodopis, returned to Mytilene, and was often lashed by Sappho in her poetry. But enough has been said on the subject of this courtesan.

3. THE CRISIS OF THE ARISTOCRACY AT CORINTH: CYPSELUS AND PERIANDER

Situations such as those alluded to by Theognis occurred in many Greek cities. The earliest and best known example is that of Corinth. Under the rule of a single extended family, the Bacchiads, and blessed with an economically advantageous location on the Isthmus of Corinth, Corinth prospered during the Archaic Period, founding colonies in Sicily, the Adriatic Sea, and northern Greece and becoming an important commercial center. Their monopoly of power and social isolation rendered the Bacchiads vulnerable, and their rule was overthrown in a rebellion led by Cypselus, a member of their family, who founded a tyranny that ruled Corinth for almost a century before being suppressed by Sparta in 587 B.C. Herodotus' account of this period appears in a speech critical of Spartan support of the overthrown Athenian tyrant Hippias (ca. 500 B.C.) that highlights the aristocratic view of tyranny as the negation of a just social and political order.[19]

The History of Herodotus

92. Such was the address of the Spartans (sc. *recommending the reestablishment of the Athenian tyranny*). The greater number of the allies listened

[19] *The History of Herodotus*, 5.92; 3.48–53 (New York, 1859–1860), trans. George Rawlinson.

without being persuaded. None however broke silence, but Sosicles the Corinthian, who exclaimed:

"Surely the heaven will soon be below, and the earth above, and men will henceforth live in the sea, and fish take their place upon the dry land, since you, Lacedaemonians, propose to put down free governments in the cities of Greece, and to set up tyrannies in their stead. There is nothing in the whole world so unjust, nothing so bloody, as a tyranny. If, however, it seems to you a desirable thing to have the cities under despotic rule, begin by putting a tyrant over yourselves, and then establish despots in the other states. While you continue yourselves, as you have always been, unacquainted with tyranny, and take such excellent care that Sparta may not suffer from it, to act as you are now doing is to treat your allies unworthily. If you knew what tyranny was as well as ourselves, you would be better advised than you now are in regard to it. The government at Corinth was once an oligarchy—a single clan, called the Bacchiads, who intermarried only among themselves, held the management of affairs. Now it happened that Amphion, one of these, had a daughter, named Labda, who was lame, and whom therefore none of the Bacchiads would consent to marry; so she was taken to wife by Aetion, son of Echecrates, a man of the township of Petra, who was, however, by descent of the race of the Lapithae, and of the house of Caeneus. Aetion, as he had no child either by this wife, or by any other, went to Delphi to consult the oracle concerning the matter. Scarcely had he entered the temple when the priestess saluted him in these words:

No one honors you now, Aetion, worthy of honor;
Labda shall soon be a mother—her offspring a rock, that will
  one day
Fall on the kingly race, and right the city of Corinth.

By some chance this address of the oracle to Aetion came to the ears of the Bacchiads, who until then had been unable to perceive the meaning of another earlier prophecy which likewise bore upon Corinth, and pointed to the same event as Aetion's prediction. It was the following:

When mid the rocks an eagle shall bear a carnivorous lion,
Mighty and fierce, he shall loosen the limbs of many beneath
  them.
Brood well upon this, all you Corinthian people,
You who dwell by fair Peirene, and beetling Corinth.

The Bacchiads had possessed this oracle for some time, but they were quite at a loss to know what it meant until they heard the response given to Aetion; then, however, they at once perceived its meaning, since the two agreed so well together. Nevertheless, though the bearing of the first prophecy was now clear to them, they remained quiet, intending to put to death the child, which Aetion was expecting. As soon therefore, as his wife was delivered, they sent ten of their number to the township where Aetion lived, with orders to make away with the baby. So the men came to Petra, and went into Aetion's house, and there asked, if they might see the child. Labda, who knew nothing of their purpose, but thought their inquiries arose from a kindly feeling towards her husband, brought the child, and laid him in the arms of one of them. Now they had agreed during their journey that whoever first got hold of the child should dash it against the ground. It happened, however, by a providential chance, that the baby, just as Labda put him into the man's arms, smiled in his face. The man saw the smile, and was touched with pity, so that he could not kill it. He therefore passed it on to his neighbor, who gave it to a third; and so it went through all the ten without any one choosing to be the murderer.

The mother received her child back, and the men went out of the house and stood near the door, and there blamed and reproached one another, especially accusing the man who had first had the child in his arms, because he had not done as had been agreed upon. At last, after spending much time this way, they resolved to go into the house again and all take part in the murder. But it was fated that evil should come upon Corinth from the progeny of Aetion. So it happened that Labda, as she stood near the door, heard all that the men said to one another. Fearful of their changing their mind, and returning to destroy her baby, she carried him off and hid him in what seemed to her the most unlikely place to be suspected, a cypsel or grain-bin. She knew that when they came back to look for the child, they would search all her house, and so indeed they did. Not finding the child after looking every where, they decided to go away and report to those by whom they had been sent that they had done their bidding. And thus they reported on their return home. Aetion's son grew up and in commemoration of the danger from which he had escaped, was named Cypselus after the grain-bin.

When he had grown up, he went to Delphi, and on consulting the oracle, received a response which was two-sided. It was the following:

> See there comes to my dwelling a fortunate man,
> Cypselus, son of Aetion, and king of the glorious Corinth,
> He and his children too, but not his children's children.

Such was the oracle; and Cypselus (ca. 657–627 B.C.) put so much faith in it that he immediately made his attempt, and thereby became master of Corinth. Having thus got the tyranny, he showed himself a harsh ruler— many of the Corinthians he drove into banishment, many he deprived of their fortunes, and a still greater number of their lives. His reign lasted thirty years, was prosperous to its end; insomuch that he left the government to Periander (ca. 627–587 B.C.), his son.

This prince at the beginning of his reign was of a milder temper than his father; but after he corresponded by means of messengers with Thrasybulus, tyrant of Miletus, he became even more savage. On one occasion he sent a herald to ask Thrasybulus what kind of government it was safest to set up in order to rule with honor. Thrasybulus led the messenger without the city, and took him into a field of wheat, through which he began to walk, while he asked him again and again concerning his trip from Corinth, while breaking off as he walked and throwing away all such ears of wheat as were higher than the rest. In this way he went through the whole field, and destroyed all the best and richest part of the crop. Then, without a word, he sent the messenger back. On the return of the man to Corinth, Periander was eager to know what Thrasybulus had advised. The messenger reported, however, that he had said nothing; and he wondered that Periander had sent him to so strange a man, who seemed to have lost his senses, since he did nothing but destroy his own property. And upon this he told how Thrasybulus had behaved at the interview. Periander, perceiving what the action meant, and knowing that Thrasybulus advised the destruction of all the leading citizens, treated his subjects from this time forward with the very greatest cruelty. Where Cypselus had spared any, and had neither put them to death nor banished them, Periander completed what his father had left unfinished. One day he stripped all the women of Corinth stark naked, for the sake of his own wife Melissa. He had sent messengers into Thesprotia to consult the oracle of the dead upon the Acheron concerning a pledge, which had been given into his charge by a stranger, and Melissa appeared, but refused to speak or tell where the pledge was. 'She was cold,' she said, 'having no clothes; the garments buried with her were of no manner of use, since they had not been burnt. And this should be her token to Periander, that what she said was true—the oven was cold when he baked his loaves in it.' When this message was brought him, Periander knew the token for he had had intercourse with the dead body of Melissa. Wherefore he immediately issued a proclamation that all the wives of the Corinthians should go to the temple of Hera. So the women dressed themselves in their best clothes, and went out, as if to a festival. Then, with the help of his guards, whom he had placed for the purpose, he stripped them one and all, making no difference between the free women and the slaves; and, taking their clothes to a pit, he called on the name of Melissa, and burnt the whole heap. When this was done, he sent a second time to the oracle, and Melissa's ghost told him where he would find the stranger's pledge. Such, Lacedaemonians, is tyranny and such are the deeds, which spring from it."

In another passage Herodotus gives further examples of Periander's legendary cruelty, describing the family chaos that followed the death of his wife and incidentally illustrating the emergence of Corinth as a major Aegean power, establishing diplomatic ties with states such as Lydia and exercising direct rule over some of its colonies, such as Corcyra.

48. The Corinthians likewise right willingly lent a helping hand towards the expedition against Samos; for a generation earlier, about the time of the seizure of the wine-bowl, they too had suffered insult at the hands of the Samians. It happened that Periander, son of Cypselus, had taken 300 boys,

children of the chief nobles among the Corcyraeans, and sent them to Alyattes for eunuchs; the men who had them in charge touched at Samos on their way to Sardis; whereupon the Samians, having found out what was to become of the boys when they reached that city, first prompted them to take sanctuary at the temple of Artemis; and after this, when the Corinthians, as they were forbidden to tear the suppliants from the holy place, sought to cut off from them all supplies of food, invented a festival in their behalf, which they celebrate to this day with the self-same rites. Each evening, as night closed in, during the whole time that the boys continued there, choirs of youths and virgins were placed about the temple, carrying in their hands cakes made of sesame and honey, in order that the Corcyraean boys might snatch the cakes, and so get enough to live upon.

49. And this went on for so long, that at last the Corinthians who had charge of the boys gave them up, and took their departure, upon which the Samians conveyed them back to Corcyra. If, now, after the death of Periander, the Corinthians and Corcyraeans had been good friends, it is not to be imagined that the former would ever have taken part in the expedition against Samos for such a reason as this; but as, in fact, the two people have always, ever since the first settlement of the island, been enemies to one another, this outrage was remembered, and the Corinthians bore the Samians a grudge for it. Periander had chosen the youths from among the first families in Corcyra, and sent them to Sardis for castration, to revenge a wrong which he had received. For it was the Corcyraeans, who began the quarrel and injured Periander by an outrage of a horrid nature.

50. After Periander had put to death his wife Melissa, it chanced that on this first affliction a second followed of a different kind. His wife had borne him two sons, and one of them had now reached the age of seventeen, the other of eighteen years, when their mother's father, Procles, tyrant of Epidaurus, asked them to his court. They went, and Procles treated them with much kindness, as was natural, considering they were his own daughter's children. At length, when the time for parting came, Procles, as he was sending them on their way, said 'Know you now, my children, who it was that caused your mother's death?' The elder son took no account of this speech, but the younger whose name was Lycophron, was sorely troubled at it—so much so that when he got back to Corinth, looking upon his father as his mother's murderer, he would neither speak to him, nor answer when spoken to, nor utter a word in reply to all his questionings. So Periander at last growing furious at such behavior, banished him from his house.

51. The younger son gone, he turned to the elder and asked him what it was that their grandfather had said to them. Then he related how kind and friendly a fashion he had received them; but, not having taken any notice of the speech, which Procles had uttered at parting, he quite forgot to mention it. Periander insisted that it was not possible this should be all—their grandfather must have given them some hint or other—and he went on pressing him, till at last the lad remembered that parting speech

and told it. Periander, after he had turned the whole matter over in his thoughts, and felt unwilling to give way at all, sent a messenger to the persons who had opened their houses to his outcast son and forbade them to harbor him. Then the boy, when he was chased from one friend, sought refuge with another, but was driven from shelter to shelter by the threats of his father, who menaced all those that took him in, and commanded them to shut their doors against him, Still as fast as he was forced to leave one house he went to another, and was received by the inmates; for his acquaintance, although in no small alarm, yet gave him shelter, as he was Periander's son.

52. At last Periander made proclamation that whoever harbored his son or even spoke to him, should forfeit a certain sum of money to Apollo. On hearing this no one any longer liked to take him in, or even to converse with him, and he himself did not think it right to seek to do what was forbidden. So, abiding by his resolve, he made his lodging in the public porticos. When four days had passed in this way, Periander seeing how wretched his son was, that he neither washed nor took any food, felt moved with compassion towards him. Wherefore, foregoing his anger, he approached him, and said, 'Which is better, my son, to fare as now you fare, or to receive my crown and all the good things that I possess, on the one condition of submitting to your father? See, now, though my own child, and lord of this wealthy Corinth, you have brought yourself to a beggar's life, because you resist and treat with anger him whom you should least oppose. If there has been a calamity, and you bear me ill will on that account, think that I too feel it, and am the greatest sufferer, in as much as it was by me that the deed was done. For yourself, now that you know how much better a thing it is to be envied than pitied, and how dangerous it is to indulge anger against parents and superiors, come back with me to your home.' With such words as these did Periander chide his son; but the son made no reply except to remind his father that he owed the god the penalty for coming and talking with him. Then Periander knew that there was no cure for the youth's malady, nor means of overcoming it; so he prepared a ship and sent him away out of his sight to Corcyra, which island at that time belonged to him. As for Procles, Periander, regarding him as the true author of all his present troubles, went to war with him as soon as his son was gone, and not only made himself master of his kingdom Epidaurus, but also took Procles himself, and carried him into captivity.

53. As time went on, and Periander came to be old, he found himself no longer equal to the oversight and management of affairs. Seeing, therefore, in his eldest son no manner of ability, but knowing him to be dull and blockish, he sent to Corcyra and recalled Lycophron to take the kingdom. Lycophron, however, did not even ask the bearer of this message a question. But Periander's heart was set upon the youth, so he sent again to him, this time by his own daughter, the sister of Lycophron, who would, he thought, have more power to persuade him than any other person. Then

she, when she reached Corcyra, spoke thus with her brother, 'Do you wish the kingdom, brother, to pass into strange hands, and our father's wealth to be made a prey, rather than yourself return to enjoy it? Come back home with me, and cease to punish yourself. It is scant gain, this obstinacy. Why seek to cure evil by evil? Mercy, remember, is by many set above justice. Many, also, while pushing their mother's claims have forfeited their father's fortune. Power is a slippery thing—it has many suitors; and he is old and stricken in years—let not your inheritance go to another.' Thus did the sister, who had been tutored by Periander what to say, urge all the arguments most likely to have weight with her brother. He however answered, that so long as he knew his father to be still alive, he would never go back to Corinth. When the sister brought Periander this reply, he sent to his son a third time by a herald, and said he would come himself to Corcyra, and let his son take his place at Corinth as heir to his kingdom. To these terms Lycophron agreed and Periander was making ready to pass into Corcyra and his to return to Corinth, when the Corcyraeans, being informed of what was taking place, to keep Periander away, put the young man to death. For this reason it was that Periander took vengeance on the Corcyraeans."

4. THE CRISIS OF THE ARISTOCRACY AT ATHENS: SOLON

Crises did not always end with the establishment of a tyrant. Instead, a lawgiver might be appointed who was empowered to impose necessary reforms and incorporate them into a written law code—one of the earliest public uses of literacy in Greece—that would become authoritative upon the end of his term of office. The best documented example of the appointment of a lawgiver is that of Athens, where a severe crisis that had brought the city to the verge of civil war was resolved by a series of reforms carried out in 594 B.C. by the aristocratic poet and lawgiver Solon. The principal source of information for the Athenian crisis was Solon's own poetry; extensive quotations from it are preserved in Aristotle's famous Constitution of Athens, *a work long thought to be lost until an ancient papyrus copy was discovered in Egypt in 1889. There is much scholarly dispute about the origins and course of the crisis, but two facts are clear. First, Solon defused the immediate problem by ending a system of sharecropping called* Hectemorage *and outlawing in Athens the practice of enslaving debtors who failed to repay their loans. Second, although Solon himself cannot be described as a democrat, he made an essential contribution to the development of the later Athenian democracy by substituting wealth for noble birth as the criterion for holding political office.[20]*

Aristotle, *The Constitution of Athens*

2. After this event there was contention for a long time between the upper classes and the populace. Not only was the constitution at this time oligarchical in every respect, but the poorer classes, men, women, and children, were

[20] Aristotle, *The Constitution of Athens* 2.5–12 (Oxford, 1892) (selections), trans. Frederick G. Kenyon.

the serfs of the rich. They were known as Pelatae and also as Hectemores, because they cultivated the lands of the rich at the rent thus indicated. The whole country was in the hands of a few persons, and if the tenants failed to pay their rent they were liable to be haled into slavery, and their children with them. All loans were secured upon the debtor's person, a custom, which prevailed until the time of Solon, who was the first to appear as the champion of the people. But the hardest and bitterest part of the constitution in the eyes of the masses was their state of serfdom. Not but what they were also discontented with every other feature of their lot; for, to speak generally, they had no part nor share in anything. . . .

5. (Since) . . . the many were in slavery to the few, the people rose against the upper class. The strife was keen, and for a long time the two parties were ranged in hostile camps against one another, till at last, by common consent, they appointed Solon to be mediator and Archon, and committed the whole constitution to his hands. . . . By birth and reputation Solon was one of the foremost men of the day, but in wealth and position he was of the middle class, as is generally agreed, and is, indeed, established by his own evidence in these poems, where he exhorts the wealthy not to be grasping.

6. As soon as he was at the head of affairs, Solon liberated the people once and for all, by prohibiting all loans on the security of the debtor's person; and in addition he made laws by which he cancelled all debts, public and private. This measure is commonly called the *Seisachtheia* (removal of burdens), since thereby the people had their loads removed from them.

7. Next Solon drew up a constitution and enacted new laws; and the ordinances of Draco ceased to be used, with the exception of those relating to murder. The laws were inscribed on the wooden stands, and set up in the King's Porch, and all swore to obey them; and the nine Archons made oath upon the stone, declaring that they would dedicate a golden statue if they should transgress any of them. This is the origin of the oath to that effect, which they take to the present day. Solon ratified his laws for 100 years; and the following was the fashion in which he organized the constitution. He divided the population according to property into four classes, just as it had been divided before, namely, *Pentacosiomedimni*, Knights, *Zeugitae*, and *Thetes*. The various magistracies, namely, the nine Archons, the Treasurers, the Commissioners for Public Contracts, the Eleven, and the Fiscal Clerks, he assigned to the *Pentacosiomedimni*, the Knights, and the *Zeugitae*, giving offices to each class in proportion to the value of their rateable property. To those who ranked among the Thetes he gave nothing but a place in the Assembly and in the juries. A man had to rank as a Pentacosiomedimnus if he made, from his own land, 500 measures, whether liquid or solid. Those ranked as Knights who made 300 measures, or, as some say, those who were able to maintain a horse. In support of the latter definition they adduce the name of the class, which may be supposed to be derived from this fact,

and also some votive offerings of early times; for in the Acropolis there is a votive offering, a statue of Diphilus, bearing this inscription:

Anthemion, the son of Diphilos, made this dedication to the gods,
when he exchanged the status of a Thete for that of a Knight (*Hippeis*).

And a horse stands in evidence beside the man, implying that this was what was meant by belonging to the rank of Knight. At the same time it seems reasonable to suppose that this class, like the *Pentacosiomedimni*, was defined by the possession of an income of a certain number of measures. Those ranked as *Zeugitae* who made 200 measures, liquid or solid; and the rest ranked as Thetes, and were not eligible for any office. Hence it is that even at the present day, when a candidate for any office is asked to what class he belongs, no one would think of saying that he belonged to the Thetes. . . .

9. Such, then, was his legislation concerning the magistracies. There are three points in the constitution of Solon which appear to be its most democratic features: first and most important, the prohibition of loans on the security of the debtor's person; secondly, the right of every person who so willed to claim redress on behalf of any one to whom wrong was being done; thirdly, the institution of the appeal to the jury-courts; and it is to this last, they say, that the masses have owed their strength most of all, since, when the democracy is master of the voting-power, it is master of the constitution. Moreover, since the laws were not drawn up in simple and explicit terms (but like the one concerning inheritances and wards of state), disputes inevitably occurred, and the courts had to decide in every matter, whether public or private. Some persons in fact believe that Solon deliberately made the laws indefinite, in order that the final decision might be in the hands of the people. This, however, is not probable, and the reason no doubt was that it is impossible to attain ideal perfection when framing a law in general terms; for we must judge of his intentions, not from the actual results in the present day, but from the general tenor of the rest of his legislation. . . .

11. When he had completed his organization of the constitution in the manner that has been described, he found himself beset by people coming to him and harassing him concerning his laws, criticizing here and questioning there, till, as he wished neither to alter what he had decided on nor yet to be an object of ill will to every one by remaining in Athens, he set off on a journey to Egypt, with the combined objects of trade and travel, giving out that he should not return for ten years. He considered that there was no call for him to expound the laws personally, but that every one should obey them just as they were written. Moreover, his position at this time was unpleasant. Many members of the upper class had been estranged from him on account of his abolition of debts, and both parties were alienated through their disappointment at the condition of things, which he had created. The mass of the people had expected him to make a complete redistribution of all property,

and the upper class hoped he would restore everything to its former position, or, at any rate, make but a small change. Solon, however, had resisted both classes. He might have made himself a despot by attaching himself to whichever party he chose, but he preferred, though at the cost of incurring the enmity of both, to be the saviour of his country and the ideal lawgiver.

12. The truth of this view of Solon's policy is established alike by common consent, and by the mention he has himself made of the matter in his poems. Thus:

> To the people I gave as much privilege as was proper, neither taking away from nor adding to their honor. As for those who had power and were preeminent in wealth, I took care that nothing shameful should happen to them. I stood firm, protecting both with my strong shield, and I allowed neither to be unjustly victorious.

Once more he speaks of the abolition of debts and of those who before were in servitude, but were released owing to the Seisachtheia:

> Which of those tasks for which I collected together the people did I give up before completing?. In the judgement of time let my best witness to these matters be black earth, great mother of the Olympian deities. I pulled up from her the boundary markers that had been planted in her everywhere. The earth that was formerly enslaved is now free. Many Athenians, who had been sold—some unjustly, some justly—I brought back to their divinely founded fatherland. Men who had fled into exile under the compulsion of debt and no longer spoke the Attic tongue because of their many wanderings, and men who endured bitter slavery here, trembling in fear at their master's whims, these men I made free. I used my power to do these things, uniting force and justice, and I accomplished what I had promised. I wrote laws equally for the bad and the good, accommodating straight justice to each. Had someone else, an evil-minded and ambitious man, taken up the goad as I did, he would not have held the people back. For if I had then done what they desired for their enemies, or what their opponents planned for them, this city would have been bereft of many men. For this reason I set up a firm defense on all sides, turning like a wolf in the midst of a pack of dogs.

5. THE CRISIS OF THE ARISTOCRACY AT ATHENS: CLEISTHENES

While Solon's reforms diffused the immediate crisis that threatened Athens at the beginning of the sixth century B.C.E., they did not end political turbulence. The next half century was marked by bitterly contested elections for the archonship and failed attempts to establish a tyranny. This turbulence only ended in 545 B.C.E. with the victory of Pisistratus, which opened a period of tyrannical government at Athens that lasted until 510 B.C.E., when Spartan intervention restored aristocratic rule. Conflict between Isagoras, who was supported by Sparta, and Cleisthenes, the head of the Alcmeonid family, over leadership of the new government led to renewed Spartan intervention and ultimately the reforms that became the foundation of the democracy of fifth-

century Athens. The first selection from Aristotle's Constitution of Athens describes the political background and details of Cleisthenes' reforms. The second selection is a quotation from the lost history of Athens of the third century B.C.E. Athenian priest and historian Philochorus intended to explain the unique Athenian institution of ostracism, which allowed Athenians to vote to exile a fellow citizen by scratching his name on an ostrakon, a piece of broden pottery. Despite the erroneous statement that the term of an ostracized person's exile was reduced from ten to five years, this passage provides the fullest and clearest surviving description of how an ostracism was conducted.

a. Cleisthenes' Reforms[21]

20. After the overthrow of the tyranny, the rival leaders in the state were Isagoras son of Tisander, a partisan of the tyrants, and Cleisthenes, who belonged to the family of the Alcmeonidae. Cleisthenes, being beaten in the political clubs, called in the people by giving the franchise to the masses. Thereupon Isagoras, finding himself left inferior in power, invited Cleomenes, who was united to him by ties of hospitality, to return to Athens, and persuaded him to "drive out the pollution," a plea derived from the fact that the Alcmeonidae were supposed to be under the curse of pollution. On this Cleisthenes retired from the country, and Cleomenes, entering Attica with a small force, expelled, as polluted, 700 Athenian families. Having effected this, he next attempted to dissolve the Council, and to set up Isagoras and 300 of his partisans as the supreme power in the state. The Council, however, resisted, the populace flocked together, and Cleomenes and Isagoras, with their adherents, took refuge in the Acropolis. Here the people sat down and besieged them for two days; and on the third they agreed to let Cleomenes and all his followers depart, while they summoned Cleisthenes and the other exiles back to Athens. When the people had thus obtained the command of affairs, Cleisthenes was their chief and popular leader. And this was natural; for the Alcmeonidae were perhaps the chief cause of the expulsion of the tyrants, and for the greater part of their rule were at perpetual war with them . . . .

21. The people, therefore, had good reason to place confidence in Cleisthenes. Accordingly, now that he was the popular leader, three years after the expulsion of the tyrants, in the archonship of Isagoras (508/7), his first step was to distribute the whole population into ten tribes in place of the existing four, with the object of intermixing the members of the different tribes, and so securing that more persons might have a share in the franchise. From this arose the saying "Do not look at the tribes" addressed to those who wished to scrutinize the lists of the old families. Next he made the Council to consist of 500 members instead of 400, each tribe now contributing fifty, whereas formerly each had sent 100. The reason why he did

Aristotle, The Constitution of Athens

---

[21] Aristotle, *The Constitution of Athens* 2.20–21 (Oxford, 1892) (selections), trans. Frederick G. Kenyon.

not organize the people into twelve tribes was that he might not have to use the existing division into trittyes; for the four tribes had twelve trittyes, so that he would not have achieved his object of redistributing the population in fresh combinations. Further, he divided the country into thirty groups of demes, ten from the districts about the city, ten from the coast, and ten from the interior. These he called trittyes; and he assigned three of them by lot to each tribe, in such a way that each should have one portion in each of these three localities. All who lived in any given deme he declared fellow demesmen, to the end that the new citizens might not be exposed by the habitual use of family names, but that men might be officially described by the names of their demes; and accordingly it is by the names of their demes that the Athenians speak of one another. He also instituted Demarchs, who had the same duties as the previously existing Naucrari; the demes being made to take the place of the naucraries. He gave names to the demes, some from the localities to which they belonged, some from the persons who founded them, since some of the areas no longer corresponded to localities possessing names. On the other hand he allowed every one to retain his family and clan and religious rites according to ancestral custom. The names given to the tribes were the ten, which the Pythia appointed out of the hundred selected national heroes.

22. By these reforms the constitution became much more democratic than that of Solon. The laws of Solon had been obliterated by disuse during the period of the tyranny, while Cleisthenes substituted new ones with the object of securing the goodwill of the masses. Among these was the law concerning ostracism. Four years after the establishment of this system, in the archonship of Hermocreon (501/0), they first imposed upon the Council of Five Hundred the oath which they take to the present day. Next they began to elect the generals by tribes, one from each tribe, while the Polemarch was the commander of the whole army. Then eleven years later, in the archonship of Phaenippus (490/89), they won the battle Marathon; and two years after this victory, when the people had now gained self-confidence, they for the first time made use of the law of ostracism. This had originally been passed as a precaution against men in high office, because Pisistratus took advantage of his position as a popular leader and general to make himself tyrant; and the first person ostracized was one of his relatives, Hipparchus son of Charmus, of the deme of Collytus, the very person on whose account especially Cleisthenes had enacted the law, as he wished to get rid of him. Hitherto, however, he had escaped; for the Athenians, with the usual leniency of the democracy, allowed all the partisans of the tyrants, who had not joined in their deeds in the time of the troubles, to remain in the city; and the chief and leader of these was Hipparchus. Then in the very next year, in the archonship of Telesinus (487/6), they for the first time since the tyranny elected, tribe by tribe, the nine Archons by lot out of the 500 candidates selected by the demes, all the earlier ones having been elected by vote . . . .

b. Ostracism[22]

Philochorus explains ostracism in the third book [of his Athenian history] as follows. "Ostracism is like this. The people determine by a preliminary vote before the eighth prytany (= February), if they will hold an ostracism. Whenever it was decided that they would hold an ostracism, the market-place was fenced in with wooden planks, and there were left open ten passages, through which people, entered by tribes, carrying their ostraka, so as to keep what they had written concealed. The nine archons and the council presided. When the votes had been counted, the person, who received the greatest number, provided not less than 6000 ostraka had been cast, had to settle his legal cases concerning his private business transactions and to leave the city within ten days for a period of ten years. Later, however, the period was reduced to five years. He could enjoy the use of his own property, provided he did not enter within a line drawn through the promontory of Euboea called Geraistos."

Philochorus,
Atthis (History of
Athens)

---

[22] Philochorus, *Die Fragmente der griechishcen Historiker* 328 F 30.

3

THE PERSIAN WARS

The Greek city-states (*poleis*) developed in an environment uniquely free of external threat thanks to the absence of a single dominant imperial power in the eastern Mediterranean for much of the first half of the first millennium B.C. That security ended with the sudden appearance in the mid-sixth century B.C. of the Persian Empire. Its first three rulers, Cyrus I (559–530 B.C.), Cambyses (530–522 B.C.), and Darius I (522–486 B.C.), created the greatest of all ancient Near Eastern empires, one that stretched from the Aegean to what is now Pakistan. Attempts to extend Persian rule to mainland Greece in 490 and 480–479 B.C. failed. In both invasions Athens bore the brunt of the Persian assault. In 490 B.C. Athens faced the invaders virtually alone at Marathon. A decade later, Athens was captured and sacked by the Persians. But together with Sparta and her allies, Athens' fleet won the key naval victory at Salamis, and a year later the Greek alliance decisively defeated the Persians on land at Plataea.

Years later the historian Thucydides remarked: "The greatest war in the past was the Persian War, yet even this was quickly decided by two battles by sea and two by land. By contrast the Peloponnesian War was a protracted struggle" (1.23). Yet it might be argued that the Persian War was not really settled by two battles. After Salamis and Plataea, Herodotus reports that at a council in Asia Minor the Greeks debated what to do about the threat of Persia in the future. Some, including the Peloponnesians, argued that Ionia should "be abandoned to the barbarians . . . for it seemed a thing impossible that they [*i.e., the Greek allies*] should be ever on the watch to guard and protect Ionia; and yet otherwise there could be no hope that the Ionians would escape the vengeance of the Persians" (9.106). Perhaps, therefore, we should see the Peloponnesian War—and for that matter many of the other wars of the Greeks down to the conquest of Persia by Alexander—as simply extensions (or consequences) in one form or another of the original struggle against Persia. Even if the Greeks—at least those who participated in the effort—were successful in fending off the Persian menace for one generation, Persia for the next century remained a threatening presence, even if not intent on conquering the Greek mainland. That presence necessitated the making and maintaining of great alliances and power blocs that the Greeks might otherwise not have had to undertake.

The problem Greece faced from a military and political viewpoint was its lack of unity. In antiquity there never was a "Greece" in the sense of a unified nation. The fifteen hundred or so Greek cities, most of them small, scattered throughout the Mediterranean and Black Sea, never came together—nor could they reasonably be expected to have come together—to form a single state with its own army, government, and administrative bureaucracy. It was not as though Greeks did not think about such possibilities. In the fourth century B.C. Aristotle asserted in a throwaway line that had the Greeks been able to attain political unity, "they would have been able to rule the world" (*Pols.* 7.1327b32–33). That was never to be the case. Instead, the story of the defense of the Greek homeland against the Persians was more a matter of the luck and bravery of the few triumphing over the betrayal, opportunism, expediency, and local antagonisms of the many. As Herodotus, the chronicler of the war, said of one Greek state with more than a touch of exasperation: "The Phocians were the only people in these parts who did not go over to the Persians, and in my opinion their motive was simply their hatred for their neighbors the Thessalians. If the Thessalians had remained loyal, no doubt the Phocians would have abandoned the Greeks" (8.30). It was the kind of comment he was to make many times in his history. As it turned out, the Phocians were to pay a high price for their decision. Herodotus reports that "the land of Phocis was entirely overrun, for the Thessalians led the Persian army through the whole of it; and wherever they went the country was wasted with fire and sword, the cities and even the temples being wilfully set alight by the troops" (8.32).

Herodotus, the "Father of History," as the Roman orator Cicero called him, was concerned, like Homer and the other epic poets, with warfare, honor, and great deeds. Unlike the poets, however, Herodotus also looked for the causes of conflict underlying wars between states. Thus, for example, he describes how Croesus, king of Lydia, lost his kingdom to the Persians as a result of a series of miscalculations and wrong assumptions, not merely because of his own moral or personal failings. Although warned by an advisor before the outbreak of the war that the Lydians had nothing to gain by going to war with the Persians, and the Persians had nothing to lose, Croesus chose to go to war anyway. After a drawn battle with the Persians, he returned to his capital at Sardis having assumed that, because it was winter, the Persians would not dare to follow him. He was wrong; they did follow him. Croesus was defeated and the Lydians lost their independence.

Herodotus was highly popular in antiquity, but at least some of his readers were uncomfortable with his frank presentation of the behavior of many prominent Greek states before and during the war. Among these Greeks he earned the title of "The Father of Lies." To them it seemed somehow unpatriotic to wash Greek dirty linen so publicly and so relentlessly. The moralist Plutarch, who could not forgive Herodotus' treatment of Thebes, one of the most important of the Greek cities to go over to the Persians, probably wrote the bizarre essay on the subject called *On the Malice of Herodotus*. Others dismissed him as a mere storyteller. It is clear, however, that Herodotus was neither a liar nor a mere teller of tales but a subtle investigator of the past, a humane and shrewd judge of human character—and an excellent storyteller. Unfortunately the Persians did not have a Herodotus to chronicle their version of the wars, nor, for that matter, even a tradition of history writing. History was an invention of the Greek enlightenment and the growth of constitutional government; it was and remains the product of free societies. Most of what we know of the Persians, except for a number of inscriptions, was written about them by others, mainly Greeks. Not all of what the Greeks had to say about the Persians was by any means hostile or even ethnocentric. As Herodotus observed, however much people know about the customs of others, they tend to prefer their own: "If one were to offer men to choose out of all the customs in the world such as seemed to them the best, they would examine the whole number, and end by preferring their own; so convinced are they that their own usages far surpass those of all others" (3.38).

A. The Persian Empire

1. THE KING AND HIS SUBJECTS: THE CYRUS CYLINDER

The Cyrus Cylinder

Cyrus the Great (ca. 560–529 B.C.), the founder of the Persian Empire, and his successors actively sought to ensure the loyalty of the religious leaders of their subjects by supporting the cults of the gods of their empire. In the Cyrus Cylinder, a cuneiform text celebrating the Persian conquest of Babylon in 539 B.C., the priests of Marduk, the chief god of Babylon, portrayed Cyrus as Marduk's tool to punish Nabonidus, the last king of Babylon, because he had neglected the city cults and festivals and introduced new gods.[1]

. . . In all lands everywhere (12) he [Marduk, chief god of Babylon] searched, he looked through them and sought a righteous prince, after his own heart, whom he took by the hand. Cyrus, king of Anshan, he called by name, to lordship over the whole world he appointed him. (13) The land of Qutu, all the Umman-manda, he cast down at his feet. The black-headed people, whom he gave his hands to conquer, (14) he took them in justice and righteousness. Marduk, the great lord, looked joyously on the caring for his people, on his pious works and his righteous heart. (15) To his city Babylon he caused him to go, he made him take the road to Babylon, going as a friend and companion at his side. (16) His numerous troops, in number unknown, like the waters of a river, marched armed at his side. (17) Without battle and conflict he permitted him to enter Babylon. He spared his city Babylon a calamity. Nabonidus, the king, who did not hear him, he delivered into his hand. (18) All the people of Babylon, of Sumer and Akkad, princes and governors, fell down before him and kissed his feet. They rejoiced in his sovereignty, their faces shone. (19)

---

[1] From Robert William Rogers, *Cuneiform Parallels to the Old Testament*, 2nd ed. (New York, 1926), pp. 380–383.

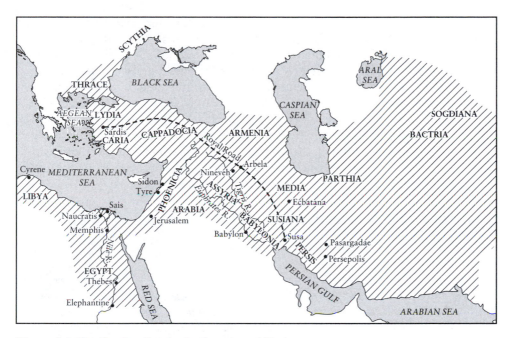

Figure 3.1 The Persian Empire in the reign of Darius.

The lord, who by his power brings the dead to life, who amid destruction and injury had protected them, they blessed him joyously, honoring his name.

(20) I am Cyrus, king of the world, the great king, the powerful king, king of Babylon, king of Sumer and Akkad, king of the four quarters of the world, (21) son of Cambyses, the great king, king of the city of Anshan, grandson of Cyrus, the great king, king of the city of Anshan; greatgrandson of Teispes, the great king, king of the city of Anshan; (22) eternal seed of royalty whose rule Bel and Nabu love, whose government they rejoice in their heart. When I made my triumphal entrance into Babylon, (23) with joy and rejoicing I took up my lordly residence in the royal palace, Marduk, the great lord, moved the noble heart of the inhabitants of Babylon to me, while I gave daily care to his worship. (24) My numerous troops marched peacefully into Babylon. In all Sumer and Akkad I permitted no enemy to enter. (25) The needs of Babylon and of all its cities I gladly took heed to. The people of Babylon [and . . .], and the dishonoring yoke was removed from them. Their dwellings, (26) which had fallen, I restored. I cleared out their ruins. Marduk, the great lord, rejoiced in my pious deeds, and (27) graciously blessed me, Cyrus, the king who worships him, and Cambyses, my own son, and all my troops, (28) while we, before him, joyously praised his exalted godhead. All the kings dwelling in palaces, (29) of all the quarters of the earth, from the Upper to the Lower sea dwelling . . . all the kings of the West-land dwelling in tents (30) brought me their heavy tribute, and in Babylon kissed my feet. From . . . to Asshur and Susa, (31) Agade, Eshnunak, Zamban, Metumu, Deri, with the territory of

the land of Gutium, the cities on the other side of the Tigris, whose sites were ancient foundations—(32) the gods, who dwelt in them, I brought them back to their places, and caused them to dwell in a habitation for all time. All their inhabitants I collected and restored them to their dwelling places. (33) And the gods of Sumer and Akkad, whom Nabonidus, to the anger of the lord of the gods, had brought into Babylon, by command of Marduk, the great lord, (34) I caused them peacefully to take up their dwelling in habitations that rejoiced the heart. May all the gods, whom I brought into their cities, (35) pray daily before Bel and Nabu for long life for me, and may they speak a gracious word for me and say to Marduk, my lord, "May Cyrus, the king who worships and Cambyses, his son, (36) their . . . I permitted to dwell in peace. . . . "

2. "BY THE GRACE OF AHURIMAZDA I AM KING": PERSIAN IMPERIAL IDEOLOGY

The Behistun inscription of Darius I

Inscribed in three languages—Old Persian, Babylonian, and Elamite—on the orders of Darius I (521–486 B.C.) three hundred feet above the ground on the face of a cliff in northern Iran, the Behistun inscription is the principal source for our understanding of the ideology of the Persian Empire. Darius I recounts in it how Ahurimazda, the Zoroastrian god of light and truth, entrusted to him rule over an enormous empire that stretched from the coast of Turkey (Ionia) in the west to the borders of India in the east (Gandara) and from Egypt in the south to the Russian steppes in the north (Saca) and enabled him to suppress the forces of evil and the "lie" represented by the false king Gomates, a story known also from the Greek historian Herodotus. Ironically, most historians now believe that despite Darius' repeated professions of "truthfulness," the Behistun inscription actually represents propaganda on the part of Darius and his allies justifying their rebellion against the family of Cyrus I. Note that for Darius the Persian Empire was a family possession blessed by God and passed on from father to son like a piece of real estate.[2]

1. I am Darius, the great king, the king of kings, the king of Persia, the king of the provinces, the son of Hystaspes, the grandson of Arsames, the Achaemenian.

2. Says Darius the king—My father was Hystaspes; the father of Hystaspes was Arsames; the father of Arsames was Ariaramnes; the father of Ariaramnes was Teispes; the father of Teispes was Achaemenes.

3. Says Darius the king—On that account we have been called Achaemenians; from antiquity we have descended; from antiquity our family have been kings.

4. Says Darius the king—There are eight of my race who have been kings before me; I am the ninth; nine of us have been kings in succession.

5. Says Darius the king—By the grace of Ahurimazda I am King; Ahurimazda has granted me the empire.

[2] "The Behistun Inscription of Darius I," Column 1,1–14, based on the translation of Henry Rawlinson. From Francis R. B. Godolphin, *The Greek Historians*, Vol. 2 (New York, 1942), pp. 623–625. (*Archaeologia*, 1853, vol. xxxiv, p. 74.)

6. Says Darius the king—These are the countries which have come to me; by the grace of Ahurimazda I have become king of them: Persia, Susiana, Babylonia, Assyria, Arabia, Egypt, those which are of the sea, Sparda, Ionia, Media, Armenia, Cappadocia, Parthia, Zarangia, Aria, Chorasmia, Bactria, Sogdiana, Gandara, Saca, Thatagush, Arachosia, and Maka; in all twenty-three provinces.

7. Says Darius the king—These are the provinces which have come to me; by the grace of Ahurimazda they have become subject to me; they have brought tribute to me. That which has been said to them by me, both by night and by day, it has been done by them.

8. Says Darius the king—Within these countries, the man who was good, him I have right well cherished. Whoever was evil, him have I utterly rooted out. By the grace of Ahurimazda, these are the countries by whom my laws have been observed. As it has been said to them by me, so by them it has been done.

9. Says Darius the king—Ahurimazda granted me the empire. Ahurimazda brought help to me, so that I gained this empire. By the grace of Ahurimazda I hold this empire.

10. Says Darius the king—This is what was done by me after that I became king. A man named Cambyses, son of Cyrus, of our race, he was here king before me. Of that Cambyses there was a brother, Bardes was his name; of the same mother, and of the same father with Cambyses. Afterwards Cambyses slew that Bardes. When Cambyses had slain Bardes, it was not known to the people that Bardes had been slain. Afterwards Cambyses proceeded to Egypt. When Cambyses had proceeded to Egypt, then the state became wicked. Then the lie became abounding in the land, both in Persia, and in Media, and in the other provinces.

11. Says Darius the king—Afterwards there was a certain man, a Magian, named Gomates. He arose from Pissiachada, the mountain named Aracadres, from thence. On the 14th day of the month Vayakhna, then it was that he arose. He thus lied to the state, "I am Bardes, the son of Cyrus, the brother of Cambyses." Then the whole state became rebellious. From Cambyses it went over to him, both Persia, and Media, and the other provinces. He seized the empire. On the 9th day of the month Garmapada, then it was he so seized the empire. Afterwards Cambyses, unable to endure, died.

12. Says Darius the king—The empire of which Gomates, the Magian, dispossessed Cambyses, that empire from the olden time had been in our family. After Gomates the Magian had dispossessed Cambyses both of Persia and Media and the dependent provinces, he did according to his desire: he became king.

13. Says Darius the king—There was not a man, neither Persian, nor Median, nor any one of our family, who would dispossess that Gomates, the Magian, of the crown. The state feared him exceedingly. He slew many people who had known the old Bardes; for that reason he slew them. "Lest they should recognize me that I am not Bardes, the son of Cyrus." No one

dared to say anything concerning Gomates, the Magian, until I arrived. Then I prayed to Ahurimazda; Ahurimazda brought help to me. On the 10th day of the month Bagayadish, then it was, with my faithful men, I slew that Gomates, the Magian, and those who were his chief followers. The fort named Sictachotes in the district of Media called Nisaea, there I slew him. I dispossessed him of the empire. By the grace of Ahurimazda I became king: Ahurimazda granted me the scepter.

14. Says Darius the king—The empire which had been taken away from our family, that I recovered. I established it in its place. As it was before, so I made it. The temples which Gomates, the Magian, had destroyed, I rebuilt. The sacred offices of the state, both the religious chants and the worship, I restored to the people, which Gomates, the Magian, had deprived them of. I established the state in its place, both Persia, and Media, and the other provinces. As it was before, so I restored what had been taken away. By the grace of Ahurimazda I did this. I arranged so that I established our family in its place. As it was before, so I arranged it, by the grace of Ahurimazda, so that Gomates, the Magian, should not supersede our family.

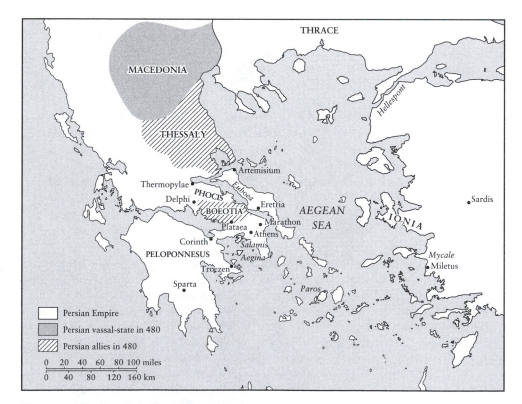

Figure 3.2 The Persian Wars.

B. The Persian Wars

1. HOW THE WARS BEGAN: THE PROBLEMS OF ARISTAGORAS

This tale of Herodotus of how the revolt among the Greeks of Asia Minor against the Persians began—and with it the Persian invasions of Greece—tells us a great deal about the perennial problem of stasis, or civil disorder, among the citizens of Greek poleis. It also reveals the kinds of relationships worked out between the Greek ruling elite and their overlords the Persians. It is a good example of Herodotus' narrative style and analytical method.[3]

The History of Herodotus

From Naxos and Miletus troubles gathered anew about Ionia. Now Naxos at this time surpassed all the other islands in prosperity, and Miletus had reached the height of its power, and was the glory of Ionia. But for two generations previously the Milesians had suffered grievously from civil disorders, which were settled by the Parians, whom the Milesians chose before all the rest of the Greeks to rearrange their government. . . . 30. Now at Naxos some of the rich men had been banished by the people (the *demos*), and had fled to Miletus. Aristagoras, son of Molpagoras, the nephew and likewise the son-in-law of Histiaeus, son of Lysagoras, who was still kept by Darius at Susa [*Histiaeus was suspected of treason and had been summoned to the capital where the Persians could keep an eye on him*], happened to be in charge of Miletus at the time of their coming. (For the power actually was in the hands of Histiaeus; but he was at Susa when the Naxians came). Now these Naxians had in times past been guest-friends (*xenoi*) of Histiaeus; and so on their arrival at Miletus they addressed themselves to Aristagoras and begged him to lend them such aid as his ability allowed, in hopes thereby to recover their country. Then Aristagoras, calculating that, if the Naxians should be restored by his help, he would be lord of Naxos, put forward the friendship with Histiaeus to cloak his views, and spoke as follows: "I cannot guarantee you sufficient troops to force you upon the Naxians against their will, since they hold the city; and I know they can bring into the field eight thousand soldiers, and have also a large number of ships of war. But I will do all that lies in my power to get you some aid, and I think I can manage it in this way. Artaphernes happens to be my friend. Now he is a son of Hystaspes, and brother to King Darius. All the sea-coast of Asia is under him, and he has a numerous army and numerous ships. I think I can prevail on him to do what we require." When the Naxians heard this, they empowered Aristagoras to manage the matter for them as well as he could, and told him to promise gifts and pay for the soldiers, which (they said) they would readily furnish, since they had great hope that the Naxians, as soon as they saw they had

[3] All translations from Herodotus provided in this chapter are based on the *History of Herodotus* (New York, 1859–1860), trans. George Rawlinson.

returned, would render them obedience, and likewise the other islanders. For at that time not one of the Cyclades was subject to King Darius.

31. So Aristagoras went to Sardis and told Artaphernes that Naxos was an island of no great size, but a fair land and fertile, lying near Ionia, and containing much treasure and a vast number of slaves. "Make war then upon this land (he said) and reinstate the exiles; for if you do this, first of all, I have very rich gifts in store for you (besides the cost of the armament, which it is fair that we who are the authors of the war should pay); and, secondly, you will bring under the power of the King not only Naxos but the other islands which depend on it—Paros, Andros, and all the rest of the Cyclades. And when you have gained these, you may easily go on against Euboea, which is a large and wealthy island not less in size than Cyprus, and very easy to bring under control. A hundred ships would be quite enough to subdue all of these." Artaphernes answered: "Truly you are the author of a plan which may bring much advantage to the House of the King, and your counsel is good in all points except the number of the ships. Instead of a hundred, two hundred shall be at your disposal when the spring comes. But the king himself must first approve the undertaking."

The History of Herodotus | *In due course King Darius approved and the expedition set off. Unfortunately, Aristagoras and the Persian commander of the ships, Megabates, quarreled and the expedition failed. Now Aristagoras was in deep trouble.*

35. And now Aristagoras found he was quite unable to make good his promises to Artaphernes, and was even hard pressed to meet the claims whereto he was liable for the pay of the troops. At the same time his fear was great, lest, owing to the failure of the expedition and his own quarrel with Megabates, he should be ousted from the government of Miletus. These manifold worries had already caused him to contemplate raising a rebellion, when the man with the marked head came from Susa, bringing him instructions on the part of Histiaeus to revolt from the King. For Histiaeus, when he was anxious to give Aristagoras orders to revolt, could find but one safe way, as the roads were guarded, of making his wishes known; which was by taking the trustiest of his slaves, shaving all the hair from off his head, and then pricking letters upon the skin, and waiting till the hair grew again. Thus accordingly he did; and as soon as his hair was grown, he dispatched the man to Miletus, giving him no other message than this: "When you come to Miletus, tell Aristagoras to shave your head, and look thereon." Now the marks on the head, as I have already mentioned, were a command to revolt. All this Histiaeus did because it irked him greatly to be kept at Susa, and because he had strong hopes that, if troubles broke out, he would be sent down to the coast to quell them, whereas, if Miletus made no movement, he did not see a chance of his ever again returning thither.

36. Such, then, were the views, which led Histiaeus to despatch his messenger; and it so chanced that all these several motives to revolt were brought to bear upon Aristagoras at one and the same time. Accordingly, at

this juncture Aristagoras held a council of his trusted friends, and laid the business before them, telling them both what he had himself purposed, and what message had been sent him by Histiaeus. At this council all his friends were of the same way of thinking, and recommended revolt, except only Hecataeus the historian. He, first of all, advised them by all means to avoid engaging in war with the king of the Persians, whose might he set forth, and whose subject nations he enumerated. As however he could not induce them to listen to this counsel, he next advised that they should do all that lay in their power to make themselves masters of the sea. "There was only one way," he said, "so far as he could see, of their succeeding in this. Miletus was, he knew, a weak state, but if the treasures in the temple at Branchidae, which Croesus the Lydian gave to it, were seized, he had strong hopes that the mastery of the sea might be thereby gained; at least it would give them money to begin the war, and would save the treasures from falling into the hands of the enemy." Now these treasures were of very great value, as I showed in the first part of my History. The assembly, however, rejected the counsel of Hecataeus, while, nevertheless, they resolved upon a revolt. . . .

2. ARISTAGORAS SEEKS HELP FROM SPARTA

Cleomenes was still king when Aristagoras, tyrant of Miletus, reached Sparta. At their interview, Aristagoras, according to the report of the Lacedaemonians, produced a bronze tablet, whereupon the whole circuit of the earth was engraved, with all its seas and rivers. Discussions began between the two; and Aristagoras addressed the Spartan king in these words: "Think it not strange, O King Cleomenes, that I have been at the pains to sail hither; for the state of affairs, which I will now recount to you, made it fitting. It is a matter of shame and grief to none so much as to us, that the sons of the Ionians should have lost their freedom, and come to be the slaves of others; but yet it touches you likewise, O Spartans, beyond the rest of the Greeks, inasmuch as you are the leaders of Greece. We beseech you, therefore, by the common gods of the Hellenes, deliver the Ionians, who are your own kinsmen, from slavery. Truly the task is not difficult; for the barbarians are an unwarlike people; and you are the best and bravest warriors in the whole world. Their mode of fighting is the following: they use bows and arrows and a short spear; they wear trousers in the field, and cover their heads with turbans. So easy are they to vanquish! Know too that the dwellers in these parts have more good things than all the rest of the world put together—gold, and silver, and brass, and embroidered garments, beasts of burden, and bond-servants—all which, if you only wish it, you may soon have for your own. . . . In the wars which you wage with your rivals of Messenia, with Argos likewise and Arcadia, about paltry boundaries and strips of land not worth much, you contend with those who have no gold, nor silver even, which often give men heart to fight and die. Must you wage such wars, and when ye might so easily be lords of Asia, will you decide otherwise?" Thus spoke Aristagoras; and Cleomenes replied to him: "Milesian stranger, three days hence I will give you an answer."

50. That was far as they got at that time. When, however, the day appointed for the answer came, and the two once more met, Cleomenes asked Aristagoras, "How many days' journey is it from the sea of the Ionians to the king's residence?" Hereupon Aristagoras, who had managed the rest so cleverly, and succeeded in deceiving the king, tripped in his speech and blundered; for instead of concealing the truth, as he ought to have done if he wanted to induce the Spartans to cross into Asia, he said plainly that it was a journey of three months. Cleomenes, hearing these words prevented Aristagoras from finishing what he had begun to say concerning the road, and said: "Milesian stranger, quit Sparta before sunset. This is no good proposal that you make to the Lacedaemonians, to conduct them a distance of three months' journey from the sea."

3. ARISTAGORAS AT ATHENS

The History of Herodotus || *The decisions made by the Athenians were among the first made under the new democratic constitution they had adopted about ten years earlier. Note Herodotus' comment on the nature of democracy that it was easier to hoodwink 30,000 people than a single individual.*

96. On the return of Hippias (*former tyrant of Athens*) to Asia from Sparta, he moved heaven and earth to set Artaphernes against the Athenians and did all that was in his power to bring Athens into subjection to himself and Darius. So when the Athenians learned what he was up to, they sent envoys to Sardis, and exhorted the Persians not to listen to the Athenian exiles. Artaphernes told them in reply that if they wished to remain safe, they must receive back Hippias. The Athenians, when this answer was reported to them, determined not to consent, and therefore made up their minds to be at open enmity with the Persians. 97. The Athenians had come to this decision, and were already in bad odor with the Persians when Aristagoras the Milesian, dismissed from Sparta by Cleomenes the Lacedaemonian, arrived at Athens. He knew that, after Sparta, Athens was the most powerful of the Greek states. Accordingly he appeared before the people, and, as he had done at Sparta, spoke to them of the good things, which there were in Asia, and of the Persian mode of combat—how they used neither shield nor spear and were very easy to conquer. All this he urged, and reminded them also that Miletus was a colony of Athens, and therefore ought to receive their help, since they were so powerful—and in the earnestness of his pleas, he cared little what he promised—until, at last, he prevailed and won them over. It seems indeed to be easier to deceive a multitude than one man—for Aristagoras, though he failed to convince Cleomenes the Lacedaemonian, succeeded with the Athenians, who were 30,000. Won by his persuasions, they voted that twenty ships should be sent to aid the Ionians, under the command of Melanthius, one of the citizens,

a man of distinction in every way. These ships were the beginning of mischief for the Greeks and for the barbarians.

The revolt that followed was a disaster for the Greeks of Asia Minor. According to Herodotus, one of the chief causes of their loss was the sloth and general fecklessness of the Ionians. Even when warned by their commander that their "fate hung on a razor's edge between being free men and slaves—and runaway slaves at that," they "reposed in the shade all day and refused to go aboard the ships and train themselves." Accordingly "when the Samians (Greek islanders allied to the Ionians) *saw that all was disorder among the Ionians" (6.12–13), they decided that the revolt was going to fail. Among other allies, they soon abandoned the Ionians to their fate. Miletus was captured and the population killed or sold into slavery.*

Figure 3.3 The vase depicts the different styles of fighting engaged in by Greeks and Persians. The nudity of the Greek is an artistic convention. In reality the warrior would have been well armored and surrounded by his fellow hoplites. Greek and Persian. Attic red-figure Oinocohe by the Chicago Painter. Francis Bartlett Donation. By permission of the Museum of Fine Arts, Boston.

4. THE BATTLE OF MARATHON

The History of
Herodotus

After their victory over the Ionian Greeks the Persians launched an expedition to punish those from the mainland of Greece who had helped in the revolt, namely the Athenians and Eretrians on the nearby island of Euboea. The usual pattern of plotting and betrayal immediately makes its appearance.

100. Meanwhile, the Eretrians learned that the Persian expedition was sailing against them, and asked the Athenians for assistance. Nor did the Athenians refuse their aid, but assigned to them as auxiliaries the 4000 landholders whom they had settled on land confiscated from the Euboeans in a previous war. At Eretria, however, things were not in a healthy state, for although they had called in the aid of the Athenians, yet they were not agreed among themselves how they should act. Some of them thought of leaving the city and taking refuge in the backwoods of Euboea, while others who looked to receiving a reward from the Persians, were making ready to betray their country. So when these things came to the ears of Aeschines, the son of Nothon, one of the first men in Eretria, he made known the whole state of affairs to the Athenians who had already arrived, and urged them to return home to their own land and not to perish with his countrymen. The Athenians followed his advice and crossing over to Oropus, in this way escaped the danger.

In due course Eretria was betrayed to the Persians, who then burned the town and sold its inhabitants into slavery. After this the Persians moved on to Attica and landed at Marathon, a plain to the north of the city. The Athenians in turn marched to Marathon and took up a defensive position there. In the meantime, they sent Pheidippides, a runner, to ask for help from the Spartans.

105. Before they left the city for Marathon the generals sent off to Sparta a herald, one Pheidippides, who was by birth an Athenian and by profession and training a long-distance runner. . . . 106. He reached Sparta the day after leaving Athens and on his arrival went before the rulers and said: "Men of Lacedaemon (*i.e., Sparta*), the Athenians beseech you to hasten to their aid, and not allow that state, which is the most ancient in all Greece, to be enslaved by the Persians. Eretria is already carried away captive, and Greece weakened by the loss of no mean city." Thus did Pheidippides deliver the message committed to him, and the Spartans wished to help the Athenians, but were unable to give them any present aid as they did not like to break their established law. It was the ninth day of the month and they could not march out of Sparta on the ninth, when the moon had not reached the full. So they waited for the full moon. . . .

Figure 3.4 This fragmentary inscription is part of a now lost monument celebrating Athenian victories in the Persian wars. The monument was set up somewhere in the center of Athens and contained two epigrams. The first epigram honored the victors in the Battle of Salamis in 480 B.C. (R. Meiggs and D. M. Lewis, *A Selection of Greek Historical Inscriptions to the End of the Fifth Century* [Oxford, 1969], no. 26):

The excellence of these men will shine an imperishable light forever
On those to whom the gods assign rewards for great deeds;
For on foot and on swift sailing ships they prevented
All Greece from seeing a day of slavery.

The second celebrated the Battle of Marathon in 490 B.C.:

There was invincible courage in their breasts, when
They raised their spears before the gates against myriads,
Repelling the army of the Persians, who wished to burn
Their famous city by the sea by force.
By permission of the American School of Classical Studies, Athens.

108. The Athenians were drawn up in order of battle in the precinct belonging to Heracles, when they were joined by the Plataeans, who came in full force to their aid. . . . 109. The Athenian generals were divided in their opinions; and some advised not to risk a battle because they were

too few to engage such a host as that of the Persians; while others were for fighting at once, and among these last was Militiades. He, therefore, seeing that opinions were divided, and that the less worthy counsel appeared likely to prevail, resolved to go to the Polemarch (*an annually chosen office; it gave the office-holder nominal command of the army*), and have a conference with him. For the man on whom the lot fell to be Polemarch, at Athens was entitled to give his vote with the ten generals, since from ancient times the Athenians allowed him an equal right in voting with them. The Polemarch at this juncture was Callimachus of Aphidnae. (*Militiades won over Callimachus, and the battle was launched.*) 111. Now as they marshaled their army on the field at Marathon, in order that the Athenian front might be of equal length with the Persian, the ranks of the center were diminished, and it became the weakest part of the line, while the wings were both made strong with a depth of many ranks. . . . 112. So when these dispositions were in place and the victims showed themselves favorable, instantly the Athenians, as soon as the command was given, charged the enemy at a run. Now the distance between the two armies was little short of a mile. The Persians, therefore, when they saw the Greeks coming on at speed, made ready to receive them, although it seemed to them the Athenians were bereft of their senses, and bent on their own destruction, for they saw a mere handful of men coming on at a run without either cavalry or archers. . . . 113. The two armies fought together on the plain of Marathon for a long time, and in the middle of the battle, where the Persians themselves and the Sacae had their place, the barbarians were victorious, and broke and pursued the Greeks into the inner country. On the two wings, however, the Athenians and the Plataeans defeated the enemy. Having done so, they allowed the routed barbarians to flee, joined their two wings into one and fell on those who had broken their own center, and defeated them. . . . 117. There fell in this battle of Marathon, on the side of the Persians about 6400 men; on that of the Athenians, 192.

A footnote to the battle: The Spartans showed up three days after the battle.

C. The Second Persian Invasion of 480 B.C.

The History of
Herodotus

The Greeks were fortunate that before the Persians could return to take revenge for Marathon, Darius, the energetic king of Persia, died and was replaced by a weaker king, Xerxes. Egypt and Babylon, the richest and most populous provinces of the empire, revolted. This forced the Persians to postpone the war of revenge against Greece for a full ten years. During these years the Athenians were lucky in that they found a great leader in Themistocles and were persuaded by him to build up their fleet. Unfortunately, the usual local rivalries, internal dissensions, and calculations of expediency weakened the Greek response.

1. THE MUDDLED GREEK RESPONSE: "IT WAS PLAIN THAT THE GREATER NUMBER OF THE STATES WOULD TAKE NO PART IN THE WAR BUT WARMLY FAVORED THE PERSIANS"

7.138. The expedition of the Persian king, though it was in name directed against Athens, in reality threatened the whole of Greece. And of this the Greeks were aware some time before, but they did not all view the matter in the same light. Some of them had given the Persians earth and water [*symbols of submission*], and were bold on that account, deeming themselves thereby secured against suffering hurt from the barbarian army. Others, who had refused compliance, were thrown into extreme alarm. For whereas they considered all the ships in Greece too few to engage the enemy, it was plain that the greater number of states would take no part in the war, but warmly favored the Persians. 139. And here I feel constrained to deliver an opinion, which most men, I know will dislike, but which as it seems to be true, I am determined not to withhold. Had the Athenians from fear of approaching danger, left their country, or had they without leaving it submitted to the power of Xerxes, there would certainly have been no attempt to resist the Persians by sea; in which case, the course of events by land would have been the following. Though the Peloponnesians might have built ever so many walls across the Isthmus, yet their allies would have fallen off from the Lacedaemonians, not by voluntary desertion, but because city after city must have been taken by the enemy fleet. And so, the Spartans, would at last have stood alone, and, standing alone would have displayed prodigies of valor, and died nobly. Either they would have done thus, or else, before it came to that extremity, seeing one Greek city after another embrace the cause of the Persians, they would have come to terms with King Xerxes. Thus either way Greece would have been brought under Persia. For I cannot understand of what possible use the walls across the Isthmus would have been if the King had mastery of the sea. If then a man should now say that the Athenians were the saviors of Greece, he would not exceed the truth. For they truly held the scales, and whichever side they chose must have carried the day. They too it was who, when they had determined to maintain the freedom of Greece, roused up that portion of the Greek people which had not gone over to the Persians and so, next to the gods, they repulsed the invader. Even the terrible oracles which reached them from Delphi, and struck fear into their hearts, failed to persuade them to fly from Greece. They had the courage to remain faithful to their land, and await the coming of the foe.

2. THEMISTOCLES AND THE "ALLIANCE OF THE WILLING"

The History of ‖ *The reference to the oracles* (end of last reading) *is to the responses the Athenians received from*
Herodotus ‖ *Delphi when they sent messengers there to consult the god. The first oracle was devastating. It told of*
　　　　　‖ *the complete destruction of Athens, including its holy places, and urged the Athenians "to flee to the*
　　　　　‖ *ends of the earth." The priests, seeing that the Athenian delegation was appalled by the first oracle,*
　　　　　‖ *suggested that they approach the priestess again. The second time they got the famous, ambiguous*
　　　　　‖ *"wooden walls" oracle.*

141. Upon this [*the Athenians had threatened not to leave the sanctuary and to*
stay there until they died], the priestess gave them a second answer, which was
the following:

Pallas Athena has not been able to soften the lord of Olympus,
Though she has often prayed to him and urged him with excellent
　　counsel.
Yet once more I address thee in words firmer than adamant.

Figure 3.5 The trireme was the preeminent Greek warship at the time of the Persian
Wars and continued to form the backbone of the navies of Greek cities until the Roman
conquest as illustrated by this second century B.C. relief of a trireme from Rhodes. The
purpose of the trireme was to ram and sink opposing warships. Powered by 170 rowers,
the trireme could achieve over 9 knots for short periods of time. Lindos, Rhodes. Photo
by Dorothy Burstein.

When the foe shall have taken whatever the limit of Cecrops
Holds within it, and all which divine Cithaeron shelters,
Then far-seeing Zeus grants this to the prayers of Athena:
Safe shall the wooden wall continue for thee and thy children.
Wait not the tramp of the horse, nor the footmen mightily moving
Over the land, but turn your back to the foe, and retire ye.
Yet shall a day arrive when ye shall meet him in battle.
Holy Salamis, thou shalt destroy the offspring of women
When men scatter the seed, or when they gather the harvest.

Some interpreted the "wooden walls" as the acropolis at Athens, which was in ancient times defended by a wooden palisade. But others, led by Themistocles, insisted that the wall referred to was the fleet. Prior to all of this, Themistocles had persuaded the Athenians to devote a find of silver in Attica to building a fleet rather than returning the profits to individual Athenians, which would normally have been the procedure.

144. Themistocles had before this given a counsel which prevailed very seasonably. The Athenians, having a large sum of money in their treasury, the produce of the mines at Laureium, were about to share it among the adult citizens, who would have received ten drachmas apiece, when Themistocles persuaded them to forbear the distribution, and build with the money 200 ships, to help them in their war against the Aeginetans. It was the breaking out of the Aeginetan war which was at this time the saving of Greece, for thereby the Athenians were forced to become a maritime power. The new ships were not used for the purpose for which they were built, but became a help to Greece in her hour of need. And the Athenians had not only these vessels ready before the war, but they likewise set to work to build more. They decided in a council, which was held after the debate upon the oracle, that, according to the advice of the god, they would embark their whole force aboard their ships, and with such Greeks as chose to join them, give battle to the barbarian invader. Such, then were the oracles, which had been received by the Athenians. 145. The Greeks who were supporters of the Hellenic cause, having assembled in one place, and there consulted together, and interchanged pledges with each other, agreed that, before any other step was taken, the feuds and enmities which existed between the different states should first of all be ended. . . .

3. THE THEMISTOCLES DECREE

This decree was found at Troezen, where most of the wives and children of the Athenians were sent for refuge. In its present form it is a third-century B.C. version of an older, possibly fifth-century original.[4]

Decree found at Troezen

[4] From R. Meiggs and D. M. Lewis, *A Selection of Greek Historical Inscriptions to the End of the Fifth Century* (Oxford, 1969), no. 23.

Gods

Resolved by council and the demos; Themistocles, the son of Neocles, from Phrearrioi, moved that: the city be placed in the hands of Athena, the mistress of the Athenians, and of all the other gods, to protect and ward off the barbarian from the land; and all the Athenians and foreigners living in Athens shall place their children and women in Troezen . . . the founder of the land; and they shall place their old men and property in Salamis; and the treasurers and priests shall remain on the acropolis, guarding the property of the gods; and all the other Athenians and adult foreigners shall embark on the two hundred ready ships and fight against the barbarian on behalf of their own freedom and that of the other Greeks together with the Lacedaimonians and Corinthians and Aeginetans and the other Greeks willing to share the risks; and beginning tomorrow the generals shall appoint two hundred trierarchs, one for each ship, from those not older than fifty years, who possess land and a house in Athens and who have legitimate sons and they shall allot the ships to them; and they shall enroll ten marines for each ship from those between twenty and thirty years of age and for archers; and they shall allot the officers when they also allot the trierarchs; and the generals shall list the rest of the crews of each ship on white boards, choosing the Athenians from the deme registers and the foreigners from the those registered with the polemarch; and they shall list them, dividing them into two hundred crews of one hundred each, and they shall write at the head of each crew the name of the trireme and the trierarch and the officers in order that each crew may know onto which trireme it is to embark; and when all the crews have been divided and allotted to the triremes, the council and the generals shall fill up all two hundred ships, after making a propitiatory sacrifice to Zeus Pankrates and to Nike and to Poseidon Asphaleios; and when the ships have been manned, one hundred of them shall go to help at Euboean Artemisium and one hundred shall remain on patrol near Salamis and the rest of Attica and defend the land; and in order that all Athenians, being united in spirit, fight against the barbarian, those exiled for ten years shall depart to Salamis and they shall remain there until the demos decides about them; and the disenfranchised. . . .

4. WHY GELON OF SYRACUSE REFUSED HELP

The History of Herodotus

The allies next sent ambassadors to various Greek states to seek their help. More often than not they were turned down. Here are Herodotus' comments regarding the refusal of aid by Gelon, the ruler of Syracuse. Herodotus recognized the difficulty of getting to the bottom of such contentious issues a generation or more after they happened. His solution was to provide two or more versions of a disputed account and leave it to the reader to decide which was right.

163. Then the Greek envoys, without having any further dealings with Gelon [*Gelon had demanded that as the price of his participation he be made commander in chief of either the army or the navy, knowing full well neither*

would be granted] sailed for home. And Gelon, who feared that the Greeks would be too weak to withstand the barbarians, but at the same time could not bring himself to go to the Peloponnese, and there, though ruler of Sicily, serve under the Lacedaemonians, developed a quite different plan. As soon as tidings reached him of the passage of the Hellespont by the Persians, he sent off three fifty oared galleys under the command of Cadmus, the son of Scythas, a native of Cos. He was to go to Delphi, taking with him a large sum of money and a stock of friendly words: there he was to watch the war, and see what turn it would take. If the barbarians prevailed, he was to give Xerxes the treasure, and with earth and water for the lands which Gelon ruled. If the Greeks won the day, he was to convey the treasure back.

However, Herodotus knew of another story, which puts Gelon's refusal to participate in a different light.

165. Those who dwell in Sicily, however, say that Gelon though he knew he must serve under the Lacedaemonians would nevertheless have come to the aid of the Greeks had it not been for Terillus, the son of Crinippus, ruler of Himera who, when driven from his city by Theron, son of Aenesidemus, ruler of Agrigentum, brought into Sicily at this very time an army of 300,000 men made up of Phoenicians, Libyans, Iberians, Ligurians, Helisycians, Sardinians, and Corsicans, under the command of Hamilcar, the son of Hanno, king of the Carthaginians. Terillus prevailed upon Hamilcar, partly as his sworn friend, but more through the zealous aid of Anaxilaus the son of Cretines, ruler of Rhegium, who, by giving his own sons to Hamilcar as hostages, induced him to make the expedition. Anaxilaus herein served his father-in-law, for he was married to the daughter of Terillus by name of Cydippe. So as Gelon could not give the Greeks any aid, he sent (they say) the sum of money to Delphi. 166. They say too, that the victory of Gelon and Theron in Sicily over Hamilcar the Carthaginian, fell out upon the very day the Greeks defeated the Persians at Salamis. . . .

Herodotus offers a similar convoluted account regarding Argos' failure to join the allies and ends with the following declaration:

152. . . . I do not deliver any opinion on the matter other than that of the Argives themselves. This, however, I know—that if every nation were to bring all its evil deeds to a given place, in order to make an exchange with some other nation, when they had all looked carefully at their neighbor's faults, they would be truly glad to carry their own back again. So, after all, the conduct of the Argives was not perhaps more disgraceful than that of the other. For myself, my duty is to report all that is said, but I am not obliged to believe it all alike—a remark which may be understood to apply to whole History.

5. THE BATTLE OF THERMOPYLAE

The History of
Herodotus

The difficulty in finding reliable allies who would actually stand and fight the Persians is illustrated by the events preceding the Battle of Thermopylae. Obstacles such as the necessity of observing the religious festivals as they occurred reveal another side of the complex situation. We have already seen how the Spartans could not leave Sparta for religious reasons when Athens was standing virtually alone at Marathon in the first invasion of 490 B.C. Now, on the eve of yet another crucial battle, the celebration of festivals again interferes with the mustering of the Greeks. The first part of the reading deals with the numbers Herodotus gives for the Greek forces at Thermopylae; they are in line with the resources of the small Greek states.

7.202. The Greeks who at this spot [*i.e., Thermopylae*] waited the coming of Xerxes were the following: from Sparta 300; from Arcadia 1,000 Tegeans and Mantineans, 500 of each people; 120 Orchomenians from Arcadian Orchomenus; and 1,000 from other cities: from Corinth, 400; from Phlius, 200; from Mycenae, 80. Such was the number from the Peloponnese. There were also present, from Boeotia, 700 Thespians and 400 Thebans. . . . 205. Leonidas [*king and therefore army commander of Sparta*] had come to Thermopylae, accompanied by the 300 men which the law assigned him, whom he had himself chosen from among the citizens, and who were all of them fathers with sons living. On his way he had taken the troops from Thebes, whose number I have already mentioned, and who were under the command of Leontiades the son of Eurymachus. The reason why he made a point of taking troops from Thebes and Thebes only was, that the Thebans were strongly suspected of having sympathies for the Persians. Leonidas therefore called on them to come with him to the war, wishing to see whether they would comply with his demand, or openly refuse, and disclaim the Greek alliance. They sent the troops although their intentions were traitorous. 206. The force with Leonidas was sent forward by the Spartans in advance of their main body, that the sight of them might encourage the allies to fight, and hinder them from going over to the Persians as it was likely they might have done had they seen the Spartans holding back. They intended presently, when they had celebrated the Carneian festival, which was what now kept them at home, to leave a garrison at Sparta, and hasten in full force to join the army. The rest of the allies also intended to act similarly; for it happened that the Olympic festival fell exactly at this same period. None of them expected that the contest at Thermopylae would be decided so speedily; wherefore they were content to send forward a mere advance guard. Such accordingly were the intentions of the allies.

207. Meanwhile the Greeks at Thermopylae, when the Persian army drew near to the entrance of the pass, became frightened and a council was held to consider a retreat. It was the wish of the Peloponnesians generally that the army should fall back upon the Peloponnese, and there guard the Isthmus. But Leonidas, when he saw how indignant the Phocians and Locrians became when they heard this plan [*their cities and lands would be abandoned by a retreat to the Isthmus*], gave his vote to remaining where they were, while

they sent envoys to the several cities to ask for help, since they were too few to make a stand against an army like that of the Persians.

The pass at Thermopylae was betrayed by a local Greek to the Persians. Nevertheless, Leonidas decided to stay while the rest of the army melted away (or, in a more favorable version, was dismissed by Leonidas himself—Herodotus reports both versions). The Thespians alone remained with him, along with the Thebans who were kept as hostages. With the exception of the Thebans, all the Greeks, including Leonidas, perished. The self-sacrifice of Leonidas and the Spartans, however, gave heart to the allies, especially after the Greeks were forced to retreat after an indecisive naval battle with the Persian fleet at nearby Artemisium.

6. ATHENS EVACUATED

8.40. Meanwhile, the Greek fleet which had left Artemisium [*after the battle there*] proceeded to Salamis, at the request of the Athenians, and there cast anchor. The Athenians had begged them to take up this position in order that they might convey their women and children out of Attica, and further might deliberate upon the course of action, which they ought to follow. Disappointed in the hopes, which they had previously entertained, they were about to hold a council concerning their present situation. For they had looked to see the Peloponnesians drawn up in full force to resist the enemy in Boeotia, but found nothing of the kind. On the contrary, they learned that the Peloponnesians, only concerning themselves about their own safety, were building a wall across the Isthmus, and intended to guard the Peloponnese, while letting the rest of Greece take its chances. . . . 41. Immediately upon their arrival, proclamation was made that every Athenian should save his children and household as best he could; whereupon some sent their families to Aegina, some to Salamis, but the greater number to Troezen. This removal was made with all possible haste, partly from a desire to obey the advice of the oracle, but still more for another reason. The Athenians say that they have in their Acropolis a huge serpent, which lives in the temple, and is guardian of the whole place. Nor do they only say this, but, as if the serpent really lived there, every month they lay out its food, which consists of a honey-cake. Up to this time the honey cake had always been consumed; but now it remained untouched. So the priestess told the people what had happened; whereupon they left Athens the more readily, since they believed that the goddess had already abandoned the citadel.

7. THE GREAT DEBATE: FIGHT AT SALAMIS OR DEFEND THE ISTHMUS OF CORINTH?

Soon after the Athenians abandoned Athens, the Persians arrived and destroyed the temples on the Acropolis.

The History of Herodotus

56. Meanwhile at Salamis, the Greeks no sooner heard what had befallen the Acropolis than they fell into such alarm that some of the captains did not even wait for the council to come to a vote [*over where to fight the Persians*], but embarked hastily on board their vessels, and hoisted sail as though they would take to flight immediately. The rest, who stayed at the council board, came to a vote that the fleet should give battle at the Isthmus. Night drew on; and the captains, dispersing from the meeting, proceeded on board their respective ships.

On his return to his ship after the meeting, the Athenian commander Themistocles was confronted by an Athenian who persuaded him that the Isthmus was indefensible and that all the individual contingents would soon give up and scatter to their individual cities. At a second council Themistocles did not present this negative argument for the fleet to stay at Salamis, but tried to persuade the Peloponnesians that, if it was their aim to keep the Persians out of the Peloponnese, it would be easier to do if they stayed and fought in the narrow waters of Salamis. His most resistant opponent was the Corinthian commander Adeimantus.

61. When Themistocles had thus spoken, Adeimantus the Corinthian again attacked him and bade him be silent since he was a man without a city. At the same time he called on Eurybiades [*the Spartan overall commander of the fleet*] not to put the question at the instance of one who had no country; and he urged Themistocles should show of what state he was an envoy, before he gave his voice with the rest. This reproach was made because the city of Athens had been taken and was in the hands of the barbarians. Thereupon Themistocles spoke many bitter things against Adeimantus and the Corinthians generally; and for proof that he had a country, reminded the captains that with two hundred ships at his command, all fully manned for battle, he had both city and territory greater than theirs; since there was no Greek state, which could resist his men should they attack it. 62. Then he turned to Eurybiades, and said with still greater warmth and earnestness, "If you stay here and behave like a brave man, all well be well—if not, you will bring Greece to ruin. For the whole fortune of the war depends on our ships. Be persuaded by my words. If not, we will take our families on board and go, just as we are, to Siris in Italy, which is ours from old, and which the prophecies declare we are to colonize some day or other. You then, when you have lost allies like us, will hereafter call to mind what I have now said." 63. At these words of Themistocles, Eurybiades changed his mind, principally, as I believe because he feared that if he withdrew the fleet to the Isthmus, the Athenians would sail away, and he knew that without the Athenians, the rest of their ships would be no match for the fleet of the enemy. He therefore decided to remain and give battle at Salamis. . . . 66. Meanwhile men of the fleet of Xerxes after they had seen the Spartan dead at Thermopylae. . . . sailed down the coast of Euboea and arrived at Phalerum [*the port of Athens*]. In my judgment, the Persian forces both by land and sea when they invaded Attica were not less numerous than

they had been on their arrival at Sepias and Thermopylae. For against the Persian loss in the storm and at Thermopylae, and again in the sea-fights off Artemisium, I set the various nations, which had since joined the King. These were the Malians, the Dorians, the Locrians and the Boeotians, each serving in full force in his army except the last, who did not number in their ranks the Thespians or the Plataeans. Together with these were the Carystians, the Andrians, the Tenians, and the other peoples of the island, who fought on the King's side except the five states already mentioned. For as the Persians penetrated farther into Greece, they were joined continually by fresh nations.

The Greek commanders continued to dither, but in the end Themistocles resolved the stalemate by sending a secret message to Xerxes that he was willing to betray the allies. He suggested that the king should block the western exits from the straits of Salamis before the Greek fleet broke up and escaped. This precipitated the battle in which the Persian fleet (actually made up mostly of Greek and Phoenician ships) was routed, and Xerxes was forced to withdraw most of his army from Greece.

8. THE BATTLE OF PLATAEA

After Salamis and Xerxes' exit from Greece, a part of the Persian army remained in Greece and wintered in Thessaly, where there was forage for their cavalry. The Persian commander was Mardonius. The Thebans urged a cynical strategy of selective bribery to sow division among the allies.

The History of Herodotus

9.1. Mardonius . . . left Thessaly, and led his army with all speed against Athens; forcing the several nations through whose land he passed to furnish him with additional troops. The chief men of Thessaly, far from repenting of the part which they had taken in the war hitherto, urged on the Persians to the attack more earnestly than ever. Thorax of Larissa in particular, who had helped to escort Xerxes on his flight to Asia, now openly encouraged Mardonius in his march upon Greece. 2. When the army reached Boeotia, the Thebans sought to induce Mardonius to make a halt: "He would not," they told him, "find anywhere a more convenient place in which to pitch his camp; and their advice to him was, that he should go no further, but fix himself there, and from there take measures to subdue all Greece without striking a blow. If the Greeks, who had held together hitherto, still continued united among themselves, it would be difficult for the whole world to overcome them by force of arms. But if you will do as we advise," they went on to say, "you will easily obtain control of all their counsels. Send presents to the men of most weight in the several states, and by so doing you will sow division among them. After that, it will be a light task, with the help of such as side with you, to bring under your control all your adversaries." Such was the advice of the Thebans: but Mardonius did not follow it.

Mardonius left Boeotia to once more enter Attica, which he found deserted. He burned the city of Athens (having previously destroyed the temples on the Acropolis) and returned to Boeotia. Meanwhile, the Spartans and their allies were dragging their feet despite promises to come to the help of the Athenians when the winter was over. Once more the Spartans were celebrating a festival, this time the Hyacinthia.

7. The truth was, the Lacedaemonians were keeping holiday at that time; for it was the feast of the Hyacinthia, and they thought nothing was as important as performing the services in honor of the god. They were also engaged in building their wall across the Isthmus, which was now so far advanced that the battlements had begun to be placed upon it. When the envoys of the Athenians, accompanied by ambassadors from Megara and Plataea, reached Sparta, they came before the Ephors, and spoke as follows: "The Athenians have sent us to you to say,—the king of the Persians has offered to give us back our country, and wishes to conclude an alliance with us on fair and equal terms, without fraud or deceit. He is willing likewise to bestow on us another country besides our own, and bids us choose any land that we like. But we, because we reverenced the God whom all Greece worships, and thought it a shameful act to betray Greece, instead of consenting to these terms, refused them; notwithstanding that we have been wronged and deserted by the other Greeks, and are fully aware that it is far more for our advantage to make peace with the Persians than to prolong the war with them. Still we shall not, of our own free will, consent to any terms of peace. Thus do we, in all our dealings with the Greeks, avoid what is base and counterfeit: while contrariwise, you, who were but now so full of fear least we should make terms with the enemy [*during the winter Mardonius had put out feelers to the Athenians through an intermediary, Alexander, King of Macedon*], having learned of what temper we are, and assured yourselves that we shall not prove traitors to our country—having brought moreover your wall across the Isthmus to an advanced state—cease altogether to have any care for us. You agreed with us to go out and meet the Persian in Boeotia; but when the time came, you were false to your word, and looked on while the barbarian host advanced into Attica. At this time, therefore, the Athenians are angered with you; and justly, for you have not done what was right. They bid you, however, make haste to send forth your army, that we may even yet meet Mardonius in Attica. Now that Boeotia is lost to us, the best place for the fight within our country, will be the plain of Thria."

8. The Ephors [*annually elected magistrates*], when they had heard this speech, delayed their answer till the next day and when the next day came until the day following. And thus they acted for ten days, continually putting off the ambassadors from one day to the next. Meanwhile the Peloponnesians generally were laboring with great zeal at the wall, and the work nearly approached completion. I can give no other reason for the conduct of the Spartans in showing themselves so anxious previously, at the time when Alexander came, that the Athenians should not join the Persians, and now being quite careless about it, except that at the former time the wall across the Isthmus was not complete, and they worked at it in great fear of the Persians,

whereas now the bulwark had been raised, and so they imagined that they had no further need of the Athenians. 9. At last the ambassadors got an answer, and the troops marched forth from Sparta, under the following circumstances. The last audience had been fixed for the ambassadors, when, the very day before it was to be given, a certain Tegean, named Chileus, a man who had more influence at Sparta than any other foreigner, learning from the Ephors exactly what the Athenians had said, addressed these words to them—"The case stands thus, O Ephors! If the Athenians are not our friends, but league themselves with the barbarians, however strong our wall across the Isthmus may be, there will be doors enough, and wide enough open too, by which the Persian may gain entrance to the Peloponnese. Grant their request then, before they make any fresh resolve, which may bring Greece to ruin." 10. Such was the counsel which Chileus gave: and the Ephors, taking the advice into consideration, determined forthwith, without speaking a word to the ambassadors from the three cities, to dispatch to the Isthmus a body of 5,000 Spartans; and accordingly they sent them forth the same night, appointing to each Spartan a retinue of seven Helots, and giving the command of the expedition to Pausanias the son of Cleombrotus. . . .

The Greek Army at Plataea was enormous by Greek standards.

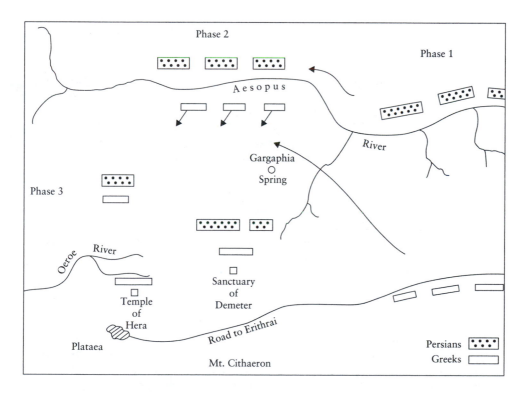

Figure 3.6 The Battle of Plataea.

28. When this matter had been arranged, the Greek army, which was in part composed of those who came at the first, in part of such as had flocked in from day to day, drew up in the following order: 10,000 Lacedaemonian troops held the right wing, 5,000 thousand of whom were Spartans; and these 5,000 were attended by a body of 35,000 Helots, who were only lightly armed— seven Helots to each Spartan. The place next to themselves the Spartans gave to the Tegeans, on account of their courage and of the esteem in which they held them. They were all fully armed, and numbered 1,500 men. Next in order came the Corinthians, 5,000 strong; and with them Pausanias had placed, at their request, the band of 300, which had come from Potidaea in Pallene. The Arcadians of Orchomenus, in number 600, came next; then the Sicyonians, 3,000; then the Epidaurians, 800; then the Troezenians, 1,000; then from Lepreum, 200; the Mycenaeans and Tirynians, 400; from Phlius, 1,000; 300 from Hermione; the Eretrians and Styreans, 600; the Chalcideans, 400; and the Ambraciots, 500. After these came the Leucadians and Anactorians, who numbered 800; the Paleans of Cephallenia, 200; the Aeginetans, 500; the Megarians, 3,000; and the Plataeans, 600. Last of all, but first at their extremity of the line, were the Athenians, who, to the number of 8,000, occupied the left wing, under the command of Aristides, the son of Lysimachus. All these, except the Helots—seven of whom, as I said, attended each Spartan—were heavy-armed troops; and they amounted to 38,700. This was the number of hoplites, or heavy-armed soldiers, which was together against the barbarian. The light-armed troops consisted of the 35,000 ranged with the Spartans, 7 in attendance upon each, who were all well equipped for war; and of 34,500 others, belonging to the Lacedaemonians and the rest of the Greeks, at the rate (nearly) of one light to one heavy armed. Thus the entire number of the light-armed was 69,500. The Greek army, therefore, which mustered at Plataea, counting light-armed as well as heavy-armed, was but 1,800 men short of 110,000; and this amount was exactly made up by the Thespians who were present in the camp; for 1,800 Thespians, being the whole number left [*i.e., after their losses at the Battle of Thermopylae*], were likewise with the army; but these men were without arms. Such was the array of the Greek troops when they took post on the Asopus.

The Greek army took up a defensive position on the hills overlooking the Asopus river and the Boeotian plain, which was dominated by the Persian cavalry. The idea was to have the Persians attack the Greek position, where their cavalry would not be of much use. Naturally, Mardonius understood this. However, a series of events led him to change his mind.

50. When the Gargaphia fountain was choked [*the Greeks could not easily get water from the Asopus because of the Persian cavalry*], the Greek commanders, seeing that the army had no longer a source of water, and observing moreover that the cavalry greatly harassed them, held a meeting on these and other matters at the headquarters of Pausanias upon the right. For besides the above-named difficulties, which were great enough, other circumstances added to their distress. All the provisions that they had brought

with them were gone; and the attendants who had been sent to fetch supplies from the Peloponnese, were prevented from returning to camp by the Persian cavalry, which had now closed the passage [*over Mt. Cithaeron to Megara*]. 51. The captains therefore held a council, whereat it was agreed, that if the Persians did not give battle that day, the Greeks should move to the Island—a tract of ground which lies in front of Plataea, at the distance of a mile and a quarter from the Asopus and the spring Gargaphia, where the army was encamped at that time. . . . They thought it best to begin their march at the second watch of the night, lest the Persians should see them as they left their station, and should follow and harass them with their cavalry. It was agreed likewise, that after they had reached the place, which the Asopus-born Oeroe surrounds, as it flows down from Cithaeron, they should dispatch, the very same night, one half of their army towards that mountain-range, to relieve those whom they had sent to procure provisions, and who were now blocked up in that region. 52. Having made these decisions, they continued during that whole day to suffer beyond measure from the attacks of the enemy's cavalry. At length when towards dusk the attacks of the cavalry ceased, and, night having closed in, the hour arrived at which the army was to commence its retreat, the greater number struck their tents and began the march towards the rear. They intended, however, to make for the place agreed upon; but in their anxiety to escape from the Persian cavalry, no sooner had they begun to move than they fled straight to Plataea; where they took up a position at the temple of Hera, which lies outside the city, at a distance of about two and a half miles from Gargaphia; and here they pitched their camp in front of the sacred building. 53. As soon as Pausanias saw a portion of the troops in motion, he issued orders to the Lacedaemonians to strike their tents and follow those who had been the first to depart, supposing that they were on their march to the place agreed upon. All the captains but one were ready to obey his orders: Amompharetus the son of Poliadas, who was leader of the Pitanate cohort, refused to move, however, saying, "He for one would not fly from the enemy, or of his own will bring disgrace upon Sparta." It had happened that he was absent from the former conference of the captains; and so what was now taking place astonished him. Pausanias and Euryanax were furious that Amompharetus would not obey them; but considered that it would be yet more monstrous, if, when he was so minded, they were to leave the Pitanates to their fate; seeing that, if they forsook them to keep their agreement with the other Greeks, Amompharetus and those with him would perish. On this account, therefore, they kept the Lacedaemonian force in its place, and made every endeavor to persuade Amompharetus that he was wrong to act as he was doing. 54. While the Spartans were engaged in these efforts to turn Amompharetus—the only man unwilling to retreat either in their own army or in that of the Tegeans—the Athenians on their side did as follows. Knowing that it was the Spartan temper to say one thing and do another, they remained quiet in their station until the army began to retreat, when they dispatched a horseman to see whether the Spartans really meant to set forth, or whether after all they had no intention of moving. The horseman was also to ask Pausanias what he wished the Athenians to do. 55. The herald on his arrival found the Lacedaemonians drawn up in their old position, and their leaders quarrelling with one another. Pausanias and Euryanax had gone on urging Amompharetus not to endanger the lives of his men by staying behind while the others drew off, but without succeeding in persuading him; until at last the dispute had waxed hot between them just at the moment when the Athenian herald arrived. At this point Amompharetus, who was still disputing, took up with both his hands a large rock, and placed it at the feet of Pausanias, saying—"With this pebble I give my vote not to run away from the strangers." (By "strangers" he meant barbarians.) Pausanias, in reply, called him a fool and a madman, and, turning to the Athenian herald, who had made the inquiries with which he was charged, bade him tell his countrymen how he was occupied, and ask them to approach nearer, and retreat or not according to the movements of the Spartans. 56. So the herald went back to the Athenians; and the Spartans continued to dispute till morning began to dawn upon them. Then Pausanias, who as yet had not moved, gave the signal for retreat—expecting (and rightly, as the event proved) that Amompharetus, when he saw the rest of the Lacedaemonians in motion, would be unwilling to be left behind. No sooner was the signal given, than all the army except the Pitanates began their march, and retreated along the line of the hills; the Tegeans accompanying them. The Athenians likewise set off in good order, but proceeded by a different way from the Spartans. For while the latter clung to the hilly ground and the skirts of Mount Cithaeron, on account of the fear which they entertained of the enemy's cavalry, the former betook themselves to the low country and marched through the plain. 57. As for Amompharetus, at first he did not believe that Pausanias would really dare to leave him behind; he therefore remained firm in his resolve to keep his men at their post; when, however, Pausanias and his troops were now some way off, Amompharetus, thinking himself forsaken in good earnest, ordered his unit to take their arms, and led them at a walk towards the main army. Now the army was waiting for them at a distance of about a mile and a quarter, having halted upon the river Moloeis at a place called Argiopius, where stands a temple dedicated to Eleusinian Demeter. They had stopped here, that, in case Amompharetus and his troops should refuse to quit the spot where they were drawn up, and should really not stir from it, they might have it in their power to move back and lend them assistance. Amompharetus, however, and his companions rejoined the main body; and at the same time the whole mass of the barbarian cavalry arrived and began to press hard upon them. The horsemen had followed their usual practice and ridden up to the Greek camp, when they discovered that the place where the Greeks had been posted hitherto was deserted. Hereupon they pushed forward without stopping, and, as soon as they overtook the enemy, pressed heavily on them.

Mardonius, seeing the confusion on the Greek side and thinking that he could rout the Greeks, left his position, crossed the river Asopus, and began the attack.

59. Mardonius crossed the Asopus, and led the Persians forward at a run directly upon the track of the Greeks, whom he believed to be in actual flight. He could not see the Athenians; for, as they had taken the way of the plain, they were hidden from his sight by the hills; he therefore led on his troops against the Spartans and the Tegeans only. When the commanders of the other divisions of the barbarians saw the Persians pursuing the Greeks so hastily, they all forthwith seized their standards, and hurried after at their best speed in great disorder and disarray. On they went with loud shouts and in a wild rout, thinking to swallow up the runaways. Meanwhile Pausanias had sent a horseman to the Athenians, at the time when the cavalry first fell upon him. . . . 61. The Athenians, as soon as they received this message, were anxious to go to the aid of the Spartans, and to help them to the uttermost of their power; but, as they were upon the march, the Greeks on the king's side, whose place in the line had been opposite theirs, fell upon them, and so harassed them by their attacks that it was not possible for them to give the help they desired. Accordingly the Spartans, and the Tegeans—whom nothing could induce to quit their side—were left alone to resist the Persians. Including the light-armed, the number of the former was 50,000; while that of the Tegeans was 3,000. Now, therefore, as they were about to engage with Mardonius and the troops under him, they made ready to offer sacrifice. The victims, however, for some time were not favorable; and, during the delay, many fell on the Spartan side, and a still greater number were wounded. For the Persians had made a rampart of their wicker shields, and shot from behind them such clouds of arrows, that the Spartans were greatly distressed. The victims continued unpropitious; till at last Pausanias raised his eyes to the Heraeum of the Plataeans, and calling the goddess to his aid, besought her not to disappoint the hopes of the Greeks. 62. As he offered his prayer, the Tegeans, advancing before the rest, rushed forward against the enemy; and the Spartans, who had obtained favorable omens the moment that Pausanias prayed, at length, after their long delay, advanced to the attack; while the Persians, on their side, left shooting, and prepared to meet them. And first the combat was at the wicker shields. Afterwards, when these were swept down, a fierce contest took place by the side of the temple of Demeter, which lasted long, and ended in a hand-to-hand struggle. The barbarians many times seized hold of the Greek spears and broke them; for in boldness and warlike spirit the Persians were not a whit inferior to the Greeks; but they were without armor, untrained, and far below the enemy in respect of skill in arms. Sometimes singly, sometimes in bodies of ten, now fewer and now more in number, they dashed upon the Spartan ranks, and so perished.

63. The fight went most against the Greeks where Mardonius, mounted upon a white horse, and surrounded by the bravest of all the Persians, the

thousand picked men, fought in person. So long as Mardonius was alive, this body resisted all attacks, and, while they defended their own lives, struck down no small number of Spartans; but after Mardonius fell, and the troops with him, which were the main strength of the army, perished, the remainder yielded to the Spartans, and fled. Their light clothing, and want of armor, were of the greatest hurt to them: for they had to contend against men heavily armed, while they themselves were without any such defense. . . .

67. As for the Greeks upon the king's side, while most of them played the coward purposely, the Boeotians, on the contrary, had a long struggle with the Athenians. Those of the Thebans who were attached to the Medes, displayed especially no little zeal; far from playing the coward, they fought with such fury that three hundred of the best and bravest among them were slain by the Athenians in this passage of arms. But at last they too were routed, and fled away—not, however, in the same direction as the Persians and the crowd of allies, who, having taken no part in the battle, ran off without striking a blow—but to the city of Thebes. 68. To me it shows very clearly how completely the rest of the barbarians were dependent upon the Persian troops, that here they all fled at once, without ever coming to blows with the enemy, merely because they saw the Persians running away. And so it came to pass that the whole army took to flight, except only the cavalry, both Persian and Boeotian. These did good service to the flying infantry, by advancing close to the enemy, and forming a barrier between the Greeks and their own fugitives. . . .

71. On the side of the barbarians, the greatest courage was shown, among the infantry, by the Persians; among the cavalry, by the Sacae; while Mardonius himself, as a man, bore off the palm from the rest. Among the Greeks, the Athenians and the Tegeans fought well; but the prowess shown by the Spartans was beyond either. Of this I have but one proof to offer, since all the three peoples overthrew the force opposed to them, which is, that the Spartans fought and conquered the best troops.

9. REVENGE FOR THERMOPYLAE: THE HUMANITY OF PAUSANIAS

78. There was a man at Plataea among the troops of the Aeginetans, whose name was Lampon; he was the son of Pytheas, and a person of the first rank among his countrymen. Now this Lampon went about this same time to Pausanias, and advised him to do an act of great wickedness. "Son of Cleombrotus," he said very earnestly, "what you have already done is passing great and glorious. By the favor of heaven you have saved Greece. . . . Now then finish your work, that your own fame may be increased thereby, and that henceforth barbarians may fear to commit outrages on the Greeks. When Leonidas was killed at Thermopylae, Xerxes and Mardonius commanded that he be beheaded and crucified. You do the like at this time to Mardonius, and you will have glory in Sparta, and likewise through the

whole of Greece. For by hanging him upon a cross you will avenge Leonidas who was your father's brother." 79. Thus spoke Lampon, thinking to please Pausanias. Pausanias answered him: "My Aeginetan friend, for your foresight and friendliness I am much beholden to you, but the counsel which you have offered is not good. First you lifted me up to the skies by your praise of my country and my achievement; then you cast me down to the ground, by bidding me maltreat the dead, and saying that thus I shall raise myself in men's esteem. Such doings befit barbarians rather than Greeks; and even in barbarians we detest them. . . . Leonidas, whom you would have me avenge is, I maintain, abundantly avenged already. Surely the countless lives taken are enough to avenge not him only but all those who fell at Thermopylae. Come not before me again with such a speech or with such counsel; and thank my forbearance that you are not now punished." Then Lampon, having received this answer, departed, and went his way.

10. THE GREEKS: THE SERPENT COLUMN

A full list of the thirty-one Greek states that actually fought against the Persians is preserved on the so-called "Serpent Column," a bronze column consisting of the bodies of three intertwined snakes that once supported a tripod. The monument was dedicated at Delphi to celebrate the Greek victory over the Persians, but was moved to Constantinople by the Roman Emperor Constantine, where it still stands in the ruins of the Hippodrome (= Race Track).

These fought the war:

Lacedaemonians, Athenians, Corinthians, Tegeates, Sicyonians, Aeginetans, Megarians, Epidaurians, Orchomenians, Phleiasians, Troezenians, Hermionians, Tirynthians, Plataeans, Thespians, Mycenaeans, Ceians, Melians, Tenians, Naxians, Eretrians, Chalcidians, Styrians, Eleians, Poteidaeans, Leucadians, Anactorians, Cythnians, Siphnians, Ambraciotes, Lepreates.

4

LIFE IN THE *POLIS*

In modern states social life is regarded as something distinct and independent of the public sphere. Most citizens spend their entire lives working for private enterprises or institutions, while their social lives revolve around clubs, unions, religious, cultural, and charitable organizations, professional or fraternal associations, and so forth. Involvement in government is likely to be minimal, limited to such matters as jury service, paying taxes, and obtaining permits for one kind of activity or another, and perhaps occasional involvement in political campaigns. It is taken for granted that government is made up of permanent administrative bodies employing large numbers of people, while very small numbers of elected individuals come and go over the years as a result of elections. During the year there are only a handful of national civic festivals.

In the case of the *polis*, most of the above needs to be reversed. There public and private realms intermingled in confusing and complicated ways. Great religious festivals, which occurred frequently throughout the year, structured, defined, and explained life for all *polis* inhabitants alike, male and female, free and slave, citizen and noncitizen. Religion was very much a public affair sponsored by the state and in turn sustaining the state. Governmental and military affairs involved proportionately larger numbers of citizens than did (or does) any other kind of polity, but there was no permanent "government." Households, the foundation of the *polis*, were inextricably involved in the full spectrum of *polis* life. *Polis* citizenship was not merely a legal matter of birth in a particular *polis*, but primarily one of moral and civic formation, first in a *polis* family and then in intermediate bodies such as the deme (local territorial divisions) and the phratry (fictive family units), membership in which came through membership in a citizen family. There was no other way, except in extraordinary circumstances, of becoming a citizen of a *polis* than by being born into one of the existing *polis* families. Only the legitimate children of such families had full access to the social, economic, religious, and political life of the city. Foreigners, no matter what their wealth or for how many generations they had lived in a *polis*, remained outsiders to much of *polis* life and its privileges. The *polis* household (or *oikos*) far exceeded the significance of the modern household in economic, social, political, and cultural terms. While it bore huge responsibilities for educating each new generation of citizens, the *polis* household had correspondingly great resources. It had none of the weak features that characterize modern households where dependency—for instance, on jobs in a nonhousehold economy—is the norm.

At its simplest, a *polis* was a small-scale agricultural community whose component parts, its households, were economically self-sufficient. The ultimate building blocks of a *polis* were, therefore, the economic units to which the citizens belonged and which supported them, their *oikoi* or "households." Economically, an *oikos* consisted of a house, a plot of one or more blocks of arable land possibly scattered in various parts of the territory of the *polis*, the tools for cultivating the land, farm animals, and perhaps a slave or two. For the most part, however, small *polis* farms could not support slaves. Socially, an *oikos* was composed of the adult male citizen, who was its head, his wife, and their children, who represented the future of the household. As was demanded by its multiple functions, the household was rigorously hierarchical and authoritarian. It prescribed precise and exact roles for all of its members, and it was understood that in the execution of these roles the members of the household found and established their individual identities. *Polis* life offered few opportunities for different economic roles—almost everyone was in some way involved in agriculture—and even fewer choices in social and cultural matters.

The household was a religious corporation with the responsibility of looking after the graves of the ancestors, performing periodic but essential family rituals, and eventually passing on these rituals to the next generation. While the household was not a formal political unit of the state, it was the source of entry into all aspects of *polis* political life. The social standing and economic resources of a particular *oikos* had an important bearing on the role played by its male members (and female ones to the extent that they played important public religious roles) in the larger political community. The reputation of the household was thus one of its most essential assets. From a practical viewpoint one of the most important resources of a household was its access to the interconnecting ties of kin, social, and political relationships that constituted *polis* life. Because no *polis* had a formal safety net, it was these connections that sustained individual households in hard times, with the expectation that such favors would be returned in kind. Ideally, a *polis* consisted of a fixed number of such economically autarkic households; laws in some cities, especially colonial cities, tried to maintain constant the number of *oikoi* by, for example, forbidding the sale of a household's original agricultural land plot.

The core of an *oikos* was the married couple. According to the *Oeconomicus*, Xenophon's fourth-century B.C. treatise on household management, marriage was a partnership of man and woman for the purpose of managing an *oikos*. Responsibilities were clearly divided. The woman's sphere was the house and all that went on within it, while the man was responsible for most of the relations between the household and the outside world. Women, however, were not confined exclusively to these private activities. Farming inevitably involved women in many of its activities, especially at harvest time, but women also had roles in small businesses connected with their domestic activities. In the public realm women had important roles in religion, one of the most significant aspects of *polis* life, in which everything was, in some way, related to religion.

Throughout Greece female deities tended to be served by women and girls. At Athens priestesses presided over more than forty major cults, and the most important priesthood in the city, that of Athena Polias, was in the hands of a woman. The *Basilinna*, the wife of the official known as the Archon Basileus, played a key role in the Anthesteria festival in honor of Dionysus. Priestesses officiated at the city's most important state festival, the Panathenaia, and served at three of the most prominent panhellenic shrines in Greece: Delphi, Dodona, and Eleusis. Women were active participants in the Eleusinian, Pythagorean, and Orphic mysteries; the cult of the Cabiri or the Great Gods on Samothrace; the rituals of Sabazios, Bendis, Cybele (the Great Mother), Adonis; and, most important of all, in the worship of Dionysus. Of the foregoing, the cults of both Bendis and Cybele were ministered to by priestesses, while the Eleusinian mysteries also involved priestesses. The religion of Dionysus had both civic and elective overtones. At Athens, as elsewhere, his worship did have institutionalized forms, as was the case in such festivals as the Lenaea and the Anthesteria, but some of the god's rites did involve bizarre (even by ancient Greek religious standards) behavior such as wild dancing, drinking, and unescorted wanderings outside the *polis* by women and young girls in the hills. In 355 B.C., during the Sacred War, the maenads (as these worshippers of Dionysos were called) of Phocis wandered at night into the agora of the enemy city of Amphissa, where they threw themselves down to sleep. While sleeping they were protected from harm by the women of Amphissa, who the next day received permission to escort them to the frontier and safety. In another incident a band of Athenian maenads were caught in a freak snowstorm on Mt. Parnassus and had to be rescued.

The Greek economic ideal was autarchy, or self-sufficiency, for both *polis* and *oikos*, in an environment of scarcity. The proper functioning of the *oikos* depended on the resources of both husband and wife. A woman brought to an *oikos* her managerial skills, wealth in the form of a dowry, and the potential for its continued survival in her sexuality. She also brought to the household her kinship network and its resources—economic, political, and other. Needless to say, a wife's role in the education of her children, the future citizens of the community, was as critical, if not more, especially in early childhood years, than that of her husband. Her failure to inculcate the norms and values of her *polis* and provide a proper role model for her children was considered shameful and would have negative consequences, not just for the children but for the household as a whole. Sexual misbehavior on her part, as is graphically demonstrated in the *Murder of Eratosthenes*, could destroy her household's reputation and confound the purity of the patrilineal descent lines that linked the *polis* and its constituent households to both their past and their future.

Although Greek law and custom fostered significant inequalities between husband and wife in most areas of social and economic life, in one area they were equals, namely, in their authority over the unfree members of their household, its slaves. Slavery was one of the central features of Greek life. The exact size of the slave population in Greece is one of the most hotly contested issues in ancient historiography, but on one point all scholars agree. Although few Greeks relied entirely on slave labor for their support, ownership of slaves was widespread throughout the society. Free Greeks and slaves worked side by side in all occupations, from the most menial to the most skilled, and slaves lived on the most intimate terms with their masters in their *oikoi*. Not surprisingly, as the *Oeconomicus* reveals, management of the household slaves was one of the chief concerns of Greek husbands and wives. The daily reality of slaves' lives is harder to grasp. Greek law afforded slaves few protections against their masters. Corporal punishment of and free sexual access to their slaves were permitted to masters (although whether the latter was socially acceptable was another matter), and the testimony of slaves was admissible in court only if extracted under torture.

Modern scholars are understandably embarrassed by the seemingly obvious contradiction between the Greek ideal of freedom and the pervasiveness of slavery in Greek life. Few Greek thinkers shared that embarrassment, but their complacency should not be surprising, since slavery was a prominent feature of all the civilizations known to the Greeks. To Greeks it seemed that there were very few, if any, really free people in non-Greek societies. There was a common saying that in the authoritarian societies of the East, only the king was free. Hence, from the ancient Greek viewpoint (as opposed to a modern one where the assumptions are reversed), the surprise was that there were, comparatively speaking, so many free people in Greece. In a world where most people were enslaved to absolute monarchs (or, in the case of Europeans, to political backwardness and barbarism), it was the freedom of the few that made Hellenic society distinct from all other known societies. Xenophon and other reformers professed to see social and economic benefits in the expansion of slavery, but other Greek thinkers, such as Plato, increasingly came to believe for both ideological and practical reasons that Greeks should not enslave Greeks. Even this view remained a utopian dream. Aristotle remarked that only when automata became available would the role of servants and slaves come to an end (*Pols.* 1.1253b33–39). Throughout Greek history the reality remained that anyone, Greek or barbarian, might, as a prisoner of war, as a victim of kidnapping, or, outside Athens, as a defaulting debtor, find himself swept up into the slave trade, a trade whose horrors Herodotus dramatically illustrates in the tale of the eunuch's revenge.

A. The Household: Family Relations

1. "WHAT IS SWEETER THAN FAMILY?"

In this speech Apollodorus is trying to persuade the jury to award him damages from the defendant Polycles. Apollodorus alleges that Polycles had failed to relieve him in a timely way from the responsibility of his trierarchy (at Athens this involved both the command and the financing of a trireme warship). As a result, Polycles was in financial difficulties. He makes an emotional appeal to the jury.[1]

Demosthenes,
Against Polycles

My mother lay sick and was at the point of death while I was away from home [*at sea on his trireme*]. . . . I was home for only six days when, after she had seen

[1] From Demosthenes, *Against Polycles* (London, 1939), 50.60–62, based on the translation of A. T. Murray.

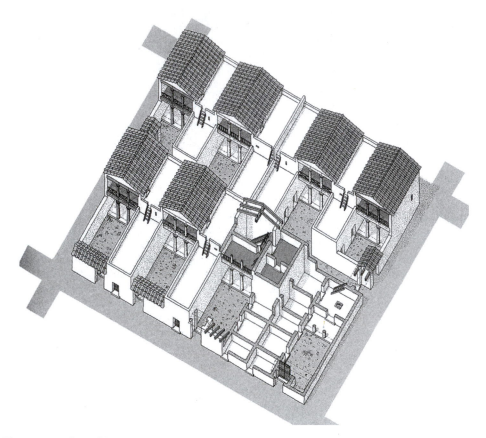

Figure 4.1 Plan of houses in Piraeus. Based on Wolfram Hoepfner and ErnstLudwig Schwandner, *Haus und Stadt im Klassischen Griechenland* (Munich, 1994), by permission.

and greeted me, she breathed her last . . . She had often sent for me before this, begging me to come to her by myself. . . . My wife, too, to whom I am deeply attached, was in poor health for a long time during my absence; my children were small and my estate was in debt; my land not only produced no crops, but that year, as you all know, the water even dried up in the wells, so that not a vegetable grew in the garden. My creditors at the expiration of the year came to collect their interest, unless the principal was paid to them according to the contract. When I heard these facts from the lips of those who came and also through letters from my relatives, how do you think I must have felt and how many tears must I have shed, while I reckoned up my present troubles and was longing to see my children and my wife, and my mother whom I had little hope of finding alive? For what is sweeter to a man than these? Why should he want to go on living if deprived of them? Although the misfortunes which had befallen me were thus grievous, I did not count my private interests of so much importance as your interests [*i.e.*, *the interests of Athens*], but felt I ought to rise above the wasting of my assets, the neglect of my household affairs, and the sickness of my wife and mother, so that no one could accuse me of deserting my post or letting my ship be useless to the state. I now implore you that, as I showed myself obedient and useful in your service, so you will now take thought of me and remembering all that I have told you. . . . you will help me when I am being wronged, will hand out punishment in your interest, and will exact repayment of the funds expended on the defendant's behalf.

2. DO PARENTS LOVE THEIR CHILDREN MORE THAN CHILDREN LOVE THEIR PARENTS?

In the Nicomachean Ethics, *Aristotle has a lot to say about relationships within families. Here are some samples. According to Aristotle, children, strictly speaking, cannot be friends with their parents because only equals can be friends.*[2]

Aristotle, *Nicomachean Ethics*

Affection (*philia*) between relatives itself seems to include a variety of species, but all appear to derive from the affection of parent for child. For parents love their children as part of themselves, whereas children love their parents as the source of their being. Also parents know their offspring with more certainty than children know their parentage; and a progenitor is more attached to progeny than progeny to progenitor, since that which springs from a thing belongs to the thing from which it springs. . . . The affection of parents exceeds that of the child in duration also; parents love their children as soon as they are born, children their parents only when time has elapsed and they have acquired understanding or at least perception. These considerations also explain why parental affection is stronger in the mother. Parents then love their children as themselves (one's offspring being as it were another self—other because separate); children love their parents as the source of their being. Brothers love each other as being from the same source, since the identity of their relations to that source identifies them with one another, which is why we speak of "being of the same blood," or "of the same stock" or the like. Brothers are therefore in a manner the same being, though embodied in separate persons. But friendship between brothers is also greatly fostered by their common upbringing and similarly of age; hence the sayings "two of an age agree," and "familiarity breeds fellowship," which is why the friendship between brothers resembles that between members of a comradeship [*in a club or fraternity*]. Cousins and other relatives derive their attachment from the fraternal relationship, since it is due to their descent from the same ancestor; and their sense of attachment is greater or less, according as the common ancestor is nearer or more remote.

[2] From Aristotle, *Nicomachean Ethics*, trans. H. Rackham (London, 1926), 8.1161b17–1162a33.

The affection of children for their parents, like that of men for the gods, is the affection for what is good and superior to oneself; for their parents have bestowed on them the greatest benefits in being the cause of their existence and rearing, and later of their education. Also the affection between parents and children affords a greater degree both of pleasure and utility than that between persons unrelated to one another, inasmuch as they have more in common in their lives.

3. THE NATURE OF YOUTH

Aristotle, *The Art of Rhetoric*

In his treatise The Art of Rhetoric, *Aristotle argues that to be effective a speaker needs (among many things) a knowledge of the emotions. This involves knowledge of human character at different stages in life from (male) youth to old age. Here is his sympathetic assessment of youth.*[3]

The young are passionate, hot-tempered, and carried away by impulse . . . they cannot endure to be slighted, and become indignant when they think they are being wronged. They are ambitious for honor, but more so for victory, for youth desires superiority, and victory is a kind of superiority. . . . They are not ill-natured but simple-natured, because they have never witnessed much depravity; confiding, because they have as yet not been often deceived; full of hope, for they are naturally as hot-blooded as those who are drunken with wine, and besides they have not yet experienced many failures. For the most part they live in hope, for hope is concerned with the future as memory is with the past. For the young the future is long, the past is short; for in the morning of life it is not possible for them to remember anything, but they have everything to hope; which makes them easy to deceive, for they readily hope. And they are more courageous, for they are full of passion and hope, and the former of these prevents them from fearing, while the latter inspires them with confidence, for no one fears when angry, and hope of some advantage inspires confidence. . . . They are high-minded, for they have not yet been humbled by life nor have they experienced the force of necessity; further, there is high-mindedness in thinking oneself worthy of great things, a feeling which belongs to one who is full of hope.

Plato, *The Republic*

Plato blamed democratic constitutions for allowing too much freedom for the young, women, and slaves. Democratic cities become "intoxicated by drinking too deeply of the unmixed wine of liberty" and end up in dictatorships. Here is what he has to say on the behavior of young men in democracies.[4]

In democracies those who obey the magistrates are reviled as willing slaves and worthless, but they commend and honor in public and private magistrates who act like subjects and subjects who act like rulers. Is it not inevitable that that in such

---

[3] From Aristotle, *The Art of Rhetoric*, trans. J. H. Freese (London, 1926), 1389a.

[4] From Plato, *The Republic*, trans. P. Shorey (London, 1935) 562d–563b.

a state, the spirit of liberty should go to extremes? . . . And this anarchical temper must penetrate into private homes . . . the father habitually tries to resemble the child and is afraid of his sons, and the son likens himself to the father and feels no awe or fear of his parents, so that he may be "free." And the metic [*resident alien*] feels himself equal to the citizen and the citizen to him, and the foreigner likewise. . . . The teacher in such a city fears and fawns upon the students and the students pay no heed to their teachers or their tutors. In general the young ape their elders and argue furiously with them in speech and action, while the old, accommodating themselves to the young, are full of specious pleasantry and graciousness, imitating the young for fear they may be thought disagreeable and authoritarian. . . .

4. HUSBANDS AND WIVES

"Children too seem to be a bond of union, and therefore childless marriages are more easily dissolved."   Plato, *The Republic*

The affection between husband and wife appears to be a natural instinct; since human beings are by nature pairing creatures even more than they are political creatures, inasmuch as the household is an earlier and more fundamental institution than the *polis,* and procreation of offspring a more general characteristic of the animal creation. So whereas with the other animals the association of the sexes aims only at continuing the species, human beings cohabit not only for the sake of begetting children but also to provide the needs of life; for with the human race division of labor beings at the outset, and man and woman have different functions. Thus, they supply each other's wants, putting their special capacities into the common stock, and so the friendship of husband and wife seems to be one of utility and pleasure combined; but it may also be based on virtue if the partners have high moral characters; for each sex has its special virtue, and this may be the ground of attraction. Children too seem to be a bond of union, and therefore childless marriages are more easily dissolved; for children are a common good possessed by both parents in common, and common property holds people together. . . .

5. MOTHERS AND SONS: "MY MOTHER IS A TRIAL"

Xenophon, a student of Socrates, wrote a book, the Memorabilia, *in defense of his teacher, who was accused of corrupting the youth of Athens by teaching them to despise their parents and introducing new gods. In refutation, Xenophon emphasized the traditionality of Socrates' teaching. Here Socrates' eldest son, Leocrates, is being taken to task for his treatment of his mother, the sharptongued Xanthippe. The reading begins with a long section (summarized here) on what mothers go through raising their children.*[5]   Xenophon, *Memorabilia*

[5] From Xenophon, *Memorabilia* or *Conversations with Socrates*, trans. E. C. Marchant (London, 1923), 2.2.5–14 (modified).

SOCRATES: The mother conceives and bears her child in suffering, risking her life . . . enduring toil day and night, with no idea of what she will get in return. Nor are parents content just to supply food, but as soon as their children seem capable of learning they teach them what they can for their good, and if they think that another is more competent to teach them anything, they send them to him at a cost and strive their utmost that the children may turn out as well as possible.

LEOCRATES: True, but even if she has done all this and far more than this, no one could stand her awful temper.

S: Which, do you think is harder to put up with—the ferocity of a wild animal or that of a mother?

L: A mother's—when she is like mine.

S: Well, now, many people get bitten or kicked by wild animals; has your mother ever done you an injury like that?

L: Well, no, but she says things one wouldn't listen to for anything in the world.

S: Indeed. How much trouble do you think you have given her by your peevish words and acts, night and day since you were a child? And how much pain when you were sick?

L: True, but I have never said or done anything to cause her shame.

S: Now do you really think it is harder for you to listen to what she says than for actors when they abuse one another in a tragedy?

L: But an actor, I suppose, doesn't think that a question put to him will lead to punishment, or that a threat means harm: so he makes light of it.

S: And why should you be annoyed? You know well that there is no malice in what your mother says to you; on the contrary, she wishes you to be blessed above all other beings—unless, indeed, you suppose that your mother is maliciously set against you?

L: Oh no, I don't think that.

S: So this mother of yours is kindly disposed towards you; she nurses you devotedly in sickness and sees that you want nothing; more than that, she prays to the gods to bless you abundantly, and makes vows on your behalf, and yet you say she is a trial! It seems to me that, if you can't endure a mother like her, you can't endure a good thing. Now tell me, is there any other being whom you feel bound to cultivate and regard? Or are you set on trying to please nobody, and obeying neither military commander nor civil magistrate?

L: Of course not! . . .

S: When you find yourself with a traveling companion on land or sea, or happen to meet anyone, is it a matter of indifference to you whether he prove to be a friend or an enemy? Or do you think his good will worth cultivating?

L: Yes, I do.

S: And yet, when you are resolved to cultivate these, you don't think courtesy is due to your mother, who loves you more than all? Don't you know that while the state ignores all other forms of ingratitude and pronounces no judgment on them, caring nothing if the recipient of a favor neglects to thank his benefactor, it inflicts penalties on a man who is discourteous to his parents. Furthermore, the state rejects him as unworthy of office, holding that it would be a sin for him to offer sacrifices on behalf of the state [*as magistrates and commanders did*] and that he is unlikely to do anything else honorably and rightly? Indeed, if one were to fail to honor his parents' graves, the state inquires into that too, when it examines candidates for office. Therefore, my boy, if you are prudent, you will pray the gods to pardon your neglect of your mother lest they in turn refuse to be kind to you, thinking you an ingrate; and you will beware of men lest all cast you out, perceiving that you care nothing for your parents, and in the end you are found without a friend. For, should men suppose you to be ungrateful to your parents, none would think you would be grateful for any kindness he might show you.

6. "EXCEPT FOR MY MOTHER I HATE THE WHOLE FEMALE SEX"

So said a character in Euripides' play Melanippe.[6] *From Homer to the end of antiquity, Greek writers celebrated marriage as a partnership of a man and woman for the successful management of a household and the continuation of a family. There is also, however, almost as continuous and strong a strain of misogyny in Greek thought, characterized by the idea that good women, whose prudence and self-control would help an* oikos *to flourish, are few and far between. The clearest expression of this aspect of Greek thought is the catalog of female stereotypes contained in the poem* On Women *by the sixth-century* B.C. *satirist Semonides of Amorgos.*[7]

Semonides of Amorgos, "On Women"

God made diverse the ways of womankind.
One he created from a hairy sow;
in her house everything's a mess of filth
rolling about untidy on the floor,
and she herself, unwashed, in dirty clothes,
eats herself fat and wallows in the muck.

One from a wicked vixen he created, expert in every trick.
She misses nothing so long as it's bad, or even if it's good:
what's good she mostly denigrates, what's bad she praises.
But her moods are changeable. . . .

Another the Olympians shaped from earth and gave a
man: a lame duck, ignorant of good and ill alike. The only
skill she knows is eating—oh, and when God sends a
frost, to pull her chair up to the fire.

Another from the sea: she has two moods. One day she
sparkles and her face is bright; a guest who sees her will
pay compliments, "No finer, fairer wife in all the world!"
Another day she's insupportable to look at or go near to,
raging mad like a bitch over her puppies, savagely at odds
with friends and enemies alike—just as the sea

[6] From Philip Vellacott, *Ironic Drama*, trans. Vellacott (Cambridge, 1975), p. 97.

[7] From M. L. West, *Greek Lyric Poetry* (Oxford, 1993), pp. 17–19.

sometimes stands motionless and harmless, a delight to
those who sail, in summertime, but sometimes rages wild
with thunderous swell rampaging to and fro. That's what
this kind of woman's like—in mood, I mean; there's no
resemblance in her looks!

Another from an obstinate grey ass,
that after thwacks and curses just consents
and does the minimum. And then she eats
in the shadows, eats at the hearth, all night, all day;
and likewise hungry for the act of love
she welcomes anyone that comes along.

One from a weasel—miserable breed, with no fair feature
or desirable or lovely or delightful to her name. She's
quite resourceless in the bed of love, making the
passenger seasick. She's a pest to neighbors with her
thieving; often, too, she eats the food that was for
sacrifice.

A fancy mare was mother to another, who baulks at
chores or anything that's hard and wouldn't touch a
millstone, lift a sieve, or clear the shit out, or sit at the
stove for fear of soot; and yet compels a man to love her.
Twice a day she takes a bath, or three times, some days;
then she puts on scent. Her long, lush hair is always
combed, and decked with flowers: hah, this sort of
woman makes a lovely sight for others, but a plague for
the man she belongs to, that's to say unless he's some big
tyrant or some sceptred king whose heart takes pride in
suchlike fripperies. . . .

One from a bee: he's lucky who gets her, for she's the
only one on whom no blame alights. Wealth grows and
prospers at her hands. Bound in affection with her
husband she grows old, her children handsome and
esteemed. Among all women she stands out; a charm
divine surrounds her. She does not enjoy sitting with
women when they talk of sex. Of all the wives that Zeus
bestows on men, this kind's the finest and most sensible.

But all those other breeds, by Zeus' design, exist and ever
will abide with men. Yes, the worst pestilence Zeus ever
made is women. Even if they look to be a helpmeet, yet
the master suffers most: the man who keeps a woman in
his house never gets through a whole day in good cheer,
nor will he soon drive Hunger from his door, that hostile
lodger, hateful deity. When with his household he seems
most content, whether by God's grace or on man's
account, she finds some fault, and girds herself for war.

Where there's a woman, they may not be keen even to welcome in a visitor. I'll tell you, she that looks the best-behaved in fact is the most rotten of them all, for while her man gawps fondly at her, oh, the neighbors' merriment: another dupe!

Yes, when the talk's of wives, each man will praise his own and criticize the other bloke's, but we don't realize it's equal shares. For Zeus made wives as his worst pestilence and fettered us in bonds unbreakable. It's long been so: remember those who fought round Troy's old city for a woman's sake and found a home in Hades, [and again those others who were murdered at their hearth . . .]

7. PROCNE'S LAMENT: THE SORROWS OF YOUNG WOMEN

In Sophocles' play Tereus, *Procne is married off to the brutal king of Thrace, Tereus. Only fragments of the play survive. In this fragment Procne is lamenting her fate—and that of other young women—who are torn from their families at a young age and married to men they hardly know.*[8]

Sophocles,
Tereus

Now I know I am nothing on my own. But I have often regarded the nature of women this way, seeing that we amount to nothing. In childhood in our father's house we live the happiest life, I think, of all mankind; for Folly always raises children in happiness. But when we have understanding and have come to youthful vigor, we are pushed out and sold away from our paternal gods and from our parents, some to foreign husbands, some to barbarians, some to joyless homes, and some to homes that are abusive.

B. Household Management

1. WOMEN'S WORK

Domestic production was an essential aspect of household activities of all families, rich and poor alike, and a vital part of the economy of the polis. *Females of the household spun wool and wove the cloth used for clothing, wall hangings, bed covers, and so on. Cloth produced in excess of household need was sold on the side (for details of this aspect of the household economy, see Chapter 5, Section E). Agricultural surplus—such as the figs mentioned in the following reading—was sold in the marketplace by women as well as men. In Aristophanes' play* Lysistrata, *the women of Athens have*

Aristophanes,
Lysistrata

[8] From Sophocles, fragment 583, *Sophocles Fragments*, trans. H. Lloyd-Jones (Cambridge, MA, 1996) (modified).

captured the Acropolis and are defending it against the Scythian archers, the quasi-police force of Athens. The heroine Lysistrata urges the women forward in mock imitation of Greek commanders, but instead of calling her troops by name, she identifies them by their occupations, with the aim of creating even more terror among the men.[9]

LYSISTRATA: Forward, my gallant companions! March forth ye vendors of grain and eggs, garlic and vegetables, keepers of taverns and bakeries. Wrench and strike and tear! Come, spew a torrent of invective and insult (*They beat the Scythians who retreat*). Enough, enough! Now retire; never strip the bodies of the slain . . . (457–461).

CLEONICE: The other day in the market I saw a cavalry captain with flowing ringlets; he was on horseback, and was packing into his helmet the broth he had just bought at an old lady's stand. Then there was this Thracian warrior who was brandishing his lance like Tereus in the play; he had scared a good woman selling figs into a perfect panic, and was gobbling up all her ripest fruit (560–564).

Demosthenes, Against Eubulides

In the following extract from a court speech, the speaker is establishing that his mother was a respectable Athenian. The fact that he and she sold ribbons in the marketplace proved nothing to the contrary.[10]

30. With regard to my mother, for they are slandering her too, I will speak of her and call witnesses in support of what I have to say. And yet, men of Athens, in reproaching us for doing business in the market, Eubulides has acted not only contrary to the state's law [*psephisma*] but also traditional laws [*nomoi*] which prescribe that anyone who reproaches a citizen, whether male or female for doing business in the market, shall be liable for prosecution for slander. 31. We acknowledge that we sell ribbons and live in a manner not of our choosing, and if in your eyes, Eubulides, this indicates that we are not Athenians, I shall prove to you the opposite—that it is not permitted to any alien to do business in the market. . . . [*the law is then cited by the clerk*] 32. And there is another tradition [*nomos*] regarding idleness under which you are liable for slander when you criticize those of us who work for a living as traders. . . . 34. When Eubulides asserts that my mother is a vendor of ribbons and that everyone knows that, he should bring forward witnesses and not just argue from hearsay. And if he claims she is an alien, he ought to examine the market records and show whether she's paid the alien's tax [*which allowed foreigners to trade in the* agora], and from what country she came. If she were a slave then her owner should have come to give evidence against her, or the one who sold her, or in their absence, someone who could prove that she had lived as a slave or had been set free. But as it is Eubulides has proved none of these things; he has merely, in my opinion, abused her

[9] From Aristophanes, *Lysistrata*, trans. anonymous, in W. J. Oates and E. O'Neill, *The Complete Greek Drama* (New York, 1938).

[10] From Demosthenes, *Against Eubulides*, 30–34.

in every conceivable way. This is what a blackmailer [*sykophantes*] does—makes charges but proves nothing!

According to Athenian tradition Solon introduced the worship of Aphrodite Pandemos ("Aphrodite of All the People") in the early sixth century B.C., *financing the cult from the profits of brothels. Although Solon's connection to the brothel tax is probably legend, in the fourth century at Athens male and female prostitutes had to pay a tax to the city. Corinth was famous for its sacred prostitutes at the temple of Aphrodite Ourania, and similar sacred prostitutes were found in other temples of Aphrodite. It is no wonder that when Dionysos planned his trip to Hades in Aristophanes'* Frogs *he asked Herakles for the following essential information.*

Tell me about the harbors; the baker's shops; the brothels; the inns; the rest areas; the springs; the roads; the cities; rooms for rent; and landladies with the fewest fleas.

2. "WHERE THERE IS NO WIFE HOUSEHOLDS ARE NEITHER ORDERLY NOR PROSPEROUS"

A female character in Euripides' play Melanippe *protests against commonplace male calumnies against women and simultaneously sums up what women did as well as what was expected of them.*[11]

Euripides,
Melanippe

Women manage households and preserve the goods, which are brought from abroad. Households where there is no wife are neither orderly nor prosperous. And in religion—I take this to be important—we women play a large part. . . . How then can it be just that the female sex should be abused? Shall not men cease their foolish reproaches, cease to blame all women alike if they meet one who is bad?

3. WOMEN AND LEGAL AFFAIRS

It is often asserted that not only were women children in the eyes of the law, but they were treated—and they acted—like children. Legally speaking, women had the status of minors, but in practice they were, in many instances, fully involved in the financial affairs of their households. In the following reading the speaker, the husband of the daughter of Polyeuctus, is making a claim against his brother-in-law, Spoudias, the husband of Polyeuctus' other daughter. The reading shows (despite its complexity) that Polyeuctus and his wife together managed their property in the interests of their daughters and that the daughters themselves took an active part in the administration of the family property. They were present at the making of their father's will, knew its contents, acted as witnesses to the authenticity of their father's sealed papers, and in the case of the speaker's wife acted independently to spend her own money. Here we are dealing with a better-off family, not the small-time

Demosthenes,
*Against
Spoudias*

[11] From Philip Vellacott, *Ironic Drama*, trans. P. Vellacott (Cambridge, 1975), p. 97.

*shopkeepers of Aristophanes (see Section B.1.). Apparently there was sufficient money involved to
make it worth taking legal measures.*[12]

Men of the jury, I now intend to provide you with details regarding the other
claims I make. The daughters received from their mother, the wife of Polyeuctus,
a bowl, which they pawned together with some pieces of jewelry. They have not
redeemed these and returned the money to the general account. . . . They also
received an awning for which there is no accounting, and many more articles of a
similar kind. And finally, although my wife advanced a mina of silver and spent
it on the funeral feast for her father, Spoudias refuses to contribute his share to
this, but keeps what he has received. . . . Regarding the house, if he maintains
that Polyeuctus was persuaded by me to order that the mortgage-markers be
set in place for the 1,000 drachmae owed me (*the mortgage transaction involving
the speaker*), yet surely, Spoudias, I did not use my influence to induce the witnesses to give false testimony in my own interest. These witnesses were present
at the betrothal of Polyeuctus' daughter to me and she knew that I received less
than the entire dowry. They heard him also when he acknowledged that he was
in my debt and also when he had introduced Leocrates as the one who should
make payment. Finally, they were present when the will was made. . . . When
Polyeuctus gave these directions in his will, the defendant's wife (*Polyeuctus'
daughter*) was present, and you may be sure that she reported to him the will of
her father, especially if he did not receive an equal share, but was significantly
disadvantaged. Spoudias was himself invited to be present so that he cannot
claim that he was kept in the dark and that we managed the affair in secrecy.
Although he was invited to attend he said that he was busy and that it would be
sufficient if his wife were present. When Aristogenes gave him a full account of
what happened, he made no comment. Although Polyeuctus lived for five days
more, Spoudias neither indicated displeasure nor objected, nor did his wife who
was present from the first on all these occasions. . . . In regard to the twenty minae
(*another debt over which there was dispute*) which he does not reveal in the account,
the defendant himself will be my most convincing witness. . . . The papers were
left by the wife of Polyeuctus as I just reported. The seals were certified both by
the defendant's wife and mine. We were both present when we broke the seals
and took copies, and then sealed up the papers again, and deposited them in the
hands of Aristogenes. . . .

4. THE EDUCATION OF A WIFE

Xenophon,
Oeconomicus

Reflecting the central place occupied by the oikos *in Greek life, the various extant classical treatises
on* oikonomia *are concerned not with the "economy" in the modern sense but with the successful
management of a household in all of its aspects. In this passage from the earliest surviving example
of such a work, the* Oeconomicus *of Xenophon, a follower of Socrates who wrote in the early fourth*

---

[12] From Demosthenes, *Against Spoudias*, 11–22.

Figure 4.2 Scholars argue about the exact interpretation of this depiction of two young women, one of whom is carrying a writing case. The simplest explanation is that she is on her way to school, being hurried along by her attendant, probably a slave. Girl going to school. Interior, kylix, red-figured, fifth century B.C. The Metropolitan Museum of Art, Rogers Fund, 1906 (06.1021.167).

century B.C., an Athenian landowner named Ischomachus is depicted as describing to Socrates how he explained to his young bride the separate but complementary roles of husband and wife in the running of a household.[13]

Socrates (he proceeded), I certainly do not spend my days indoors, if for no other reason, than that my wife is quite capable of managing our domestic affairs without my aid.

Ah! (said I), Ischomachus, that is just what I should like particularly to learn from you. Did you yourself educate your wife to be all that a wife should be, or when you received her from her father and mother was she already proficient and well skilled to discharge the duties appropriate to a wife?

Well skilled! (he replied). What proficiency was she likely to bring with her, when she was not quite fifteen at the time she wedded me, and during the whole

[13] Xenophon, *Oeconomicus* 7.3–6 (selections). From *The Works of Xenophon*, Vol. 3, trans. H. G. Dakyns (London, 1890).

prior period of her life had been most carefully brought up to see and hear as little as possible, and to ask the fewest questions? Or do you not think one should be satisfied, if at marriage her whole experience consisted in knowing how to take wool and make a dress, and seeing how her mother's slaves had their daily spinning-tasks assigned them? For (he added), as regards control of appetite and self-indulgence, she had received the soundest education, and that I take to be the most important matter in the bringing-up of man or woman.

The Reasons for Marriage

Soc. Tell me, Ischomachus, what you first taught her. To hear that story would please me more than any description of the most splendid gymnastic contest or horse-race you could give me.

Why, Socrates (he answered), when after a time she had become used to me, that is, was domesticated sufficiently to play her part in a discussion, I put to her this question: "Did it ever strike you to consider, dear wife, what led me to choose you as my wife among all women, and your parents to entrust you to me of all men? It was certainly not from any difficulty that might beset either of us to find another spouse. That I am sure is evident to you. No! it was with deliberate intent to discover, I for myself and your parents on your behalf, the best partner for managing a household and for children we could find, that I sought you out, and your parents, acting to the best of their ability, made choice of me. If at some future time God grant us to have children, we will take counsel together how best to bring them up, for that too will be a common interest, and a common blessing if happily they shall live to fight our battles and we find in them hereafter support when we ourselves are old. But at present there is our house here, which belongs alike to both. It is common property, for all that I possess goes by my will into the common fund, and in the same way all that you deposited was placed by you in the common fund. We need not stop to calculate in figures which of us contributed most, but rather let us lay to heart this fact, that whichever of us proves the better partner, he or she at once contributes what is most worth having. . . . "

The Unique Talents of Men and Women

"But what is there that I can do," my wife inquired, "which will help to increase our joint estate?"

"Assuredly," I answered, "try to do as well as possible what Heaven has given you a natural gift for and which the law approves."

"And what may these things be?" she asked.

"To my mind they are not the things of least importance," I replied, "unless the things which the queen bee in her hive presides over are of trivial importance to the bee community; for the gods" (so Ischomachus assured me, he continued), "the gods, my wife, would seem to have exercised much care and judgment in compacting that twin-system which goes by the name of male and female, so as to secure the greatest possible advantage to the pair. Since no doubt the underlying principle of the bond is first and foremost to perpetuate through procreation the species of living creatures; and next, as the outcome of this bond, for human beings at any rate, a provision is made by which they may have sons and daughters to support them in old age. Finally, since humans do not live outdoor like cattle, they have need of shelter.

"But whereas both of these, the indoor and the outdoor occupations alike, demand new toil and new attention, to meet the case," I added, "God made provision from the first by shaping, as it seems to me, the woman's nature for indoor and the man's for outdoor occupations. Man's body and soul He furnished with a greater capacity for enduring heat and cold, wayfaring and military marches; or, to repeat, He laid upon his shoulders the outdoor works. While in creating the body of woman with less capacity for these things," I continued, "God would seem to have imposed on her the indoor works; and knowing that He had implanted in the woman and imposed upon her the nurture of new-born babes, He endowed her with a larger share of affection for the new-born child than He bestowed upon man. And since He had imposed on woman the guardianship of the things imported from without, God, in His wisdom, perceiving that a fearful spirit was no detriment to guardianship, endowed the woman with a larger measure of circumspection than He bestowed on man. Knowing further that he to whom the outdoor works belonged would need to defend them against malign attack, He endowed the man in turn with a larger share of courage."

The Duties of Men and Women

"Now, being well aware of this, my wife," I added, "and knowing well what things are laid upon the two us by God Himself, must we not strive to perform, each in the best way possible, our respective duties? Law, too, gives her consent— law and the usage of mankind, by sanctioning the marriage of man and wife; and just as God ordained them to be partners in their children, so the law establishes their common ownership of house and estate. Custom, moreover, proclaims as beautiful those excellences of man and woman with which God gifted them at birth. Thus for a woman to bide tranquilly at home rather than roam abroad is no dishonor; but for a man to remain indoors, instead of devoting himself to outdoor pursuits, is a thing discreditable. But if a man does things contrary to the nature given him by God, the chances are, such insubordination escapes not the eye of Heaven: he pays the penalty, whether of neglecting his own works, or of performing those appropriate to woman." . . .

"Yes," I answered, "you will need in the same way to stay indoors, dispatching to their work without those of your domestics whose work lies there. Over those whose appointed tasks are done indoors, it will be your duty to preside; yours to receive the stuffs brought in; yours to apportion part for daily use, and yours to make provision for the rest, to guard and garner it so that the outgoings destined for a year may not be expended in a month. It will be your duty, when the wools are introduced, to see that clothing is made for those who need; your duty also to see that the dried wheat is in good condition and edible. . . . "

"But there are other cares, you know, and occupations," I answered, "which are yours by right, and these you will find agreeable. This, for instance: to take some slave who knows naught of carding wool and to make her proficient in the art, doubling her usefulness; or to receive another quite ignorant of housekeeping or of service, and to render her skillful, loyal, serviceable, till she is worth her weight in gold; or again, when occasion serves, you have it in your power to requite by kindness the well-behaved whose presence is a blessing to your house; or maybe to chasten the bad character, should such a one appear. But the greatest joy of all will be to prove yourself my better; to make me your faithful follower; knowing no dread lest as the years advance you should decline in honor in your household, but rather trusting that, though your hair turn gray, yet, in proportion as you come to be a better helpmate to myself and to the children, a better guardian of our home, so will your honor increase throughout the household as mistress, wife, and mother, daily more dearly prized. Since," I added, "it is not through excellence of outward appearance, but by reason of the luster of virtues shed forth upon the life of man, that increase is given to things beautiful and good."

That, Socrates, or something like that, as far as I may trust my memory, records the earliest conversation which I held with her.

5. MANAGING OBSTREPEROUS CHILDREN

Plato, *Laws*

In the Laws, *Plato's tract on the second-best state (the best was the one described in the* Republic*), Plato offers some unprogressive ideas on child psychology and education.*[14]

With the return of daylight, the children should go to their teachers; for just as no sheep or other grazing beast ought to live without a herdsman, so children cannot live without a tutor, nor slaves without a master. Of all wild creatures, the child is the most intractable, for in spite of the fact that it is above all other animals because it has at least the beginnings of reason, yet it remains unrestrained. It is a treacherous, sly and most insolent animal. Therefore the child must be tied up, as it were, with many bridles, first, when he leaves the care of nurse and mothers, with tutors to guide his childish ignorance, and after that with teachers of all sorts of subjects and lessons, treating him as becomes a freeborn child. On the other hand he must still be treated as a slave and any free man that meets him shall punish the child himself (and his tutor or teacher if any of them does wrong). And if anyone thus meets them and fails to punish them duly, he shall in the first place be liable to dishonor; and the supervisor who is chosen as president over children shall keep his eye on the man who has met with wrong doings mentioned and has failed to inflict the needed punishment at all, or else to inflict it rightly.

[14] From Plato, *Laws* 808d–e, trans. R. G. Bury (London, 1925).

6. THE SHORT SAD LIFE OF A GOOD WOMAN: THE EPITAPH OF SOKRATEA OF PAROS

Although in her second-century B.C. *epitaph Sokratea seems to speak in her own voice to passersby, it, like the rest of the burial equipment, would have been commissioned by her husband and, therefore, reflects his assessment of his wife's character and life.*[15]

Epitaph of
Sokratea

Nikander was my father, Paros my fatherland, and Sokratea was my name. Parmenion, husband, laid me in my tomb and granted this favor to me to serve as a memorial also to future generations of a life lived in good repute. The irresistible Erinys of childbirth separated unhappy me from my pleasant life through a hemorrhage. I could not even succeed in bringing my child into the light through my labors, but he lies in my womb among the dead.

C. Slaves and Slavery

1. "THE BEST AND MOST NECESSARY POSSESSIONS"

Homer said that slavery destroys half a man's manhood. The Greeks viewed slaves as essential to the successful functioning of a household, but they did not indulge in the illusion that slaves were happy in their lot. Greek literature once included a significant number of works devoted to advising owners how to manage this important but dangerous form of property. None of these works survive, but a good idea of their content is provided by the discussion of slavery in the Oeconomica, *a late fourth-century* B.C. *treatise on household management written by an unknown member of Aristotle's school.*[16]

Aristotle,
Oeconomica

Of possessions the first in importance, the most necessary, the best, and the most relevant to the subject of household management is man. For this reason, it is necessary that slaves be trained to be reliable.

There are two types of slaves: overseers and workers. Since we see that education creates young people with characters of various sorts, it is necessary that one rear carefully those slaves to whom tasks similar to those of freemen are to be assigned.

A master's conduct toward his slaves should be such as to not encourage either insolence or slackness. He should grant a large share of respect to the more responsible slaves and an abundance of food to the workers. Since wine makes even freemen insolent and many nations withhold it even from free men, as the

[15] *Inscriptiones Graecae* 12.5.310, lines 3–10.

[16] From Ps. Aristotle, *Oeconomica* 1.5.

Carthaginians do during a military campaign, it is clear that slaves should be given no wine or very little.

The life of a slave has three aspects: work, punishment, and food. For a slave to not be punished nor made to work but to be fed makes him insolent. But for a slave to work and experience punishment but not to receive food is outrageous and makes a slave weak. What remains, therefore, is to furnish both work and food in sufficient amounts. For it is not possible to govern people who are not paid, and for slaves their pay is their food. The same thing occurs in the case of slaves as happens with regard to other kinds of persons: whenever things do not get better for those who improve and there is no prize for excellence and penalty for badness, they become worse. For this reason, it is necessary to exercise careful supervision, allocating food, clothing, leisure, and punishment to or withholding them from each slave according to his merit in word and deed. Acting this way, masters will follow the example of doctors in the matter of medicine, noting only that food is not medicine because it is always present.

The best kind of slaves for work are those that are neither extremely timid nor extremely brave, for both types cause problems. Those who are too timid do not endure, and those who are very spirited are not easy to manage.

A limit should be set to everything. For it is right and advantageous that freedom be set as a reward. Slaves will willingly work whenever they are offered a reward and the period of their enslavement is specified. Masters should look on the bearing of children as a source of hostages for the good behavior of their slaves.

An owner ought not to have many slaves of the same ethnic background in a household, a rule that also holds true for cities. One should offer sacrifices and provide sources of pleasure more on account of slaves than of freemen, because the reasons such things exist concern them more than they do freemen.

2. "WE HAVE MISTRESSES FOR OUR PLEASURE": SEX AND SLAVERY IN THE *OIKOS*

Antiphon,
*Against a
Stepmother*

A fourth-century B.C. orator observed, "We have mistresses for our pleasure, concubines to serve our person, and wives to bear us legitimate children." Freedom of sexual access by masters to their slaves is one of the basic characteristics of all slave systems. Both the tension created in the oikos *by this situation and the insecurity of the life of even the most privileged slave are illustrated in the fifth-century B.C. Athenian orator Antiphon's vivid account of how a scheming woman exploited the anxieties of a slave girl to bring about the death of her husband.[17]*

Our house has an upper room, which Philoneos, a respectable man and a friend of my father, used to occupy whenever he was in Athens. He had a concubine, whom he was intending to set up as a prostitute. My step-mother, having learned of this, made a friend of the woman; and when she got to know of the wrong Philoneos was planning to do her, she sent for her. When she came, my step-mother told

[17] From Antiphon, *Against a Stepmother*, 14–20.

her that she, too, was being wrongly treated by my father; and that if the woman would do as she said, she would be able to restore the love Philoneos had for her, and also my father's love for herself. Her role, she said was to devise the plan while the slave-girl was to carry it out. She asked her therefore if she was willing to act as her helper, and the woman promised to do so—very readily, I imagine.

Later, it happened that Philoneos had to go down to Peiraeus (*the port of Athens*) for sacrificial rites in honor of Zeus Ctesius (*Zeus the Guardian of Property*) and since at the same time my father was preparing for a voyage to Naxos it seemed like an excellent idea to Philoneos that he should make the same trip serve a double purpose: that he should accompany my father, his friend, down to the harbor, and at the same time, after the sacrificial rites, entertain him to a feast. Philoneos's concubine went with them, to help with the sacrifice and the banquet.

When they arrived at the port, Philoneos performed the sacrifice appropriately. When the religious ceremony was over, the slave-girl began to debate with herself as to how and when she should administer the drug, whether before dinner or after dinner. The result of her deliberation was that she decided to administer the drug after dinner, thus carrying out the instructions of my step-mother—that Clytemnestra (*the wife and murderess of Agamemnon*).

The whole story of the dinner would be too long for me to tell or you to hear; but I shall try to relate the rest to you in the fewest possible words, that is, how the actual administration of the poison took place. When they had finished dinner, they naturally—as one of them was sacrificing to Zeus Ctesius and entertaining a guest, and the other was about to set off on a voyage and was dining with his friend—they naturally began to offer libations, and burn incense. As she was serving them the wine for the libation—a libation that was accompanied by prayers destined, alas! gentlemen, not to be fulfilled—Philoneos' concubine poured in the poison. And in the belief that she was doing something clever, she gave the bigger dose to Philoneos, thinking that perhaps the more she gave him, the more he would love her. She still did not know that she had been deceived by my step-mother, and did not find out until she was already involved in disaster. She poured in a smaller dose for my father.

The two men poured their libations and then, taking in hand that which was to destroy them, they each drained their last draught. Philoneos died instantly, but my father was seized with an illness from which he died in three weeks. For this, the woman who helped has paid the penalty for her offence, in which she was an innocent accomplice: she was handed over to the public executioner after being broken on the wheel. But the woman who was the real cause, who thought up and engineered the deed—she will pay the penalty now, if you and the gods so decree.

3. HOW TO BECOME A SLAVE: BE IN THE WRONG PLACE AT THE WRONG TIME

Greek slave law emphasized the potentially hereditary nature of slavery. The reality, however, was that most slaves had not been born into that status but became slaves through some accident: capture

Demosthenes, *Against Nicostratus*

in war, kidnapping, sale to satisfy a debt, and so on. Nevertheless, despite its importance to Greek social and economic life, little evidence survives concerning the ancient slave trade. A rare insight into this aspect of Greek life is provided by the fourth-century B.C. orator Apollodorus, who recounts how the Athenian farmer Nicostratus was kidnapped by a warship from the neighboring city of Aegina and enslaved while pursuing several of his own slaves, who had run away.[18]

4. I have known this man Nicostratus, jurors, who is my neighbor and my contemporary, for a long time. When my father died and I began to live in the country, where I still live, we had many dealings with each other, because we are neighbors and contemporaries. As time passed, we developed very good feelings for each other, and I was so well inclined toward him, that he never failed to receive from me whatever he needed. He likewise was helpful to me in watching over and managing my affairs, and whenever I happened to be away either on public service as a trierarch (*the commander and financial sponsor of a trireme warship*) or for some personal business, I left him in charge of all matters concerning my farm.

5. While I was serving as trierarch near the Peloponnesus, I had to transport from there to Sicily the ambassadors, whom the people had chosen. The voyage was on short notice. I wrote to him, accordingly, that I was leaving and would not be able to come home lest I delay the ambassadors. I also instructed him to watch over and manage my affairs at home just as in previous times. 6. During my absence three slaves ran away from his farm. Two of them I had given him and one he had bought. While he was pursuing them, he was captured by a trireme, brought to Aegina, and sold there. When I returned—I was still in command of my trireme—Deinon, his brother, came to me, and told me of Nicostratus' misfortune. He also told me that, although Nicostratus had written letters to him, he himself had not gone after him because of the lack of travel money. And he told me at the same time that he had heard that Nicostratus was in very bad circumstances.

7. When I had heard these things, I was moved by his misfortune, and I gave his brother Deinon three hundred drachmas for travel money and immediately sent him to Nicostratus. After he returned home, Nicostratus came to me first thing, and greeted me and praised me because I had provided his brother with travel money. He also bewailed his misfortune and, condemning his relatives, he asked me for help, just as before I had been a true friend to him. In tears he said that he had been ransomed for twenty-six minas and he urged me to contribute to the ransom. 8. When I heard these things, I pitied him, seeing at the same time that he was in a bad state. He also showed me the sores on his limbs from the fetters, of which he still has the scars, but if you order him to show them, he will be unwilling. I answered him that, just as I was a true friend to him before, so also now I would help him in his misfortune. I would forgive the three hundred drachmas, which I had given to his brother as travel money so that he could go to him; and I would advance him a thousand drachmas toward the ransom as a loan. 9. And I did

---

[18] From Ps. Demosthenes, *Against Nicostratus*, 53.4–11.

not merely promise him this in word and not do it in fact; but, although I was not prosperous because of my dispute with Phormion and the loss to him of the property, which my father had left me, I brought to Theocles, who had then had a bank, cups and a gold crown, which I still had from my inheritance, and I told him to give Nicostratus a thousand drachmas, and I gave this money to him as a gift, and I admit that I gave it to him. . . .

10. A few days later, however, he approached me in tears and said that the strangers, who had loaned him the ransom, were demanding payment from him; and that according to the contract he had thirty days to pay it back or he would owe double the amount. Moreover, no one wished to buy his farm, which was next to mine, or give him a loan on it. For his brother, Arethousius, whose slaves were mentioned earlier, would not allow anyone to buy it or make a loan on it, on the ground that the money was owed to him.

11. "You, therefore," he said, "provide me with the balance of the money before the thirty days are up in order that the thousand drachmas which I have paid not be lost and I become liable to seizure. And," he said, "After I pay off the strangers, I will obtain a loan from my friends, and pay you back what you loaned me. And you know," he said, "that the laws order that a person who has been ransomed from enemies shall belong to the ransomer, if he does not repay the ransom."

4. THE SLAVE TRADE: A EUNUCH'S REVENGE

Further evidence concerning the operation of the ancient slave trade is provided by Herodotus' capsule biography of Hermotimus, a eunuch of the Persian King Xerxes, and the revenge he took on the man responsible for his enslavement.[19]   *The History of Herodotus*

104. Xerxes likewise sent away at this time one of the principal of his eunuchs, a man named Hermotimus, a Pedasian, who was bidden to take charge of his sons. Now the Pedasians inhabit the region above Halicarnassus, and it is related of them that in their country the following circumstance happens. When a mischance is about to befall any of their neighbors within a certain time, the priestess of Athena in their city grows a long beard. This has already taken place on two occasions.

105. The Hermotimus of whom I spoke above was, as I said, a Pedasian, and he, of all men whom we know, took the most cruel vengeance on the person who had done him an injury. He had been made a prisoner of war, and when his captors sold him, he was bought by a certain Panionius, a native of Chios, who made his living by a most nefarious traffic. Whenever he could get any boys of unusual beauty, he castrated them and, carrying them to Sardis or Ephesus, sold them for large sums of money, for the barbarians value eunuchs more than others since they regard them as more

[19] From Herodotus, *The History of the Persian Wars* 8.104–106 (New York, 1859–1860), trans. G. Rawlinson.

trustworthy. Many were the slaves that Panionius, who made his living by the practice, had thus treated, and among them was this Hermotimus of whom I have here made mention. However, he was not without his share of good fortune, for after a while he was sent from Sardis, together with other gifts, as a present to the king. Nor was it long before he came to be esteemed by Xerxes more highly than all his eunuchs.

106. When the king was on his way to Athens with the Persian army and abode for a time at Sardis, Hermotimus happened to make a journey upon business into Mysia; and there, in a district that is called Atarneus but that belongs to Chios, he chanced to fall in with Panionius. Recognizing him at once, he entered into a long and friendly talk with him wherein he counted up the numerous blessings he enjoyed through his means, promised him all manner of favors in return, if he would bring his household to Sardis and live there. Panionius was overjoyed and, accepting the offer made him, came presently and brought with him his wife and children. Then Hermotimus, when he had got Panionius and all his family into his power, addressed him in these words: "You, who make a living by viler deeds than anyone else in the whole world, what wrong to you or yours had I or any of mine done, that you should have made me nothing and no longer a man? Surely you thought that the gods took no note of your crimes. But they in their justice have delivered you, the doer of unrighteousness, into my hands; and now you cannot complain of the vengeance which I am resolved to take on you."

After these reproaches, Hermotimus commanded the four sons of Panionius to be brought and forced the father to castrate them with his own hand. Unable to resist, he did as Hermotimus required; and then his sons were made to treat him in the self-same way. So in this way there came to Panionius requital at the hands of Hermotimus.

D. The *Polis* and the Household

1. THE MURDER OF ERATOSTHENES

Lysias, *On the Killing of Eratosthenes*

Few documents illustrate so clearly the connection between household and state, oikos *and* polis, *as the following speech written by the orator Lysias for a defendant in a murder trial. It was probably composed sometime in the early fourth century* B.C. *The defendant, Euphiletus, claims that he was justified in killing Eratosthenes, whom he caught in the act of adultery with his wife. Euphiletus has now been brought to trial by the relatives of the dead man.*

Euphiletus does not claim that he acted out of passion but rather because the laws enjoined him to kill his wife's lover in the name of the good of the polis. *This is odd by modern standards because in most contemporary states adultery is regarded as a private matter between consenting adults. In the* polis, *however, households were essential subunits of the state, and an attack on one of them was equivalent to an attack on the state itself. Adultery, which undermined the foundation of the household, was thus seen as a dangerous public as well as a private offense. There was passion involved, but it was mostly felt on behalf of the destroyed household, the loss of honor suffered by the husband, the confusion cast upon the legitimacy of the children and therefore their citizenship, inheritance rights, their right to the family name, the ancestral gods, and so on. A cuckolded husband was not just an object of humor (or perhaps sympathy), but an injured man who had lost face and therefore power and influence in society because he had been shown publicly to be unable to defend his own household—hence the attraction of homicide for Euphiletus. It restored his honor and standing in the community, although there was a danger that the jury might think he had killed Eratosthenes for other reasons, such as a grudge or for money. Another danger was the perpetuation of a vendetta between the families involved. On balance, Athenians apparently believed that it was better to hope these outcomes could be avoided rather than, as Euphiletus claimed, "total impunity be granted to men who commit outrages against married women."[20]*

Introductory Remarks

In judging this case, gentlemen of the jury, I would be only too pleased to have you disposed to me as you would be towards yourselves in a similar situation. I am sure that if you had the same opinions about others as you do about yourselves not one of you would fail to be indignant at what has been done; on the contrary you would all regard the penalties appointed for those who resort to such practices as too mild. And these feelings would be found, not only amongst you, but throughout Greece: for in the case of this crime alone, under both democracy and oligarchy, the same satisfaction is accorded to the weakest against the strongest. Hence the lowest in status gets the same treatment as the highest. Such is the abomination all men hold for this outrage. You are all, I imagine, of the same opinion regarding the severity of the penalty; not one of you is so easy-going as to think it right that those who are guilty of such acts should obtain pardon, or that they deserve only light penalties. What I need to show, I believe, is that Eratosthenes committed adultery with my wife, and not only corrupted her but inflicted disgrace upon my children and an outrage on myself by entering my house; that this was the one and only enmity between him and me; that I did not do what I did for the sake of money so as to raise myself from poverty to wealth; and that all I seek to gain now is satisfaction accorded by our laws. I will therefore tell you the whole story from the beginning; I shall omit nothing, but will tell the truth. For I consider that my sole salvation rests on my telling you, if I am able, the whole of what has occurred.

The Narrative of Events

Athenians, when I decided to marry, and brought my wife into my house, my first attitude was neither to bother her too much nor to leave her too free to do just as she pleased. I kept a watch on her as far as possible and gave her such attention as was reasonable. But when a child was born to me, from then on I began to trust her and placed all my affairs in her hands, assuming that this was the most perfect proof of affection. It is true that in the early days, Athenians, she was the most

---

[20] From Lysias, *On the Killing of Eratosthenes* (London, 1930), based on the translation of W. R. M. Lamb.

excellent of wives; she was a clever and frugal housekeeper, and kept everything in the best of order. But as soon as I lost my mother, her death became the cause of all my troubles. For it was in attending her funeral that my wife was seen by this man, who in time corrupted her. He kept a look out for the slave-girl who went to the market, and through her was able to reach her mistress and so brought about her ruin.

Now in the first place I must explain to you, gentlemen of the jury (for I need to give you these particulars), my house has two floors, the upper being equal in space to the lower, with the women's quarters above and the men's below. When the child was born to us, his mother nursed him; and in order that, each time that it had to be washed, she might avoid the risk of descending by the stairs, I took over the upstairs room and the women had the ground floor. By this time it had become such an habitual thing that my wife would often leave me and go down to sleep with the child, so as to be able to feed it and stop it crying. Things went on in this way for a long time, and I never suspected, but was simple-minded enough to suppose that my own wife was the most faithful wife in the city. Time went on, gentlemen; I came home unexpectedly from the country, and after dinner the child started crying and complaining, because, as I later learned, the slave girl was deliberately hurting it. So I told my wife to go down and feed the baby to stop its howling. At first she refused, as though delighted to see me home again after so long; but when I began to be angry and insisted she go, she said "Yes, so that you may have a go at the slave girl. Once before, too, when you were drunk, you pulled her about." I laughed at this, while she got up, went out of the room, and closed the door, pretending it was a joke, and turned the key in the lock [*supposedly to keep the slave girl out*]. I, without giving a thought to the matter, or having any suspicion, went to sleep gladly after my return from the country. Towards daytime she came and unlocked the door. I asked why the doors made a noise in the night; she claimed that the child's lamp had gone out, and she had lit it again at our neighbor's. I said nothing, thinking that this was what happened. But it caught my attention, gentlemen, that she had put make up on, though her brother had died not thirty days before. Even so, however, I said nothing and left the house in silence.

After this, gentlemen of the jury, an interval occurred during which I was left quite unaware of my own injuries. Then, one day, I was approached by an old woman who was secretly, as I later learned, sent by a lady with whom that man [*Eratosthenes*] had had an affair. This woman was angry with him and felt herself wronged because he no longer visited her as regularly as before, and she was on the look out to find what was the cause. So the old woman encountered me (she was waiting for me near my house), and said,—"Euphiletus, do not think it is because I am a busy body that I have approached you. The man who is shaming you and your wife also happens to be our enemy. If, therefore, you take the slave girl who goes to market and waits on you, and torture her, you will learn all. It is," she said, "Eratosthenes of Oe who is doing this; he has debauched not only your wife, but many others besides; he makes a profession of it." With these words, gentlemen, she took herself off.

I was at once disturbed. All that had happened came to my mind, and I was filled with suspicion. I thought first of how I was locked in my bedroom, and then remembering how on that night the inner and outer doors made a noise, which had never occurred before, and how it struck me that my wife had put on makeup. All these things came into my mind, and I was filled with suspicion. Returning home, I told the servant-girl to follow me to the market, and taking her to the house of an intimate friend, I told her I was fully informed of what was going on in my house. "So it is up to you, I said, to choose as you please between two things—either to be whipped and put to work in the mill and never have any rest from miseries of that sort or else to speak out the whole truth and, instead of suffering any harm, obtain my pardon for your transgressions. Tell no lies, but speak the whole truth." The girl at first denied it, and told me to do what I pleased, for she knew nothing. But when I mentioned the name of Eratosthenes and said that he was the man who visited my wife, she was dismayed, supposing that I had exact knowledge of everything. At once she threw herself down at my knees, and having got my pledge that she should suffer no harm, she accused him, first, of approaching her after the funeral, and then told how at last she became his messenger; how my wife in time was persuaded, and by what means she procured his entrances, and how at the Thesmophoria, while I was in the country, she went off to the temple with his mother. And the girl gave an exact account of everything else that had occurred. When the whole story was finished, I said, "See that nobody at all gets knowledge of this; otherwise, nothing in our arrangement with me will hold good. And I insist that you show me their guilt in the very act. I want no words, but demonstrated actions, if it really is so." She agreed to do this.

After this, four or five days passed as I shall conclusively demonstrate. But first I wish to relate what took place on the last day. I had an intimate friend named Sostratus. After sunset I met him as he came from the country. As I knew that, because of the hour, he would find none of his circle at home, I invited him to have dinner with me. We came to my house, climbed the stairs to the upper room, and had dinner. When he had made a good meal, he left me and departed; then I went to bed. Eratosthenes, gentlemen, entered, and the slave girl aroused me at once, and told me that he was in the house. Telling her to look after the door, I descended and went out in silence. I called on one friend after another, and found some at home, while others were out of town. I took with me as many as I could among those who were available, and returned to the house. We got torches from the nearest shop, and—because the slave girl had left the door open—we went in. We pushed open the door of the bed-room, and the first of us to enter were in time to see him lying down by my wife; those who followed saw him standing naked on the bed. I gave him a blow, gentlemen, which knocked him down, and pulling round his hands behind his back, tied them together. I asked him why he had the insolence to enter my house. He admitted his guilt, but then begged and implored me not to kill him, and to accept a sum of money instead. To this I replied,—"It is not I who am going to kill you, but our city's law, which you have transgressed and regarded as of less account than your pleasures, choosing rather to commit this foul offence against my wife and my children than to obey the laws like a decent man."

Thus it was, gentlemen, that this man incurred the fate that the laws set down for those who do such things. He had not been dragged into my house from the street, nor had he taken refuge at my hearth, as my opponents claim. For how could he have done so, when it was in the bedroom that he was struck and fell down then and there, and I tied his arms, and so many persons were in the house that he could not escape them, as he had neither weapons of steel nor wood nor anything else with which he might have beaten off those who had entered? But, gentlemen, I think you know as well as I that those who are wrong doers do not acknowledge that their enemies speak the truth, but lie and use other such devices to foment anger in their hearers against those whose acts are just. So, first read the law. [*The law of Solon that an adulterer caught in the act may be put to death is read. Witnesses are presented and then another law on the same subject found on the hill where the ancient court of the Areopagus met is read.*]

You hear, gentlemen, how the Court of the Areopagus itself, to which has been assigned, in our own as in our fathers' time, the trial of suits for murder, has expressly stated that whoever takes this vengeance on an adulterer caught in the act with his wife shall not be convicted of murder. And so strongly was the law-giver convinced of the justice of this in the case of married women, that he even applied the same penalty in the case of mistresses, who are of less account. Now surely it is clear that, if he had available any heavier punishment than this for the case of married women, he would have imposed it. But in fact, as he was unable to devise a severer one for the seduction of wives, he ordained that it should be the same for that of mistresses also. Please read this law besides. (*The law is read.*)

The Distinction Between Rape and Seduction

You hear, gentlemen, how the law directs that, if anyone indecently assaults a free man or child, he shall be liable to double damages, while if he so debauches a woman, in any of the cases where it is permitted to kill him, he is subject to the same rule. Thus the lawgiver, gentlemen, considered that those who commit rape deserve a lesser penalty than those who use persuasion. For these latter he pre-scribed death, whereas for rapists he doubled the damages, considering that those who achieve their ends by force are hated by the persons forced, while those who used persuasion corrupted thereby their victims' souls, thus making the wives of others more closely attached to themselves than to their husbands, and got the whole house into their hands, and caused uncertainty as to whose the children really were, the husbands' or the adulterers'. In view of all this the author of the law made death their penalty.

Therefore gentlemen I not only stand acquitted of wrongdoing by the laws, but am also directed by them to take this satisfaction. It is for you to decide whether the laws are to be effective or of no account. For to my way of thinking every city makes its laws in order that on any matter on which we have doubt we may resort to them and inquire what we should do. And so it is that in cases like the present the laws themselves exhort the wronged parties to exact this penalty. I call upon you to support their opinion: otherwise, you will be giving adulterers such license that you will encourage thieves as well to call themselves adulterers since they will feel assured that, if they plead this reason in their defense, and allege that they enter other men's houses for this purpose, nobody will touch them. For everyone will know that the laws on adultery have been nullified, and that they need to fear only your verdict because this has supreme authority over all the city's affairs.

Refutation of Opponents' Arguments

Do not consider, gentlemen, what my opponents say: they accuse me of ordering the slave girl on that day to go and fetch the young man. Now gentlemen, I could have held myself justified in using any possible means to catch the corrupter of my wife. Admittedly if I had bidden the girl fetch him, when words alone had been spoken and no act had been committed, I should have been in the wrong. But if, when once he had gained all his ends, and had frequently entered my house, I had then used any possible means to catch him, I should have considered myself quite in order. And observe how on this point also they are lying; you will see it easily in this way.

As I told you, sirs, before, Sostratus was a friend of mine, on intimate terms with me. He met me as he came from the country about sunset, and had dinner with me, and when he had enjoyed a good meal, he left. Now in the first place, gentlemen, you must bear this in mind: if on that night I had planned to entrap Eratosthenes, which was more to my advantage—to go and take my dinner elsewhere with Sostratus, or to bring him as my guest to dinner with me? Certainly in the latter case Eratosthenes would have been less likely to venture entering my house. And in the second place, do you suppose that I should have let my dinner-guest go and leave me there alone without support, and not rather have asked him to stay so that he might stand by me in taking vengeance upon the adulterer? Then again, gentlemen, do you not think that I should have sent word to my intimate acquaintances in the day-time, and asked them assemble at the house of one of my friends living nearest to me, rather than have waited till the moment of making my discovery to run round in the night, without knowing whom I should find at home, and who were away? Thus I called on Harmodius, and one other, who were not in town—of this I was not aware—and others, I found, were not in. But those whom I could I took along with me. Yet if I had foreknown this, do you not think that I should have called up some slaves and passed the word to my friends, in order that I might have gone in myself with all possible safety,—for how could I tell whether he too had some weapon?—and so I might have had as many witnesses as possible with me when I took my vengeance? But as in fact I knew nothing of what was to befall on that night, I took with me those whom I could. Now let my witnesses come forward in support of all this. [*The witnesses testify.*]

You have heard the witnesses, gentlemen. Examine the affair in the following way in your own minds, asking yourselves whether any enmity has ever arisen before this between me and Eratosthenes. I say you will find none. For he had neither subjected me to slanderous impeachment, nor attempted to have me exiled from the city, nor brought any private suit against me, nor was he aware of any wrongdoing which I was so afraid of being divulged that I was intent on killing him; nor by doing this did I have any hope of getting money from anywhere: for there are people who plot each other's death for such purposes. So far, indeed, from either abuse or a drunken brawl or any other quarrel having occurred between us, I had never even seen the man before that night. For what object, then, should I run so grave a risk, unless I had received from him the greatest of injuries? Why, again, did I choose to summon witnesses for my wicked act, when it was open to me, if I was thus criminally intent on his destruction, to have none of them privy to it?

The Penalty Was for the Sake of the *Polis*

I therefore, gentlemen, do not regard this penalty as having been exacted in my own private interest, but in that of the whole city. For those who behave in that way, when they see the sort of prizes offered for such transgressions, will be less inclined to trespass against their neighbors, if they see that you also take the same view. Otherwise it were better far to erase our established laws, and ordain others which will inflict the penalties on men who keep watch on their own wives, and will allow full immunity to those who would debauch them. This would be a far juster way than to let the citizens be entrapped by the laws. These may command a man, on catching an adulterer, to deal with him in whatever way he pleases, but the trials are found to be more dangerous to the wronged parties than to those who, in defiance of the laws, dishonor the wives of others. For I am now risking the loss of life, property and all else that I have, because I obeyed the city's laws.

2. THE DEMOS MUST BE PURE: ATHENIAN LAWS ON PEDERASTY

Aeschines,
*Against
Timarchus*

Aristocratic attitudes were marked by a deep suspicion and hostility to the demos and its lifestyle. The feeling was reciprocated by the demos, especially with regard to pederasty, the ritualized homoerotic relationship between an older male and an adolescent boy, which was a central feature of Greek aristocratic life. Although even Solon, the founding father of the democracy, celebrated pederasty in a famous couplet—"until he loves a boy in the lovely bloom of youth, desiring his thighs and sweet mouth"—Athenian laws on pederasty reveal an equally strong unease with this aspect of aristocratic life, viewing it as a potential threat to the purity and health of the demos itself.[21]

Consider how much attention that ancient lawgiver, Solon, gave to morality, as did Draco and the other lawgivers of those days. First, you recall, they laid down laws to protect the morals of our children, and they expressly prescribed what were to be the habits of the freeborn boy, and how he was to be brought up; then they legislated for the adolescents, and next for the other age-groups in succes-

[21] Aeschines, *Against Timarchus* 6–7, 9–20. From *The Speeches of Aeschines*, trans. C. D. Adams (London, 1919).

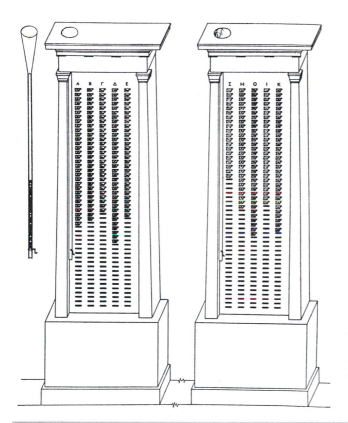

Figure 4.3 (a) The cleroterion was a foolproof lottery machine devised to produce jury pools that were a random cross section of the voting population. A much simplified explanation of how it worked is as follows. Each juror had a ticket, which was inserted in one of the slots. Black and white balls were dropped into a hopper at the top of the machine and mixed. As they came out of the opening at the bottom (b) (an opening can be seen in the actual fragment of the cleroterion), their color determined the columns to be chosen or rejected. Fragment of a third-century B.C. cleroterion. Courtesy of the American School of Classical Studies, Athens.

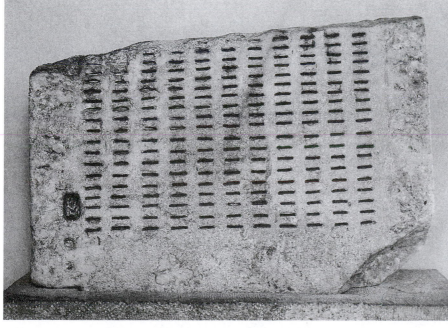

sion, including in the provision, not only private citizens, but also the public men. And when they had inscribed these laws, they gave them to you in trust, and made you their guardians. . . .

In the first place, consider the case of the teachers. Although the very livelihood of these men, to whom we necessarily entrust our own children, depends on their good character, while the opposite conduct on their part would mean poverty, yet it is plain that the lawgiver distrusts them; for he expressly prescribes, first, at what time of day the free-born boy is to go to the school-room; next, how many other boys may go there with him, and when he is to go home. He forbids the teacher to open the school-room, or the gymnastic trainer the wrestling school, before sunrise, and he commands them to close the doors before sunset; for he is exceedingly suspicious of their being alone with a boy, or in the dark with him. He prescribes what children are to be admitted as pupils, and their age at admission. He provides for a public official who shall superintend them, and for the oversight of slave-attendants of school boys. He regulates the festivals of the muses in the school-rooms, and of Hermes in the wrestling-schools. Finally, he regulates the companionships that the boys may form at school, and their cyclic dances. He prescribes, namely, that the choragus, a man who is going to spend his own money for your entertainment, shall be a man of more than forty years of age when he performs this service, in order that he may have reached the most temperate time of his life before he comes into contact with your children.

These laws, then, shall be read to you, to prove that the lawgiver believed that it is the boy who has been well brought up that will be a useful citizen when he becomes a man. But when a boy's natural disposition is subjected at the very outset to vicious training, the product of such wrong nurture will be, as he believed, a citizen like this man Timarchus. . . .

Now after this, fellow citizens, he lays down laws regarding crimes which, great as they undoubtedly are, do actually occur, I believe, in the city. For the very fact that certain unbecoming things were being done was the reason for the enactment of these laws by the men of old. At any rate the law says explicitly: if any boy is let out for hire as a prostitute, whether it be by father or brother or uncle or guardian or by any one else who has control of him, prosecution is not to lie against the boy himself, but against the man who let him out for hire, and against the other, it says, because he hired him. And the law has made the penalties for both offenders the same. Moreover, the law frees a son, when he has become a man, from all obligation to support or to furnish a home to a father by whom he has been hired out for prostitution; but when the father is dead, the son is to bury him and perform the other customary rites. . . .

But what other law has been laid down for the protection of our children? The law against panders (= *pimps*). For the lawgiver imposes the heaviest penalties if any person act as pander in the case of a freeborn child or a freeborn woman.

And what other law? The law against outrage, which includes all such conduct in one summary statement, wherein it stands expressly written: if any one outrage a child . . . or a man or woman, or any one, free or slave, or if he commit any unlawful act against any one of these. Here the law provides prosecution for outrage, and it prescribes what bodily penalty he shall suffer, or what fine he shall pay. . . .

Now perhaps someone, on first hearing this law, may wonder for what possible reason this word "slaves" was added in the law against outrage. But if you reflect on the matter, fellow citizens, you will find this to be the best provision of all. For it was not for the slaves that the lawgiver was concerned, but he wished to accustom you to keep a long distance away from the crime of outraging free men, and so he added the prohibition against even the outraging of slaves. In a word, he was convinced that in a democracy that man is unfit for citizenship who outrages any person whatsoever. And I beg you, fellow citizens, to remember this also, that here the lawgiver is not yet addressing the person of the boy himself but those who are near him, father, brother, guardian, teachers, and in general those who have control of him. But as soon as the young man has been registered in the list of citizens, and knows the laws of the state, and is now able to distinguish between right and wrong, the lawgiver no long addresses another, Timarchus, but now the man himself. And what does he say? "If any Athenian," he says, "shall have prostituted his person, he shall not be permitted to become one of the nine archons," because, no doubt, that official wears the wreath; "nor to discharge the office of priest," as being not even clean of body; "nor shall he act as an advocate for the state," he says, "nor shall he ever hold any office whatsoever, at home or abroad, whether filled by lot or by election; nor shall he be a herald or an ambassador"—nor shall he prosecute men who have served as ambassadors, nor shall he be a hired accuser—"nor ever address council or assembly," not even though he be the most eloquent orator in Athens. And if any one act contrary to these prohibitions, the lawgiver has provided for criminal process on the charge of prostitution, and prescribed the heaviest penalties therefore.

E. Religion in the Classical *Polis*

1. THE AFFAIR OF THE HERMS

The overt rationalism of works such as The Old Oligarch's essay on the Athenian constitution and the Melian dialogue (see Chapter 5, Section C5) can easily lead to the belief that religion was of little significance in fifth-century B.C. Greek culture. The same impression is conveyed by the seeming materialism of many Greek religious documents. Thus, a fourth-century B.C. Athenian decree concerning the proper conduct of sacrifices at the Panathenaea is devoted mostly to regulating the distribution of the meat from the sacrifices, specifying that

> *five portions of meat are to be allocated to the Prytanes, three to the nine Archons and the Treasurer of Athena, one to the Sacrificers, and three to the Generals and the Taxiarchs; the usual*

portions are to be given to those Athenians participating in the procession and to the girls who are basket-bearers, and the rest of the meat is to be distributed to the Athenians.[22]

A very different assessment of the religious feelings of the Athenian populace is suggested, however, by Thucydides' account of the hysteria that gripped Athens in 415 B.C., on the eve of the Athenian invasion of Sicily, as a result of the mutilation of the Herms—the vandalizing of the fetishlike pillars with a human head and an erect male genital organ that stood in front of most Athenian homes and were believed to promote fertility.[23]

28. Certain metics and servants gave information, not indeed about the Hermae, but about the mutilation of other statues which had shortly before been perpetrated by some young men in a drunken frolic; they also said that the mysteries were repeatedly profaned by the celebration of them in private houses, and of this impiety they accused, among others, Alcibiades. A party who were jealous of his influence over the people, which interfered with the permanent establishment of their own, thinking that if they could get rid of him they would be supreme, took up and exaggerated the charges against him, clamorously insisting that both the mutilation of the Hermae and the profanation of the mysteries were part of a conspiracy against the democracy, and that he was at the bottom of the whole affair. In proof they alleged the excesses of his ordinary life, which were unbecoming in the citizen of a free state.

The hysteria reached its peak a year later in 414 B.C., when the Athenians, suspecting that the mutilation of the Herms was the work of plotters against the democracy, authorized the mass arrest and detention of the suspects.

53. There they found that the vessel Salaminia had come from Athens to fetch Alcibiades, who had been put upon his trial by the state and was ordered home to defend himself. With him were summoned certain of his soldiers, who were accused, some of profaning the mysteries, others of mutilation of the Hermae. For after the departure of the expedition the Athenians prosecuted both enquiries as keenly as ever. They did not investigate the character of the informers, but in their suspicious mood listened to all manner of statements and seized and imprisoned some of the most respectable citizens on the evidence of wretches; they thought it better to sift the matter and discover the truth, and they would not allow even a man of good character against whom an accusation was brought to escape without a thorough investigation, merely because the informer was a rogue. For the people, who had heard by tradition that the tyranny of Pisistratus and his sons ended in great oppression, and knew moreover that their power was overthrown, not by Harmodius or any efforts of their own, but by the Lacedaemonians, were in a state of incessant fear and suspicion. . . .

[22] From *Inscriptiones Graecae* 2² .334.

[23] Thucydides, *The History of the Peloponnesian War* 5.27–28, 53, 60. From B. Jowett, *Thucydides Translated*, Vol. 2 (Oxford, 1900).

60. The Athenian people, recalling these and other traditions of the tyrants which had sunk deep into their minds, were suspicious and savage against the supposed profaners of the mysteries; the whole affair seemed to them to indicate some conspiracy aiming at oligarchy or tyranny. Inflamed by these suspicions, they had already imprisoned many men of high character. There was no sign of returning quiet, but day by day the movement became more furious and the number of arrests increased. At last one of the prisoners, who was believed to be deeply implicated, was induced by a fellow-prisoner to make a confession—whether true or false I cannot say; opinions are divided, and no one knew at the time, or to this day knows, who the offenders were. His companion argued that even if he were not guilty he ought to confess and claim a pardon; he would thus save his own life and at the same time deliver Athens from the prevailing state of suspicion. His chance of escaping would be better if he confessed his guilt in the hope of a pardon than if he denied it and stood his trial. So he gave evidence against both himself and others in the matter of the Hermae. The Athenians were delighted at finding out what they supposed to be the truth: they had been in despair at the thought that the conspirators against the democracy would never be known, and they immediately liberated the informer and all whom he had not denounced. The accused they brought to trial, and executed such of them as could be found. Those who had fled they condemned to death, and promised a reward to any one who would kill them. No one could say whether the sufferers were justly punished, but the beneficial effect on the city at the time was undeniable.

2. THE FESTIVALS: "A MAN SHOULD SPEND HIS WHOLE LIFE AT PLAY"

Plato provides one of the few ancient, analytical explanations of why the festivals were so important to the life of the polis. *He begins by explaining why dance is natural and then goes on to elaborate: we honor the gods by dancing; they are our leaders in the chorus. Sacrificing, singing, and dancing are the most important of human activities.*[24]   Plato, *The Laws*

Now these forms of childhood training which consist in right discipline in regard to pleasure and pain, grow slack and wear off to a great extent in the course of men's lives. Hence the gods took pity on the human race thus born to misery and ordained religious festivals as periods of recreation from its troubles. And they have granted the Muses, Apollo the master of Music, and Dionysus as the companions in their feasts so that, by having the gods share in their holidays, they might be made whole again, finding nourishment in these feasts with the gods. We should now see whether the theory explaining this, which is constantly repeated nowadays, is true or not. It says that children, almost without exception are incapable of keeping body or voice quiet; they are always trying to move and to cry out, jumping and skipping and delighting in dances and games and

[24] From Plato, *The Laws* (London, 1926), 653d–654b; 803c–e, based on the translation of R. G. Bury.

uttering noises of every kind as they play with each other. And whereas all other animals have no sense of order and disorder in their movement (which we term rhythm and harmony), to us human beings the very gods, who were given to us as we said, as fellow chorus members, have granted the gift of pleasurable perception of rhythm and harmony. Thus they cause us to move and lead our choruses linking us one with another by means of songs and dances. The term "chorus" gets its name from the "charms" or "cheer" [*a play on words in Greek*] that naturally comes with it. . . .

By an uneducated person we mean a person who is without training in choral activity while the "educated" man has been trained to take part in a chorus . . . and of course a performance by a chorus is a combination of singing and dancing. This means that the well educated man will be able to both to sing and dance well. . . .

What I claim is this—that man ought to be serious about serious things, and not about trivialities and that the object really worthy of all serious and blessed effort is God. I believe that while man has been created as the plaything of God, and the best part of him is really just that. So I say that every man and woman ought to live their lives in accordance with this character, engaging in the best possible pastimes, quite other than they do now. . . . We should live out our lives at play— sacrificing, singing and dancing—so as to be able to win Heaven's favor and to repel our foes and vanquish them in battle. A man will achieve both these aims if he sings and dances in the way we've outlined. . . .

Children are educated by seeing adults praying, sacrificing, and participating in festivals.[25]

While still infants and sucklings children heard stories chanted to them from the lips of their nurses and mothers. The stories were sung partly for entertainment but also in full earnest and the same stories were repeated in prayers at sacrifices. They saw spectacles which illustrated them, of the kind which the young delight to see and hear when performed at sacrifices; and their own parents praying with the utmost seriousness for themselves and their families in the firm conviction that their prayers and supplications were addressed to gods who really did exist. At the rising and setting of the sun and moon the children heard and saw the prostrations and devotions of Greeks and foreigners, in happiness and misery alike, directed to these luminaries not as though they were gods, but as though they most certainly were gods beyond the shadow of doubt.

3. LOCAL FESTIVALS

Sacrifices offered in the deme of Thorikos during Boedromion

In the fifth and fourth centuries B.C. *120 days or 33% of the calendar were devoted to city-wide festivals at Athens. This may seem a lot, but an even larger number of festivals and sacrifices were held at*

[25] From Plato, *Laws* (London, 1926), 887d–e, based on the translation of R. G. Bury.

Figure 4.4 It is commonly claimed that Greek women had no roles in public life. This is certainly true of legislative and judicial affairs, but the assertion ignores the importance of religion in which women had major roles. At Athens, for instance, priestesses presided at more than forty major cults. The most important priesthood in the city, that of Athena Polias, was in the hands of a woman. Women at Dionysiac festival. The Chicago Painter. Greek, Attic Stamnos (Wine Jar), ca. 450 B.C., terracotta, red-figure, 14⅝ in. (37 cm). Gift of Philip Armour and Charles L. Hutchinson, 1889.22 detail. Photography © The Art Institute of Chicago.

the local or deme level. The following reading gives the sacrifices to be offered in the deme of Thorikos during Boedromion (September–October) to various gods, goddesses, heroes, and heroines.[26]

In Boedromion festival of the Proerosia: for Zeus Poleius, a choice sheep; women acclaiming the god, a piglet brought for holocaust sacrifice; for the worshipper the priest will provide a dinner; for Kephalos, a choice sheep; for Prokris, an offering tray; for Thorikos, a choice sheep; for the Heroines of Thorikos, an offering tray; at Sounion for Poseidon, a choice lamb; for Apollo, a choice goat; for Kourotrophos, a choice female piglet; for Demeter, a full grown victim; for Zeus Herkeios, a full grown victim; for Kourotrophos, a piglet . . . ; at the salt-marsh [?] for Poseidon, a full grown victim; for Apollo, a piglet.

[26] From L. B. Zaidman and P. Schmitt Pantel, *Religion in the Ancient Greek City* (Cambridge, 1992), p. 82, by permission of Cambridge University Press.

4. ATHENA NIKE PRIESTESS

The importance of women in Greek religion is underlined by the fact that throughout Greece female deities tended to be served by women and girls. At Athens the city's principal cult of Athena was headed by a female priestess, the priestess of Athena Polias, patron goddess of Athens. Some deities were served by priestesses who were chosen annually and by lot, as was the priestess of Athena Nike.

[—]kos proposed [for Athena Ni]ke a priestess who [. . .] [12 letters missing]. [F]rom all Athenian women shall be [appointed], and the sanctuary shall have whatever doors Kallikrates designs; the *poletai* [*officials who contracted out city work*] shall let the contract out for hire during the prytany of the tribe Leontis. The priestess shall be paid 50 drachmae (a year) and the legs and hides from the public sacrifices.[27]

5. XENOPHON CONSULTS THE DELPHIC ORACLE[28]

Xenophon, *Anabasis*

Already in the Iliad *and the* Odyssey *it is clear that the Greeks believed that communication between men and gods was possible. Such communication could occur either indirectly by means of omens, such as unusual or out of place natural phenomena like thunder on a clear day or malformed births, or directly by dreams or, more importantly, through oracles such as that of Apollo at Delphi in Central Greece. At Delphi the actual oracle was a middle aged peasant woman through whom the god was believed to speak in trance-inspired utterances that were interpreted by the prophetes (= spokesperson) and turned over to the inquirer as the reply to his question. This procedure gave rise to the idea that the oracles took the form of riddles or were ambiguous such as the famous answer to the Lydian king Croesus, who was told that if he crossed the Halys River (to attack the Persians), a great kingdom would fall, and, of course, one did—his own. In actuality, questions were normally posed to the god in a form that permitted only a "yes or no" answer or an otherwise simple response, and this allowed, as this passage from Xenophon's* Anabasis *indicates, the inquirer to frame his question so as to force the god to give him the answer he desired.*

Now there was in the army a certain man, an Athenian, Xenophon, who had accompanied Cyrus, neither as a general, nor as an officer, nor yet as a private soldier, but simply on the invitation of an old friend, Proxenus. This old friend had sent to fetch him from home, promising, if he would come, to introduce him to Cyrus, "whom," said Proxenus, "I consider to be worth my fatherland and more to me."

Xenophon, having read the letter, consulted Socrates the Athenian, whether he should accept or refuse the invitation. Socrates, who had a suspicion that the State of Athens might in some way look askance at any friendship with Cyrus, whose zealous co-operation with the Lacedaemonians against Athens in the war

---

[27] From M. Crawford and D. Whitehead, *Archaic and Classical Greece* (Cambridge, 1983), p. 297, by permission of Cambridge University Press.

[28] Xenophon, *Anabasis* 3.1.5 (London and New York 1890–97), trans. H. G. Dakyns.

was not forgotten, advised Xenophon to go to Delphi and there to consult the god as to the desirability of such a journey. Xenophon went and put the question to Apollo, to which of the gods he must pray and do sacrifice, so that he might best accomplish his intended journey and return in safety, with good fortune. Then Apollo answered and told him to what gods he must sacrifice, and when he had returned home he reported to Socrates the oracle. But he, when he heard, blamed Xenophon that he had not, in the first instance, inquired of the god, whether it were better for him to go or to stay, but had taken on himself to settle that point affirmatively, by inquiring straightway, how he might best perform the journey. "Since, however," continued Socrates, "you did so put the question, you should do what the god enjoined." Thus, and without further ado, Xenophon offered sacrifice to those whom the god had named, and set sail on his voyage.

6. PERSONAL RELIGION: XENOPHON'S TEMPLE TO ARTEMIS

Because of his lack of sympathy for the restored Athenian democracy, Xenophon left Athens shortly after the Peloponnesian War, becoming one of the mercenary soldiers who were a prominent feature of fourth-century B.C. Greece. After participating in Cyrus the Younger's unsuccessful revolt against his brother Artaxerxes II in 401 B.C. and then fighting on the Spartan side against Athens in the 390s B.C., for which he was exiled from his homeland, Xenophon retired to a country estate near Sparta. In this passage he recounts his devotion to the goddess Artemis and the intimate connection between her and his life in exile.[29]

Xenophon,
Anabasis

At this time and place they divided the money accruing from the sale of the captives [*i.e., captured by Cyrus the Younger's Greek mercenaries*]; and a tithe selected for Apollo and Artemis of the Ephesians was divided between the generals, each of whom took a portion to guard for the gods, Neon the Asinaean taking on behalf of Cheirisophus. Out of the portion, which fell to Xenophon, he caused a dedication offering to Apollo to be made and dedicated among the treasures of the Athenians at Delphi. It was inscribed with his own name, and that of Proxenus, his friend, who was killed with Clearchus. The gift for Artemis of the Ephesians was, in the first instance, left behind by him in Asia at the time when he left that part of the world himself with Agesilaus on the march into Boeotia. He left it behind in charge of Megabyzus, the sacristan of the goddess, thinking that the voyage on which he was starting was likely to be dangerous. In the event of his coming out of it alive, he charged Megabyzus to restore to him the deposit; but should any evil happen to him, then he was to cause to be made and dedicate on his behalf to Artemis, whatsoever thing he thought would be pleasing to the goddess.

In the days of his banishment, when Xenophon was now established by the Lacedaemonians as a colonist in Scillus, a place, which lies on the main road to Olympia, Megabyzus arrived on his way to Olympia as a spectator to attend the games, and restored to him the deposit. Xenophon took the money and bought for

---

[29] Xenophon, *Anabasis* 5.4. (London and New York 1890–97), trans. H. G. Dakyns.

the goddess a plot of ground at a point indicated to him by the oracle. The plot, it so happened, had its own Selinus river flowing through it, just as at Ephesus the river Selinus flows past the temple of Artemis, and in both streams fish and mussels are to be found. On the estate at Scillus there is hunting and shooting of all sorts of beasts of the chase.

Here with the sacred money he built an altar and a temple, and ever after, year by year, tithed the fruits of the land in their season and sacrificed to the goddess, while all the citizens and neighbors, men and women, shared in the festival. The goddess herself provided for the banqueters meat and loaves and wine and sweet-meats, with portions of the victims sacrificed from the sacred pasture, as also of those which were slain in the chase. For Xenophon's own sons, with the sons of the other citizens, always made a hunting excursion against the festival day, in which any grown men who liked might join. The game was captured partly from the sacred district itself, partly from Pholoe, pigs and gazelles and stags. The place lies on the direct road from Lacedaemon to Olympia, about two and one-half miles from the temple of Zeus in Olympia, and within the sacred enclosure there is meadow-land and wood-covered hills, suited to the breeding of pigs and goats and cattle and horses, so that even the pack-animals of the people passing to the feast fare sumptuously. The shrine is girdled by a grove of cultivated trees, yielding dessert fruits in their season. The temple itself is a facsimile on a small scale of the great temple at Ephesus, and the image of the goddess is like the golden statue at Ephesus, save only that it is made, not of gold, but of cypress wood. Beside the temple stands a column bearing this inscription:

> The place is sacred to Artemis. He who holds it and enjoys the fruits of it is bound to sacrifice yearly a tithe of the produce. And from the residue thereof to keep in repair the shrine. If any man fail in any of this, the goddess herself will look to the matter.

F. War and Warfare in the *Polis*

1. THE SPARTAN ARMY

Plutarch,
Lycurgus

Plutarch's description of the Spartan army, written centuries after the decline of Sparta, reflects an idealizing view of that city felt by many intellectuals attracted to the orderly nature of its constitution, which seemed to have none of the vices manifested by democratic Athens.[30]

When the army was drawn up in battle array, and the enemy near, the king sacrificed a goat, commanded the soldiers to set their garlands on their heads, and the

---

[30] From Plut. Lyc. 22.3–23.

pipers to play the tune of the hymn to Castor, and himself began to sing the paean of advance. It was at once a magnificent and terrible sight to see them march on to the tune of their flutes, without any disorder in their ranks, any lack of resolve in their minds, or change in their faces, calmly and cheerfully moving with the music to the deadly fight. Men in this mood were not likely to be possessed with fear or carried away by fury, but with the deliberate valor of hope and certainty, as if some divinity were in charge and guiding them.

The king was always accompanied by an athlete who had been crowned in the Olympic games. Regarding this custom it is said that a Spartan once refused a valuable bribe, which was offered to him upon condition that he would not compete. But after beating his opponent after much effort, some of the spectators asked him, "Spartan, what have you gained from your victory?" he replied, smiling, "I shall fight at the side of the king."

After the Spartans had routed an enemy, they pursued them until they were certain of victory, and then they sounded a retreat, thinking it not right and unworthy of a Greek people to cut men in pieces, who had given up and abandoned all resistance. This manner of dealing with their enemies was not only magnanimous but was politically wise also, for, knowing that they killed only those who made resistance, and gave quarter to the rest, their enemies generally thought it best to flee than to stand be annihilated.

2. A HOPLITE BATTLE: MANTINEIA

Fought in 418 B.C. during a lull in the Peloponnesian War, the battle of Mantineia was essentially a struggle for control of the Peloponnese between Argos, Mantineia, and Elis on one side and Sparta and its allies on the other. The Athenians were acting in support of the former group. Their involvement technically did not violate the peace that had been temporarily established in 421 B.C., and their contribution was halfhearted. Ancient battlefield casualties are notoriously untrustworthy. Here Thucydides makes an effort to establish the size of the two armies. The reading reflects both the methodical and cautious approach of the historian as well as the relatively small number of casualties. Fourteen hundred killed for an engagement that Thucydides characterizes as the "greatest that had occurred for a very long time" does not seem large. The relatively small number of casualties reflects the traditional approach to hoplite fighting before the military revolution of the next century. The professionalism of the Spartans who constituted the core of the "Lacedaemonians" and the excellent tactical control their general Agis exercised over them are very much in evidence in the reading.[31]

Thucydides,
The History of the Peloponnesian War

In this battle the left wing was composed of the Sciritae (*a subject people of the Spartans*), who in the Lacedaemonian army always have that post to themselves alone. Next to them were the soldiers Brasidas had used in Thrace, including the Neodamodes (*freed helots*). The companies (*lochoi*) of the Lacaedaemonians them-

[31] From Thucydides, *The Peloponnesian War*, 5.67–74, based on the translation of Richard Crawley (London, 1910).

selves were positioned beside these, with the Arcadians of Heraea at their side. After these were Maenalians, and on their right wing the Tegeans with a few of the Lacedaemonians at the extremity. Their cavalry was posted on both wings. Such was the Lacedaemonian formation.

The line of battle of their opponents was as follows. On the right wing (*the post of honor*) were the Mantineans because the battle was taking place in their country, and next to them were the allies from Arcadia. Then came the thousand picked men of the Argives, to whom the state had given a long course in military training at public expense; next to them were the rest of the Argives, and their allies, the Cleonaeans and Orneans. The Athenians were on the extreme left; they had their own cavalry with them.

Such were the order and composition of the two combatants. The Lacedaemonian army looked the largest, but it would be difficult to determine with accuracy the numbers of either army, or of the units composing it. Owing to the secrecy of their government the number of the Lacedaemonians was not known. On the other hand, since men are so apt to brag about the forces of their country, the estimate of their opponents was not trusted. The following calculation, however, makes it possible to give an estimate of the numbers of the Lacedaemonians present upon this occasion. There were seven companies (*lochoi*) in the field without counting the Sciritae, who numbered six hundred men. In each company there were four pentecostyies, and in each pentecosty four enomoties. The first rank of each enomoty was composed of four soldiers. As to the depth, although they had not been all drawn up alike, but as each captain chose, they were generally ranged eight deep. Hence, the first rank along the whole line, exclusive of the Sciritae, consisted of four hundred and forty-eight men (*thus, 3,585 Lacedaemonians plus 600 Sciritae*).

The armies being now on the point of engaging, each contingent received some words of encouragement from its own commander. The Mantineans were reminded that they were going to fight for their country and to avoid returning to the experience of servitude after having tasted that of empire; the Argives, that they would contend for their hegemony, to regain their once equal share of Peloponnese of which they had been so long deprived, and to punish an enemy and a neighbor for a thousand wrongs; the Athenians, the glory of gaining the honors of the day with so many and brave allies in arms, and that a victory over the Lacedaemonians in the Peloponnese would cement and extend their empire, and would besides preserve Attica from all invasions in the future. These were the incitements addressed to the Argives and their allies. The Lacedaemonians meanwhile, man to man and with their war-songs in the ranks, exhorted each brave comrade to remember what he had learnt before. They were well aware that safety was to be found in long training rather than any brief verbal exhortation, however well it was delivered.

After they joined in battle, the Argives and their allies advanced in haste and fury, while the Lacedaemonians moved slowly and to the music of many flute-players—a standing institution in their army that has nothing to do with religion, but is meant to make them advance evenly, stepping in time, without breaking their order, as large armies have a tendency to do in the moment of engaging.

Just before the battle lines met, King Agis resolved upon the following maneuver. All armies are alike in this. On going into action their right wing gets forced out and tends to overlap their adversary's left. The reason for this is that fear makes each man do his best to shelter his unarmed side with the shield of the man next him on the right, thinking that the closer the shields are locked together the better he will be protected. The man primarily responsible for this is the first upon the right wing, who is always striving to withdraw from the enemy his unarmed side; and the same apprehension makes the rest follow him. On this occasion the Mantineans reached with their wing far beyond the Sciritae, and the Lacedaemonians and the Tegeans still farther beyond the Athenians, as their army was the largest. Agis, afraid of his left being surrounded, and thinking the Mantineans outflanked it too far, ordered the Sciritae and Brasideans to move from their place in the ranks and make the line even with the Mantineans, and told the polemarchs Hipponoidas and Aristocles to fill up the gap thus formed, by throwing themselves into it with two companies taken from the right wing. Agis thought that his right would still be strong enough and to spare, and that the line in front of the Mantineans would gain solidarity.

However, as he gave these orders at the moment of the collision of the armies, and at short notice, it so happened that Aristocles and Hipponoidas would not move over, for which offense they were afterwards banished from Sparta as having been guilty of cowardice. The enemy meanwhile closed before the Sciritae (whom Agis on seeing that the two companies did not move over ordered them to return to their place) had time to fill up the breach in question. Now it was, however, that the Lacedaemonians, utterly worsted in respect of skill, showed themselves as superior in point of courage. As soon as they came to close quarters with the enemy, the Mantinean right broke their Sciritae and Brasidean opponents and burst in with their allies and the thousand picked Argives into the unclosed breach, cut up and surrounded the Lacedaemonians, and drove them in full retreat to the wagons, killing some of the older men on guard there. The rest of the Lacedaemonians, together with their allies, and especially the center where the three hundred so-called knights (*they actually fought on foot*), fought around King Agis, fell on the older men of the Argives and the five companies so named, and on the Cleonaeans, the Orneans and the Athenians next to them and instantly routed them. The greater number did not wait to strike a blow, but gave away the moment the enemy came on them. Some were trodden under foot in their fear of being overtaken by their assailants.

The army of the Argives and their allies having given way in this quarter was now completely cut in two, and the Lacedaemonian and Tegean right simultaneously closed round the Athenians with the troops that outflanked them. The Athenians were now between two fires, being surrounded on one side and already defeated on the other. Indeed they would have suffered more severely than any other part of the army but for the support of the cavalry which they had with them. Agis also on seeing the danger to his left opposed to the Mantineans and the thousand Argives, ordered all the army to advance to the support of the defeated wing. While this took place, as the enemy moved past and slanted away from them, the Athenians escaped at their leisure and with the beaten Argive division. Meanwhile the Mantineans and their allies and the picked body of Argives ceased to press the enemy, and seeing their friends defeated and the Lacedaemonians in full advance upon them, took to flight. Many of the Mantineans perished, but the bulk of the Argive contingent escaped. The flight and retreat, however, were neither hurried nor long. The Lacedaemonians fought long and stubbornly until they have routed their enemy, but once they have done this, they do not pursue for long or very far.

Such was the battle, as nearly as possible as I have described it. It was the greatest that had occurred for a very long while among the Hellenes, and involved the most important states. The Lacedaemonians took up a position in front of the enemy's dead and immediately set up a trophy and stripped the slain. They took up their own dead and carried them back to Tegea, where they buried them. They restored those of the enemy dead under truce. The Argives, Orneans, and Cleonaeans lost seven hundred killed; the Mantineans two hundred, and the Athenians and Aeginetan settlers also two hundred with both their generals. On the side of the Lacedaemonians, the allies did not suffer any loss worth speaking of. As to the Lacedaemonians themselves it was difficult to learn the truth. It is said, however, that there were killed about three hundred of them.

G. The Place of Warfare in the *Polis*: Some Philosophical Reflections

1. "ALL STATES ARE BY NATURE FIGHTING AN UNDECLARED WAR WITH ALL OTHER STATES"

Plato, *Laws*

So said the Cretan Cleinias, one of the three speakers in Plato's famous dialogue, The Laws. *Cleinias' claim, however, was not an assertion of fact but of ideology, aimed at justifying his own state's type of constitution, which heavily emphasized preparation for war. It should not be understood as a statement about public opinion on the subject in Greece, although many Greeks might have agreed with him. The Athenian, the principal figure in the dialogue, challenges Cleinias' claim: "You seem to imagine that a well-governed state ought to be so ordered as to conquer all other states in war: am I right in supposing this to be your meaning?" Cleinias agrees with this assessment: "Certainly; and our Lacedaemonian (Spartan) friend (the third speaker in the dialogue), if I am not mistaken, will agree with me." Later in the dialogue the Athenian goes into greater detail as to why organizing a state around war-making is a mistake. All the speakers agree, however, that self-defense is a necessity for all states.*[32]

[32] From Plato, *Laws* 625d–626b, based on the translation of B. Jowett (London, 1892).

CLEINIAS: "I think, Stranger, that the aim of our customs is easily grasped by anyone. Look at the physical character of our country: Crete is not like Thessaly, which is a large plain. For this reason Thessalians have horsemen while we have runners. The roughness of the terrain in our country is more adapted to movement on foot, and if you have runners, you must have light arms for no one can carry heavy weights while running. Bows and arrows are convenient because they are light. Now all these customs of Crete have been made with a view to war, and the legislator who made them appears to me to have looked to this in all his arrangements. The common meals, if I am not mistaken, were instituted by him for a similar reason, because he saw that for as long as soldiers are on campaign they are, by the nature of the situation, forced to eat their meals together for the sake of mutual protection. He seems to me to have thought the majority opinion was foolish in not understanding that all men are always at war without cessation with other states. Thus, if in war there ought to be common meals and certain officers and men be regularly appointed as guards, the same practices should be continued in peace. For what men in general term peace would be said by him to be nothing other than a fiction and in reality every state is in a natural state of perpetual, if undeclared, war with every other state. And if you look closely you will find that this was the intention of our Cretan legislator. All institutions, private as well as public, were arranged by him with a view to war. In giving them he was under the impression that no possessions or institutions are of any value to him who is defeated in battle, for all the good things of the conquered pass into the hands of the conquerors.

The following assertion by the Athenian, rejecting Cleinias' explanation, is probably close to Plato's own views.

ATHENIAN: I remember and you will remember, what I said at first, that a statesman and legislator ought to make laws with a view to wisdom, while you, on the other hand, were arguing that the good lawgiver ought to make laws only with a view to war. And to this I replied that there were four virtues, but upon your view of them only one was the aim of legislation, whereas you ought to take into consideration all virtue, and especially that which comes first, and is the leader of all the rest. This is good practical judgment, strength of mind and opinion, together with the affection and desire that come with them. And now the argument returns to the same point, and I say once more, as a joke if you like, or in earnest if you like that the prayer of a fool is full of danger, being likely to end in the opposite of what he desires (*a Greek proverb*). And if you would rather receive my words in earnest, I am willing that you should; and you will find, I suspect, as I have said already, that not cowardice was the cause of the ruin of the Dorian kings (*both Sparta and Crete were Dorian states*) and of their whole design, nor ignorance of military matters, either on the part of the rulers of their subjects; but their misfortunes were due to their vices in general, and especially their ignorance of what was most important in human affairs. That was then, and is still, and always will be the case, as I will endeavor, if you will allow me, to make out and demonstrate as well as I am able to you who are my friends, in the course of my argument.

2. "PEACE IS THE END OF WAR, LEISURE OF WORK"

Aristotle, *Politics*

Like Plato, Aristotle too criticized states such as Crete and Sparta, which organized themselves principally for war and then had difficulty coping with peace. However, he comes at the subject from a somewhat different angle. Good citizens should be well rounded and prepared for success in what he calls "work," i.e., practical life (ascholia), as well as leisure (scholē). Courage is an important and necessary virtue, but taken in isolation it leads to a kind of brutal, uncivil culture.[33]

Experience supports the testimony of theory, that it is the duty of the lawgiver to study how he may frame his legislation both with regard to warfare and in other spheres for the object of leisure and peace. Most military states remain safe while at war but perish when they have won their empire. Like iron they lose their keen temper in times of peace. The legislator is at fault for he did not educate them to be able to employ leisure. . . . [It] has been said repeatedly, peace is the end of war, and leisure of work. But the virtues useful for leisure and for its employment are not only those that operate during leisure but also in work, for a lot of essentials are necessary for leisure. Therefore, it is proper for the state to be self-restrained, brave and steadfast since, as the proverb goes, there is no leisure for slaves, and those who cannot face danger bravely are the slaves of their assailants. Accordingly, courage and steadfastness are needed for work, love of wisdom for leisure, and temperance and justice for both leisure and work. This is especially true in times of leisure, for war compels men to be just and self-restrained, whereas the enjoyment of prosperity and peaceful leisure tend to make them arrogant. Therefore much justice and much self-restraint are needed by those who are thought to be very prosperous and who enjoy everything the world counts as blessings. . . . The more such people are at leisure and have an abundance of such blessing, the more they will need wisdom, self-restraint and justice. It is clear therefore that a state that is to be happy and morally excellent must share in these virtues. If it is disgraceful not to be capable of using well our good things in general, it is even more disgraceful not to be capable of using them in times of leisure, and although demonstrating ourselves good men when engaged in work and war, in times of peace and leisure to seem to be no better than slaves. Therefore we must not cultivate virtue after the manner of the state of Sparta. The superiority of the Spartans over other races does not lie in their holding a different opinion from others as to what things are the greatest goods, but rather in their believing that these are obtained by means of one particular virtue. . . .

[33] From Aristotle, *Politics*, 7.1334a–b, 8.1338b, based on the translation of H. Rackham (London, 1932).

Now at the present time some of the states with the reputation of paying closest attention to the education of children, produce in them an athletic habit to the detriment of their bodily appearance and growth, while the Spartans, although they have avoided this error, yet make their boys animal in nature by their laborious exercises, in the belief that this is most contributory to manly courage. Yet, as has often been said, it is not right to regulate education with a view to one virtue only, or to this one most of all. And even if courage was the principal objective of their education, the Spartans have not been able to figure out how to achieve it. For neither in the lower animals nor in the case of foreign races is courage associated with the most ferocious, but rather with the gentler and lion-like temperaments. . . . And again we know that even the Spartans, although so long as they continued by themselves in their laborious exercises they surpassed all others both in gymnastics and in military contests; for they used not to excel because they drilled their young men in this fashion but only because they trained and their adversaries did not. Consequently honor and not animal ferocity should have the principal role, for it is not a wolf nor one of the other wild animals that will venture upon any noble hazard, but rather a good man. But those who let boys pursue these hard exercises too much and turn them out without education in necessary things, in effect render them banausic and thus useful for only one function of citizenship, and even for this task training them worse than others do, as our argument proves.[34]

---

[34] *Banausic* is the Greek word used for any occupation or form of work that limited human development. This could be either an all-engrossing form of professionalism or a job that completely absorbed a person's time and talent to the exclusion of other activities. Most often, however, the term referred to physical labor.

5

THE PELOPONNESIAN
WAR AND THE MILITARY
REVOLUTION

The Greek victory over the Persians left many unresolved problems, the principal one being the question of leadership. It was clear to many Greeks that the jealously guarded, freewheeling independence of their *poleis* had almost lost them the war. An opinion was reported by Thucydides to the effect that the only thing that had actually saved the Greeks from destruction was the fact that the Persians made more mistakes than they did. Plato had another version of the war: "If one were to tell the history of the Persian War many nasty charges would have to be brought against Greece; in fact it would be right to say that Greece made no defense of itself at all were it not for the joint actions of Athenians and Spartans in resisting the threatened enslavement."[1] There was no assurance that the next time the Greeks would be so lucky. Persia was not going to go away. It remained an active threat, always meddling, always probing. The Greek states had to make a decision about how they were going to cope with this situation. But were they flexible enough to adjust? This was a deeper problem: Was the freedom of Greece as a whole compatible with the freedom of its individual states? In the end it was the tragedy of the Greeks of the *polis* age that they were unable to preserve both sets of freedoms.

The prestige that Sparta enjoyed after the battle of Plataea suggested that it should remain the head of the Greek alliance, but neither the logic of the military situation nor Sparta's own constitution would permit this. There was the further problem that, after the battles of Marathon and Salamis, Sparta now had a potential rival in Greece: Athens. Sparta was a hothouse society, so tightly organized that its citizens could not survive long as Spartans outside its immediate environment. This fact was brought home immediately after the war by the heavy-handed behavior of the Spartan supreme commander Pausanias, which alienated the allies. More important than the inability of individual Spartans to survive outside Sparta was the inability of the Spartan army to operate for long periods away from home. After Plataea, defense against the Persians did not call for massive land armies, but rather for both large and small fleet operations against widely scattered targets. Persian garrisons contin-

---

[1] Plato, *Laws*, 3.692e.

ued to maintain footholds in Europe for fifteen years or more after Plataea, and the Persians were still able to control large segments of Greek Asia through cooperative tyrants and oligarchies. Major naval offensives were a possibility, and the Greeks had to be prepared to handle massive fleet concentrations of three hundred or more ships. What was needed was a well-informed central organization that could coordinate strategy and concentrate the scattered forces of Greece to counter the enemy's great strength—in short, centralized command and control over military resources.

Other factors also made it difficult for a state such as Sparta to provide leadership to the Greeks after the repulse of the Persians. First, the theater of war was now the eastern and northern Aegean, not mainland Greece, where Sparta had traditionally operated. Then, whereas almost any city could field a hoplite phalanx, the same was not true of a fleet of triremes. Sparta was least endowed with the resources necessary to sustain a navy. Ships were extremely expensive. Large crews were needed to operate them, and large sums of money were required merely to keep the fleet in existence. The state that aspired to naval power had to have either a large population, a lot of money, or both. Naval warfare tended to favor (as it still does) the development of large fleets by the few states that possessed the necessary resources. It is not surprising that by mid-century only Athens, Lesbos, Chios, and Samos were making significant contributions in ships to the anti-Persian alliance, with Athens predominating.

Although the Greek league headed by Sparta remained intact, Athens—with the enthusiastic support of the Greeks in the east—created another alliance, the Delian League, in the winter of 478–477 B.C. Its purpose was both offensive and defensive. It aimed to preserve Greek freedom and to conduct active reprisals against the Persian Empire to obtain plunder to offset the expenses of the league. During the next half century the Delian League grew to almost two hundred members, but as the Persian threat receded, the Delian League gradually changed from an association of free allies into an Athenian empire. Along with the growth of Athens' imperial power, there was increased tension between Athens and Sparta, its chief rival for preeminence in Greece, until war broke out in 431 B.C. and lasted until 404 B.C., with an uneasy peace in the middle from 421 to 413 B.C.

Our principal source for the war is the great historian Thucydides. Thucydides served Athens as one of the ten generals elected in 424 B.C., but having failed against the Spartans in the north of Greece, he was exiled and returned to Athens only after the Peloponnesian War. His dominant viewpoint, not so much his reporting of the events of the war, is hard to escape. Thucydides' history is one of the finest pieces of intellectual analysis of all time, but it is not a history in the modern sense of the term. In addition to presenting the facts accurately, Thucydides sought also to penetrate the surface of individual events to discover the universal and permanent laws concealed in them and to reveal causes that lead predictably to the same results. For example, he pointed out that although Athens might be universally hated because it wielded almost total power throughout Greece, this was not because of anything peculiar to the nature of Athens or the Athenian people, but because of the nature of power itself, which has its own laws and generates the same kind of reaction no matter who possesses it. War and justice, he concluded, cannot coexist; the powerful oppress the weak, and all states act in their own self-interest. He sought to lay bare the underlying but hidden structures of the state and the various constraints these imposed on its citizens in the conduct of interstate relations. Events for him were not right or wrong, good or evil. He did not view them in ethical or moral terms, but rather as questions of fact: What are the causes of conflict? What courses do social revolutions take once they begin? That people or states act from expedience or use whatever power they have at their disposal is not weighed for its good or evil consequences; Thucydides merely determined whether it was a fact. People and states must act according to their natures, and Thucydides' practical aim was to unravel the nature of both and leave the answer as a guide ("as an eternal possession," was his expression) to future generations.

The length and intensity of the Peloponnesian War and the wars that followed tended to push upwards the demands of warfare, especially in terms of skills and economic resources. The almost ritualistic hoplite battles of the past in which small, relatively unskilled phalanxes confronted each other gave way to more complex encounters in which, in addition to hoplites, light infantry, cavalry, slingers, archers, and other specialized arms had a role. The quality of fortifications improved, adding further complexity to the military equation. As in the past, fleets of warships were enormously expensive to maintain.

Poverty had always driven young Greeks to seek military service as mercenaries. Arcadia was well known as a place of recruitment of such mercenaries. After the Peloponnesian War there were thousands of soldiers who had known little other than warfare during their lifetimes. Persia drew on large numbers of these mercenaries for its wars, as did tyrants throughout the Greek world. Jason of Pherae was said to have had 6000 at his disposal, and in an attempt to unseat his brother as king of Persia, Cyrus the Younger had little difficulty in rounding up 10,000 Greek veterans. It was next to impossible for the ordinary small state whose defense rested on its small, citizen-soldier phalanx to keep up with the new developments. Gradually the whole foundation—material and ideological—of the *polis* as a self-sustaining community was undermined. The larger states fared better, since with their greater economic resources they could hire mercenaries to complement their citizen phalanxes and fleets, but in the new arms race even such states as Athens and Syracuse found themselves unable to compete. The future was to be one in which only the largest leagues and monarchies could be successful.

A. The Rise of Athens

1. THE GOLDEN AGE: LOOKING AT THE PAST

Diodorus | *The idea that the unexpected Greek victory over the Persians in 480–479 B.C. not only saved Greece from slavery but also ushered in a cultural "Golden Age" is not just a modern view. It was also how the Greeks interpreted the history of this period, as is illustrated by this selection from the universal history of the first-century B.C. historian Diodorus. Whether his interpretation was accurate is another question. Clearly his remarks regarding cultural development apply mainly to Athens. Even there Diodorus intensified the picture of the fifth century B.C. as a period of extraordinary cultural achievement by anachronistically including in it such fourth-century* B.C. *luminaries as the philosophers Plato and Aristotle and the rhetorician Isocrates.*[2]

A person would rightly feel perplexed who considered the inconsistency of human life. For none of the agreed-on goods are found to be given to men in perfect form nor are any of the ills absolutely free of some advantage. This can be shown by considering past events, especially the greatest. For the campaign of Xerxes, the king of the Persians, caused the greatest fear among the Greeks because of the huge size of his army, since the stake for which they were about to fight was their enslavement. They all assumed that they would suffer a similar fate as the Greek cities of Asia which had been enslaved previously. But when the war, contrary to expectation, came to an unanticipated conclusion, not only did the inhabitants of Greece escape from danger, but they gained great fame, and every Greek city was filled with such abundance that all were astounded at their reversal of fortune. For the next fifty years Greece experienced a great surge of prosperity. In this period the arts flourished because of the abundance, and the greatest artists known to posterity existed then, among whom was the sculptor Pheidias. Education also advanced greatly, and philosophy and rhetoric were highly esteemed by all the Greeks, but especially by the Athenians. The philosophers included Socrates, Plato, and Aristotle; the orators, Pericles and Isocrates together with the students of Isocrates. There were also famous generals: Miltiades, Themistocles, Aristides, Cimon, Myronides, and many others. . . . The Athenians especially advanced in repute and vigor and became renowned throughout the world. For they increased their power to such a degree that without the Spartans and the Peloponnesians they defeated, on their own, great Persian forces on both land and sea and so humbled the famed Persian Empire that they compelled the Persians to sign a treaty freeing all the cities in Asia.

2. "FOR WITHOUT EQUAL MILITARY POWER IT IS IMPOSSIBLE FOR ALLIES TO HAVE EQUAL OR SIMILAR SAY IN POLICY-MAKING": THE REALITY OF ATHENIAN POWER

Diodorus could have made more explicit the connection between Athens' economic and cultural flourishing in the fifth century B.C. *and its new-found military clout. Athenians in that age were energized by their unexpected success in the Persian Wars and were quite willing to use their military influence whenever self-interest seemed to indicate its need. The first instance of muscle flexing occurred immediately after the retreat of the Persians when the Athenians reoccupied their devastated city and the Spartans sought to dissuade them from rebuilding their walls. The Spartans argued speciously that walled cities would only help the Persians if they returned again, and that indeed all walled cities outside the Peloponnese should have their fortifications destroyed. The Athenian leader Themistocles outfoxed the Spartans, and the walls were rebuilt without the Spartans being able to intervene. At an assembly of the irritated Spartans, Thucydides gives the gist of how (supposedly)*

Thucydides, *The Peloponnesian War*

---

[2] From Diodorus 12.1–2.

Themistocles justified Athenian actions. The remainder of the reading deals with the formation of the Delian League and its gradual transition from alliance to empire.[3]

91. Themistocles, coming before the Spartans, finally told them openly that the Athens was now provided with walls and could protect her own citizens. Henceforward, if the Spartans or their allies wished at any time to negotiate, they must deal with the Athenians as with men who knew quite well what was for their own and the common good of Greece. When they boldly resolved to leave their city and take to their ships [*during the second Persian invasion*], they did not first ask the advice of the Spartans, and when the two states met in council, their own judgment had been as good as that of any one. And now they had arrived at the opinion that it was better far, and would be more advantageous for themselves and for the whole body of allies, that their city should have a wall. For without equal military power it was impossible for allies to have equal or similar say in councils. Either all the allies should pull down their walls, or they should acknowledge that the Athenians were in the right.

3. THE STRATEGIC THINKING OF THEMISTOCLES

Thucydides,
*The Peloponnesian
War*

93. In such hurried fashion did the Athenians rebuild the walls of their city. To this day the structure shows evidence of haste. The foundations are made up of all sorts of stones, in some places unshaped, and laid just as each worker brought them; there were many columns too, taken from graves, and many old stones already cut, inserted in the work. The circuit of the city was extended in every direction, and the citizens, in their desire to complete the design, spared nothing. Themistocles also persuaded the Athenians to finish the fortifications of Piraeus, of which he had made a beginning in his year of office as Archon. The situation of the place, which had three natural harbors, was excellent and now that the Athenians had become seafarers, he thought that a good harbor would greatly contribute to the extension of their power. For he was the first to dare to say that the Athenians must make the sea their domain, and he lost no time in laying the foundations of their empire. By his advice, they built the wall of such a width that two wagons carrying the stones could meet and pass on the top; this width may still be traced at the Piraeus. Inside there was no rubble or mortar, but the whole wall was made up of large stones hewn square, which were clamped on the outer face with iron and lead. The wall, however, was completed to not more than half what he had originally intended. He had hoped that the very size of the wall would paralyze the designs of an enemy, and he thought that a handful of the least effective soldiers would be sufficient for its defense, while the rest might man the fleet. His mind was turned in this direction,

[3] From Thucydides, *The Peloponnesian War*, trans. B. Jowett (Oxford, 1900) (revised).

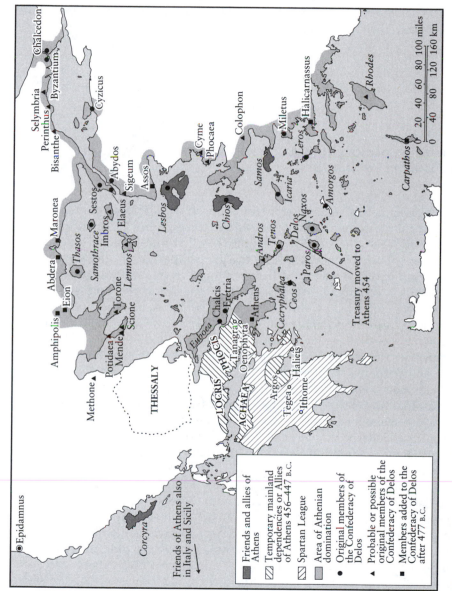

Figure 5.1 The Athenian Empire at its height.

I believe, from observing that the Persians had met fewer obstacles by sea than by land. The Piraeus appeared to him to be of more real consequence than the upper city. He was fond of saying the Athenians that if they were hard pressed they should go to the Piraeus and fight all their enemies at sea. Thus the Athenians built their walls and restored their city immediately after the retreat of the Persians.

B. The Delian League

1. "THEY HAD ENOUGH OF THE PERSIAN WAR": THE SPARTANS AND THE DELIAN LEAGUE

Thucydides,
The Peloponnesian
War

94. Pausanias the son of Cleombrotus was now sent from Peloponnese with twenty ships in command of the Hellenic forces; thirty Athenian ships and a number of the allies sailed with him. They first made an expedition against Cyprus, of which they subdued the greater part; and afterwards against Byzantium, which was in the hands of the Persians, and was taken while he was still in command. 95. He had already begun to be oppressive, and the allies were offended by him, especially the Ionians and others who had been recently freed from Persian control. So they appealed to their kinsmen the Athenians and begged them to be their leaders, and to protect them against Pausanias, if he attempted to oppress them. The Athenians took the matter up and prepared to interfere, being fully resolved to manage the confederacy in their own interests. In the meantime the Lacedaemonians summoned Pausanias to Sparta, intending to investigate certain reports which had reached them; for he was accused of numerous crimes by Greeks returning from the Hellespont, and he appeared to exercise his command more after the fashion of a tyrant than of a general. His recall occurred at the very time when the hatred which he inspired had induced the allies, with the exception Peloponnesians, to transfer themselves to the Athenians. On arriving at Lacedaemon he was punished for the wrongs which he had done to individuals, but he had been also accused of conspiring with the Persians, and of this, which was the principal charge and was generally believed to be proven, he was acquitted. The government however did not continue him in his command, but sent in his place Dorcis and certain others with a small force. To these the allies refused obedience, and Dorcis, seeing the state of affairs, returned home. Henceforth the Lacedaemonians sent out no more commanders, for they were afraid that those who they appointed would be corrupted, as they had found to be the case with Pausanias; they had had enough of the Persian War; and they thought that the Athenians were fully able to lead, and at that time believed them to be their friends.

2. "THE ALLIES BROUGHT ALL THIS ON THEMSELVES": FROM LEAGUE TO EMPIRE

96. Thus the Athenians by the good-will of the allies, who detested Pausanias, obtained the leadership. They immediately fixed which of the cities should supply money and which of them ships for the war against the Persians, the avowed object being to compensate themselves and the allies for their losses by devastating the King's country. Then was first instituted at Athens the office of Hellenic treasurers who received the tribute, for so the contribution was termed. The amount was originally fixed at 460 talents. The island of Delos was the treasury and the meetings of the allies were held in the temple. 97. At first the allies were independent and deliberated in a common assembly under the leadership of Athens. But in the interval between the Persian and the Peloponnesian Wars, by their military success and by their policy in dealing with the barbarian, with their own rebellious allies and with the Peloponnesians who came across their path from time to time, the Athenians made immense strides in power. I have gone out of the way to speak of this period because the writers who have preceded me treat either of Hellenic affairs previous to the Persian invasion or of that invasion itself. The intervening portion of history has been omitted by all of them with the exception of Hellanicus; and he, where he has touched upon it in his Attic history, is very brief, and inaccurate in his chronology. The narrative will also serve to explain how the Athenian empire grew up.

98. First of all under the leadership of Cimon, the son of Miltiades, the Athenians besieged and took from the Persians Eion upon the Strymon and sold the inhabitants into slavery. The same fate befell Scyros, an island in the Aegean inhabited by Dolopes; this they colonized themselves. They also carried on a war with the Carystians of Euboea who, after a time, capitulated; the other Euboeans took no part in the war. The Naxians revolted, and the Athenians made war against them and reduced them by blockade. This was the first of the allied cities which was enslaved contrary to Hellenic law; the turn of the others came later.

99. The causes which led to the defections of the allies were of different kinds, the principal being their neglect to pay the tribute or to furnish ships, and, in some cases, the refusal to provide military service. For the Athenians were exacting and oppressive, using coercive measures towards men who were neither willing nor accustomed to bear the hardships of military service. And for other reasons they soon began to prove less agreeable leaders than at first. They no longer campaigned on terms of equality with the rest of the confederates, and they had no difficulty in reducing them when they revolted. Now the allies brought all this upon themselves; for the majority of them disliked military service and being absent from home. Accordingly, they agreed to contribute a regular sum of money instead of ships, with the result that the Athenian navy was proportionally increased, while the allies were always untrained and unprepared for war when they revolted.

Thucydides, *The Peloponnesian War*

3. ARISTOTLE ON THE ORGANIZATION OF THE ATHENIAN EMPIRE

Aristotle, *The Constitution of Athens*

The Aristotelian Constitution of Athens *is the only surviving* politeia *out of the 158 Greek and non-Greek constitutions Aristotle and his students assembled for the purpose of political analysis. It provides useful information on the actual numbers of Athenians dependent on tribute from the empire. Since the vast majority of Greek poleis were very small—in the range of 700 to 1000 households—Athens' preponderance among Greek states can easily be appreciated.*[4]

23. The leaders of the people during this period [*i.e., after the Persian wars*] were Aristides, son of Lysimachus, and Themistocles, son of Neocles, of whom the latter appeared to devote himself to the conduct of war, while the former had the reputation of being a clever statesman and the most upright man of his time. Accordingly the one was usually employed as general, the other as political adviser. The rebuilding of the fortifications they conducted in combination, although they were political opponents; but it was Aristides who, seizing the opportunity afforded by the discredit brought upon the Lacedaemonians by Pausanias, guided the public policy in the matter of the defection of the Ionian states from the alliance with Sparta. It follows that it was he who made the first assessment of tribute from the various allied states, two years after the battle of Salamis, in the archonship of Timosthenes; and it was he who took the oath of offensive and defensive alliance with the Ionians. . . . 24. After this, seeing the state growing in confidence and much wealth accumulated, Aristides advised the people to lay hold of the leadership of the league, and to quit the country districts and settle in the city. He pointed out to them that all would be able to gain a living there, some by service in the army, others in the garrisons, others by taking a part in public affairs; and in this way they would secure the leadership. This advice was taken; and when the people had assumed the supreme control they proceeded to treat their allies in a more imperious fashion, with the exception of the Chians, Lesbians, and Samians. These they maintained to protect their empire, leaving their constitutions untouched, and allowing them to retain whatever dominion they then possessed. They also secured an ample maintenance for the mass of the population in the way which Aristides had pointed out to them. Out of the proceeds of the tributes and the taxes and the contributions of the allies more than 20,000 persons were maintained. There were 6,000 jurymen, 1,600 bowmen, 1,200 Knights, 500 members of the Council, 500 guards of the dockyards, besides fifty guards in the Acropolis. There were some 700 magistrates at home, and some 700 abroad. Further, when they subsequently went to war, there were in addition 2,500 heavy-armed troops, twenty guard-ships, and other ships which collected the tributes, with crews amounting to 2,000 men, selected by lot; and besides these there were the persons maintained at the Prytaneum, and orphans, and jailers, since all these were supported by the state.

[4] Aristotle, *The Constitution of Athens* 23–24, trans. Frederick G. Kenyon (Oxford, 1892).

C. The Athenian Empire

1. THE LOGIC OF POSSESSING AN EMPIRE

"The Old Oligarch" is the name given by scholars to an anonymous author who, in the 430s or 420s B.C., wrote a short essay attempting to explain, possibly as a rhetorical exercise, the reasons for the paradoxical success of the Athenian democracy. Using the principle of "enlightened self-interest," he demonstrated that the Athenian poor, the backbone of the Athenian navy, knowingly supported the "bad" democracy because a "good" government would deprive them of a share in government and the benefits it provided. Besides demonstrating how the "People" benefited from the possession of an empire, "The Old Oligarch" provides a vivid picture of the prosperous, cosmopolitan society of mid-fifth-century B.C. Athens.[5]

The Constitution of Athens by "The Old Oligarch"

Democracy and the Poor

1. Now, as for the constitution of the Athenians, and the type or manner of constitution which they have chosen, I praise it not, in so far as the very choice involves the welfare of the baser folk as opposed to that of the better class. I repeat, I withhold my praise so far; but, given the fact that this is the type agreed upon, I propose to show that they set about its preservation in the right way; and that those other transactions in connection with it, which are looked upon as blunders by the rest of the Hellenic world, are the reverse.

   In the first place, I maintain, it is only just that the poorer classes and the common people of Athens should be better off than the men of birth and wealth, seeing that it is the people who man the fleet, and have brought the city her power. The steersman, the boatswain, the lieutenant, the look-out-man at the prow, the shipwright—these are the people who supply the city with power far more than her heavy infantry and men of birth and quality. This being the case, it seems only just that offices of state should be thrown open to every one both in the ballot and the show of hands, and that the right of speech should belong to any one who likes, without restriction. For, observe, there are many of these offices which, according as they are in good or in bad hands, are a source of safety or of danger to the People, and in these the People prudently abstains from sharing; as, for instance, it does not think it incumbent on itself to share in the functions of the general or of the commander of cavalry. The commons recognizes the fact that in forgoing the personal exercise of these offices, and leaving them to the control of the more powerful citizens, it secures the balance of advantage to itself. It is only those

---

[5] From *The Constitution of Athens* by "The Old Oligarch," trans. H. G. Dakyns (London and New York, 1890–1897).

departments of government which bring pay and assist the private estate that the People cares to keep in its own hands.

In the next place, in regard to what some people are puzzled to explain—the fact that everywhere greater consideration is shown to the base, to poor people and to common folk, than to persons of good quality—so far from being a matter of surprise, this, as can be shown, is the keystone of the preservation of the democracy. It is these poor people, this common folk, this worse element, whose prosperity, combined with the growth of their numbers, enhances the democracy. Whereas, a shifting of fortune to the advantage of the wealthy and the better classes implies the establishment on the part of the commons of a strong power in opposition to itself. In fact, all the world over, the cream of society is in opposition to the democracy. Naturally, since the smallest amount of intemperance and injustice, together with the highest scrupulousness in the pursuit of excellence, is to be found in the ranks of the better class, while within the ranks of the People will be found the greatest amount of ignorance, disorderliness, rascality,—poverty acting as a stronger incentive to base conduct, not to speak of lack of education and ignorance, traceable to the lack of means which afflicts the average of mankind.

The Plight of the Rich in the Democracy

Another point is the extraordinary amount of license granted to slaves and resident aliens at Athens, where a blow is illegal, and a slave will not step aside to let you pass him in the street. I will explain the reason of this peculiar custom. Supposing it were legal for a slave to be beaten by a free citizen, or for a resident alien or freedman to be beaten by a citizen, it would frequently happen that an Athenian might be mistaken for a slave or an alien and receive a beating; since the Athenian People is not better clothed than the slave or alien, nor in personal appearance is there any superiority. Or if the fact itself that slaves in Athens are allowed to indulge in luxury, and indeed in some cases to live magnificently, be found astonishing, this too, it can be shown, is done of set purpose. Where you have a naval power dependent upon wealth we must perforce be slaves to our slaves, in order that we may get in our slave-rents, and let the real slave go free. Where you have wealthy slaves it ceases to be advantageous that my slave should stand in awe of you. In Lacedaemon my slave stands in awe of you. But if your slave is in awe of me there will be a risk of his giving away his own moneys to avoid running a risk in his own person. It is for this reason then that we have established an equality between our slaves and free men; and again between our resident aliens and full citizens, because the city stands in need of her resident aliens to meet the requirements of such a multiplicity of arts and for the purposes of her navy. That is, I repeat, the justification of the equality conferred upon our resident aliens.

The common people put a stop to citizens devoting their time to athletics and to the cultivation of music, disbelieving in the beauty of such training, and recognizing the fact that these are things the cultivation of which is beyond its power. On the same principle, in the case of the choregia, the management of athletics, and the command of ships, the fact is recognized that it is the rich man who trains the chorus, and the People for whom the chorus is trained; it is the rich man who is naval commander or superintendent of athletics, and the People that profits by their labors. In fact, what the People looks upon as its right is to pocket the money. To sing and run and dance and man the vessels is well enough, but only in order that the People may be the gainer, while the rich are made poorer. And so in the courts of justice, justice is not more an object of concern to the jurymen than what touches personal advantage.

The Advantages of Empire

To speak next of the allies, and in reference to the point that emissaries from Athens come out, and, according to common opinion, calumniate and vent their hatred upon the better sort of people, this is done on the principle that the ruler cannot help being hated by those whom he rules; but that if wealth and respectability are to wield power in the subject cities the empire of the Athenian People has but a short lease of existence. This explains why the better people are punished with infamy, robbed of their money, driven from their homes, and put to death, while the baser sort are promoted to honor. On the other hand, the better Athenians protect the better class in the allied cities. And why? Because they recognize that it is to the interest of their own class at all times to protect the best element in the cities. It may be urged that if it comes to strength and power the real strength of Athens lies in the capacity of her allies to contribute their money quota. But to the democratic mind it appears a higher advantage still for the individual Athenian to get hold of the wealth of the allies, leaving them only enough to live upon and to cultivate their estates, but powerless to harbor treacherous designs.

Again, it is looked upon as a mistaken policy on the part of the Athenian democracy to compel her allies to voyage to Athens in order to have their cases tried. On the other hand, it is easy to reckon up what a number of advantages the Athenian People derives from the practice impugned. In the first place, there is the steady receipt of salaries throughout the year derived from the court fees. Next, it enables them to manage the affairs of the allied states while seated at home without the expense of naval expeditions. Thirdly, they thus preserve the partisans of the democracy, and ruin her opponents in the law courts. Whereas, supposing the several allied states tried their cases at home, being inspired by hostility to Athens, they would destroy those of their own citizens whose friendship to the Athenian People was most marked. But besides all this the democracy derives the following advantages from hearing the cases of her allies in Athens. In the first place, the one per cent tax levied in Piraeus is increased to the profit of the state; again, the owner of a lodging-house does better, and so, too, the owner of a pair of beasts, or of slaves to be let out on hire; again, heralds and criers are a class of people who fare better owing to the sojourn of foreigners at Athens. Further still, supposing the allies had not to resort to Athens for the hearing of cases, only the official representative of the imperial state would be held in honor, such as the general, or trierarch, or ambassador. Whereas now every single individual among the allies is forced to pay flattery to the People of Athens because he knows that he must betake himself to Athens and win or lose his case at the bar, not of any stray set of judges, but of the sovereign People itself, such being the law and custom at Athens. He is compelled to behave as a suppliant in the courts of justice, and when some juryman comes into court, to grasp his hand. For this reason, therefore, the allies find themselves more and more in the position of slaves to the people of Athens.

2. As to the heavy infantry, an arm the deficiency of which at Athens is well recognized, this is how the matter stands. They recognize the fact that, in reference to the hostile power, they are themselves inferior, and must be, even if their heavy infantry were more numerous. But relatively to the allies, who bring in the tribute, their strength even on land is enormous. And they are persuaded that their heavy infantry is sufficient for all purposes, provided they retain this superiority. Apart from all else, to a certain extent fortune must be held responsible for the actual condition. The subjects of a power which is dominant by land have it open to them to form contingents from several small states and to muster in force for battle. But with the subjects of a naval power it is different. As far as they are groups of islanders it is impossible for their states to meet together for united action, for the sea lies between them, and the dominant power is master of the sea. And even if it were possible for them to assemble in some single island unobserved, they would only do so to perish by famine. And as to the states subject to Athens which are not islanders, but situated on the continent, the larger are held in check by need and the small ones absolutely by fear, since there is no state in existence which does not depend upon imports and exports, and these she will forfeit if she does not lend a willing ear to those who are masters by sea. In the next place, a power dominant by sea can do certain things which a land power is debarred from doing; as, for instance, ravage the territory of a superior, since it is always possible to coast along to some point, where either there is no hostile force to deal with or merely a small body; and in case of an advance in force on the part of the enemy they can take to their ships and sail away. Such a performance is attended with less difficulty than that experienced by the relieving force on land. Again, it is open to a power so dominating by sea to leave its own territory and sail off on as long a voyage as you please. Whereas the land power cannot place more than a few days' journey between itself and its own territory, for marches are slow affairs; and it is not possible for an army on the march to have food supplies to last for any great length of time. Such an army must either march through friendly territory or it must force a way by victory in battle. The voyager meanwhile has it in his power to disembark at any point

where he finds himself in superior force, or, at the worst, to coast by until he reaches either a friendly district or an enemy too weak to resist. Again, those diseases to which the fruits of the earth are liable as visitations from heaven fall severely on a land power, but are scarcely felt by the naval power, for such sicknesses do not visit the whole earth everywhere at once. So that the ruler of the sea can get in supplies from a thriving district. And if one may descend to more trifling particulars, it is to this same lordship of the sea that the Athenians owe the discovery, in the first place, of many of the luxuries of life through intercourse with other countries. So that the choice things of Sicily and Italy, of Cyprus and Egypt and Lydia, of Pontus (= the Black Sea) or Peloponnese, or wherever else it be, are all swept, as it were, into one center, and all owing, as I say, to their maritime empire. And again, in process of listening to every form of speech, they have selected this from one place and that from another—for themselves. So much so that while the rest of the Greeks employ each pretty much their own peculiar mode of speech, habit of life, and style of dress, the Athenians have adopted a composite type, to which all sections of Hellas, and the foreigner alike, have contributed.

As regards sacrifices and temples and festivals and sacred enclosures, the People sees that it is not possible for every poor citizen to do sacrifice and hold festival, or to set up temples and to inhabit a large and beautiful city. But it has hit upon a means of meeting the difficulty. They sacrifice—that is, the whole state sacrifices—at the public cost a large number of victims; but it is the People that keeps holiday and distributes the victims by lot among its members. Rich men have in some cases private gymnasia and baths with dressing-rooms, but the People takes care to have built at the public cost a number of palaestras, dressing-rooms, and bathing establishments for its own special use, and the mob gets the benefit of the majority of these, rather than the select few or the well-to-do.

As to wealth, the Athenians are exceptionally placed with regard to Greek and foreign communities alike, in their ability to hold it. For, given that some state or other is rich in timber for shipbuilding, where is it to find a market for the product except by persuading the ruler of the sea? Or, suppose the wealth of some state or other to consist of iron, or maybe of bronze, or of linen yarn, where will it find a market except by permission of the supreme maritime power? Yet these are the very things, you see, which I need for my ships. Timber I must have from one, and from another iron, from a third bronze, from a fourth linen yarn, from a fifth wax. Besides which they will not suffer their antagonists in those parts, to carry these products elsewhere, or they will cease to use the sea. Accordingly I, without one stroke of labor, extract from the land and possess all these good things, thanks to my supremacy on the sea; while not a single other state possesses the two of them. Not timber, for instance, and yarn together, the same city. But where yarn is abundant, the soil will be light and devoid of timber. And in the same way bronze and iron will not be products of the same city. And so for the rest, never two, or at best three, in one state, but one thing here and another thing there. Moreover, above and beyond what has been said, the coastline of every mainland presents, either some jutting promontory, or adjacent island, or narrow strait of some sort, so that those who are masters of the sea can come to moorings at one of these points and wreak vengeance on the inhabitants of the mainland.

The Economic Advantages of Democracy

3. I repeat that my position concerning the constitution of the Athenians is this: the type of constitution is not to my taste, but given that a democratic form of government has been agreed upon, they do seem to me to go the right way to preserve the democracy by the adoption of the particular type which I have set forth.

But there are other objections brought, as I am aware, against the Athenians, by certain people, and to this effect. It not seldom happens, they tell us, that a man is unable to transact a piece of business with the council or the People, even if he sit waiting a whole year. Now this does happen at Athens, and for no other reason save that, owing to the immense mass of affairs, they are unable to work off all the business on hand and dismiss the applicants. And how in the world should they be able, considering in the first place that they, the Athenians, have more festivals to celebrate than any other state throughout the length and breadth of Greece? (*During these festivals, of course, the transaction of any sort of affairs of state is still more out of the question.*) In the next place, only consider the number of cases they have to decide, what with private suits and public causes and scrutinies of accounts, more than the whole of the rest of mankind put together; while the council of elders has multifarious points to advise upon concerning peace and war, concerning ways and means, concerning the framing and passing of laws, and concerning the matters affecting the state perpetually occurring, and endless questions touching the allies; besides the receipt of the tribute, the superintendence of dockyards and temples. Can, I ask again, any one find it at all surprising that, with all these affairs on their hands, they are unequal to doing business with all the world?

But some people tell us that if the applicant will only address himself to the senate or the People with a bribe in his hand he will do a good stroke of business. And for my part I am free to confess to these gainsayers that a good many things may be done at Athens by dint of money; and I will add, that a good many more still might be done, if the money flowed still more freely and from more pockets. One thing, however, I know full well, that as to transacting with every one of these applicants all he wants, the state could not do it, not even if all the gold and silver in the world were the inducement offered.

Here are some of the cases which have to be decided on. Some one fails to fit out a ship: judgment must be given. Another puts up a building on a piece of public land: again judgment must be given. Or, to take another class of cases: adjudication has to be made between the patrons of choruses for the Dionysia, the Thargelia, the Panathenaea, the Prometheia, and the

Hephaestia, year after year. Also as between the trierarchs, 400 of whom are appointed each year, of these, too, any who choose must have their cases adjudicated on, year after year. But that is not all. There are various magistrates to examine and approve and decide between; there are orphans whose status must be examined; and guardians of prisoners to appoint. These, be it borne in mind, are all matters of yearly occurrence; while at intervals there are exemptions and abstentions from military service which call for adjudication, or in connection with some other extraordinary misdemeanor, some case of outrage and violence of an exceptional character, or some charge of impiety. A whole string of others I simply omit; I am content to have named the most important part with the exception of the assessments of tribute which occur, as a rule, at intervals of four years.

There is another point in which it is sometimes felt that the Athenians are ill advised, in their adoption, namely, of the less respectable party, in a state divided by faction. But if so, they do it advisedly. If they chose the more respectable, they would be adopting those whose views and interests differ from their own, for there is no state in which the best element is friendly to the people. It is the worst element which in every state favors the democracy—on the principle that like favors like. It is simple enough then. The Athenians choose what is most akin to themselves. Also on every occasion on which they have attempted to side with the better classes, it has not fared well with them, but within a short interval the democratic party has been enslaved, as for instance in Boeotia; or, as when they chose the aristocrats of the Milesians, and within a short time these revolted and cut the people to pieces; or, as when they chose the Lacedaemonians as against the Messenians, and within a short time the Lacedaemonians subjugated the Messenians and went to war against Athens.

I seem to overhear a retort, "No one, of course, is deprived of his civil rights at Athens unjustly." My answer is, that there are some who are unjustly deprived of their civil rights, though the cases are certainly rare. But it will take more than a few to attack the democracy at Athens, since you may take it as an established fact, it is not the man who has lost his civil rights justly that takes the matter to heart, but the victims, if any, of injustice. But how in the world can any one imagine that many are in a state of civil disability at Athens, where the People and the holders of office are one and the same? It is from iniquitous exercise of office, from iniquity exhibited either in speech or action, and the like circumstances, that citizens are punished with deprivation of civil rights in Athens. Due reflection on these matters will serve to dispel the notion that there is any danger at Athens from persons visited with disfranchisement.

2. ATHENS AND HER SUBJECTS: THE CASE OF ERYTHRAE

Aristotle and "The Old Oligarch" clearly illustrate the intimate involvement of Athenians of all social classes in the ongoing management of the Athenian Empire. A rare insight into the situation   The Erythrae Decree *of Athens' allies is provided by the so-called Erythrae Decree. Erythrae, a Greek city on the west coast of modern Turkey, overthrew its Persian-supported tyrant in the mid-450s B.C. and joined the Delian League. The Athenian decree translated here is essentially the "constitution" of the new Erythraean democracy.[6]*

. . . [*So and so*] made the motion. The Erythraeans are to bring sacrificial victims to the Great Panathenaea. The victims are to be worth not less than three minas and the sacrificers are to allocate to each of the Erythraeans who may be present a portion of the meat worth one drachma. If the sacrificial victims that are brought are not worth three minas as has been prescribed, the sacrificers are to buy sacrificial victims and the costs are to be assigned to the Erythraean people. As for the meat, anyone who wishes may take some.

The Council of the Erythraeans, which is to be chosen by the lot, shall number 120 men. Each person who is designated by lot shall undergo scrutiny in the Council of the Erythraeans. No one may be a councilor who is less than 30 years of age, nor may a foreigner be a councilor. Convicted violators shall be liable to prosecution. No one may be a councilor more than once every four years. The [*Athenian*] Overseers and garrison commander shall now conduct the allocation and establish the Council, but in the future the Council and the garrison commander shall do it. Before entering office, each of those who are to serve as councilors for the Erythraeans shall swear an oath by Zeus, Apollo, and Demeter, invoking destruction on himself if he swears falsely and on his children, and he shall swear the oath over burning victims. Each councilor shall serve according to the established law. If he does not, he shall pay a fine of one thousand drachmas and pay not less to the Erythraean people. The Erythraean Council shall swear the following oath:

> I will be the best and most just councilor that I can for the Erythraean people and the Athenians and the allies, and I will not revolt from the Athenian people or from the allies of the Athenians, neither on my own initiative nor persuaded by another. Nor will I defect on my own initiative or persuaded by anyone else, nor will I welcome back on my own initiative or persuaded by anyone else any of those who fled into exile to the Persians without the approval of the Athenians and the people, nor will I drive into exile any of those who remain in Erythrae without the approval of the Athenians and the people.
>
> If any Erythraean kills another Erythraean, let him die if he is convicted. But if he goes into exile, let him be exiled from the whole Athenian alliance, and let his property be confiscated by the Erythraean people. And if anyone is convicted of seeking to betray Erythrae to the tyrants, let him and his children be killed with impunity. But if his children are supporters of the Erythraean people and the Athenians, they shall be acquitted, and, after having forfeited all of the property of their condemned father, let them regain half of that property and let the other half become public property.

---

[6] From *Inscriptiones Graecae* 1².10.

Figure 5.2 Built in the mid-fifth century B.C. on a low hill overlooking the agora that was the site of metalworking establishments, the temple of Hephaestus, patron god of craftsmen, marked the beginning of the great program of temple building at Athens that found its climax in the Parthenon and the other temples on the Acropolis. The excellent preservation of the temple of Hephaestus is due to its consecration as the church of St. George in the seventh century A.D. Photo by Stanley Burstein.

3. IMPERIAL IDEOLOGY: PERICLES' FUNERAL ORATION

No systematic defense of the Athenian democracy comparable to the critique of "The Old Oligarch" survives. However, it was traditional for leading Athenian politicians to praise Athens and her achievements on one occasion, namely, the public funeral for those who had died fighting for the city. The most famous such speech was delivered in 431 B.C. by Pericles, one of the chief architects of the Athenian empire, in honor of those killed during the first year of the Peloponnesian War. The only extant record of this speech is contained in Thucydides' History of the Peloponnesian War. Although scholars dispute the faithfulness of Thucydides' version to what Pericles actually said, it does provide a vivid image of Athens and her democratic ideals at the peak of her imperial power.[7]

Thucydides, *The History of the Peloponnesian War*

Athens and Her Dead

35. "Most of those who have spoken here before me have commended the lawgiver who added this oration to our other funeral customs; it seemed to

[7] From Thucydides, *The History of the Peloponnesian War* 2.35–46, trans. B. Jowett (Oxford, 1900) (modified).

them a worthy thing that such an honor should be given at their burial to the dead who have fallen on the field of battle. But I should have preferred that, when men's deeds have been brave, they should be honored in deed only, and with such an honor as this public funeral, which you are now witnessing. Then the reputation of many would not have been imperiled on the eloquence or want of eloquence of one, and their virtues believed or not as he spoke well or ill. For it is difficult to say neither too little nor too much; and even moderation is apt not to give the impression of truthfulness. The friend of the dead who knows the facts is likely to think that the words of the speaker fall short of his knowledge and of his wishes; another who is not so well informed, when he hears of anything which surpasses his own powers, will be envious and will suspect exaggeration. Mankind are tolerant of the praises of others so long as each hearer thinks that he can do as well or nearly as well himself, but, when the deed is beyond him, jealousy is aroused and he begins to be incredulous. However, since our ancestors have set the seal of their approval upon the practice, I must obey, and to the utmost of my power shall endeavor to satisfy the wishes and beliefs of all who hear me.

36. "I will speak first of our ancestors, for it is right and becoming that now, when we are lamenting the dead, a tribute should be paid to their memory. There has never been a time when they did not inhabit this land, which by their valor they have handed down from generation to generation, and we have received from them a free state. But if they were worthy of praise, still more were our fathers, who added to their inheritance, and after many a struggle transmitted to us their sons this great empire. And we ourselves assembled here to-day, who are still most of us in the vigor of life, have chiefly done the work of improvement, and have richly endowed our city with all things, so that she is sufficient for herself both in peace and war. Of the military exploits by which our various possessions were acquired, or of the energy with which we or our fathers drove back the tide of war, Greek or barbarian, I will not speak; for the tale would be long and is familiar to you. But before I praise the dead, I should like to point out by what principles of action we rose to power, and under what institutions and through what manner of life our empire became great. For I conceive that such thoughts are not unsuited to the occasion, and that this numerous assembly of citizens and strangers may profitably listen to them.

Athenian Democracy: "Under What Institutions Our Empire Became Great"

37. "Our form of government does not enter into rivalry with the institutions of others. We do not copy our neighbors, but are an example to them. It is true that we are called a democracy, for the administration is in the hands of the many and not of the few. But while the law secures equal justice to all alike in their private disputes, the claim of excellence is also recognized; and when a citizen is in any way distinguished, he is preferred to the public service, not as a matter of privilege, but as the reward of merit. Neither is

poverty a bar, but a man may benefit his country whatever be the obscurity of his condition. There is no exclusiveness in our public life, and in our private lives we are not suspicious of one another, nor angry with our neighbor if he does what he likes; we do not put on sour looks at him which, though harmless, are not pleasant. While we are thus unconstrained in our private affairs, a spirit of reverence pervades our public acts; we are prevented from doing wrong by respect for the magistrates and for the laws, having an especial regard to those which are ordained for the protection of the injured, whether they are actual statutes or belong to those unwritten laws which cannot be broken without bringing public disgrace upon their transgressors.

38. "And we have not forgotten to provide for our weary spirits many relaxations from toil; we have regular games and sacrifices throughout the year; at home the style of our life is refined; and the delight which we daily feel in all these things helps to banish melancholy. Because of the greatness of our city the fruits of the whole earth flow in upon us; so that we enjoy the goods of other countries as freely as of our own.

40. "For we are lovers of the beautiful, yet with economy, and we cultivate the mind without loss of manliness. Wealth we employ, not for talk and ostentation, but when there is a real use for it. To admit poverty with us is no disgrace; the true disgrace is in doing nothing to avoid it. An Athenian citizen does not neglect the state because he takes care of his own household; and even those of us who are engaged in business have a very fair idea of politics. We alone regard a man who takes no interest in public affairs, not as a harmless, but as a useless character; and if few of us are originators, we are all sound judges of a policy. The great impediment to action is, in our opinion, not discussion, but the want of that knowledge which is gained by discussion preparatory to action. For we have a peculiar power of thinking before we act and of acting too, whereas other men are courageous from ignorance but hesitate upon reflection. And they are surely to be esteemed the bravest spirits who, having the clearest sense both of the pains and pleasures of life, do not on that account shrink from danger. In doing good, again, we are unlike others; we make our friends by conferring, not by receiving favors. Now he who confers a favor is the firmer friend, because he aims by kindness to keep alive the memory of an obligation; while the recipient is less warm in his feelings, because he knows that in requiting another's generosity he will not be winning gratitude but only paying a debt. We alone do good to our neighbors not upon a calculation of interest, but in the confidence of freedom and in a frank and fearless spirit.

41. "To sum up: I say that Athens is the school of Greece, and that the individual Athenian in his own person seems to have the power of adapting himself to the most varied forms of action with the utmost versatility and grace. This is no passing and idle word, but truth and fact; and the assertion is verified by the position to which these qualities have raised the state. For in the hour of trial Athens alone among her contemporaries is superior to the report of her. No enemy who comes against her is indignant at the

reverses which he sustains at the hands of such a city; no subject complains that his masters are unworthy of him. And we shall assuredly not be without witnesses: there are mighty monuments of our power which will make us the wonder of this and of succeeding ages; we shall not need the praises of Homer or of any other panegyrist whose poetry may please for the moment, although his representation of the facts will not bear the light of day. For we have compelled every land and every sea to open a path for our valor, and have everywhere planted eternal memorials of our friendship and of our enmity. Such is the city for whose sake these men nobly fought and died; they could not bear the thought that she might be taken from them; and every one of us who survive should gladly toil on her behalf.

The Nature of True Heroism: "The Whole Earth Is the Sepulchre of Famous Men."

42. "I have dwelt on the greatness of Athens because I want to show you that we are contending for a higher prize than those who enjoy none of these privileges, and to establish by clear proof the merit of these men whom I am now commemorating. Their loftiest praise has already been spoken. For in magnifying the city I have magnified them and men like them whose virtues made her glorious. And of how few Greeks can it be said as of them, that their deeds when weighed in the balance have been found equal to their fame. It seems to me that a death such as theirs has been gives the true meaning of a man's worth; it may be the first revelation of his virtues, but is at any rather their final seal. For even those who come up short in other ways may justly plead the valor with which they have fought for their country; they have blotted out the evil with the good, and have benefited the state more by their public services than they have injured it by their private actions. None of these men were enervated by wealth or hesitated to resign the pleasures of life; none of them put off the evil day in the hope, natural to poverty, that man, thought poor, may one day become rich. But, deeming that the punishment of their enemies was sweeter than any of these things, and that they could fall in no nobler cause, they determined at the hazard of their lives to be honourably avenged, and let their wishes and hopes wait. They resigned to hope their unknown chance of happiness; but in the face of death they resolved to rely on themselves alone. And when the moment came they were ready to resist and suffer, rather than to fly and save their lives. They ran away from the word of dishonor, but on the battlefield their feet stood fast, and in an instant, at the height of their fortune, they passed away from the scene, not of their fear, but of their glory.

43. "Such was the end of these men; they were worthy of Athens, and the living need not desire to have a more heroic spirit, although they may pray for a less fatal outcome for themselves. The value of such a spirit is not to be expressed in words. Any one can discourse to you for ever about the advantages of a brave defence which you know already. But instead of listening to him I would have you day by day fix your eyes upon the greatness of Athens, until you become filled with love of her; and when

you are impressed by the spectacle of glory, reflect that this empire has been acquired by men who knew their duty and had the courage to do it, who in the hour of conflict had the fear of dishonor always present to them, and who, if ever they failed in an enterprise, would not allow their virtues to be lost to their country, but freely gave their lives to her as the fairest offering which they could present at her feast. The sacrifice which they collectively made was individually repaid to them; for they received again each one for himself a praise which grows not old, and the noblest of all sepulchres—I speak not of that in which their remains are laid, but of that in which they glory survives, and is proclaimed always and on every fitting occasion. For the whole earth is the sepulchre of famous men; not only are they commemorated by columns and inscriptions in their own country, but in foreign lands there dwells also an unwritten memorial of them, cut not on stone but in the hearts of men. Make them your examples, and esteeming courage to be freedom and freedom to be happiness, do not weight too nicely the perils of war. The unfortunate who has no hope of a change for the better has less reason to thrown away his life than the prosperous who, if he survive, is always liable to change for the worse, and to whom any accidental fall makes the most serious difference. To a man of spirit, cowardice and disaster coming together are far more bitter than death striking him unperceived at a time when he is full of courage and animated by the general hope.

Advice to the Living

44. "Therefore I do not now commiserate the parents of the dead who stand here; I would rather comfort them. You know that your life has been passed amid manifold vicissitudes; and that they may be deemed fortunate who have gained most honor, whether an honorable death like theirs, or an honorable sorrow like yours, and whose days have been so ordered that the term of their happiness is likewise the term of their life. I know how hard it is to make you feel this, when the good fortune of others will too often remind you of the gladness which once lightened your hearts. And sorrow is felt at the want of those blessings, not which a man never knew, but which were a part of his life before they were taken from him. Some of you are of an age at which they may hope to have other children, and they ought to bear their sorrow better; not only will the children who may hereafter be born make them forget their own lost ones, but the city will be doubly a gainer. She will not be left desolate, and she will be safer. For a man's counsel cannot have equal weight or worth, when he alone has no children to risk in the general danger. To those of you who have passed their prime, I say, 'Congratulate yourselves that you have been happy during the greater part of your days; remember that your life of sorrow will not last long, and be comforted by the glory of those who are gone. For the love of honor alone is ever young, and not riches, as some say, but honor is the delight of men when they are old and useless.'

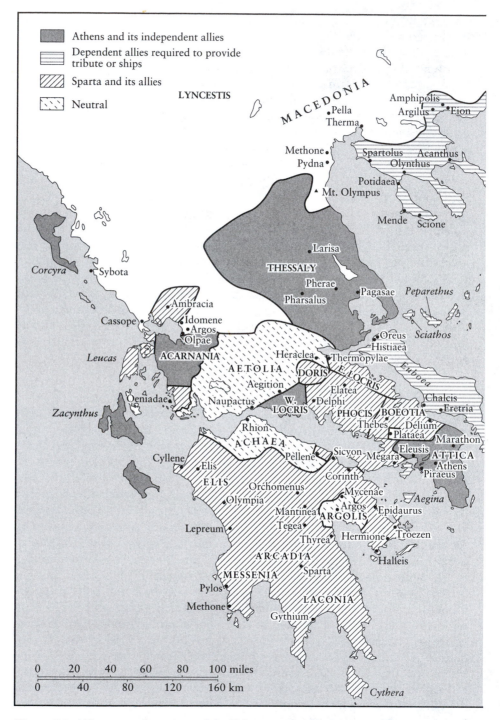

Figure 5.3 Alliances at the outset of the Peloponnesian War.

180

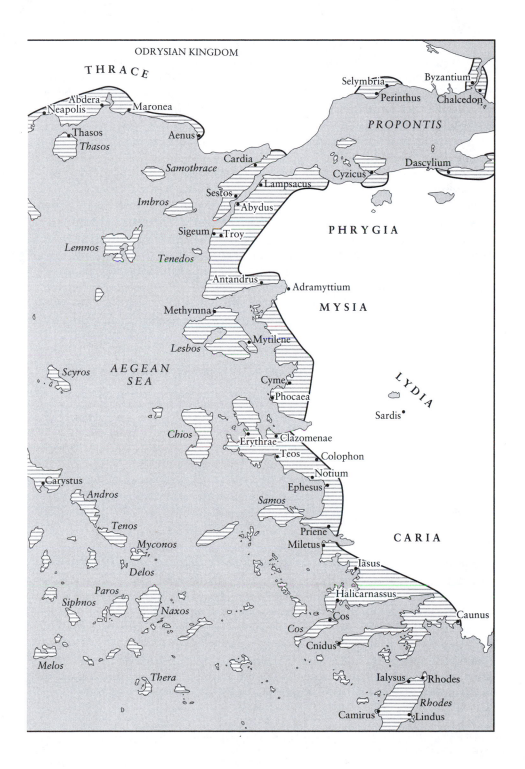

ODRYSIAN KINGDOM

THRACE

Abdera
Neapolis
Maronea

Thasos
Thasos

Aenus

Samothrace

Cardia

Imbros

Sestos
Abydus

Lampsacus

Selymbria
Perinthus

Byzantium
Chalcedon

PROPONTIS

Cyzicus

Dascylium

Sigeum • Troy

PHRYGIA

Lemnos

Tenedos

Antandrus

Adramyttium

MYSIA

Methymna

Lesbos

Mytilene

AEGEAN
SEA

Scyros

Cyme

Phocaea

LYDIA

Sardis

Chios

Erythrae • Clazomenae
Teos
Colophon
Notium

Carystus

Andros

Tenos

Myconos

Delos

Samos

Ephesus

Priene
Miletus

CARIA

Iasus

Paros
Siphnos

Naxos

Halicarnassus
Cos
Cos

Caunus

Cnidus

Melos

Thera

Ialysus • Rhodes

Rhodes

Camirus

Lindus

45. "To you who are the sons and brothers of the departed, I see that the struggle to emulate them will be an arduous one. For all men praise the dead, and, however pre-eminent your virtue may be, hardly will you be thought, I do not say to equal, but even to approach them. The living have their rivals and detractors, but when a man is out of the way, the honor and good-will which he receives is unalloyed. And if I am to speak of womanly virtues to those of you who will henceforth be widows, let me sum them up in one short admonition: To a woman not to show more weakness than is natural to her sex is a great glory, and not to be talked about for good or for evil among men.

46. "I have paid the required tribute, in obedience to the law, making use of such fitting words as I had. The tribute of deeds has been paid in part; for the dead have been honorably interred, and it remains only that their children should be maintained at the public charge until they are grown up: this is the solid prize with which, as with a garland, Athens crowns her sons living and dead, after a struggle like theirs. For where the rewards of virtue are greatest, there the noblest citizens are enlisted in the service of the state. And now, when you have duly lamented, every one his own dead, you may depart."

4. THE BLOODY REVOLUTION AT CORCYRA: "WAR IS A HARD MASTER"

Thucydides, *The History of the Peloponnesian War*

Support for democratic factions, as we have seen in the "The Old Oligarch" and Erythrae Decree, was a characteristic feature of Athenian policy during the decades prior to the outbreak of the Peloponnesian War in 431 B.C. Sparta, likewise, intervened in the internal affairs of other cities wherever it could, particularly in the Peloponnese. In this passage, the historian Thucydides gives a dramatic account of how in 427 B.C. this aspect of the rivalry between Athens and Sparta led to the total disruption of normal social and political relations in the city of Corcyra on the island of Corfu in the Adriatic Sea.[8]

79. The Corcyraeans, who were afraid that the victorious enemy would sail to the city and have recourse to some decisive measure, such as taking on board the prisoners in the island, conveyed them back to the temple of Hera and guarded the city. But the Peloponnesians, although they had won the battle, did not venture to attack the city, but returned to their station on the mainland with thirteen Corcyraean ships which they had taken. On the next day they still hesitated, although there was great panic and confusion among the inhabitants. It is said that Brasidas advised Alcidas to make the attempt, but he had not an equal vote with him. So they only disembarked at the promontory of Leucimne and ravaged the country.

---

[8] From Thucydides, *The History of the Peloponnesian War* 3.79–83, 85, trans. B. Jowett (Oxford, 1900) (modified).

80. Meanwhile the people of Corcyra, dreading that the fleet of the Peloponnesians would attack them, held a parley with the other faction, especially with the suppliants, in the hope of saving the city; they even persuaded some of them to go on board the fleet; for the Corcyraeans still contrived to man 30 ships. But the Peloponnesians, after devastating the land till about midday, retired. And at nightfall the approach of 60 Athenian vessels was signaled to them from Leucas. These had been sent by the Athenians under the command of Eurymedon, the son of Thucles, when they heard of the revolution and of the intended expedition of Alcidas to Corcyra.

81. The Peloponnesians set out that very night on their way home, keeping close to the land and transporting the ships over the Leucadian isthmus, that they might not be seen sailing round. When the Corcyraeans perceived that the Athenian fleet was approaching while that of the enemy had disappeared, they took the Messenian troops, who had hitherto been outside the walls, into the city and ordered the ships which they had manned to sail round into the Hyllaic harbor. These proceeded on their way. Meanwhile they killed any of their enemies whom they caught in the city. On the arrival of the ships, they disembarked those whom they had induced to go on board and killed them; they also went to the temple of Hera and, persuading about 50 of the suppliants to stand their trial, condemned them all to death. The majority would not come out, and, when they saw what was going on, destroyed one another in the enclosure of the temple where they were, except a few who hung themselves on trees or put an end to their own lives in any other way that they could. And during the seven days which Eurymedon after his arrival remained with his 60 ships, the Corcyraeans continued slaughtering those of their fellow-citizens whom they deemed their enemies; they professed to punish them for their designs against the democracy, but in fact some were killed from motives of personal enmity, and some, because money was owing to them, by the hands of their debtors. Every form of death was to be seen; and everything, and more than everything, that commonly happens in revolutions, happened then. The father slew the son, and the suppliants were torn from the temples and slain near them; some of them were even walled up in the temple of Dionysus, and there perished. To such extremes of cruelty did revolution go; and this seemed to be the worst of revolutions, because it was the first.

82. For not long afterwards nearly the whole Greek world was in commotion; in every city the Greek chiefs of the democracy and of the oligarchy were struggling, the one to bring in the Athenians, the other the Spartans. Now in time of peace, men would have had no excuse for introducing either, and no desire to do so; but, when they were at war, the introduction of a foreign alliance on one side or the other to the hurt of their enemies and the advantage of themselves was easily effected by the dissatisfied party. And revolution brought upon the cities of Greece many terrible calamities, such as have been and always will be while human nature remains the same, but which are more or less aggravated and differ in character with every new

combination of circumstances. In peace and prosperity both states and individuals are actuated by higher motives, because they do not fall under the dominion of imperious necessities; but war, which takes away the comfortable provision of daily life, is a hard master and tends to assimilate men's characters to their conditions.

When troubles had once begun in the cities, those who followed carried the revolutionary spirit further and further and determined to outdo the report of all who had preceded them by the ingenuity of their enterprises and the atrocity of their revenges. The meaning of words had no longer the same relation to things but was changed by them as they thought proper. Reckless daring was held to be loyal courage; prudent delay was the excuse of a coward; moderation was the disguise of unmanly weakness; to know everything was to do nothing. Fanaticism was the true quality of a man. Cautious plotting, a justifiable means of self-defense. The advocate of extreme measures was always trusted, and his opponent suspected. He who succeeded in a plot was deemed knowing, but a still greater master in craft was he who detected one. On the other hand, he who plotted from the first to have nothing to do with plots was a breaker up of parties and acting in fear of the enemy. In a word, he who could outstrip another in a bad action was applauded, and so was he who encouraged to evil one who had no idea of it. The tie of party was stronger than the tie of blood, because a partisan was more ready to dare without asking why. (For party associations are not based upon any established law, nor do they seek the public good; they are formed in defiance of the laws and from self-interest.) The seal of good faith was not divine law, but fellowship in crime. If an enemy when he was in the ascendant offered fair words, the opposite party received them, not in a generous spirit, but by a jealous watchfulness of his actions. Revenge was dearer than self-preservation. Any agreements sworn to by either party, when they could do nothing else, were binding as long as both were powerless. But he who on a favorable opportunity first took courage, and struck at his enemy when he saw him off his guard, had greater pleasure in a perfidious than he would have had in an open act of revenge; he congratulated himself that he had taken the safer course, and also that he had overreached his enemy and gained the prize of superior ability. In general the dishonest more easily gain credit for cleverness than the simple for goodness; men take a pride in the one but are ashamed of the other.

The cause of all these evils was the love of power, originating in avarice and ambition, and the party-spirit which is engendered by them when men are fairly embarked in a contest. For the leaders on either side used specious names, the one party professing to uphold the constitutional equality of the many, the other the wisdom of an aristocracy, while they made the public interests, to which in name they were devoted, in reality their prize. Striving in every way to overcome each other, they committed the most monstrous crimes; yet even these were surpassed by the magnitude of their revenges which they pursued to the very utmost, neither party observing any definite limits of either justice or public expediency, but both alike making the caprice of the moment their law. Either by the help of an unrighteous sentence, or grasping power with the strong hand, they were eager to satiate the impatience of party-spirit. Neither faction cared for religion; but any fair pretence which succeeded in effecting some odious purpose was greatly lauded. And the citizens who were of neither party fell a prey to both; either they were disliked because they held aloof, or men were jealous of their surviving.

83. Thus revolution gave birth to every form of wickedness in Greece. The simplicity which is so large an element in a noble nature was laughed to scorn and disappeared. An attitude of perfidious antagonism everywhere prevailed; for there was no word binding enough, nor oath terrible enough to reconcile enemies. Each man was strong only in the conviction that nothing was secure; he must look to his own safety and could not afford to trust others. Inferior intellects generally succeeded best. For, aware of their own deficiencies, and fearing the capacity of their opponents, for whom they were no match in powers of speech, and whose subtle wits were likely to anticipate them in contriving evil, they struck boldly and at once. But the cleverer sort, presuming in their arrogance that they would be aware in time, and disdaining to act when they could think, were taken off their guard and easily destroyed. . . .

85. Such were the passions which the citizens of Corcyra, first of all Greeks, displayed towards one another. After the departure of Eurymedon and the Athenian fleet the surviving oligarchs, who to the number of 500 had escaped, seized certain forts on the mainland and thus became masters of the territory on the opposite coast which belonged to Corcyra. Thence issuing forth, they plundered the Corcyraeans in the island and did much harm, so that there was a great famine in the city. They also sent ambassadors to Sparta and Corinth, begging that they might be restored, but, failing of their object, they procured boats and auxiliaries, and passed over to Corcyra, about 600 in all; then, burning their boats that they might have no hope but in the conquest of the island, they went into Mount Istone, and building a fort there, became masters of the country to the ruin of the inhabitants of the city.

5. "JUSTICE ENTERS THE DISCUSSION ONLY WHEN THE PARTIES ARE EQUAL": THE MELIAN DIALOGUE

In 416 B.C. Athens attacked the island of Melos, a colony of Sparta that, according to Thucydides, had been neutral in the Peloponnesian War. After a brief siege, the Athenians captured the city, executed its male population, sold the rest of the Melians into slavery, and resettled the island with their own citizens. A hundred years later the fate of Melos was still cited as a prime example of the excesses of Athenian imperialism. In the following selection Thucydides uses the negotiations between the Athenians and the Melians as the occasion to analyze the nature and application of imperial power. Although it is doubtful that either the Athenians or Melians used the exact arguments ascribed to them by Thucydides, the "Melian Dialogue," with its scorn for arguments based

Thucydides, *The History of the Peloponnesian War*

on religious tradition and its invocation of the "Laws of Nature," is a remarkable example of fifth-century B.C. *rationalism applied to the analysis of political action.*[9]

84. In the ensuing summer, Alcibiades sailed to Argos with twenty ships and seized any of the Argives who were still suspected to be of the Spartan faction, 300 in number; and the Athenians deposited them in the subject islands near at hand. The Athenians next made an expedition against the island of Melos with 30 ships of their own, six Chian, and two Lesbian, 1,200 hoplites and 300 archers besides twenty mounted archers of their own, and about 1,500 hoplites furnished by their allies in the islands. The Melians are colonists of the Sparta who would not submit to Athens like the other island-ers. At first they were neutral and took no part. But when the Athenians tried to coerce them by ravaging their lands, they were driven into open hostilities. The generals, Cleomedes the son of Lycomedes and Tisias the son of Tisimachus, encamped with the Athenian forces on the island. But before they did the country any harm, they sent envoys to negotiate with the Melians. Instead of bringing these envoys before the people, the Melians desired them to explain their errand to the magistrates and to the chief men. They spoke as follows:

85. "Since we are not allowed to speak to the people, lest, no doubt, they should be deceived by seductive and unanswerable arguments which they would hear set forth in a single uninterrupted oration (for we are perfectly aware that this is what you mean in bringing us before a select few), you who are sitting here may as well make assurance yet surer. Let us have no set speeches at all, but do you reply to each several statement of which you disapprove, and criticize it at once. Say first of all how you like this mode of proceeding."

86. The Melian representatives answered: "The quiet interchange of explanations is a reasonable thing, and we do not object to that. But your warlike movements, which are present not only to our fears but to our eyes, seem to belie your words. We see that, although you may reason with us, you mean to be our judges, and that at the end of the discussion, if the justice of our cause prevail and we therefore refuse to yield, we may expect war; if we are convinced by you, slavery."

87. *Athenians*: No, but if you are only going to argue from fancies about the future, or if you meet us with any other purpose than that of looking your circumstances in the face and saving your city, we have done; but if this is your intention we will proceed.

88. *Melians*: It is an excusable and natural thing that men in our position should have much to say and should indulge in many fancies. But we admit

---

[9] From Thucydides, *The History of the Peloponnesian War* 5.84–116, trans. B. Jowett (Oxford, 1900) (modified).

that this conference has met to consider the question of our survival; and therefore let the argument proceed in the manner which you propose.

89. *Athenians*: Well, then, we Athenians will use no fine words; we will not go out of our way to prove at length that we have a right to rule because we overthrew the Persians, or that we attack you now because we are suffering any injury at your hands. We should not convince you if we did; nor must you expect to convince us by arguing that, although a colony of the Spartans, you have taken no part in their expeditions, or that you have never done us any wrong. But you and we should say what we really think, and aim only at what is possible, for we both alike know that into the discussion of human affairs the question of justice enters only where the pressure of necessity is equal, and that the powerful exact what they can and the weak grant what they must.

90. *Melians*: Well, then, since you set aside justice and invite us to speak of expediency, in our judgment it is certainly expedient that you should respect a principle which is for the common good; and that to every man when in peril a reasonable claim should be accounted a claim of right, and any plea which he is disposed to urge, even if failing of the point a little, should help his cause. Your interest in this principle is quite as great as ours, inasmuch as you, if you fall, will incur the heaviest vengeance and will be the most terrible example to mankind.

91. *Athenians*: The fall of our empire, if it should fall, is not an event to which we look forward with dismay; for ruling states such as Sparta are not cruel to their vanquished enemies. And we are fighting not so much against the Spartans as against our own subjects who may some day rise up and overcome their former masters. But this is a danger which you may leave to us. And we will now endeavor to show that we have come in the interests of our empire, and that in what we are about to say we are seeking only the preservation of your city. For we want to make you ours with the least trouble to ourselves, and it is for the interests of us both that you should not be destroyed.

92. *Melians*: It may be your interest to be our masters, but how can it be ours to be your slaves?

93. *Athenians*: To you the gain will be that by submission you will avert the worst; and we shall be all the richer for your preservation.

94. *Melians*: But must we be your enemies? Will you not receive us as friends if we are neutral and remain at peace with you?

95. *Athenians*: No, your enmity is not half so mischievous to us as your friendship; for the one is in the eyes of our subjects an argument of our power, the other of our weakness.

96. *Melians*: But are your subjects really unable to distinguish between states in which you have no concern and those that are chiefly your own colonies and in some cases have revolted and been subdued by you?

97. *Athenians*: Why, they do not doubt that both of them have a good deal to say for themselves on the score of justice, but they think that states like

yours are left free because they are able to defend themselves, and that we do not attack them because we dare not. So that your subjection will give us an increase of security as well as an extension of empire. For we are masters of the sea, and you who are islanders, and insignificant islanders too, must not be allowed to escape us.

98. *Melians*: But do you not recognize another danger? For, once more, since you drive us from the plea of justice and press upon us your doctrine of expediency, we must show you what is for our interest, and, if it be for yours also, may hope to convince you: Will you not be making enemies of all who are now neutrals? When they see how you are treating us, they will expect you some day to turn against them; and if so, are you not strengthening the enemies whom you already have and bringing upon you others who, if they could help, would never dream of being your enemies at all?

99. *Athenians*: We do not consider our really dangerous enemies to be any of the peoples inhabiting the mainland, who, secure in their freedom, may defer indefinitely any measures of precaution which they take against us, but islanders who, like you, happen to be under no control, and all who may be already irritated by the necessity of submission to our empire—these are our real enemies, for they are the most reckless and most likely to bring themselves as well as us into a danger which they cannot but foresee.

100. *Melians*: Surely then, if you and your subjects will brave all this risk, you to preserve your empire and they to be quit of it, how base and cowardly would it be in us, who retain our freedom, not to do and suffer anything rather than be your slaves?

101. *Athenians*: Not so, if you calmly reflect: for you are not fighting against equals to whom you cannot yield without disgrace, but you are taking counsel whether or not you shall resist an overwhelming force. The question is not one of honor but of prudence.

102. *Melians*: But we know that the fortune of war is sometimes impartial, and not always on the side of numbers. If we yield now, all is over; but if we fight, there is yet a hope that we may stand upright.

103. *Athenians*: Hope is a good comforter in the hour of danger, and when men have something else to depend upon, although hurtful, she is not ruinous. But when her spendthrift nature has induced them to stake their all, they see her as she is in the moment of their fall, and not till then. While the knowledge of her might enable them to beware of her, she never fails. You are weak and a single turn of the scale might be your ruin. Do not you be thus deluded; avoid the error of which so many are guilty, who, although they might still be saved if they would take the natural means, when visible grounds of confidence forsake them, have recourse to the invisible, to prophecies and oracles and the like, which ruin men by the hopes which they inspire in them.

104. *Melians*: We know only too well how hard the struggle must be against your power, and against fortune, if she does not mean to be impartial. Nevertheless we do not despair of fortune; for we hope to stand as high

as you in the favor of heaven, because we are righteous, and you against whom we contend are unrighteous; and we are satisfied that our deficiency in power will be compensated by the aid of our allies the Spartans; they cannot refuse to help us, if only because we are their kinsmen, and for the sake of their own honor. And therefore our confidence is not so utterly blind as you suppose.

105. *Athenians*: As for the gods, we expect to have quite as much of their favor as you: for we are not doing or claiming anything which goes beyond common opinion about divine or men's desires about human things. Of the gods we believe, and of men we know, that by a law of their nature wherever they can rule they will. This law was not made by us, and we are not the first who have acted upon it; we did but inherit it, and shall bequeath it to all time, and we know that you and all mankind, if you were as strong as we are, would do as we do. So much for the gods; we have told you why we expect to stand as high in their good opinion as you. And then as to the Spartans—when you imagine that out of very shame they will assist you, we admire the simplicity of your idea but we do not envy you the folly of it. The Spartans are exceedingly virtuous among themselves and according to their national standard of morality. But, in respect of their dealings with others, although many things might be said, a word is enough to describe them; of all men whom we know they are the most notorious for identifying what is pleasant with what is honorable, and what is expedient with what is just. But how inconsistent is such a character with your present blind hope of deliverance!

106. *Melians*: That is the very reason why we trust them; they will look to their interest and therefore will not be willing to betray the Melians, who are their own colonists, lest they should be distrusted by their friends in Hellas and play into the hands of their enemies.

107. *Athenians*: But do you not see that the path of expediency is safe, whereas justice and honor involve danger in practice, and such dangers the Lacedaemonians seldom care to face?

108. *Melians*: On the other hand, we think that whatever perils there may be, they will be ready to face them for our sakes and will consider danger less dangerous where we are concerned. For if they need to act we are close at hand, and they can better trust our loyal feeling because we are their kinsmen.

109. *Athenians*: Yes, but what encourages men who are invited to join in a conflict is clearly not the good-will of those who summon them to their side, but a decided superiority in real power. To this no men look more keenly than the Lacedaemonians; so little confidence have they in their own resources that they attack their neighbors only when they have numerous allies, and therefore they are not likely to find their way by themselves to an island when we are masters of the sea.

110. *Melians*: But they may send their allies: the Cretan sea is a large place; and the masters of the sea will have more difficulty in overtaking

vessels which want to escape than the pursued in escaping. If the attempt should fail they may invade Attica itself, and find their way to allies of yours whom Brasidas did not reach: and then you will have to fight, not for the conquest of a land in which you have no concern, but nearer home, for the preservation of your confederacy and of your own territory.

111. *Athenians*: Help may come from Sparta to you as it has come to others, and should you ever have actual experience of it, then you will know that never once have the Athenians retired from a siege through fear of a foe elsewhere. You told us that the safety of your city would be your first care, but we remark that, in this long discussion, not a word has been uttered by you which would give a reasonable man expectation of deliverance. Your strongest grounds are hopes deferred, and what power you have is not to be compared with that which is already arrayed against you. Unless after we have withdrawn, you mean to come, as even now you may, to a wiser conclusion, you are showing a great want of sense. For surely you cannot dream of flying to that false sense of honor which has been the ruin of so many when danger and dishonor were staring them in the face. Many men with their eyes still open to the consequences have found the word honor too much for them and have suffered a mere name to lure them on, until it has drawn down upon them real and irretrievable calamities; through their own folly they have incurred a worse dishonor than fortune would have inflicted upon them. If you are wise, you will not run this risk; you ought to see that there can be no disgrace in yielding to a great city which invites you to become her ally on reasonable terms, keeping your own land and merely paying tribute; and that you will certainly gain no honor if, having to choose between two alternatives, safety and war, you obstinately prefer the worse. To maintain our rights against equals, to be politic with superiors, and to be moderate towards inferiors is the path of safety. Reflect once more when we have withdrawn, and say to yourselves over and over again that you are deliberating about your one and only country, which may be saved or may be destroyed by a single decision.

112. The Athenians left the conference: the Melians, after consulting among themselves, resolved to persevere in their refusal and answered as follows, "Men of Athens, our resolution is unchanged, and we will not in a moment surrender that liberty which our city, founded 700 years ago, still enjoys; we will trust to the good-fortune which, by the favor of the gods, has hitherto preserved us, and for human help to the Spartans, and endeavor to save ourselves. We are ready however to be your friends, and the enemies neither of you nor of the Spartans, and we ask you to leave our country when you have made such a peace as may appear to be in the interest of both parties."

113. Such was the answer of the Melians; the Athenians, as they quitted the conference, spoke as follows, "Well, we must say, judging from the decision at which you have arrived, that you are the only men who deem the future to be more certain than the present, and regard things unseen as

already realized in your fond anticipation, and that the more you cast your-selves upon the Lacedaemonians and fortune, and hope, and trust them, the more complete will be your ruin."

114. The Athenian envoys returned to the army, and the generals, when they found that the Melians would not yield, immediately com-menced hostilities. They surrounded the town of Melos with a wall, dividing the work among the several contingents. They then left troops of their own and of their allies to keep guard both by land and by sea, and retired with the greater part of their army; the remainder carried on the blockade. 115. About the same time the Argives made an inroad into Phliasia and lost nearly 80 men, who were caught in an ambuscade by the Phliasians and the Argive exiles. The Athenian garrison in Pylos took much spoil from the Spartans; nevertheless the latter did not renounce the peace and go to war, but only notified by a proclamation that if any one of their own people had a mind to make reprisals on the Athenians he might. The Corinthians next declared war upon the Athenians on some private grounds, but the rest of the Peloponnesians did not join them. The Melians took that part of the Athenian wall which looked towards the agora by a night assault, killed a few men, and brought in as much grain and other necessaries as they could; they then retreated and remained inactive. After this the Athenians set a better watch. So the summer ended. 116. In the fol-lowing winter the Lacedaemonians had intended to make an expedition into the Argive territory, but finding that the sacrifices which they offered at the frontier were unfavorable, they returned home. The Argives, sus-pecting that the threatened invasion was instigated by citizens of their own, apprehended some of them; others, however, escaped. About the same time the Melians took another part of the Athenian wall, for the fortifications were insufficiently guarded. Whereupon the Athenians sent fresh troops, under the command of Philocrates the son of Demeas. The place was now closely invested, and there was treachery among the citi-zens themselves. So the Melians were induced to surrender at discretion. The Athenians thereupon put to death all who were of military age and made slaves of the women and children. They then colonized the island, sending thither 500 settlers of their own.

D. Opposition to the Peloponnesian War at Athens

The play Peace *was composed by Aristophanes for the festival of Dionysus in 421 B.C.* Lysistrata *was probably written for the Lenaea festival in 411 B.C. In both, the playwright attacks the propo-nents of the war and advocates a negotiated settlement between Athens and Sparta. In* Peace *the hero Trygaeus flies to heaven on a beetle to ask why the gods want to destroy Greece. He discovers that the gods have moved out of heaven, leaving the ogre War, who has buried Peace, in charge.*

Aristophanes, *Peace*

Trygaeus manages to unearth Peace and bring her back to Athens. The first reading here is the prayer that Trygaeus offers to her. In Lysistrata *the heroine by that name (Lysistrata means "disbander of armies") proposes a sex strike and the occupation of the Acropolis to control the funds necessary for the continuation of the war (second reading).*[10]

1. PRAYER TO PEACE

TRYGAEUS: Oh! Peace, mighty queen, venerated goddess, thou who presidest over choruses and weddings, deign to accept the sacrifices we offer thee.

SLAVE: Receive it, greatly honored mistress, and behave not like adulterous wives, who half open the door to entice men and draw back when they are stared at, only to appear once more when they're gone. But do not thou act like this to us.

TRYGAEUS: No, but like an honest woman, show thyself to thy worshippers, who have been pining for thee all these thirteen years. Hush the noise of battle, be a true Lysimacha[11] to us. Put an end to suspicions, to this claptrap that set us to defying one another. Cause the Greeks once more to taste the pleasant beverage of friendship and temper all hearts with the gentle feelings of forgiveness. Make excellent commodities flow to our markets, fine heads of garlic, early cucumbers, apples, pomegranates and nice little coats for the slaves. Make them bring geese, ducks, pigeons and larks from Boeotia and baskets of eels from Lake Copais. We shall rush to buy them, disputing their possession with Morychus, Teleas, Glaucetes (*all well-known politicians*), and every other glutton. Melanthius (*a rival playwright*) will arrive at the market last of all; they'll say, "No more eels, all sold!" and then he'll start groaning and exclaiming as in his monologue of *Medea*, "I am dying, I am dying! Alas! I have let those hidden in the beet (*i.e., the eels*) escape me!" And won't we laugh? These are the wishes, mighty goddess, which we pray thee to grant. (*To the Slave*) Take the knife and slaughter the sheep like a master cook.

SLAVE: But that's not right.

TRYGAEUS: Why not?

SLAVE: Surely blood cannot please Peace! Let us not spill blood on her altar.

TRYGAEUS: Oh, alright. Go and sacrifice the sheep in the house. . . .

2. LYSISTRATA'S SOLUTION TO WAR

Aristophanes,
Lysistrata

MAGISTRATE: And how, pray, would you women be able to sort out the present tangled mess and restore peace in all the cities of Greece?

LYSISTRATA: It's the easiest thing in the world!

[10] From Aristophanes, *Peace* 974–1022; *Lysistrata* 565–594.

[11] "Lysimacha" means "releaser from battles." It was the name of the current priestess of the goddess Athena Polias.

MAGISTRATE: How? I'm curious to know.

LYSISTRATA: It's like a ball of wool when it's all tangled, we pass the spindle across and through the skein, now this way, now that way. That's how we'll finish off the war. We'll send embassies hither and thither and everywhere to *dis*entangle matters!

MAGISTRATE: And is it with your yarn, and your skeins, and your spindles, you could settle so many bitter enmities, you silly women?

LYSISTRATA: If only you had common sense, you would always do in politics the same as we do with our yarn.

MAGISTRATE: How's that? I'd like to see.

LYSISTRATA: First we wash the yarn to separate the grease and filth; do the same with all bad citizens, sort them out and beat them out with sticks—they're the refuse of the city. Then for all such as clump and knot themselves together to snag government jobs and offices, we must card them thoroughly and pluck their heads; then to bring them all to the same standard, pitch them pell-mell into the same basket, resident aliens or no, allies, debtors to the state, all mixed up together. Then, as for our colonies, you must think of them as so many isolated hanks; find the ends of the separate threads, draw them to a center here, wind them into one, make one great hank of the lot, out of which the public can weave itself a good, stout tunic.

MAGISTRATE: Is it not a sin and a shame to see these women carding and winding the State, who have no part in the burdens of war?

LYSISTRATA: What! Accursed man! Why, it's a far heavier burden to us than to you. In the first place, we bear sons who go off to fight—

MAGISTRATE: Enough said! Do not remind us of our miseries.

LYSISTRATA: —then, secondly, instead of enjoying the pleasures of love and making the best of our youth and beauty, we sleep alone far from our husbands who are all with the army. But say no more of ourselves; what pains me is to see our young women grow old in lonely grief.

MAGISTRATE: Don't men grow old too?

LYSISTRATA: That's not the same thing. When a man comes home he can quickly find a young wife even though he has grey hair. But a woman has only one summer; if she doesn't make hay while the sun shines, no one will afterwards want to marry her, and she spends her days consulting oracles that never send her a husband.

E. Defeat and Hard Times:
Athens after the Peloponnesian War

The Peloponnesian War ended in 404 B.C. with the defeat of Athens by Sparta, the loss of Athens' empire, and the replacement of the democracy by a narrow oligarchy supported by Sparta, the so-called "Thirty." The brutal regime of the "Thirty," which the philosopher Plato said made the

Xenophon,
Memorabilia

democracy seem a "Golden Age," lasted less than a year. The social and economic dislocations that resulted from the devastation of the war and forced repatriation of Athenians, who had been settled on land in the empire seized from rebellious allies and subjects, lasted into the early fourth century B.C. *The straitened circumstances of late fifth-century* B.C. *Athens challenged traditional Greek ideas concerning the proper roles of men and women and the nature of work. In this selection from his* Memorabilia, *Xenophon shows Socrates offering practical advice to a formerly prosperous Athenian who was suddenly saddled with the need to support fourteen female relatives.*[12]

Soc: You seem to have some trouble on your mind, Aristarchus; if so, you should share it with your friends. Perhaps together we might lighten the weight of it a little.

Aristarchus answered: Yes, Socrates, I am in sore straits indeed. Ever since the party strife declared itself in the city, what with the rush of people to Piraeus, and the wholesale banishments, I have been fairly at the mercy of my poor deserted female relatives. Sisters, nieces, cousins, they have all come flocking to me for protection. I have fourteen free-born souls, I tell you, under my single roof, and how are we to live? We can get nothing out of the soil—that is in the hands of the enemy; nothing from my house property, for there is scarcely a living soul left in the city; my furniture? no one will buy it; money? there is none to be borrowed—you would have a better chance to find it by looking for it on the road than to borrow it from a banker. Yes, Socrates, to stand by and see one's relatives die of hunger is hard indeed, and yet to feed so many at such a pinch impossible.

After he had listened to the story, Socrates asked: How comes it that Ceramon, with so many mouths to feed, contrives not only to furnish himself and them with the necessaries of life, but to realize a handsome surplus, whilst you being in like plight are afraid you will one and all perish of starvation for want of the necessaries of life?

Ar: Why, bless your soul, do you not see he has only slaves and I have free-born souls to feed?

Soc: And which should you say were the better human beings, the free-born members of your household or Ceramon's slaves?

Ar: The free souls under my roof without a doubt.

Soc: Is it not a shame, then, that he with his baser folk to back him should be in easy circumstances, while you and your far superior household are in difficulties?

Ar: To be sure it is, when he has only a set of handicraftsmen to feed, and I my liberally educated household.

Soc: What is a handicraftsman? Does not the term apply to all who can make any sort of useful product or commodity?

Ar: Certainly.

<hr>

[12] Xenophon, *Memorabilia* 2.7–8, trans. H. G. Dakyns (London and New York, 1890–1897).

Soc: Barley meal is a useful product, is it not?

Ar: Preeminently so.

Soc: And loaves of bread?

Ar: No less.

Soc: Well, and what do you say to cloaks for men and for women—tunics, mantles, vests?

Ar: Yes, they are all highly useful commodities.

Soc: Then your household do not know how to make any of these?

Ar: On the contrary, I believe they can make them all.

Soc: Then you are not aware that by means of the manufacture of one of these alone—his barley meal store—Nausicydes not only maintains himself and his domestics, but many pigs and cattle besides, and realizes such large profits that he frequently contributes to the state liturgies [*for example, the training of choruses for the festivals or the equipping of warships, expenses which the well-off were expected to bear*]; while there is Cyrêbus, again, who, out of a bread factory, more than maintains the whole of his establishment and lives in the lap of luxury; and Dêmeas of Collytus gets a livelihood out of a cloak business, and Menon as a mantle-maker, and so, again, more than half the Megarians by the making of vests.

Ar: Bless me, yes! They have got a set of barbarian fellows, whom they purchase and keep, to manufacture by forced labor whatever takes their fancy. My kinswomen, I need not tell you, are free-born ladies.

Soc: Then, on the ground that they are free-born and your kinswomen, you think that they ought to do nothing but eat and sleep? Or is it your opinion that people who live in this way—I speak of free-born people in general—lead happier lives, and are more to be congratulated, than those who give their time and attention to such useful arts of life as they are skilled in? Is this what you see in the world, that for the purpose of learning what it is well to know, and of recollecting the lessons taught, or with a view to health and strength of body, or for the sake of acquiring and preserving all that gives life its charm, idleness and inattention are found to be helpful, whilst work and study are simply a dead loss? Pray, when those relatives of yours were taught what you tell me they know, did they learn it as barren information which they would never turn to practical account, or, on the contrary, as something with which they were to be seriously concerned some day, and from which they were to reap solid advantage? Do human beings in general attain to well-tempered manhood by a course of idling, or by carefully attending to what will be of use? Which will help a man the more to grow in justice and uprightness, to be up and doing, or to sit with folded hands revolving the ways and means of existence? As things now stand, if I am not mistaken, there is no love lost between you. You cannot help feeling that they are costly to you, and they must see that you find them a burden? This is a perilous state of affairs, in which hatred and bitterness have every prospect of increasing, whilst the preexisting bond of affection is likely to be snapped.

But now, if only you allow them free scope for their energies, when you come to see how useful they can be, you will grow quite fond of them, and they, when they perceive that they can please you, will cling to their benefactor warmly. Thus, with the memory of former kindnesses made sweeter, you will increase the grace which flows from kindnesses tenfold; you will in consequence be knit in closer bonds of love and domesticity. If, indeed, they were called upon to do any shameful work, let them choose death rather than that; but now they know, it would seem, the very arts and accomplishments which are regarded as the loveliest and the most suitable for women; and the things which we know, any of us, are just those which we can best perform, that is to say, with ease and expedition; it is a joy to do them, and the result is beautiful. Do not hesitate, then, to initiate your friends in what will bring advantage to them and you alike; probably they will gladly respond to your summons.

Well, upon my word (Aristarchus answered), I like so well what you say, Socrates, that though hitherto I have not been disposed to borrow, knowing that when I had spent what I got I should not be in a condition to repay, I think I can now bring myself to do so in order to raise a fund for these works.

Thereupon a loan was taken out, wools were purchased; the good man's relatives set to work, and even whilst they breakfasted they worked, and on and on till work was ended and they supped. Smiles took the place of frowns: they no longer looked askance with suspicion, but full into each other's eyes with happiness. They loved their kinsman for his kindness to them. He became attached to them as helpmates; and the end of it all was, he came to Socrates and told him with delight how matters fared; "and now," he added, "they tax me with being the only drone in the house, who sits and eats the bread of idleness." . . .

VIII.—At another time chancing upon an old friend whom he had not seen for a long while, he greeted him thus:

Soc: What quarter of the world do you hail from, Euthërus?

The other answered: From abroad, just before the close of the war; but at present from the city itself. You see, since we have been denuded of our possessions across the frontier, and my father left me nothing in Attica, I must needs bide at home, and provide myself with the necessaries of life by means of bodily toil, which seems preferable to begging from another, especially as I have no security on which to raise a loan.

Soc: And how long do you expect your body to be equal to providing the necessaries of life for hire?

Euth: Goodness knows, Socrates—not for long.

Soc: And when you find yourself an old man, expenses will not diminish, and yet no one will care to pay you for the labor of your hands.

Euth: That is true.

Soc: Would it not be better then to apply yourself at once to such work as will stand you in good stead when you are old—that is, address yourself to some large proprietor who needs an assistant in managing his estate? By superintending his works, helping to get in his crops, and guarding his property in general, you will be a benefit to the estate and be benefited in return.

I could not endure the yoke of slavery, Socrates! (he exclaimed).

Soc: And yet the heads of departments in a state are not regarded as adopting the badge of slavery because they manage the public property, but as having attained a higher dignity of freedom rather.

Euth: In a word, Socrates, the idea of being held to account to another is not at all to my taste.

Soc: And yet, Euthërus, it would be hard to find a work which did not involve some liability to account; in fact it is difficult to do anything without some mistake or other, and no less difficult, if you should succeed in doing it immaculately, to escape all unfriendly criticism. I wonder now whether you find it easy to get through your present occupations entirely without reproach. No? Let me tell you what you should do. You should avoid censorious persons and attach yourself to the considerate and kind-hearted, and in all your affairs accept with a good grace what you can and decline what you feel you cannot do. Whatever it be, do it heart and soul, and make it your finest work. There lies the method at once to silence fault-finders and to minister help to your own difficulties. Life will flow smoothly, risks will be diminished, provision against old age secured.

F. The Military Revolution

The Peloponnesian War (431–404 B.C.) had the side effect of producing a generation of Greeks schooled in the latest techniques of warfare. The level of military skills rose throughout Greece, and the older, more traditional, almost ritualistic style of battle conducted by citizen-soldiers gave way to military professionalism at every level from ordinary infantryman to commanding general. In the next go-round of intercity warfare, the self-sufficiency of the hoplite phalanx came into question after light infantry (peltasts) demonstrated their effectiveness against individual hoplite units at the battle of Lechaeum in 390 B.C. Light infantry, however, were usually mercenaries and therefore constituted an expense that the average small state found difficult to meet. It remained for an outsider, Philip II the King of Macedonia, to unite all the novel elements of the military revolution and create a wholly new style of waging war.

1. OLD AND NEW FORMS OF WARFARE

In a series of famous speeches begun in 351 B.C. and known as the "Philippics," the Athenian orator Demosthenes tried to persuade Athens that Philip of Macedon was a serious threat to its independence. In the Third Philippic, probably given in 341 B.C., Demosthenes urged the Athenians to send additional support to an expedition sent earlier to secure the Hellespont, Athens' lifeline to the grain-producing regions of the Black Sea. In the course of the speech he reminded his hearers, the Athenians, that the old days of warfare were over and that they needed to wake up to the fact.[13]

Demosthenes, *Philippic*

[13] From Demosthenes, *Philippic* 3.47–50.

In my opinion, while nearly all the arts have advanced, nothing has undergone greater change and development from the old days than the art of war. First off, I have heard that the Spartans of a century ago would, like everyone else, spend the summer season of four or five months invading and laying waste the countryside of their enemies with their hoplites and citizen levies, and then return home again. They were so old-fashioned—rather, so statesmanlike—that they never bought off their enemies, and their manner of waging war was open and according to tradition. But now, you no doubt understand that the destruction is, more often than not, caused by traitors, and does not result from regular pitched battles. You will also have heard that Philip roams at will not because of his phalanx of hoplites, but because he campaigns with light-armed troops, cavalry, archers, mercenaries, and the like. When he uses these to attack a state suffering from factional disorder, and when mutual distrust prevents anyone from going out to defend its lands, he brings up his siege machinery and besieges the city. And I don't have to tell you that "summer" or "winter" makes no difference to him; he campaigns at any time of the year he pleases.

2. IPHICRATES: A MILITARY REVOLUTIONARY

Cornelius Nepos,
Life of Iphicrates

A pioneer in the use of new form of infantry warfare was the Athenian general Iphicrates, who introduced critical reforms in peltast weaponry and tactics. His readiness to serve both Greek and non-Greek employers foreshadowed the commanders of professional mercenary bands that are so prominent a feature of fourth-century B.C. and Hellenistic warfare and the condotierri of the Renaissance.[14]

1. Iphicrates, the Athenian, gained renown by his great deeds, but still more by his knowledge of the art of war; for not only was he a leader comparable with the greatest of his own time, but not even among the men of earlier days was there anyone who surpassed him. Indeed, a great part of his life was spent in warfare, he often commanded armies, and he never lost a battle through his own fault. It was always by knowledge of war that he gained his victories, and his knowledge was so great that he introduced many novelties in military equipment, as well as many improvements. For example, he changed the arms of the infantry. While before he became commander they used very large shields, short spears and little swords, he on the contrary exchanged *peltae*, or Thracian shields, for the round ones (for which reason the infantry have since been called peltasts), in order that the soldiers might move and charge more easily when less burdened. He doubled the length of the spear and increased that of the swords; he changed the character of their breastplates, giving them linen ones in place of bronze cuirasses or chain armor. In that way he made the soldiers more active; for while he diminished the weight of their armor, he contrived to protect their bodies equally

[14] From Cornelius Nepos, *Life of Iphicrates*.

well without overloading them. 2. He waged war with the Thracians; he restored Seuthes, an ally of the Athenians, to his throne. At Corinth [during the Corinthian War] such was the strictness of his command of the army, that no troops in Greece were better drilled or more obedient to their leader; and he made them form the habit, when the signal for battle had been given by the commander, without waiting for an officer's command to take their places in such good order that each man seemed to have been assigned his position by a most skilful general. It was with that army that he annihilated a Spartan regiment (*see next reading*), a feat which was highly praised all over Greece. On another occasion in that same war he put all their forces to flight, an exploit by which he gained great glory. When Artaxerxes wished to make war on the king of Egypt, he asked the Athenians for Iphicrates as one of his generals, to command an army of twelve thousand mercenaries. That army the Athenian trained so thoroughly in all varieties of military discipline, that just as in days of old the soldiers of Fabius were called true Romans, so "soldiers of Iphicrates" became a title of the greatest honor among the Greeks. Again, having gone to the aid of the Lacedaemonians, he thwarted the designs of Epaminondas (*the Theban general who defeated the Spartans at the Battle of Leuctra in 371 B.C. and followed up the victory with an invasion of Sparta*); for if his arrival had not been imminent, the Thebans would not have left Sparta until they had taken and burned the city.

3. He had, in addition to nobility of soul and great size of body, the aspect of one born to command, so that his appearance alone inspired admiration in all men; but, as Theopompus has recorded, he was not steadfast enough in effort and he lacked endurance: nevertheless, he was a good citizen and the soul of honor. This was manifest both on other occasions and especially in protecting the children of Amyntas, the Macedonian; for after his death Eurydice, the mother of Perdiccas and Philippus, took refuge with Iphicrates with these two boys, and was defended with all his power. He lived to a good old age, enjoying the devotion of his fellow-citizens. Only once did he have occasion to defend himself against a capital charge; that was during the war with the allies in company with Timotheus, and he was acquitted. He left a son Mnestheus, the offspring of a Thracian woman, the daughter of King Cotus. When Mnestheus was once asked whether he thought more of his father or of his mother, he answered: "My mother." When everyone expressed surprise at his reply, he added: "I have good reason for that; for my father did everything in his power to make me a Thracian; my mother, on the contrary, made me an Athenian."

3. A STUNNING REVERSAL: LIGHT INFANTRY DEFEAT HEAVY INFANTRY AT LECHAEUM

After the Peloponnesian War some of Sparta's old allies, principally the Corinthians and Thebans, turned against her. Athens joined them, and the Corinthian War (395–387 B.C.) resulted. One | Xenophon, *Hellenica skirmish at Lechaeum, the port of Corinth, demonstrated the effectiveness of well-trained light infantry* (peltasts) *against even the best hoplites.*[15]

Now the disaster to the Spartan division happened in this way. It was the unvaried custom of the men of Amyclae (*one of the villages that made up Sparta*) to return home for the feast of the Hyacinthia, to join in the sacred hymn, a custom not to be interrupted either by active service or absence from home or for any other reason. So, too, on this occasion Agesilaus had left behind all the Amyclaeans serving in any part of his army at Lechaeum. At the right moment the general in command of the garrison of Lechaeum had posted the garrison troops of the allies to the guard the walls during his absence. He put himself at the head of his division of heavy infantry with the cavalry division, and led the Amyclaeans past the walls of Corinth. When he arrived at a point within three miles of Sicyon, the Spartan commander turned back in the direction of Lechaeum with his heavy infantry regiment, 600 strong, giving orders to the cavalry commander to escort the Amyclaeans with his division as far as they required, and then to turn and overtake him. It cannot be said that the Spartans were ignorant of the large number of enemy light troops and heavy infantry that were inside Corinth, but owing to their previous successes they arrogantly presumed that no one would pick a fight with them.

Within Corinth, however, the fewness of the Spartans—a thin line of heavy infantry unsupported by light infantry or cavalry—had been noted. Callias, the son of Hipponicus, who was in command of the Athenian hoplites, and Iphicrates at the head of his peltasts, saw no risk in attacking with these light troops. If the Spartans continued their march by the high road, they could be cut-up by showers of javelins on their exposed right flanks, but if they were tempted to respond to the attacks, the peltasts, the nimblest of all light troops, would easily slip out of the reach of the hoplites. With this plan in mind, they led out their troops. While Callias drew up his heavy infantry in line at no great distance from the city, Iphicrates and his peltasts made a dash at the Spartan division.

The Spartans were soon within range of the javelins. Here a man was wounded, and there another killed. Each time orders were given to the attendant shield-bearers to pick up the men and bear them to Lechaeum. These were the only members of the Spartan regiment who were, strictly speaking, saved. Then the Spartan commander ordered the younger men to charge and drive off their assailants. No matter how they attacked, however, they gained nothing; not a man could come within javelin range of the peltasts. Being heavy infantry opposed to light troops, before they could get to close quarters the enemy's command to retire sounded, and as soon as the Spartans fell back, scattered as they were because of the charge they made where each man's speed had told, Iphicrates and his men turned right about and renewed the javelin attack. Other peltasts running alongside the Spartan division, harassed their exposed flanks.

[15] From Xenophon, *Hellenica* 4.4.14–17, trans. H. G. Dakyns (London and New York, 1890–1897), modified.

At the very first charge the peltasts had shot down nine or ten Spartans. Encouraged by this success, they pressed on them with increasing audacity. These attacks told so severely that the Spartan commander gave the order a second time (and this time for more of the younger men) to charge. The order was promptly obeyed, but on retiring they lost more men than of the first occasion, and it was not until the pick and flower of the division had fallen that they were joined by the returning cavalry in whose company they once again attempted a charge. The light infantry gave way, but the attack of the cavalry was weakly enacted. Instead of pressing home the charge until they had killed at least some of the enemy, they kept their horses abreast of their heavy infantry skirmishers, charging and wheeling side-by-side.

Again and again the monotonous tale of attacking and being killed repeated itself, except that as their own ranks grew thinner and their courage ebbed, the courage of their assailants grew bolder and their numbers increased. In desperation the Spartans massed compactly upon the narrow slope of a hillock, distant a quarter mile or so from the sea and a couple of miles perhaps from Lechaeum. Their friends in Lechaeum, seeing their difficulty, embarked in ships and sailed around until they were immediately under the hillock. And now, in despair, being so sorely troubled as man after man dropped dead, and unable to strike a blow, to crown their distress they saw the enemy's heavy infantry advancing. Then they took to flight. Some of them threw themselves into the sea. Others—a mere handful—escaped to Lechaeum with the cavalry. The death-roll, including those who fell in the second and final fights, must have numbered 250 slain, or thereabouts. Such is the tale of the destruction of the Spartan regiment. . . .

Since such a calamity was unusual for the Spartans, a widespread mourning fell upon the whole army, those alone excepted whose sons or fathers or brothers had died at their posts. The bearing of these resembled conquerors, as with bright faces they moved freely to and fro, glorying in their domestic sorrow. . . .

4. MERCENARIES AT WAR

For centuries Greeks had served in the armies of Middle Eastern states as mercenaries. In 401 B.C. Cyrus, the Persian commander of Asia Minor, organized a coup using Greek mercenaries against his brother, the reigning King of Persia, Artaxerxes II. Among the 10,000 Greeks recruited was a student of Socrates, the Athenian Xenophon, who wrote an account of Cyrus' expedition. While en route to Persia, Epyaxa, queen of the Cilicians, asked Cyrus for a display of his army.[16]

Xenophon, *Anabasis*

The Cilician queen, it is said, begged Cyrus to exhibit his army for her. Cyrus was only too glad to make such an exhibition, and held a review of the Greeks and non-Greek soldiers in the plain. He ordered the Greeks to draw up their lines and post themselves in their customary battle order, each general marshalling his

[16] From Xen. *Anab.* 1.3.14–18.

own battalion. Accordingly they drew up four deep. The right was held by Menon and his contingent; on the left was Clearchus and his men; in the center were the remaining generals and their companies. Cyrus first inspected the nonGreeks who marched past in troops of horse and companies of infantry. He then inspected the Greeks, driving past them in his chariot, with the queen in her carriage. The troops wore bronze helmets, purple tunics, and greaves, with their shields uncovered.

After he had driven past the whole body, Cyrus drew up his chariot in front of the center of the battle-line, and sent his interpreter Pigres to the generals of the Greeks, with orders to present arms and to advance along the whole front. This order was repeated by the generals to their men; and at the sound of the trumpet, with their shields forward and spears at rest, they advanced. The pace quickened, and with a shout the soldiers spontaneously broke into a run making for the camp. At the sight the non-Greeks panicked and the Cilician queen fled in her carriage. The merchants in the camp market place left their wares and took to their heels. The Greeks meanwhile came into the camp with a roar of laughter. What astounded the queen was the brilliance and order of the armament, but what pleased Cyrus was the terror inspired by the Greeks in the hearts of the non-Greeks.

5. A TWO-EDGED SWORD: MERCENARY TROOPS AND THEIR EMPLOYERS

Aeneas Tacticus,
On Siegecraft

The efficiency of mercenary troops over traditional citizen hoplites and their willingness to fight for any employer encouraged their use in both wars and civil strife. Their use also, however, carried with it risks for the cities that employed them, as Aeneas Tacticus reveals in this passage.[17]

If allied forces are admitted into the city they should never be stationed together, but should be separated in the manner already suggested and for the same reasons. In the same way those who are to make use of mercenary troops should always have citizens under arms surpassing these mercenaries in number and power, otherwise both the citizens and the state are at their mercy. A danger of this sort befell the Chalcedonians (*a Greek city in the Bosporus*) while in a state of siege, due to the presence of allied forces sent by the people of Cyzicus, their allies. When the Chalcedonians were deliberating upon measures affecting their interest, the troops of the garrison said that they would not consent unless it seemed advantageous to the people of Cyzicus as well, so that the garrison within the walls was much more terrible to the Chalcedonians than was the besieging enemy. One must, therefore, never admit into a city an alien force greater than that already available to the citizens, and the state employing mercenaries must always be much superior to them in strength, since it is not safe to be outnumbered by aliens nor to be in the power of mercenaries, as actually happened to the inhabitants of Heraclea Pontica; for, by bringing in more hired troops than they should, they first made away with those of the opposing faction, but later brought

---

[17] From Aeneas Tacticus, *On Siegecraft*, 11.14; 12.3.

destruction to themselves and the state, being forced into subjection to the man who introduced the mercenaries.

6. THE NEED FOR WALLS

It was a commonplace among Greeks that armies, not walls, made for the best defense of a city. In the Laws *Plato has the Athenian speaker say that he agreed that it was wise that the Spartans left their walls "sleeping in the ground and did not wake them up." He cites an unidentified poet for saying that walls should be made of "bronze and iron" rather than stone and earth (778d–e). Ever the realist, Aristotle challenges this view, pointing to the changed times of the fourth century B.C. and the practical need for walls. The following is from book 7 of the* Politics, *where he describes how the ideal city ought to be constructed.[18]*

Aristotle,
Politics

As regards walls, those who argue that cities which place special emphasis on bravery should not have them, hold too old fashioned a view—especially when it is clear that cities that do indulge in that form of pretension are refuted by actual experience. It is true that against an evenly matched foe and one little superior in numbers it is not honorable to try to seek security by the strength of one's fortifications. But it may possibly happen that the superior number of the attackers may be too much for the mere human valor of the smaller defending force, and if the city is to survive and not to suffer disaster or arrogant treatment, the securest fortification of walls must be reckoned the most militarily practical, particularly in view of the inventions that have now been made with regard to missile accuracy and artillery for sieges. To choose not to build walls around a city is like selecting a site for a city that makes it easy to invade and clearing away the high ground. It would be similar to not providing walls for a private dwelling on the grounds that such walls would make its inhabitants cowardly.

---

[18] From Aristotle, *Politics* 7.1330b–1331a.

6

INTELLECTUAL DEVELOPMENTS
IN THE CLASSICAL AGE

The *Physis/Nomos* Debate

A major debate over cultural values, politics, and society took place in Athens and elsewhere in the Greek world beginning about the middle of the fifth century B.C. It focused on the question of the kind of authority that sustained the ethical values of a society: What laws and customs bound individuals once they stepped outside their individual communities or states? Were moral obligations and commands based on changeable tradition or on something more permanent and universal? The debate was stimulated by a number of causes. Greeks had been traveling around the Mediterranean and the Black Sea for centuries and brought back to their home states information, sometimes far-fetched, about how other peoples behaved in their marriage practices, religious beliefs, eating habits, and so on. Another contributing factor was the development of a critical, questioning style of political culture that came into being as a result of the growth of free, constitutional government throughout the Greek world. If political matters were to be questioned and debated in public, why not debate every other aspect of daily life, including moral standards?

As early as the seventh century, serious thought was being given in some intellectual circles to the natural world. What was matter? Did it come into being, or was it eternal? How did change come about in material things? What was the nature (*physis*) of the stars and planets? By the mid-fifth century, Greek thinkers extended their analytical focus to include human nature and human society. The "sophistic" movement, as it was dubbed, made this shift in philosophical focus more than just an intellectual affair, because it addressed the basic issue of what constituted a good society and, correspondingly, what was the proper education for such a society and who should conduct it?

The new approaches alarmed different groups in Greek society. Parents suspected that their authority to raise their children as they saw fit was being undermined by some teachers who claimed that that the gods were fictions and that there was no fixed morality or absolute truth. All moral rules, said the professors, were simply ad hoc arrangements made up by individual societies, usually with the aim of keeping ordinary people in line. The sophist Thrasymachus of Chalcedon argued that justice was simply the advantage of the stronger members in each society. Each government, he said, "frames its laws for its own advantage, a democracy creates democratic laws, a tyranny autocratic laws and so on. In legislating this way the rulers claim that what is 'just,' that is to say, their own advantage, is justice for their subjects, and anyone who breaks the law is punished as a lawbreaker and a criminal."[1] Slave owners were shocked when they were told by some of the new thinkers that slavery was unjust and that it was unnatural to enslave human beings. "No one is born a slave," claimed the sophist Alcidamas. "Man is the measure of all things," proclaimed Protagoras, one of the most prominent of the sophists, meaning that human laws and social practices are man-made artifacts. With regard to the existence of God, he could not say definitely whether He existed or not. Hippias of Elis pushed this assertion a step further by insisting that law (*nomos*) was a "tyrant which forced men to do many things contrary to nature (*physis*)." Phaleas of Chalcedon made a logical inference about human conventions when he commented that maldistribution of wealth was at the root of all the social strife in the states of Greece. It could be remedied, he proposed, by making the properties of citizens equal. Democritus of Abdera suggested that the *polis*, which Greeks revered as the acme of human development, in fact limited human experience. "To the wise man," he said, "the whole world is open; the good person has the entire world as his country." Diogenes of Sinope, the founder of Cynicism, made this approach the basis of a countercultural way of life, which influenced Greek society for centuries.

Broadly conceived, the sophistic movement was clearly not monolithic. There were radicals at either end of the spectrum. At one extreme some "conventionalists" espoused a form of relativism that attached little weight to any ethical system and found any and all forms of society equally acceptable. At the other end was the absolutism of the extreme "naturalists," who could be just as dogmatic in their criticism of existing ethical systems and the societies based on them. "Moderates" could also be found, among them Plato, Protagoras, and Aristotle. A key figure in the debate was the complex and towering figure of Socrates. Unfortunately he left no writings and so is not able to speak to us directly but only through the refracted (and frequently distorting) prisms of the many who wrote about him. The intellectual movement brought into being by the remarkable thinkers of the Greek world of the late Archaic and Classical periods remained vigorous for centuries, influencing the development of Roman law and laying the foundation for the flowering of the modern tradition of human rights.

A. The Conventionalist Argument

1. "THERE IS NO NATURAL STANDARD OF JUSTICE": AN OVERVIEW FROM PLATO

In this reading Plato gives a one-sided overview of the sophistic movement, lumping all sophists together in an unflattering portrait. The reading, although skewed, is useful in that it reflects the   Plato, *Laws*

---

[1] Plato, *Republic* 338d–e. Such opinions were not unusual in Greek political discourse. Thrasymachus' contribution was to elevate a commonplace into a theoretical principle.

expansion of philosophic interest during the fifth century B.C. from the natural word to the realm of human nature and society. Plato begins with the speculations of the natural philosophers of earlier generations and claims that their influential speculations led naturally and directly to the present unfortunate situation where moral beliefs had no certain foundation. The speaker is "The Athenian," the main figure in the dialogue known as the Laws.[2]

ATHENIAN: . . . Fire and water, earth and air, they say [*i.e., the older thinkers in their demythologized, nontheistic cosmology*] all exist by nature and chance and none of them by art. By means of these elements which are wholly inanimate the bodies which come next—namely, the earth, sun, moon and stars—have been brought into existence. Driven by their respective forces all these elements move at random, and as they meet together and combine appropriately—hot with cold, dry with moist, soft with hard—there results all such necessary mixtures as come about from the chance combinations of these opposites. In this way and by these means the whole of the heavens and all that is in the heavens, and all animals, too, and plants were brought into being. . . . All this, they assert, was not due to reason, nor to any god nor art, but owing as we have seen, to nature and chance.

   As a later product of these, comes art, and it, being mortal itself and of mortal birth, begets later playthings which have little reality in truth, being images of a sort like the arts themselves—images such as painting begets, and music, and the arts which accompany these. Those arts which really produce something serious—like medicine, agriculture and gymnastics—are such as produce their effect by working in concert with nature. Politics, they say, shares little with nature, but is mostly an art. In like manner legislation is not based on nature but on art and its enactments are artificial.

CLEINIAS: What do you mean?

A: The first statement, my dear sir, which, these people make about the gods is that they exist by art and not by nature. They are artificial creations produced by certain legal fictions which differ from place to place, according as each people agreed among themselves when making their laws. They assert, moreover, that there is one class of things good by nature, and another class of things good by convention. As for justice, there is no natural standard by which things are just or unjust. Men are constantly in dispute about such things and continually altering them, and whatever alteration they make at any time is at that time authoritative, though it owes its existence to legislative contrivance, and not in any way to nature. All these, my friends, are views which young people imbibe from men reputedly wise, both prose writers and poets. They maintain that the height of justice is to succeed by force. This is why young people are afflicted with a plague of impiety, and take it that the gods, such as the law commands us to believe in, do not exist. This is why civic dissensions arise when these teachers attract the young to the

[2] From Plato, *Laws* 889b–890b, trans. R. G. Bury (London, 1926) (modified).

kind of life that is "right according to nature"—that is, a life that essentially consists in being in control of others instead of being of service to them as the laws command.

C: What a horrible picture you have painted, O Athenian, and what widespread corruption of the young in the state at large as well as in private families.

2. CALLICLES' SUPERMAN: "RIGHT IS THE ADVANTAGE OF THE STRONGER OVER THE WEAKER"

In Plato's dialogue, the Gorgias, *the speaker Callicles presents the expressly nihilistic and immoral-*   Plato, *Gorgias*
ist views of the radical wing of the sophist movement referred to in the previous reading. According
to these sophists, all ethical rules are mutable arrangements made up by individual societies. To the
extent that anything is "by nature" or natural law, it is the pursuit of self-interest. This alone is
a "law of nature." Plato is the first known writer to actually use the term "law of nature" and is
usually credited with its invention.[3]

CALLICLES: For the most part these two—nature and convention—are opposed to each other. . . . In my view conventions are made by weaklings who are in the majority. So it is with a view to themselves and their own interest that they make their laws and distribute their praise and blame. They intimidate the stronger sort of folk who are able to do well in society. To prevent them from doing well they say that such ability is base and unjust, and that wrongdoing consists precisely in this effort to get advantage over one's neighbors. Being inferior themselves they are well content to see themselves on a footing of equality with their betters. So this is why by convention it is termed unjust and evil to aim at an advantage over the majority, and why they call it wrong doing. But nature, in my opinion, herself proclaims the fact that it is right for the better to have advantage over the worse, and the able over the feebler. It is obvious in many cases that this is so, not only in the animal world, but among the states and races collectively of men—namely, that right has been decided to consist in the sway and advantage of the stronger over the weaker. What kind of right did Xerxes have to march against Greece, or his father against Scythia, or any of the innumerable cases of this sort of thing one might mention? Surely these men were acting in accordance with nature.

I would go even farther and say they were following the law of nature—though perhaps not the kind of law which is made by us. For our method is to mould the best and the strongest among us from infancy like tame lions, and utterly enthrall them by our spells and witchcraft, and enslave them by telling them that men ought to be equal and that such equality is what is fair and just. But, I imagine that when some man arises with a nature of sufficient force, he shakes off all that we have taught him, bursts his bonds, and breaks free; he tramples underfoot our

[3] From Plato, *Gorgias* 483a–484b, trans. W.R.M. Lamb (London, 1925) (modified).

codes and drugs, our charms and "laws," which are all against nature. Thus our slave rises in revolt and shows himself our master, and there dawns the full light of natural justice.

3. PROTAGORAS: VIRTUE IS TAUGHT BY PARENTS, TEACHERS, AND THE LAWS

Plato, *Protagoras*

Other sophists were moderate ethical relativists, not extremists like Callicles. They held that all states had their own systems of ethical values, which were good because they were tailored to the needs of their individual states. Naturally these values could be taught like any other subject or art. Protagoras was one of the most prominent proponents of this view and is given the principal role in Plato's dialogue named after him. In this reading Protagoras argues that in civic society all must share to some extent in virtue, because no society can exist without some measure of virtue. Unfortunately, virtue is not innate but needs to be taught—but indeed can be taught—by parents, teachers, the laws of the state, even society itself. In opposition to Protagoras, Socrates took the paradoxical position that virtue could not be taught by these traditional agencies. Understandably, this doctrine led to confusion as to what he actually believed as well as real antagonism on the part of those who felt threatened by his public proclamation of this subversive thesis.[4]

PROTAGORAS: [Virtue is not] innate or spontaneous, but is something taught and acquired after careful preparation by those who acquire it. . . . In all cases of evils which men think to have befallen their neighbors by nature or fortune, no one is upset with those so afflicted, or reproves or lectures or punishes them in the hope of changing them; one merely pities them. Who, for instance, is such a fool as to try to do anything of this sort to the ugly, the puny or the weak? I assume this is so because men know that it is by nature and fortune that people are endowed with both good and bad characteristics. But it is a different matter with the good things people are supposed to get by application and practice and teaching. Where these are lacking in anyone and only their opposite evils prevail, here surely there is reason for anger and punishment and reproof. Such, for example, are injustice and impiety, and in short all that is contrary to civic virtue. Clearly because such good qualities are to be acquired by application and learning, it is acceptable to be angry with one's neighbor and reprove him.

   If you will consider punishment, Socrates, and what control it has over wrongdoers, the facts will demonstrate that men agree among themselves that virtue can be acquired. No one punishes a wrong-doer as a result of reflecting on past wrong doing or punishes him for that reason, unless one takes blind vengeance like a wild beast. The rational man does not avenge himself for past offence, since he cannot undo what has been done. Instead, he looks to the future and aims at

[4] From Plato, *Protagoras* 323c–324c; 325c–326e; 328a, trans. W.R.M. Lamb (London, 1924) (modified).

preventing that same person and others who see him punished, from doing wrong again. If he holds this view he must also believe that virtues come by training: for you observe that he punishes to deter.

Parents' Role in Education

[Parents] teach and admonish their children from their earliest years to the last days of their lives. As soon as a child understands what is said to him, the nurse, the mother, the tutor, and the father himself strive hard that the child may excel, and as he says or does anything they teach and impress upon him that "this is right and this is wrong, this is honorable this is dishonorable, this is holy, this is unholy," and generally that he is to do this and not do that. If he readily obeys, this is all to the good; but if not, they treat him as a bent and twisted piece of wood and straighten him with threats and blows.

Schools for the Better-Off

After this they send them to school and charge the master to be more concerned with their children's good behavior than with their letters and musical performance. The masters take pains accordingly and the children when they have learnt their letters and are getting to understand the written word as before they did only the spoken, are furnished with works of good poets to read as they sit in class, and are made to learn them off by heart. In these poems they find many warnings, many descriptions and praises and eulogies of good men in times past, that the child in envy may imitate them and yearn to become as they. Similarly the music-masters take pains to instill self-restraint, and see that their young charges do not go wrong. When they learn to play the lyre, they are taught the works of another set of good poets, the song-makers, the lyric poets, while the master accompanies them on the lyre; and they insist on familiarizing the boys' souls with the rhythms and scales, that they may gain in civility, and by advancing in rhythmic and harmonic grace may become more resourceful in speech and action; for the whole of a man's life requires the graces of rhythm and harmony. Again, over and above all this, people send their sons to a trainer so that their improved bodies may serve their now well developed minds, and that they may not be forced by bodily weaknesses to play the coward in wars and other duties. This is what people do, who are most able; and the most able are the wealthiest. Their sons begin school at the earliest age, and are freed from it at the latest.

The Laws Teach Everyone

And when they are released from their schooling the city next compels them to learn the laws and to live according to them as after a pattern, that their conduct may not be swayed by their own heedlessness. When writing teachers first draw letters in faint outline with the pen for their less advanced pupils, and then give them a copy book and make them write according to the guidance of their lines, so the city sketches out for them the laws devised by good lawgivers of old and constrains them to govern and be governed according to them. Anyone who steps outside these borders is punished. . . .

Virtue, Therefore, Can Be Taught

Seeing then that so much care is taken in the matter of private and public virtue, do you wonder, Socrates, and make it a great difficulty that virtue may be taught? Surely there is no reason to wonder at that: you would have far greater reason if virtue were not teachable. . . . Thus it is with virtue. If there is someone who excels us ever so little in showing the way to virtue, we must be thankful. Such a one I take myself to be, somewhat better than other men in the gift of assisting people to become good and true, and giving full value for the fee that I charge, even more than full value as the learner himself admits it. For this reason I have arranged my charges according to the following arrangement: when anyone has had lessons from me, if he is satisfied he pays the sum I ask; if not, he may go to a temple, and state on oath the value he sets on what has learnt, and then pay me that amount.

B. The Naturalist Argument

1. ANTIPHON: GREEKS AND BARBARIANS ARE THE SAME BY NATURE

Antiphon
on slavery

Another branch of the sophistic movement appealed to nature as opposed to convention. Human goodness or excellence was not the product of the values and customs of this or that ethnic group or nation; it was the same wherever human beings were to be found. Goodness, accordingly, consisted in adhering to universally valid norms of behavior. This branch of sophism gave birth to the ideas of cosmopolitanism (i.e., the belief that we should think of ourselves not as citizens of a particular state or nation but of the cosmos, the world); the unity of mankind; natural law and natural rights. These ideas were later built up into major philosophical principles by Stoic philosophers. The first reading is from the sophist Antiphon, a contemporary of Socrates. An opinion common among some Greeks at the time held that barbarians, i.e., non-Greeks, were slaves by nature or at least slavish in the customs.[5]

Justice is not to violate the laws of the city in which one is a citizen. Therefore a man will act in accordance with justice if he upholds the law (*nomos*) when he is in the presence of witnesses, but obeys the laws of nature (*physis*) when no one is present. The reason for this is that the decrees of man-made laws are artificial constructs, while those of nature are by necessity. The compulsion of a city's laws derives from consent, whereas the force of the natural law is not a matter of agreement or consent. Accordingly, if a man violates the city's legal code and escapes

[5] From H. Diels and W. Kranz, *Die Fragmente der Vorsokratiker*, Berlin 1951, B44.

the notice of the rest of his fellow citizens who agreed to the code, he avoids both disgrace and penalty. (Obviously, if the law-breaking is noticed he does not escape). On the other hand, if he violates any one of the inherent demands of nature, even if no one notices, the evil is no less, and if everyone notices, the harm is greater still. The reason for this is that the injury he suffers is not just a matter of the loss of public opinion, but in truth [*meaning that the offender damages his soul or his personhood*].

Antiphon goes on to point out the ineffectiveness of man-made laws in comparison with the laws of nature.

We reverence and honor those people who are of noble ancestry but not those of lesser households. In acting this way we treat each other like barbarians when in reality, by nature, we all have the same nature in all things, barbarians and Greeks alike. The proof of this is to be seen when we consider the things that are natural and necessary to all humankind. These things are available to everyone in the same way, whether barbarian or Greek. Thus we all use our mouth and nostrils to breathe and eat with our hands. . . .

2. SOPHOCLES, EMPEDOCLES, AND ALCIDAMAS: UNIVERSALLY VALID NORMS EXIST

Aristotle in his work on rhetoric cites a number of thinkers who believed in universally valid norms of justice.[6]

Aristotle, *The Art of Rhetoric*

Let us now classify just and unjust actions generally, starting from what follows. Justice and injustice have been defined in reference to laws and persons in two ways. Now there are two kinds of laws, particular and general. By particular laws I mean those established by each people in reference to themselves, which again are divided into written and unwritten; by general laws I mean those based upon nature. In fact, there is a general idea of just and unjust in accordance with nature, as all men in a manner understand, even if there is neither communication nor agreement between them. This is what Antigone in Sophocles evidently means, when she declares that it is just by nature, though forbidden by edict, to bury Polynices [*her brother, who was killed while attacking his native city, Thebes*]:

> For neither today nor yesterday, but from all eternity these statutes live and no man knoweth whence they came.

And as Empedocles says in regard to not killing that which has life, for this is not right for some and wrong for others,

---

[6] From Aristotle, *The Art of Rhetoric*, 1373b, trans. J. H. Freese (London, 1926) (modified).

But a universal precept, which extends without a break throughout the wide-ruling sky and boundless earth.

Alcidamas also speaks of this precept in his play *The Messenians*:

God has left all men free; nature has made none a slave.

3. ARISTOTLE: INTRINSICALLY EVIL ACTS

Aristotle,
*Nicomachean
Ethics*

Aristotle's own position is not easy to pin down. In the first reading, where he argues that some actions are intrinsically evil, he seems to be opposed to relativism and on the side of the natural-ists. The first reading occurs in the middle of his discussion of virtue, which he defines as the mean between two extremes. The second suggests that Aristotle was in some respects closer to the main-stream sophist idea that justice was conventional. The ideal state did not exist, and the best one could hope for was the improvement of existing states. It was extremely difficult, he felt, to judge whether individual laws were or were not in conformity with nature. In the third reading Aristotle establishes the shared etymology of nomisma *(money, coins) and* nomos, *which demonstrates that money is both "conventional" (different states have different coins), and something natural, namely the needs or wants of people.*

[1] Virtue then is a settled disposition of the mind determining the choice of actions and emotions, consisting essentially in the observance of the mean relative to us, this being determined by principle, that is as the man of good practical judgment would determine it. And it is a mean state between two vices, one of excess and one of defect. . . .

However, not every action or emotion admits of the observance of a due mean. Indeed the very names of some directly imply evil, for instance, spite, shamelessness, envy, and among actions, adultery, theft, murder. All these and similar actions and feelings are regarded as being bad in themselves, not because of an excess or deficiency on their part. It is impossible therefore ever to be right in doing them; one must always be wrong. Nor does right or wrong in their case depend on the circumstances, for instance whether one commits adultery with the right woman, at the right time, and in the right manner; the mere commission of any of them is wrong. One might as well suppose there could be a due mean and excess and deficiency in acts of injustice or cowardice or self-indulgence, which would imply that one could have a medium amount of excess and of deficiency, an excessive amount of excess and a deficient amount of deficiency. But just as there can be no excess or deficiency in temperance and justice, because the mean is, in a sense an extreme, so there can be no observance of the mean nor excess nor deficiency in the corresponding vicious acts mentioned above, but however they are committed, they are wrong.[7]

---

[7] From Aristotle, *Nicomachean Ethics* 2.6.1107a1–27, trans. H. Rackham (London, 1926) (modified).

[2] A rule of justice is natural that has the same validity everywhere, and does not depend on our accepting it or not. A rule is conventional that in the first instance may be settled in one way or the other indifferently, though having once been settled it is not indifferent. For example, that the ransom of a prisoner should be a mina or that a sacrifice should consist of a goat and not two sheep, and any regulations enacted for particular cases as for instance the sacrifice in honor of Brasidas (*hero of Amphipolis, a town near Aristotle's birthplace, Stagira*), and some ordinances in the nature of special decrees.

Some people think that all rules of justice are merely conventional, because whereas a law of nature is immutable and has the same validity everywhere, as fire burns both here and in Persia, rules of justice are seen to vary. That rules of justice vary is not absolutely true, but only with qualifications. Among the gods indeed it is perhaps not true at all; but in our world, although there is such a thing as natural law, yet everything is capable of change. For example the right hand is naturally stronger than the left, yet it is possible for some persons to be born ambidextrous. The same distinction will hold good in all matters; though what sort of things that admit of variation are as they are by nature, and what are merely customary and conventional, it is not easy to see, inasmuch as both alike are capable of change. But nevertheless some things are ordained by nature and others not.

The rules of justice based on convention and expedience are like standard measures. Grain and wine measures are not equal in all places, but are larger in wholesale and smaller in retail markets. Similarly the rules of justice ordained not by nature but by man are not the same in all places, since forms of government are not the same, though in all places there is only one form of government that is natural, namely the best form.[8]

[3] All commodities exchanged must be able to be compared in some way. It is to meet this requirement that men have introduced money. Money constitutes in a manner a middle term, for it is a measure of all things, and so of their superior or inferior value, that is to say, how many shoes are equivalent to a house or to a given quantity of food. . . . It is therefore necessary that all commodities shall be measured by some one standard, and this one standard is in reality "demand" or "need" which is what holds everything together, since if men cease to have wants or if their wants alter, exchange will go on no longer, or will be on different lines. But demand or need has come to be conventionally represented by money; this is why money is called *nomisma* (customary currency), because it does not exist by nature but by custom (*nomos*), and can be altered and rendered useless at will.[9]

Aristotle, *Politics*

---

[8] From Aristotle, *Nicomachean Ethics* 5.7–8.1134b18–1135a5 (London, 1926), following Rackham's translation of Richards emendations.

[9] From Aristotle, *Politics* 5.1133a19–31, trans. Rackham (London, 1926) (modified).

4. MAKING FUN OF THE PHILOSOPHERS: ARISTOPHANES

Aristophanes,
The Clouds

That the ideas running through the nomos/physis *debate were not limited to the world of philosophers and professors is suggested by the following reading from Aristophanes' play,* The Clouds. *In the play a cunning old farmer named Strepsiades tries to escape from his creditors by taking lessons from "Socrates," supposedly a sophist selling his smarmy services for a fee. Here is a sample of what he got.*[10]

STREPSIADES (*puzzled*):   But look—Zeus, up on Olympus, don't you count him a god?

SOCRATES (*incredulous, scornful*):   Zeus? What rubbish! There's no Zeus!

STREPSIADES (*awestruck*):   What? Well! (*Recovering countenance a bit*) Who makes the rain? You just tell me that, for a start!

SOCRATES (*gesture towards the chorus of the comedy, who represent Clouds*):   They do, of course. I'll explain. The evidence is overwhelming. Have you ever seen rain without clouds? But, on your theory it ought to rain out of a clear sky, with no clouds in sight.

STREPSIADES (*impressed*):   Well, by God, that certainly fits with what you were saying. Do you know, honestly, I always thought it was Zeus pissing through a sieve! (*Cackles, then worried again*) But tell me—who does the thundering? That's what gives me the willies!

SOCRATES: They thunder—(*portentously*) in *random motion*.

STREPSIADES: Well, you do have some ideas! But how do you mean?

SOCRATES (*adopting lecturing manner*):   When they are charged with fluid, and the laws of physics set them in movement, they hang low, laden with rain—through the laws of physics—and then, laden, they collide with each other and split—crash!

STREPSIADES: But who makes all those laws to get them moving? Isn't it Zeus?

SOCRATES: Oooooh no! It is *Atmospheric Rotation*.

STREPSIADES: Well, I never realized Zeus wasn't there any longer, but it was Rotation in charge. (*Suspiciously*) But—you still haven't explained to me about the noise, the thunder.

SOCRATES: Didn't I tell you that when the clouds are filled with water they collide with each other and produce a noise by virtue of their density?

STREPSIADES (*a little pugnaciously*):   Well, what's the reason for thinking that?

SOCRATES (*patiently*):   I'll explain with reference to your own experience. Have you ever filled yourself up with stew at a festival and then felt a bit funny in your guts, when a rumbling and bubbling runs all through them?

STREPSIADES: By God I have, and they give me terrible trouble when they're upset, and that bit of stew starts thundering—it's a terrible noise. Quiet-like at

---

[10] From Kenneth Dover, trans., *The Greeks* (Austin, University of Texas, 1980), pp. 104–105. Used by permission.

first—ppp! ppp! Then it steps it up—pppPP! And when I go and shit, it's *thunder*—ppppPPPPP!!!—just like the clouds!

SOCRATES: Well, just think what a fart you can produce from that puny belly of yours; and doesn't it stand to reason that the air above us (*points solemnly*)—infinite—can do a great crash of thunder? That, incidentally, is why the words "crash" and "crap" resemble each other.

C. The Threat of Socrates

Why Socrates (469–399 B.C.) constituted so grave a threat to Athens that some of its most important leaders wanted to have him either executed or exiled has puzzled readers of the ancient sources of his trial for centuries. To begin with, there are difficulties with the sources themselves. Contemporaries of Socrates like Plato and Xenophon give accounts of the great philosopher and his trial that are inconsistent with each other, not to mention with versions of "Socrates" such as that of Aristophanes (Section B.4.). A political pamphlet ascribed to a sophist by the name of Polykrates (Section C.2.) may have generated Plato's and Xenophon's defenses of Socrates. Other than the surviving dialogues of Plato and Xenophon, about a dozen other authors wrote dialogues that feature Socrates. Of these, however, only fragments survive.

The charges against Socrates, "refusing to recognize the gods the state recognizes; introducing other new divinities; and corrupting the youth,"[11] have always been well known. The three accusations add up to a single accusation: impiety. However, the precise meaning and nature of Socrates' "impiety," and whether the charges actually concealed a more important political agenda, have been endlessly debated. This much at least seems clear. Athens, and the Greek world in general, had undergone major political, military, social, and cultural developments during the fifth century. As often happens in periods of change, traditional institutions had difficulty in adjusting. Socrates became a focal point at Athens for the clash between old and new. In his "Socratic" discussions, the self-proclaimed gadfly of Athens embarrassed many of its leading lights publicly while challenging all existing institutions and encouraging his listeners (he claimed to have no pupils and that he was not a teacher) to do likewise.

One of the most touchy of the subjects Socrates dealt with was the question of how values should and could be transmitted to the young—the central endeavor and problem facing all societies. Who should educate? Socrates trashed all who were traditionally supposed to "educate": parents, the laws, teachers, sophists, good men, prominent citizens, famous heroes of the past, and the wealthy. Some of his younger listeners picked up his approach and with gusto challenged the wisdom of their elders and the authority of traditional values. In the context of a lost war (the Peloponnesian War) followed by a civil war, this was a dangerous undertaking. Although an amnesty protected political dissidents after the civil war, there was nothing to stop charges of what many saw as the waging of an insidious cultural war against accepted values. Despite all the threats, Socrates showed no hint of mending his ways. His god, he claimed, kept him on the right

---

[11] Diogenes Laertius 2.40.

track, not by positively prescribing actions, but by prohibiting them. His self-sufficient, arrogant individualism and his appeal to a private source of authority militated against the communitarian traditions of polis *society.*

1. SOCRATES AND ANYTUS

Plato, *Meno*

Anytus, Socrates' future (and most prominent) accuser, features in Plato's dialogue The Meno. *Meno, a young man looking to improve his role as a citizen (though not of Athens) and a manager of his household, asks Socrates how excellence can be taught, and Socrates responds by saying that he cannot answer because he does not know what excellence is. At the conclusion of the dialogue Anytus joins the discussion and is invited by Socrates to participate. Socrates demonstrates that parents cannot transmit their own virtue to their children. After the usual Socratic back and forth, Anytus leaves, warning Socrates not to run people down or slander the good people of Athens. The discussion begins with the question of who can teach excellence. Socrates suggests, ironically, that the sophists might be able to perform this task. The reading is a good example of Socrates' approach and his use of irony.*[12]

SOCRATES: Now there is an opportunity for you [*Anytus*] to join me in consultation on my friend Meno here. He has been declaring to me for some time, Anytus, that he desires to have that wisdom and virtue whereby men keep their household or their city in good order, honor their parents, and know when to welcome and when to send off properly citizens and strangers as befits a good man. Now tell me, to whom ought we properly send him for lessons in this virtue? Or is it clear enough, from our argument just now, that he should go to those men who profess to be teachers of virtue and advertise themselves as the common teachers of Greeks, and who are ready to instruct anyone who chooses in return for fees charged on a fixed scale.

ANYTUS: To whom are you referring, Socrates?

S: Surely you know them as well as anyone; they are the men whom people call sophists.

A: For heavens sake don't use that term. May no kinsman or friend of mine, whether of this city or another, be seized with such madness as to let himself be infected with the company of these men; they are a manifest ruin and a corrupting influence on whoever has anything to do with them.

S: What, Anytus? Of all the people who set out to understand how to do us good, do you mean to single out these as conveying not merely no benefit, such as the rest can give, but actually corruption to anyone placed in their hands and in return for this service openly claim they should be paid! Indeed, I cannot believe you, for I know of one man, Protagoras, who amassed more money by his craft as a sophist than did the sculptor Pheidias—a man famous for the noble works he produced—or for that matter any ten other sculptors. A mender of old shoes, or a patcher up of clothes, who made the shoes or clothes

---

[12] From Plato, *Meno* 91a–95a, trans. B. Jowett (London, 1892) (modified).

worse than he received them, could not have remained thirty days undetect-
ed, and would very soon have starved; whereas during more than forty years,
Protagoras was corrupting all Greece, and sending his disciples from him
worse than he received them, and he was never found out! . . . And not only
Protagoras, but many others are well spoken of, some of whom lived before
him and others are still living. Are we to suppose from what you have said
that they deceived and corrupted the youth consciously or unconsciously? Can
those who were presumed by many to be the wisest men of Greece have been
so out of their minds?

A: Mad? No, Socrates. Rather the young men who gave them their money, and
still more their relatives and guardians, were out of their minds. Even more to
blame were the states that allowed the sophists entry and did not expel them,
whether they were foreigners or one of themselves.

S: Has any one of the sophists wronged you Anytus? What makes you so angry
at them?

A: Heavens, no! I have never in my life had anything to do with any of them, nor
would I let any of my family have anything to do with them either.

S: Then you have absolutely no experience of them?

A: And don't want any, ever.

S: Then, my good friend, how can you know whether a thing is good or bad of
which you are wholly ignorant?

A: Easily. The fact is I know what kind of people these sophists are whether I
have experience of them or not.

*Having dismissed out-of-hand the sophists as teachers of virtue, Anytus is invited to say who is
capable of teaching the young how to live properly. (Bear in mind that Socrates was popularly
thought to be a sophist himself, although he did not charge for his interrogations.)*

A: Why single out individuals? Any Athenian gentleman taken at random will
do him more good than the sophists would if he follows his advice.

S: And did these gentlemen develop their fine qualities spontaneously, and
without having been taught by anyone are able, nonetheless, to teach others that
which they had never learned themselves?

A: I expect they must have learned from the previous generation of good men
like themselves. You can't deny that there have been many good men in this
city.

S: True, indeed, Anytus. And many good statesmen have been and still are in
the city of Athens. But I want to know whether they have proved to be good
teachers besides possessing their own virtue. That is the question, not whether there are or have been, good men here, but whether virtue can be taught.
And our inquiry into this problem resolves itself into the question: Did the
good men of our own and of former times know how to transmit to another
man the virtue in respect of which they were good, or is it something not to
be transmitted? That is the question Meno and I have been discussing all this
time. Look at the matter in your own way of speaking: would you not say that

Themistocles [*a major architect of Greek resistance during the second Persian invasion*] was a good man?

A: Yes, indeed; none better.

S: And if any man ever was a teacher of his own virtue, he especially was a good teacher of his?

A: Yes—if he wanted to.

S: But would he not have wanted to? He would, at any rate have desired to make his own son a good man and a gentleman; he could not have been jealous of him, or have intentionally abstained from imparting to him his own virtue. Did you never hear that he made his son Cleophantus a famous horseman and had him taught to ride upright on horseback and hurl a javelin and perform many other marvelous feats? In anything which could be learned from a master he was well trained. Surely you must have heard all this from your elders?

A: I have.

S: Then no one could say that he showed any want of natural ability?

A: Very likely not.

S: But have you ever heard anybody, young or old, say that Cleophantus, son of Themistocles, was a wise or good man, as his father was?

A: Certainly not.

S: And if virtue could have been taught, would his father Themistocles have sought to train him in these minor accomplishments, and allowed him who, as you must remember, was his own son, to be no better than his neighbors in those qualities in which he himself excelled?

A: Indeed, indeed, I think not.

S: Well, there you have a fine teacher of virtue who, you admit, was one of the best men of past times. Let us take another, Aristeides son of Lysimachus [*another famous Athenian of the Second Persian War period*]. Do you not admit that he was a good man?

Socrates repeats the process with Aristeides' son and the sons of other famous Athenians, such as Pericles and Thucydides, son of Melesias. None of their sons could be shown to measure up to their fathers in terms of virtue. He concludes that virtue cannot be taught. At this point Anytus responds with a warning to Socrates and leaves the discussion.

A: Socrates, I think that you are too ready to speak evil of men: and if you will take my advice, I would recommend you to be careful. Perhaps there is no city in which it is not easier to do men harm than to do them good, and this is certainly the case at Athens, as I believe that you know.

S: O Meno, I think that Anytus is in a rage. And he may well be in a rage, for he thinks, in the first place that I am defaming these gentlemen; and in the second place, he is of the opinion that he is one of them himself. But some day he will know what is the meaning of defamation, and if he ever does, he will forgive me.

In his trial Socrates was defamed by his accusers, Anytus among them. Whether Anytus later repented is not known. Perhaps. A tradition has it that he was exiled when the Athenians came to their senses.

2. THE SOPHIST POLYKRATES' PAMPHLET

A version of the charges against Socrates comes from a pamphlet by a sophist by the name of Polykrates. The pamphlet itself has been lost, but some ancient sources are thought to quote from it. It strips away the charge of impiety and focuses on what a significant number of Athenians must have thought was the real reason why Socrates was brought to trial. It might also help explain why he lost his case when he was condemned by a majority of the five hundred of his fellow citizens who constituted his judges.[13]

|| Xenophon, *Memorabilia*

The accuser claimed that Socrates taught sons to treat their fathers with contempt. He persuaded them that he made his companions wiser than their fathers. He said that the law allowed a son to put his father in prison if he convinced a jury that he was insane; and this was a proof that it was lawful for the wiser to keep the more ignorant in jail.

D. Socrates' Defense: "I Shall Obey God Rather Than You"

The portion of Socrates' defense provided in this reading comes from Plato's version of the trial of the great philosopher. It is not a historical transcript of Socrates' speech, but a cleverly developed defense composed by his greatest admirer. Guided by his daimonion *(i.e., his personal divine spirit), Socrates insists that he has a responsibility to "philosophize," that is to spend his life "exhorting any one whom I meet and saying to him after my manner: 'You, my friend,—a citizen of the great and mighty and wise city of Athens,—are you not ashamed of heaping up the greatest amount of money and honor and reputation, and caring so little about wisdom and truth and the greatest improvement of the soul, which you never regard or heed at all?' "[14] If that's all Socrates did, it is hard to see why he excited so much antagonism—annoyance, perhaps, but not hatred.*

|| Plato, *Apology*

Scholars differ among themselves as to the weight to be given to religious, political, and social elements in the jury's decision to condemn Socrates to death. Apparently all three elements were involved. It would seem that the jury did not see Socrates as a gentle, absent-minded professor, harmlessly speculating about nature, human society, good behavior, and so on, but as emblematic of a force that was undermining traditional cultural values, and in particular the role of parents

---

[13] From Xen. *Memorabilia* 1.2.59, trans. E. C. Marchant (London, 1923) (modified).

[14] Plato, *Apology* 29d–e, trans. B. Jowett (London, 1892).

in educating their children. This force was viewed as also undermining the laws and customs of the city, which were supposed to help parents in their task of preparing the next generation of children for their lives as citizens. His remark, to the effect that the public life of the citizen was worthless—"for he who will fight for the right, if he would live even for a brief space, must be a private citizen, not a public man"[15]*—must have been felt as arrogant by his jurors who in this very instance were exercising their role as public figures—citizens, that is—in the administration of justice. His disregard for the Athenian democracy, "the many," runs through the speech. His "philosophizing" may have struck the "the many" as something other than exhorting people not to worry about wealth and take care of their souls. Nevertheless, the defense is a moving account, constructed by Plato, of Socrates as Athens' dedicated, self-appointed ethical ombudsman.*[16]

SOCRATES: I have said enough in answer to the charge of Meletus: any elaborate defense is unnecessary; but I know only too well how great is the hostility I have incurred. This is what will be my destruction if I am destroyed—not Meletus, nor yet Anytus—but the envy and detraction of the many, which has been the death of many good men, and will probably be the death of many more; there is no danger of my being the last of them. Perhaps some one will say: "Are you not ashamed, Socrates, of a course of life which is likely to bring you to an untimely end? To him I may fairly answer: "There you are mistaken: a man who is good for anything ought not to calculate the chance of living or dying; he ought only to consider whether in doing anything he is doing right or wrong—acting the part of a good man or of a bad." Whereas, upon your view, the heroes who fell at Troy were not good for much, and the son of Thetis [*i.e., Achilles*] above all, who altogether despised danger in comparison with enduring disgrace; and when he was so eager to slay Hector, his goddess mother said to him, that if he avenged his companion Patroclus, and slew Hector, he would die himself. "Fate," she said, in these or the like words, "waits for you next after Hector." He, on receiving this warning, utterly despised danger and death, and instead of fearing them, feared rather to live in dishonor, and not to avenge his friend. "Let me die forthwith," he replies, "and be avenged of my enemy, rather than stay here by the curved ships, a laughing-stock and a burden of the earth." Had Achilles any thought of death and danger?

Wherever a man's place is, whether it is the place which he has chosen or that in which he has been placed by a commander, there he ought to remain in the hour of danger; he should not think of death or of anything but of disgrace. And this, O men of Athens, is a true saying. Strange, indeed, would be my conduct, if I who, when I was ordered by the generals whom you chose to command me at Potidaea and Amphipolis and Delium [*battles fought during the Peloponnesian War, where Socrates distinguished himself*] remained where they placed me, like

---

[15] Plato, *Apology* 32a, trans. B. Jowett (London, 1892).

[16] From Plato, *Apology* 28a–32a, trans. B. Jowett (London, 1892) (modified).

any other man, facing death—if now, when, as I conceive and imagine, God orders me to fulfill the philosopher's mission of searching into myself and other men, I were to desert my post through fear of death, or any other fear, that would indeed be shocking, and I might justly be arraigned in court for denying the existence of the gods, if I disobeyed the oracle because I was afraid of death, fancying that I was wise when I was not wise. For the fear of death, gentlemen, is nothing else than to think one is wise when one is not; it is pretence of knowing the unknown. In truth no one knows whether death may not be the greatest good. But people fear it as if they knew that it was the greatest evil. Is not this ignorance, which thinks that it knows what it does not, surely ignorance of a disgraceful sort?

Perhaps in this respect also I believe myself to differ from men in general, and may perhaps claim to be wiser than they are:—that whereas I know but little of the world below, I do not suppose that I know. But I do know that to do injustice to, and disobey him who is better, whether God or man, is evil and dishonorable, and I will never fear or avoid a possible good rather than a certain evil. And therefore if you let me go now, and are not convinced by Anytus, who said that since I had been prosecuted I must be put to death (or if not that I ought never to have been prosecuted at all); and that if I escape now, your sons will all be utterly ruined by listening to my words—if you say to me, "Socrates, this time we will do as Anytus says, and you shall be let off, but upon one condition, that you are not to enquire and philosophize in this way any more, and that if you are caught doing so again you shall die." If this was the condition on which you let me go, I should reply: "Men of Athens, I honor and love you; but I shall obey God rather than you, and while I have life and strength I shall never cease from the practice and teaching of philosophy, exhorting any one whom I meet and saying to him after my manner: "You, my friend,—a citizen of the great and mighty and wise city of Athens,—are you not ashamed of heaping up the greatest amount of money and honor and reputation, and caring so little about wisdom and truth and the greatest improvement of the soul, which you never regard or heed at all?" And if the person with whom I am arguing, says: "Yes, I do care," then I do not leave him or let him go at once, but I proceed to interrogate and examine and cross-examine him, and if I think that he has no virtue in him, but only says that he has, I reproach him with undervaluing the greater, and overvaluing the less. And I shall repeat the same words to every one whom I meet, young and old, citizen and alien, but especially to the citizens, inasmuch as they are my brethren. For know that this is the command of God; and I believe that no greater good has ever happened in the state than my service to the God. For I do nothing but go about persuading you all, old and young alike, not to take thought for your bodies or your properties, but first and chiefly to care about the greatest perfection of the soul. I tell you that virtue is not created by money, but that from virtue comes money and every other good of man, public as well as private.

This is my teaching, and if this is the doctrine which corrupts the youth, then it must be injurious. But if any one says that this is not my teaching, he is speaking an untruth. Wherefore, O men of Athens, I say to you, "Do as Anytus bids or not as Anytus bids, and either acquit me or not; but whichever you do, understand that I shall never alter my ways, not even if I have to die many times."

Men of Athens, do not interrupt, but hear me; there was an understanding between us that you should hear me to the end: I have something more to say, at which you may be inclined to cry out; but I believe that to hear me will be good for you, and therefore I beg that you will not cry out. I would have you know, that if you kill such an one as I am, you will injure yourselves more than you will injure me. Nothing will injure me, not Meletus nor yet Anytus—they cannot, for a bad man is not permitted to injure a better than himself. I do not deny that Anytus may, perhaps, kill him, or drive him into exile, or deprive him of civil rights; and he may imagine, and others may imagine, that he is inflicting a great injury upon him: but there I do not agree. For the evil of doing as he is doing—the evil of unjustly taking away the life of another—is greater far.

And now, O men of Athens, I am not going to argue for my own sake, as you may think, but for yours, that you may not sin against the God by condemning me, who am his gift to you. For if you kill me you will not easily find a successor to me, who, if I may use such a ludicrous figure of speech, am a sort of gadfly, given to the state by God; and the state is a great and noble steed who is lazy in his motions owing to his very size, and requires to be stirred into life. I am that gadfly which God has attached to the state, and all day long and in all places am always fastening upon you, arousing and persuading and reproaching you. You will not easily find another like me, and therefore I would advise you to spare me. I dare say that you may feel out of temper (like a person who is suddenly awakened from sleep), and you think that you might easily strike me dead as Anytus advises, and then you would sleep on for the remainder of your lives, unless God in his care of you sent you another gadfly. . . .

Someone may wonder why I go about in private giving advice and busying myself with other people's affairs, but do not venture to come forward in public and advise the state. I will tell you why. You have heard me speak at different times and in different places of an oracle or sign [*daimonion*] which comes to me, and is the divinity which Meletus ridicules in the indictment. This sign, which is a kind of voice, first began to come to me when I was a child; it always forbids but never commands me to do anything which I am going to do. This is what deters me from being a politician. And rightly, as I think. For I am certain, O men of Athens, that if I had engaged in politics, I should have perished long ago, and done no good either to you or to myself. And do not be offended at my telling you the truth: for the truth is, that no man who conscientiously opposes you or any other multitude, and prevents many lawless and unrighteous deeds from happening in the state, will save his life; for he who will fight for the right, if he would live even for a brief space, must be a private citizen, not a public man.

E. Diogenes the Cynic

Diogenes (ca. 412–ca. 321 B.C.) was exiled from his native Sinope on the Black Sea, having been accused, so tradition has it, of having adulterated the coinage there. He spent the rest of his life in exile at Corinth and Athens. The accusation of debasing the currency was seen by supporters and critics alike as emblematic of his dedication throughout his life to subverting contemporary civic values.

    More than perhaps any other philosophy, that of Diogenes demonstrated the logical extreme to which naturalism could be elevated over conventionalism. According to Diogenes, the main obstacles to a virtuous life stemmed from conventional behavior. Hence the goal of philosophy was to liberate the individual from the shackles of work, marriage, raising children, good manners, military service, voting, paying taxes, etc. Wealth, power, and worldly reputation should be rejected; all social, racial, and sexual distinctions should be ignored. The ideal of life was to be found not in a city or a civilized state, but in human society before it became complex and urbanized. Since man was an animal, Diogenes' aim was to duplicate a life as close as possible to that of the natural life of animals—and of the gods who were also free from human conventions. All natural functions were to be performed without shame in public; only a minimum of material possessions should be had; the individual should be able to endure heat and cold with indifference. Thus liberated from the burdens of possessions and obligations to society, the individual could achieve perfect self-sufficiency and freedom. However, this was not the self-sufficiency of slovenly living, because for Diogenes the ultimate form of self-sufficiency was the practice of natural virtues. Because the narrowness of citizenship in an individual polis *was to be rejected, Diogenes declared himself to be a citizen of the world, a* cosmopolites—*convenient for someone who lived in exile and was thus without any actual civic obligations other than those of a* metic. *The accusation of "adulterating the coinage" in his native city was often resurrected, but Diogenes embraced the charge, claiming that, metaphorically speaking, undermining existing value systems was, in fact, his life's work.*[17]

He would wonder that musicians should tune the strings of the lyre, while leaving the dispositions of their own souls discordant; that mathematicians should gaze at the sun and the moon, but overlook matters close at hand; that the orators should make a fuss about justice in their speeches, but never practice it (6.27–28). . . . He described himself as a hound (*kyôn*—hence Cynicism, *"doglike"*) which all men praise, although none of its admirers, he added, dared go hunting with. When someone boasted that at the Pythian games he had vanquished men, Diogenes replied, "No, I defeat men; you defeat slaves" (6.33). To those who said to him: "You are old; take a rest," he said, "What? If I were running in the stadium, ought I to slacken my pace when approaching the finish line? Ought I not rather to put on speed?" (6.34).

Diogenes
Laertius, *Lives
of Eminent
Philosophers*

---

[17] From Diogenes Laertius, *Lives of Eminent Philosophers*, trans. R. D. Hicks (London, 1925).

He used to call the demagogues the lackeys of the people. . . . He lit a lamp in broad daylight and said, as he went about, "I am looking for a man." (6.41) Dionysius the Stoic says that after the Battle of Chaeronea [*where the Macedonians under Philip II defeated the Athenians and Thebans*] he was seized and dragged off to Philip and being asked who he was, replied, "A spy upon your insatiable greed" (6.43). Once he saw the officials of a temple leading away someone who had stolen a bowl belonging to the treasurers, and said, "The great thieves are leading away the little thief" (6.45). When someone declared that life is an evil he corrected him: "Not life itself, but living badly" (6.55). He was returning from Olympia, and when somebody inquired whether there was a great crowd, "Yes," he said, "a great crowd, but few who could be called men" (6.60). Asked where he came from he said: "I am a citizen of the world" (6.63). Seeing a young man behaving effeminately, "Are you not ashamed," he said, that your own intention about yourself should be worse than nature's: for nature made you a man, but you are forcing yourself to play the woman" (6.65). To a man who was urgently soliciting a prostitute he said, "Why, foolish man, are you at such pains to gain your suit, when it would be better for you to lose it" (6.66).

Education according to Diogenes is moderation for the young, consolation for the old, wealth for the poor, and an ornament for the rich (6.68). Being asked what was the most beautiful thing in the world he replied, "Freedom of speech" (6.68).

He used to say that training was of two kinds, mental and physical. By constant physical exercise perceptions are formed which secure freedom of movement for the performance of virtuous actions. The one half of this course of mental and physical training is incomplete without the other, good health and strength being just as much included among the essential things whether for body or soul. He would bring forward indisputable evidence to show how easily from gymnastic training we arrive at excellence . . . taking the example of flute-players and athletes he would say what surpassing skill they acquire by incessant toil. Yet if they had transferred their efforts to the training of the mind, how certainly their labors would have achieved their proper end and been productive (6.70).

Nothing in life, however, he maintained, has any chance of succeeding without strenuous practice; and this is capable of overcoming anything. Accordingly, instead of useless toils men should choose such as nature recommended, and thereby live happily. Yet such is their madness that they choose to be miserable. For even the despising of pleasure is itself most pleasurable, when we are habituated to it; and just as those accustomed to a life of pleasure feel disgust when they pass over to the opposite experience, so those whose training has been the opposite kind derive more pleasure from despising pleasure than from the pleasures themselves. This was the gist of his conversation; and it was plain that he acted accordingly, adulterating currency in very truth, allowing convention no such authority as he allowed to natural right, and asserting that the manner of life he lived was the same as that of Heracles when he preferred liberty to everything (6.71).

He maintained that all things are the property of the wise. . . . He would argue: All things belong to the gods. The gods are friends of the wise and friends share all property in common; therefore all things are the property of the wise. . . . He would ridicule good birth and fame and all such distinctions calling them showy ornaments of vice. The only true commonwealth was, he said, that which is as wide as the universe. He advocated community of wives, recognizing no other marriage than a union of the man who persuades with the woman who consents. And for this reason he thought too sons should be held in common (6.72).

7

THE FOURTH CENTURY

Greek historians have traditionally viewed the fourth century B.C. as a period of decline after the "Golden Age" of the fifth century B.C. In terms of Greek culture this is a surprising interpretation. The fourth century B.C. was one of the most creative periods in Greek history. Not only did some of the greatest Greek artists and writers, including the sculptor Praxiteles, the orator Demosthenes, and the dramatist Menander, work in the fourth century B.C., but so also did the founders of the major philosophical schools: Diogenes, Plato, Aristotle, Epicurus, and Zeno. If the fourth century B.C. was not a time of cultural decline, it was definitely a period of political crisis and dramatic change in Greece. The roots of the century's problems lay in the Peloponnesian War.

As the Athenian historian Thucydides pointed out, the Peloponnesian War was the Greeks' "Great War," greater by far than the Trojan War and Persian War both in the scale of the fighting and the devastation it inflicted on Greece. Population fell sharply throughout Greece. Athens alone may have lost half its male citizens, and even the victor Sparta had to resort increasingly to mobilizing helots to fulfill its manpower needs. Everywhere farms were ruined, trade declined sharply, and cities were destabilized. Recovery in the new century was slow and difficult. Severe episodes of stasis broke out at Argos and other cities, leading to an unprecedented rise in the number of political exiles and the reappearance throughout the Greek world of tyrants such as Clearchus, whose dynasty ruled the city of Heraclea in the Black Sea for more than three quarters of a century. The situation was aggravated by the ambitions of the principal *poleis* to appropriate for themselves the hegemonic position Athens had enjoyed in the fifth century B.C. For almost four decades Sparta, Athens, and Thebes vied for preeminence in the Aegean, only to have their rivals combine against them and frustrate their plans. The result was exhaustion of the major cities, political and military stalemate, and the failure of the Greek cities to cooperate when a serious foreign threat appeared about the mid-fourth century B.C. for the first time in over a century.

The threat came from an unexpected source. The Persian Empire had been the great power of the Greek world for almost two centuries. Although the Persian attempt to conquer Greece in 480/79 B.C. had failed, Persia remained a potent force in Greek affairs well into the fourth century B.C., supporting Sparta in the Peloponnesian War, Sparta's enemies in the 390s B.C., and imposing peace on the Greeks in the King's Peace in 387 B.C. With their attention focused on their own internal struggles and their traditional enemy Persia, the Greek states ignored until it was too late the rise of a new power in the north Balkans: Macedon. In little more than twenty years the Macedonian king Philip II transformed Macedon from a weak and chronically unstable state into the most formidable military power in the Balkans, mistress of an empire that extended from the Danube River in the north to central Greece. Athens and Thebes belatedly awoke to the threat and attempted to repel Philip II but were decisively defeated in the Battle of Chaeronea in 338 B.C., opening the way to Macedonian domination of all Greece. By the late 320s B.C., Philip II's son Alexander III had consolidated his hold on Greece and invaded and conquered the Persian Empire, extending Macedonian power to western India and destroying the political system that had governed Greek life for more than two centuries.

A. The Decline and Fall of Sparta

1. SOCIAL PROBLEMS AT SPARTA: THE CONSPIRACY OF CINADON

Sparta's imperial preeminence in the decades immediately following the Peloponnesian War increased stresses already present in Spartan society. Several factors—the influx of wealth from the empire, the decrease in Spartan manpower resulting from losses during the Peloponnesian War and the conflicts of the 390s B.C., and the concentration of land encouraged by changes in Spartan law allowing heiresses to inherit kleroi—*combined to undermine the vaunted "equality" of the Spartan citizens. Dramatic evidence of the resulting fissures in Spartan society is provided by Xenophon's account of the abortive conspiracy organized by the "inferior" Cinadon—an individual of Spartan birth who failed to successfully complete the agoge—ca. 394 B.C.[1]*

Xenophon,
Hellenica

Now Agesilaus had not been seated on the throne one year when, as he sacrificed one of the appointed sacrifices in behalf of the city, the soothsayer warned him, saying, "The gods reveal a conspiracy of the most fearful character." When the king sacrificed a second time, he said, "The aspect of the victims is now even yet more terrible." When he had sacrificed for the third time, the soothsayer exclaimed, "O Agesilaus, the sign is given to me, even as though we were in the very midst of the enemy." Thereupon they sacrificed to the deities who avert evil and work salvation, and so barely obtained good omens and ceased sacrificing. Nor had five days elapsed after the sacrifices were ended, before one came bringing information to the ephors of a conspiracy, and named Cinadon

---

[1] Xenophon, *Hellenica* 3.3.4. From Xenophon, *Hellenica*, trans. Henry G. Dakyns (London and New York, 1892).

as the ringleader, a young man who was strong of body and soul, but not one of the peers. Accordingly the ephors questioned their informant, "How say you the occurrence is to take place?" He who gave the information answered, "Cinadon took me to the limit of the market-place, and bade me count how many Spartans there were in the market-place; and I counted—king, and ephors, and elders, and others—maybe forty. 'But tell me, Cinadon,' I said to him, 'why have you asked me to count them?' and he answered me, 'Those men, I would have you know, are your enemies; and all those others, more than 4,000, congregated there are your natural allies.' Then he took and showed me in the streets, here one and there two of our enemies, as we chanced to come across them, and all the rest our natural allies; and so again running through the list of Spartans to be found in the country districts, he still kept emphasizing the same point: 'Look you, on each estate there is one enemy—the master—and all the rest allies.'" The ephors asked, "How many do you reckon are in the secret of this matter?" The informant answered, "On that point also he gave me to understand that there were by no means many in their secret who were prime movers of the affair, but those few to be depended on. 'And to make up,' said he, 'we ourselves are in their secret, all the rest of them—Helots, enfranchised, inferiors, provincials, one and all. Note their demeanor when Spartans chance to be the topic of their talk. Not one of them can conceal the delight it would give him if he might eat up every Spartan raw.'" Then, as the inquiry went on, the question came, "And where did they propose to find arms?" The answer followed, "He explained that those of us, of course, who are enrolled in regiments have arms of our own already, and as for the mass—he led the way to the war foundry, and showed me scores and scores of knives, of swords, of spits, hatchets, and axes, and reaping-hooks. 'Anything or everything,' he told me, 'which men use to dig in the earth, cut timber, or quarry stone, would serve our purpose; indeed, the instruments used for other crafts would in nine cases out of ten furnish weapons enough and to spare, especially in dealing with unarmed antagonists.'" Once more being asked what time the affair was to come off, he replied his orders were not to leave the city.

As the result of their inquiry the ephors were persuaded that the man's statements were based upon things he had really seen, and they were so alarmed that they did not even venture to summon the Little Assembly, as it was named; but holding informal meetings among themselves—a few senators here and a few there—they determined to send Cinadon and others of the young men to Aulon, with instructions to apprehend certain of the inhabitants and Helots, whose names were written on the scytale. He had further instructions to capture another resident in Aulon; this was a woman, the most beautiful in the place—supposed to be the arch-corruptress of all Lacedaemonians, young and old, who visited Aulon. It was not the first mission of the sort on which Cinadon had been employed by the ephors. It was natural, therefore, that the ephors should entrust him with the scytale on which the names of the suspects were inscribed; and in answer to his inquiry which of the young men he was to take with him, they said, "Go and order the eldest of the commanders of horse to let you have six or seven who chance to be there." But they had taken care to let the commander know whom he was to send, and that those sent should also know that their business was to capture Cinadon. Further, the authorities instructed Cinadon that they would send three wagons to save bringing back his captives on foot—concealing as deeply as possible the fact that he, and he alone, was the object of the mission. Their reason for not securing him in the city was that they did not really know the extent of the mischief; and they wished, in the first instance, to learn from Cinadon who his accomplices were before these latter could discover they were informed against and effect their escape. His captors were to secure him first, and having learned from him the names of his confederates, to write them down and send them as quickly as possible to the ephors. The ephors, indeed, were so much concerned about the whole occurrence that they further sent a company of cavalry to assist those going to Aulon. As soon as the capture was effected, and one of the horsemen was back with the list of names taken down on the information of Cinadon, they lost no time in apprehending the soothsayer Tisamenus and the rest who were the principals in the conspiracy. When Cinadon himself was brought back and cross-examined, and had made a full confession of the whole plot, his plans, and his accomplices, they put to him one final question, "What was your object in undertaking this business?" He answered, "I wished to be inferior to no man in Lacedaemon." Let that be as it might, his fate was to be taken out forthwith in irons, just as he was, and to be placed with his two hands and his neck in the collar, and so under scourge and goad to be driven, himself and his accomplices, round the city. Thus, these men suffered the appropriate penalty for their offences.

2. SPARTA AT ITS PEAK: THE KING'S PEACE (386 B.C.)

In the early 390s B.C. Sparta sought to regain the high ground it had enjoyed during much of the Peloponnesian War by intervening in Anatolia to "liberate" the Greek cities it had surrendered to Persia in exchange for aid against Athens. The result was the Corinthian War (394–386 B.C.), in which Persia supported an alliance of Athens, Corinth, Thebes, and others against Sparta. The war ended when Sparta resolved its disputes with Persia, becoming the guarantor of the so-called "King's Peace," the first of the fourth-century B.C. "Common Peace" agreements, which sought to guarantee the autonomy of the Greek city states. Sparta's exploitation of the autonomy clause of the King's Peace to weaken its various enemies, including Thebes, undercut the hopes for peace aroused by the King's Peace, setting the stage for the conflict that would end Sparta's position as the preeminent Greek military power.[2]

Xenophon,
Hellenica

The Athenians could not but watch with alarm the growth of the enemy's fleet, and began to fear a repetition of their former misfortune. To be trampled under foot by the hostile power seemed indeed no remote possibility, now that the Lacedaemonians had procured an ally in the person of the Persian monarch, and

[2] Xenophon, *Hellenica*, 5.1.30. From Xenophon, *Hellenica*, trans. Henry G. Dakyns (London and New York, 1892).

they were in little less than a state of siege themselves, pestered as they were by privateers from Aegina. On all these grounds the Athenians became passionately desirous of peace. The Lacedaemonians were equally disgusted with the war for various reasons—what with their garrison duties, one detachment at Lechaeum and another at Orchomenus, and the necessity of keeping guard over the states, if loyal, not to lose them, if disaffected, to prevent their revolt; not to mention the endless cycle of problems around Corinth. So again the Argives had a strong appetite for peace; they knew that the army had been called out against them, and, it was plain, that no fictitious alteration of the calendar would any longer stand them in good stead. Hence, when Tiribazus issued a summons calling on all who were willing to listen to the terms of peace sent down by the king to present themselves, the invitation was promptly accepted. When they had gathered, Tiribazus pointed to the king's seal attached to the document, and proceeded to read the contents, which ran as follows:

> The king, Artaxerxes, deems it just that the cities in Asia, with the islands of Clazomenae and Cyprus, should belong to himself; the rest of the Hellenic cities he thinks it just to leave independent, both small and great, with the exception of Lemnos, Imbros, and Scyros, which three are to belong to Athens as of old. Should any of the parties concerned not accept this peace, I, Artaxerxes, will war against him or them, with those who share my views. This will I do by land and by sea, with ships and with money.

After listening to the above declaration the ambassadors from the several states proceeded to report the same to their respective governments. One and all of these took the oaths to ratify and confirm the terms unreservedly, with the exception of the Thebans, who claimed to take the oaths in behalf of all Boeotians. This claim Agesilaus repudiated: unless they chose to take the oaths in precise conformity with the words of the king's edict, which insisted on the future autonomy of each state, small or great, he would not admit them. To this the Theban ambassadors made no other reply, except that the instructions they had received were different. "Pray go, then," Agesilaus retorted, "and ask the question; and you may inform your countrymen that if they will not comply, they will be excluded from the treaty." The Theban ambassadors departed, but Agesilaus, out of hatred to the Thebans, took active measures at once. Having got the consent of the ephors he forthwith offered sacrifice. The offerings for crossing the frontier were propitious, and he pushed on to Tegea. From Tegea he dispatched some of the knights right and left to visit the Perioeci and hasten their mobilization, and at the same time sent commanders of allied brigades to the various cities on a similar errand. But before he had started from Tegea the answer from Thebes arrived: the point was yielded, they would suffer the states to be independent. Under these circumstances the Lacedaemonians returned home, and the Thebans were forced to accept the truce unconditionally, and to recognize the autonomy of the Boeotian cities. But now the Corinthians would not dismiss the garrison of the Argives. Accordingly Agesilaus had a word of warning for both. To the former he said that if they did not dismiss the Argives, and to the latter, if they did not quit Corinth, he would march an army into their territories. The terror of both was so great that the Argives marched out of Corinth, and Corinth was once again left to herself; whereupon the butchers and their accomplices in the deed of blood determined to retire from Corinth, and the rest of the citizens welcomed back their late exiles voluntarily.

Now that the transactions were complete, and the states were bound by their oaths to abide by the peace sent down to them by the king, the immediate result was a general disarmament, military and naval forces being alike disbanded; and *so* it was that the Lacedaemonians and Athenians, with their allies, found themselves in the enjoyment of peace for the first time since the period of hostilities subsequent to the demolition of the walls of Athens. From a condition which, during the war, can only be described as a sort of even balance with their antagonists, the Lacedaemonians now emerged; and reached preeminence consequent upon the Peace of Antalcidas, so called. As guarantors of the peace presented to Hellas by the king, and as administrators personally of the autonomy of the states, they had added Corinth to their alliance; they had obtained the independence of the states of Boeotia at the expense of Thebes, which meant the gratification of an old ambition; and lastly, by calling out the army in case the Argives refused to evacuate Corinth, they had put a stop to the appropriation of that city by the Argives.

3. THE FOUNDATION OF THE SECOND ATHENIAN LEAGUE (377 B.C.)

Sparta's arbitrary exploitation of her position as guarantor of the King's Peace during the 380s and early 370s B.C. led various cities to turn to Athens for protection, reviving Athenian dreams of reestablishing her fifth-century B.C. empire. In 377 B.C. Athens formalized her growing network of alliances into a general alliance embracing many of the Aegean islands and much of central and northern Greece. The ostensible purpose of this new alliance, which historians call the "Second Athenian League," was to uphold the King's Peace. The inscription translated here is the general invitation to Greek states to join the new alliance. Notable is Athens' effort to disarm suspicion by promising to refrain from actions that had generated hostility in the fifth century: levying of tribute, installation of garrisons, establishment of cleruchies, and acquisition by Athenians of property in the empire.[3]

General invitation to join the Second Athenian League

In the archonship of Nausinicus, Callibius, son of Cephisophon, of Paeania, was secretary.

In the seventh prytany, that of (the tribe) Hippothontis, it has pleased the council and the people,—Charinus of Athmonon presided; Aristoteles made the motion:—

That, with good fortune to the Athenians and their allies, and in order that the Lacedaemonians may allow the Greeks to live in quiet, free and

---

[3] *I.G.* 2².43. From G. W. Botsford and E. G. Sihler, *Hellenic Civilization* (New York: Columbia University Press, 1915), pp. 391–394.

autonomous, and to possess their respective territories in security . . . be it
decreed by the people:—

That if any of the Greeks or of the barbarians dwelling on the mainland or of the
islanders, except such as are subjects of the King, wish to be allies of the Athenians
and of their allies, they may become such while preserving their freedom and
autonomy, using the form of government that they desire, without either admit-
ting a garrison or receiving a commandant or paying tribute, and upon the same
terms as the Chians, the Thebans, and the other allies. In favor of those who make
an alliance with the Athenians and with the allies, the (Athenian) people shall
release all the Athenians' landed possessions, whether public or private, that may
chance to be in the territory of those who make the alliance; and [the Athenians]
shall give assurances to this effect. If with regard to the cities that make the alliance with the Athenians, there chance to be at Athens inscriptions of a prejudi-
cial character, the council holding office for the time being shall have authority
to destroy them. From the date of the archonship of Nausinicus (= 378/7 B.C.) it
shall not be allowable for any Athenian, either on behalf of the state or as a private
person, to acquire either a house or a piece of land in the territories of the allies,
whether by purchase or by mortgage, or in any other way. If anyone shall undertake to purchase or acquire or take property on mortgage, in any way whatsoever,
any ally who wishes may lay an information against him before the delegates of
the allies; and the delegates, after selling the property, shall give one half (of the
proceeds) to the informer, and the other half shall belong to the common fund of
the allies. If anyone shall go to war against the members of the alliance, whether
by land or by sea, the Athenians and the allies shall give aid to the party attacked,
both by land and by sea, with all their might, according to their ability. If anyone,
whether magistrate or private citizen, shall propose or put to vote a motion contrary to this decree with the effect of annulling any of the provisions of this decree,
he himself shall incur loss of civil rights, and his property shall be confiscated, one
tenth of it for the Goddess (Athena) and he shall be tried before the Athenians
and the allies on the charge of destroying the alliance. The punishment shall be
death or banishment from the domain of the Athenians and the allies; and if he is
sentenced to death, he shall not be buried in Attica or in the territory of the allies.
The secretary of the council shall inscribe this decree on a stone stele and shall
place it by (the statue of) Zeus the Deliverer. The money for inscribing the stele,
sixty drachmas, shall be given by the treasurers of the Goddess from the fund of
ten talents. There shall be inscribed on this stele the names both of the cities now
in the alliance and of any that may join it. Furthermore, the people shall choose
immediately three envoys to go to Thebes and, so far as they can, to induce the
Thebans to take good measures.

   The following were chosen: Aristoteles of Marathon, Pyrrhander of Anaphlys-
tus, Thrasybulus of Collytus.

   The following cities are allies of the Athenians:—

Chios, Tenedos	Thebes
Mytilene	Chalcis

Methymna	Eretria
Rhodes, Poeessa	Arethusa
Byzantium	Carystus
Perinthus	Icos
Peparethos	Pall . . .
Sciathos	
Maronea	
Dion	
Paros, O . . .	
Athenae, P . . .	

(Here follows a fragment of another motion made by Aristoteles). (On the left face of the stone the following names are written in a single column):

The democracy of Corcyra, Abdera, Thasos, the Chalcidians in Thrace, Aenus, Samothrace, Dicaeopolis, the Acarnanians, Pronni in Cephallenia, Alcetas, Neoptolemus, [Jason (*erased*)], Andros, Tenos, Hestiaea, Myconos, Antissa, Eresus, Astraeus, Iulis in Ceos, Carthaea, Coresia, Elaeus, Amorgos, Selymbria, Siphnos, Sicinos, Dion in Thrace, Neapolis, the democracy of Zacynthus living in Nellus.

4. THE BATTLE OF LEUCTRA AND THE END OF SPARTAN PRIMACY (371 B.C.)

Tension between Sparta and Thebes continued throughout the 380s and 370s B.C., with Sparta attempting to use the autonomy clause of the King's Peace to undermine Theban primacy in the Boeotia. Hostilities came to a head in 372 B.C., when a Spartan army led by the king Cleombrotus invaded Boeotia, only to be decisively defeated by Theban forces led by one of the most creative generals in Greek history, Epaminondas. Sparta's heavy caualities—the king and four hundred Spartans were killed—aggravated the decline in the number of Spartan citizens, but what converted the Battle of Leuctra into one of the critical events of Greek history was the aftermath. Epaminondas followed up his victory by invading the Peloponnesus and freeing the Messenian helots, thereby reestablishing an independent Messenia for the first time in over three centuries and leaving Sparta humiliated and impoverished.[4]

Xenophon,
Hellenica

In consequence of the peace (*i.e., the general peace of 371 B.C.*) the Athenians proceeded to withdraw their garrisons from the different states, and sent to recall Iphicrates with his fleet; besides which they forced him to restore everything captured subsequent to the oaths taken at Lacedaemon. The Lacedaemonians acted differently. Although they withdrew their governors and garrisons from the other states, in Phocis they did not do so. Here Cleombrotus was quartered with his army, and had sent to ask directions from the home authorities. A speaker, Prothous, maintained that their business was to disband the army in accordance

[4] Xenophon, *Hellenica* 6.4. From Xenophon, *Hellenica*, trans. Henry G. Dakyns (London and New York, 1892).

with their oaths, and then to send round invitations to the states to contribute what each felt individually disposed, and lay such sum in the temple of Apollo; after which, if any attempt to hinder the independence of the states on any side were manifested, it would be time enough then again to invite all who cared to protect the principle of autonomy to march against its opponents. "In this way," he added, "I think the good-will of heaven will be secured, and the states will suffer least annoyance." But the Assembly, on hearing these views, agreed that this man was talking nonsense. An unseen power, as it would seem, was already driving them onwards; so they sent instructions to Cleombrotus not to disband the army, but to march straight against the Thebans if they refused to recognize the autonomy of the states (*i.e., of the Boeotian League*). . . .

The Spartan king soon perceived that, so far from leaving the Boeotian states their autonomy, the Thebans were not even preparing to disband their army, clearly in view of a general engagement; he therefore felt justified in marching his troops into Boeotia. The point of entry which he adopted was not that which the Thebans anticipated from Phocis, and where they were keeping guard at a defile; but, marching through Thisbae by a mountainous and unsuspected route, he arrived before Creusis, taking that fortress and capturing twelve Theban war-vessels besides. After this achievement he advanced from the seaboard and encamped in Leuctra on Thespian territory. The Thebans encamped on a rising ground immediately opposite at no great distance, and were supported by no allies except the Boeotians.

At this juncture the friends of Cleombrotus came to him and urged upon him strong reasons for delivering battle. "If you let the Thebans escape without a battle," they said, "you will run great risks of suffering the extreme penalty at the hands of the state. People will call to mind against you the time when you reached Cynoscephalae and did not ravage a square foot of Theban territory; and again, a subsequent expedition when you were driven back foiled in your attempt to make an entry into the enemy's country—while Agesilaus on each occasion found his entry by Mount Cithaeron. If then you have any care for yourself, or any attachment to your fatherland, you must march against the enemy." That was what his friends urged. As to his opponents, what they said was, "Now our fine friend will show whether he really is so concerned on behalf of the Thebans as he is said to be."

Cleombrotus, hearing these words, felt driven to join battle. On their side the leaders of Thebes calculated that, if they did not fight, their provincial cities would hold aloof from them and Thebes itself would be besieged; while, if the people of Thebes failed to get supplies, there was every prospect that the city itself would turn against them; and, seeing that many of them had already tasted the bitterness of exile, they came to the conclusion that it was better for them to die on the field of battle than to renew that experience. Besides this they were somewhat encouraged by the recital of an oracle which predicted that the Lacedaemonians would be defeated on the spot where the monument of the virgins stood, who, as the story goes, being raped by certain Lacedaemonians, had slain themselves. This sepulchral monument the Thebans decked with ornaments before the battle.

Furthermore, tidings were brought them from the city that all the temples had opened of their own accord; and the priestesses asserted that the gods revealed victory. Again, from the Heracleium men said that the arms had disappeared, as though Heracles himself had sallied forth to battle. It is true that another interpretation of these marvels made them out to be one and all the artifices of the leaders of Thebes. However this may be, everything in the battle turned out adverse to the Lacedaemonians; while fortune herself lent aid to the Thebans and crowned their efforts with success. Cleombrotus held his last council whether to fight or not, after the morning meal. In the heat of noon a little wine goes a long way; and people said that it had a somewhat provocative effect on their spirits.

Both sides were now arming, and there were the unmistakable signs of approaching battle, when, as the first incident, there issued from the Boeotian lines a long train bent on departure—these were the furnishers of the market, a detachment of baggage bearers, and in general such people as had no inclination to join in the fight. These were met on their retreat and attacked by the mercenary troops under Hiero, who got round them by an encircling movement. The mercenaries were supported by the Phocian light infantry and some squadrons of Heracleote and Phliasian cavalry, who fell upon the retiring train and turned them back, pursuing them and driving them into the camp of the Boeotians. The immediate effect was to make the Boeotian portion of the army more numerous and closer packed than before. The next feature of the combat was that in consequence of the flat space of plain between the opposing armies, the Lacedaemonians posted their cavalry in front of their squares of infantry, and the Thebans followed suit. Only there was this difference; the Theban cavalry was in a high state of training and efficiency, owing to their war with the Orchomenians and again their war with Thespiae, while the cavalry of the Lacedaemonians was at its worst at this period. The horses were reared and kept by the wealthiest members of the state; but whenever the army was called out, an appointed trooper appeared who took the horse with any sort of arms which might be presented to him, and set off on the expedition at a moment's notice. Moreover, these troopers were the least able-bodied of the men: raw recruits set simply astride their horses, and devoid of soldierly ambition. Such was the cavalry of either antagonist.

The heavy infantry of the Lacedaemonians, it is said, advanced by sections three-files abreast, allowing a total depth to the whole line of not more than twelve. The Thebans were formed in close order of not less than fifty shields deep, calculating that victory gained over the king's division of the army implied the easy conquest of the rest.

Cleombrotus had hardly begun to lead his division against the foe when, before in fact the troops with him were aware of his advance, the cavalry had already come into collision, and that of the Lacedaemonians was speedily worsted. In their flight they became involved with their own heavy infantry; and to make matters worse, the Theban regiments were already attacking vigorously. Still strong evidence exists for supposing that Cleombrotus and his division were, in the first instance, victorious in the battle, if we consider the fact that they could never have picked him up and brought him back alive unless his vanguard had been masters of the situation for the moment.

When, however, Deinon the polemarch and Sphodrias, a member of the king's council, with his son Cleonymus, had fallen, then it was that the cavalry and the polemarch's adjutants, as they are called, with the rest, under pressure of the mass against them, began retreating; and the left wing of the Lacedaemonians, seeing the right borne down in this way, also swerved. Still, in spite of the numbers slain, and broken as they were, as soon as they had crossed the trench which protected their camp in front, they grounded arms on the spot whence they had rushed to battle. This camp, it must be borne in mind, did not lie at all on the level, but was pitched on a somewhat steep incline. At this juncture there were some of the Lacedaemonians who, looking upon such a disaster as intolerable, maintained that they ought to prevent the enemy from erecting a trophy, and try to recover the dead not under a truce but by another battle. The polemarchs, however, seeing that nearly 1,000 men of the total Lacedaemonian troops were slain; seeing also that of the 700 Spartans themselves who were on the field something like 400 lay dead; aware, further, of the despondency which reigned among the allies, and the general disinclination on their parts to fight longer (a frame of mind not far removed in some instances from positive satisfaction at what had taken place) under the circumstances, I say, the polemarchs called a council of the ablest representatives of the shattered army and deliberated as to what should be done. Finally the unanimous opinion was to pick up the dead under a truce, and they sent a herald to treat for terms. The Thebans after that set up a trophy and gave back the bodies under a truce.

After these events, a messenger was despatched to Lacedaemon with news of the calamity. He reached his destination on the last day of the festival of the Naked Youths, just when the chorus of grown men had entered the theatre. The ephors heard the mournful tidings with grief and pain, as was inevitable; but for all that they did not dismiss the chorus, but allowed the contest to run out its natural course. What they did was to deliver the names of those who had fallen to their friends and families, with a word of warning to the women not to make any loud lamentation but to bear their sorrow in silence; and the next day it was a striking spectacle to see those who had relations among the slain moving to and fro in public with bright and radiant looks, while of those whose friends were reported to be living barely a man was to be seen, and these went about with lowered heads and scowling brows, as if in humiliation.

5. THE DECLINE OF SPARTA: WHY?

For almost three centuries Sparta had been the preeminent military power in Greece. Military success encouraged other Greeks to admire Sparta and its unique lifestyle and to overlook its internal problems while holding it up as a counterpoise to democratic Athens. Sparta's defeat in the Battle of Leuctra and subsequent collapse militarily and economically stripped away the veil, prompting a new critical attitude toward Sparta and efforts to explain the causes of Sparta's dramatic decline and fall. The pro-Spartan Athenian expatriate Xenophon located the cause in the moral failings of contemporary Spartans, their unwillingness to live up to the strict requirements of the Lycurgan system; while Aristotle looked to Lycurgus' laws themselves, identifying what he considered deficiences within them concerning the treatment of women's property and structural problems within Spartan society resulting from them.

Xenophon: The Decline of Sparta and the Spartan Ideal[5]

Now, if the question be put to me whether the laws of Lycurgus remain still to this day unchanged, that indeed is an assertion which I should no longer venture to maintain; knowing, as I do, that in former times the Lacedaemonians preferred to live at home on moderate means, content to associate exclusively with themselves rather than to play the part of governor-general in foreign states and to be corrupted by flattery; knowing further, as I do, that formerly they dreaded to be detected in the possession of gold, whereas nowadays there are not a few who make it their glory and their boast to be possessed of it. I am very well aware that in former days alien acts were put in force for this very object. To live abroad was not allowed. And why? Simply in order that the citizens of Sparta might not take the infection of dishonesty and light-living from foreigners; whereas now I am very well aware that those who are reputed to be leading citizens have but one ambition, and that is to live to the end of their days as governors-general on a foreign soil. The days were when their sole anxiety was to fit themselves to lead the rest of Greece. But nowadays they concern themselves much more to wield command than to be fit themselves to rule. And so it has come to pass that whereas in old days the states of Hellas flocked to Lacedaemon seeking her leadership against the supposed wrongdoer, now numbers are inviting one another to prevent the Lacedaemonians again recovering their empire. Yet, if they have incurred all these reproaches, we need not wonder, seeing that they are so plainly disobedient to the god himself and to the laws of their own lawgiver Lycurgus.

Xenophon, The Constitution of the Spartans

Aristotle: Women and the Failure of Spartan Society[6]

Again, the license of the Lacedaemonian women defeats the intention of the Spartan constitution, and is adverse to the happiness of the state. For, a husband and a wife being each a part of every family, the state may be considered as about equally divided into men and women; and, therefore, in those states in which the condition of the women is bad, half the city may be regarded as having no laws. And this is what has actually happened at Sparta; the legislator wanted to make the whole state hardy and temperate, and he has carried out his intention in the

Aristotle, Politics

---

[5] Xenophon, *The Constitution of the Spartans* 14. From Xenophon, *The Constitution of the Spartans*, trans. Henry G. Dakyns (London and New York, 1892).

[6] Aristotle, *Politics* 2.9, 1269b–1270b. From Aristotle, *Politics*, trans. Benjamin Jowett (Oxford, 1885).

case of the men, but he has neglected the women who live in every sort of intemperance and luxury. The consequence is that in such a state wealth is too highly valued, especially if the citizens fall under the dominion of their wives, after the manner of most warlike races, except the Celts and a few others who openly approve of male lovers. The old mythologer would seem to have been right in uniting Ares and Aphrodite, For all warlike races are prone to the love either of men of women. This was exemplified among the Spartans in the days of their greatness; many things were managed by their women. But what difference does it make whether women rule or the rulers are ruled by women?

The result is the same. Even in regard to courage, which is of no use in daily life, and is needed only in war, the influence of the Lacedaemonian women has been most mischievous. The evil showed itself in the Theban invasion, when, unlike the women in other cities, they were utterly useless and caused more confusion than the enemy. This license of the Lacedaemonian women existed from the earliest times, and was only what might be expected. For, during the wars of the Lacedaemonians, first against the Argives, and afterwards against the Arcadians and Messenians, the men were long away from home, and, on the return of peace, they gave themselves into the legislator's hand, already prepared by the discipline of a soldier's life (in which there are many elements of virtue), to receive his enactments. But, when Lycurgus, as tradition says, wanted to bring the women under his laws, they resisted, and he gave up the attempt. These then are the causes of what then happened, and this defect in the constitution is clearly to be attributed to them. We are not, however, considering what is or is not to be excused, but what is right or wrong, and the disorder of the women, as I have already said, not only gives an air of indecorum to the constitution considered in itself, but tends in a measure to foster avarice.

The mention of avarice naturally suggests a criticism of the inequality of property. While some of the Spartan citizens have quite small properties, others have very large ones; hence the land has passed into the hands of a few. And this is due also to faulty laws; for, although the legislator rightly holds up to shame the sale or purchase of an inheritance, he allows anybody who likes to bequeath it. Yet both practices lead to the same result. And nearly two-fifths of the whole country are held by women; this is owing to the number of heiresses and to the large dowries which are customary. It would surely have been better to have given no dowries at all, or, if any, but small or moderate ones. As the law now stands, a man may bestow his heiress on any one whom he pleases, and, if he dies intestate, the privilege of giving her away descends to his heir. Hence, although the country is able to maintain 1500 cavalry and 30,000 hoplites, the whole number of Spartiates fell below 1000. The result proves the faulty nature of their laws respecting property; for the city sank under a single defeat; the want of men was their ruin. There is a tradition that, in the days of their ancient kings, they were in the habit of giving the rights of citizenship to strangers, and therefore, in spite of their long wars, no lack of population was experienced by them; indeed, at one time Sparta is said to have numbered not less than 10,000 citizens. Whether this statement is true or not, it would certainly have been better to have maintained their numbers by the equalization of property. Again, the law which relates to the procreation of children is adverse to the correction of this inequality. For the legislator, wanting to have as many Spartans as he could, encouraged the citizens to have large families; and there is a law at Sparta that the father of three sons shall be exempt from military service, and he who has four from all the burdens of the state. Yet it is obvious that, if there were many children, the land being distributed as it is, many of them must necessarily fall into poverty.

B. The Crisis of the *Polis* in Fourth-Century B.C. Greece

1. FIFTH-COLUMN ACTIVITY IN GREEK CITIES

Fears of fifth-column activities are not limited to our times. The chronic military and social instability in fourth-century B.C. Greece exposed poleis *to unprecedented risk of attack. One result was increased fear of subversion by discontented social groups who might conspire with foreign enemies. In this passage Aeneas Tacticus—an Arcadian general and author of* On Siegecraft, *the earliest surviving Greek military manual—discusses possible sources of subversion and suggests methods to protect against them.[7]*

Aeneas Tacticus,
On Siegecraft

Furthermore, proclamations such as these are to be issued from time to time to frighten and deter conspirators. The free population and the ripe crops are to be brought into the city, authority being given to anyone so disposed to lead away or carry off from the country, without fear of punishment, the possessions of anyone who disobeys this regulation. The usual festivals are to be celebrated in the city, and private gatherings shall not take place, either by day or by night, but those which are really necessary may be held in the town-hall, the council-chamber, or other public place. A soothsayer shall not make sacrifice on his own account without the presence of a magistrate. Men shall not dine in common but each in his own house, except in the case of a wedding or a funeral feast, and then only upon previous notice to the authorities.

If there are any citizens in exile, announcement is to be made what is to be done with each citizen, stranger, or slave who may try to leave. And if any person associate with any of the exiles, or in dealing with any of them, send or receive letters, there is to be a definite risk or even a penalty awaiting him. Outgoing and incoming letters shall be brought to censors before being sent out or delivered. Men who have more than one equipment of arms shall return a list of them, and no one shall send any weapon out of the city or receive such as security. Soldiers may not be hired nor may one serve for hire without the permission of

---

[7] Aeneas Tacticus, *On Siegecraft*, 10.3–6. From Aeneas Tacticus, Asclepiodotus, Onasander, trans. Illinois Greek Club (Cambridge, MA, 1928).

Figure 7.1 Siege technology improved greatly during the fourth century B.C. and the early Hellenistic Period. Greek cities responded to the growing effectiveness of siege technology such as towers, battering rams, and catapults by replacing at great expense the brick walls of the archaic and early classical periods with increasingly elaborate stone fortifications. One of the best preserved examples of these new fortifcations is the fortress of Aigosthena at the eastern end of the Gulf of Corinth, which guarded the road from Boeotia through the territory of Megara to the Peloponnesus. Ironically, the improvement in defenses increased reliance on fifth-column activities such as those described by Aeneas Tacticus to capture cities. Photo by Stanley Burstein.

the authorities. No citizen or resident alien shall take passage on a ship without a passport, and orders shall be given that ships shall anchor near gates designated in what follows. Strangers arriving shall carry their weapons unconcealed and ready at hand, and immediately upon arrival shall be disarmed, while no one, not even the innkeepers, shall receive them without permission from the authorities, who shall record also in whose house any persons are, when they take lodging; and at night inns must be locked from the outside by the authorities. From time to time vagrants among these strangers shall be publicly expelled. Citizens of neighboring states, however, residing in the city for the sake of education or for some other special purpose, shall be registered. Not everyone who wishes may converse with public embassies representing cities, princes, or armies, but there must always be present certain of the most trusted citizens who shall stay with the ambassadors so long as they remain. For the importer of whatever the city lacks, grain or oil or anything else, profits shall be specified in proportion to the amount of his importations, and he shall be honored with a crown, and the shipmaster shall be granted allowance for the hauling up and down of his vessel.

Frequent calls to arms shall be given and all strangers in the town shall at this time assemble in a specified place or remain indoors; if, however, one of them shall appear elsewhere, a penalty shall be prescribed for him as a malefactor. At a given signal their stores and shops shall be closed and their lights extinguished, and no one else shall come in. Whenever it is necessary for anyone, he may go out with a lantern, until orders are issued to the contrary. For whoever points out anyone conspiring against the city, or reports anyone as doing any of the things above-mentioned, a reward in money shall be announced, and the reward shall be displayed openly in the market-place or on an altar or in a temple, in order that men may the more readily venture to report any violation of the provisions mentioned.

2. POLITICAL REVOLUTION IN ARGOS

The atmosphere of fear and suspicion evoked by Aeneas Tacticus' discussion of subversion was not theoretical. In 371 B.C. the city of Argos was convulsed by a political crisis that became a byword for the breakdown of civic order and violence.[8]   ‖ Diodorus

While these events were taking place, civil strife and slaughter occurred in the city of the Argives on a scale greater than had ever been recorded among other Greeks. This revolution was called by the Greeks "club-law," gaining this appellation because of the manner of death imposed.

The civil strife occurred for this reason. The city of the Argives was democratically governed and demagogues were inciting the populace against those who were preeminent in wealth and reputation. The persons who were being attacked joined together and decided to suppress the people. When some of those thought to be involved in the conspiracy were tortured, some of the others, fearing that they also would be punished with torture, killed themselves. One, who confessed under torture and received a guarantee of immunity, became an informer and denounced thirty of the most distinguished citizens. Without carefully investigating all the accused, the people executed them and confiscated their property. As many other individuals came under suspicion and the demagogues made false accusations, the people were excited to such a degree that they condemned to death all the accused, who were many and very wealthy. More than 1200 of the most influential Argives were killed. The people also did not spare the demagogues. Because of the magnitude of the catastrophe, the demagogues, fearful that something unexpected might befall them, ceased their accusations. The mob, however, thinking it had been abandoned by them, and aroused for this reason, killed all the demagogues. They, therefore, just as if some divinity was taking vengeance, met with appropriate retribution, and the people, when its fury ceased, returned to normality.

[8] Diodorus 15.57–58.

3. MERCENARIES AND EXILES: THE TYRANNY OF CLEARCHUS OF HERACLEA PONTICA (364–352 B.C.)

Justin, *Philippic History*

Civil strife generated employment for both mercenaries and exiles, who became ready recruits for commanders of mercenary bands. A prime example of this phenomenon is the tyranny established in the Black Sea city of Heraclea Pontica by Clearchus, a political exile in the service of the Persians, who had been introduced into the city by its oligarchic government to destroy their political opponents, only to be overthrown in turn by their agent. Clearchus' victory, however, continued the cycle as his former employers joined the ever-growing number of exiles hoping and scheming to return to their homes.[9]

Among many other evils they endured also that of tyranny; for when, on the populace violently clamoring for an abolition of debts, and a division of the lands of the rich, the subject was long discussed in the council, and no settlement of it was devised, they (i.e. the oligarchs) at last sought assistance against the commons, who were grown riotous by too long idleness, from Timotheus general of the Athenians, and afterwards from Epaminondas general of the Thebans. As both, however, refused their request, they had recourse to Clearchus, whom they themselves had exiled; such being the urgency of their distresses, that they recalled to the guardian ship of his country him whom they had forbidden to enter his country. But Clearchus, being rendered more desperate by his banishment, and regarding the dissension among the people as a means of securing to himself the government, first sought a secret interview with Mithridates, the enemy of his countrymen, and made a league with him on the understanding that when he was re-established in his country, he should, on betraying the city into his hands, be made lieutenant-governor of it. But the treachery which he had conceived against his countrymen, he afterwards turned against Mithridates himself; for on returning from banishment, to be as it were the arbiter of the disputes in the city, he, at the time appointed for delivering the town to Mithridates, made Mithridates himself prisoner, with a party of his friends, and released him from captivity only on the receipt of a large sum of money. And as, in this case, he suddenly changed himself from a friend into an enemy, so, in regard to his countrymen, he soon, from a supporter of the council's cause, became a patron of the common people, and not only inflamed the populace against those who had conferred his power upon him, and by whom he had been recalled into his country and established in the citadel, but even exercised upon his benefactors the most atrocious inflictions of tyrannical cruelty. Summoning the people to an assembly, he declared that he would no longer support the senate in their proceedings against the populace, but would even interpose his authority, if they persisted in their former severities; and that, if the people thought themselves able to check the tyranny of the senate, he would retire with his soldiers, and take no further part in their dissensions; but that, if they distrusted their ability to make

[9] Justin, *Philippic History* 16.4–5. From *Justin, Cornelius Nepos, and Eutropius*, trans. John Selby Watson (London, 1890).

resistance, he would not be wanting to aid them in taking revenge. They might therefore, he added, determine among themselves; they might bid him withdraw, if they pleased, or might request him to stay as a sharer in the popular cause. The people, induced by these fair speeches, conferred on him the supreme authority, and, while they, incensed at the power of the senate, surrendered themselves, with their wives and children, as slaves to the power of a single tyrant, Clearchus then apprehended sixty councilors (the rest had taken flight), and threw them into prison. The people rejoiced that the council was overthrown, and especially that it had fallen by means of a leader among the councilors, and that, by a reverse of fortune, their support was turned to their destruction. Clearchus, by threatening all his prisoners with death, made the price offered for their ransom the higher; and, after receiving from them large sums of money, as if he would secretly withdraw them from the violence threatened by the people, despoiled those of their lives whom he had previously despoiled of their fortunes.

Learning, soon after, that war was prepared against him by those who had made their escape (several cities being moved by pity to espouse their cause), he gave freedom to their slaves; and that no affliction might be wanting to distress the most honorable families, he obliged their wives and daughters to marry their slaves, threatening death to such as refused, that he might thus render the slaves more attached to himself, and less reconcilable to their masters. But such marriages were more intolerable to the women than immediate death; and many, in consequence, killed themselves before the nuptial rites were celebrated, and many in the midst of them, first killing their new husbands, and delivering themselves from dishonorable sufferings by a spirit of noble virtue. A battle was then fought, in which the tyrant, being victorious, dragged such of the senators as he took prisoners before the faces of their countrymen in triumph. Returning into the city, he threw some into prison, stretched others on the rack, and put others to death; and not a place in the city was unvisited by the tyrant's cruelty. Arrogance was added to severity, insolence to inhumanity. From a course of continued good fortune, he sometimes forgot that he was a man, sometimes called himself the son of Zeus. When he appeared in public, a golden eagle, as a token of his parentage, was carried before him; he wore a purple robe, buskins like kings in tragedies, and a crown of gold. His son he named Ceraunos (*"Thunderbolt"*), to mock the gods, not only with false statements, but with impious names. Two noble youths, Chion and Leonides, incensed that he should dare to commit such outrages, and desiring to deliver their country, formed a conspiracy to put him to death. They were disciples of Plato the philosopher, and being desirous to exhibit to their country the virtue in which they were daily instructed by the precepts of their master, placed fifty of their relations, as if they were their attendants, in ambush; while they themselves, in the character of men who had a dispute to be settled, went into the citadel to the tyrant. Gaining admission, as being well known, the tyrant, while he was listening attentively to the one that spoke first, was killed by the other. But as their accomplices were too late in coming to their support, they were overpowered by the guards; and hence it happened that though the tyrant was killed, their country was not liberated. Satyrus, the brother of Clearchus, made himself tyrant in a similar way; and for many years, with various successive changes, the Heracleans continued under the yoke of tyrants.

4. CAN THE *POLIS* BE SAVED? SUGGESTED SOLUTIONS

The crises of the fourth century B.C. encouraged an extraordinary outburst of creative social and political thought about how poleis *might regain stability. Aeneas Tacticus'* On Siegecraft, *with its suggestions about how cities should deal with internal and external subversion, exemplifies the efforts of patriotic citizens to find pragmatic solutions to such problems. Other thinkers proposed more radical approaches. In his oration* To Philip, *the Athenian rhetorician Isocrates proposes to export the crisis, inviting Philip II of Macedon to conquer territory from Persia on which Greek exiles could be settled in new and prosperous cities. In his autobiographical seventh letter, the philosopher Plato tries to justify his withdrawal from traditional politics and suggests that the only way to restore good government to Greece is for philosophers to govern states or for statesmen to become philosophers. Finally, in his essay* Ways and Means, *the Athenian soldier and man of letters Xenophon suggests that Athens rely on its natural resources and economic advantages to restore prosperity to the city.*

Isocrates: Salvation through Empire[10]

Isocrates,
To Philip

From many considerations you may realize that you ought to act in this way, but especially from the experiences of Jason, For he, without having achieved anything comparable to what you have done, won the highest renown, not from what he did, but from what he said; for he kept talking as if he intended to cross over to the continent and make war upon the King. Now since Jason by use of words alone advanced himself so far, what opinion must we expect the world will have of you if you actually do this thing; above all, if you undertake to conquer the whole empire of the King, or, at any rate, to wrest from it a vast extent of territory and sever from it—to use a current phrase—"Asia from Cilicia to Sinope"; and if, furthermore, you undertake to establish cities in this region, and to settle in permanent abodes those who now, for lack of the daily necessities of life, are wandering from place to place and committing outrages upon whomsoever they encounter? If we do not stop these men from banding together, by providing sufficient livelihood for them, they will grow before we know it into so great a multitude as to be a terror no less to the Hellenes than to the barbarians. But we pay no heed to them; nay, we shut our eyes to the fact that a terrible menace which threatens us all alike is waxing day by day. It is therefore the duty of a man who is high-minded, who is a lover of Hellas, who has a broader vision than the rest of the world, to employ these bands in a war against the barbarians, to strip from that empire all the territory which I defined a moment ago, to deliver these homeless wanderers from the ills by which they are afflicted and which they inflict

---

[10] Isocrates, *To Philip* 119–123, 132, 139. From Isocrates, trans. George Norlin (Cambridge, MA, 1928).

upon others, to collect them into cities, and with these cities to fix the boundary of Hellas, making of them buffer states to shield us all. For by doing this, you will not only make them prosperous, but you will put us all on a footing of security. If, however, you do not succeed in these objects, this much you will at any rate easily accomplish,—the liberation of the cities which are on the coast of Asia. . . .

Consider also what a disgrace it is to sit idly by and see Asia flourishing more than Europe and the barbarians enjoying a greater prosperity than the Hellenes; and, what is more, to see those who derive their power from Cyrus, who as a child was cast out by his mother on the public highway, addressed by the title of "The Great King," while the descendants of Heracles, who because of his virtue was exalted by his father to the rank of a god, are addressed by meaner titles than they. We must not allow this state of affairs to go on; so, we must change and reverse it entirely. . . .

Now I am not unaware that many of the Hellenes look upon the King's power as invincible. Yet one may well marvel at them if they really believe that the power which was subdued to the will of a mere barbarian—an ill-bred barbarian at that—and collected in the cause of slavery, could not be scattered by a man of the blood of Hellas, of ripe experience in warfare, in the cause of freedom—and that too although they know that while it is in all cases difficult to construct a thing, to destroy it is, comparatively, an easy task.

Plato: Philosophers as the Vanguard of Revolution[11]

In the days of my youth my experience was the same as that of many others. I thought that as soon as I should become my own master I would immediately enter into public life. But it so happened, I found, that the following changes occurred in the political situation. | Plato, *Letter 7*

In the government then existing, reviled as it was by many, a revolution took place; and the revolution was headed by fifty-one leaders, of whom eleven were in the City and ten in the Piraeus—each of these sections dealing with the market and with all municipal matters requiring management—and Thirty were established as irresponsible rulers of all. Now of these some were actually connections and acquaintances of mine; and indeed they invited me at once to join their administration, thinking it would be congenial. The feelings I then experienced, owing to my youth, were in no way surprising: for I imagined that they would administer the State by leading it out of an unjust way of life into a just way, and consequently I gave my mind to them very diligently, to see what they would do. And indeed I saw how these men within a short time caused men to look back on the former government as a golden age; and above all how they treated my elderly friend Socrates, whom I would hardly scruple to call the most just of men then living, when they tried to send him, along with others, after one of the citizens, to fetch him by force that he might be put to death—their object being that Socrates, whether he wished or no, might be made to share in their political actions; he, however, refused to obey and risked the uttermost penalties rather than be a partaker in their

---

[11] Plato, *Letter 7*, 324C–326B. From Plato, vol. 7, trans. R. G. Bury (Cambridge, MA, 1929).

unholy deeds. So when I beheld all these actions and others of a similar grave kind, I was indignant, and I withdrew myself from the evil practices then going on. But in no long time the power of the Thirty was overthrown together with the whole of the government which then existed. Then once again I was really, though less urgently, impelled with a desire to take part in public and political affairs. Many deplorable events, however, were still happening in those times, troublous as they were, and it was not surprising that in some instances, during these revolutions, men were avenging themselves on their foes too fiercely; yet, notwithstanding, the exiles who then returned exercised no little moderation. But, as ill-luck would have it, certain men of authority summoned our comrade Socrates before the law-courts, laying a charge against him which was most unholy, and which Socrates of all men least deserved; for it was on the charge of impiety that those men summoned him and the rest condemned and slew him—the very man who on the former occasion, when they themselves had the misfortune to be in exile, had refused to take part in the unholy arrest of one of the friends of the men then exiled.

When, therefore, I considered all this, and the type of men who were administering the affairs of State, with their laws too and their customs, the more I considered them and the more I advanced in years myself, the more difficult appeared to me the task of managing affairs of State rightly. For it was impossible to take action without friends and trusty companions; and these it was not easy to find ready to hand, since our State was no longer managed according to the principles and institutions of our forefathers; while to acquire other new friends with any facility was a thing impossible. Moreover, both the written laws and the customs were beingcorrupted, and that with surprising rapidity. Consequently, although at first I was filled with an ardent desire to engage in public affairs, when I considered all this and saw how things were shifting about anyhow in all directions, I finally became dizzy; and although I continued to consider by what means some betterment could be brought about not only in these matters but also in the government as a whole, yet as regards political action I kept constantly waiting for an opportune moment; until, finally, looking at all the States which now exist, I perceived that one and all they are badly governed; for the state of their laws is such as to be almost incurable without some marvelous overhauling and good-luck to boot. So in my praise of the right philosophy I was compelled to declare that by it one is enabled to discern all forms of justice both political and individual. Wherefore the classes of mankind (I said) will have no cessation from evils until either the class of those who are right and true philosophers attains political supremacy, or else the class of those who hold power in the States becomes, by some dispensation of Heaven, really philosophic.

Xenophon: Outgrowing the Problem[12]

Xenophon, *Ways and Means*

As . . . it has been maintained by certain leading statesmen in Athens that the recognized standard of right and wrong is as high at Athens as elsewhere, but that,

[12] Xenophon, *Ways and Means* 1–3. From Xenophon, *Ways and Means*, trans. Henry G. Dakyns (London and New York, 1892).

owing to the pressure of poverty on the masses, a certain measure of injustice in their dealing with the allied cities could not be avoided; I set myself to discover whether by any manner of means it were possible for the citizens of Athens to be supported solely from the soil of Attica itself, which was obviously the most equitable solution. For if so, herein lay, as I believed, the antidote at once to their own poverty and to the feeling of suspicion with which they are regarded by the rest of Hellas.

I had no sooner begun my investigation than one fact presented itself clearly to my mind, which is that the country itself is made by nature to provide the amplest resources. . . . Indeed it would be scarcely irrational to maintain that the city of Athens lies at the center, not of Hellas merely, but of the habitable world. So true is it, that the farther we remove from Athens the greater the extreme of heat or cold to be encountered; or to use another illustration, the traveler who desires to traverse the confines of Hellas from end to end will find that, whether he voyages by sea or by land, he is describing a circle, the center of which is Athens.

Once more, this land though not literally sea-girt has all the advantages of an island, being accessible to every wind that blows, and can invite to its bosom or waft from its shore all products, since it is peninsular; while by land it is the emporium of many markets, as being a portion of the continent. . . .

All these advantages . . . may, I believe, be traced primarily to the soil and position of Attica itself. But these natural blessings may be added to: in the first place, by a careful handling of our resident alien population. And, for my part, I can hardly conceive of a more splendid source of revenue than lies open in this direction. Here you have a self-supporting class of residents conferring large benefits upon the state, and instead of receiving payment themselves, contributing on the contrary by a special tax. Nor, under the term careful handling, do I demand more than the removal of obligations which, while they confer no benefit on the state, have an air of inflicting various disabilities on the resident aliens. And I would further relieve them from the obligation of serving as hoplites side by side with the citizen proper; since, beside the personal risk, which is great, the trouble of quitting trades and homesteads is no trifle. Incidentally the state itself would be benefited by this exemption, if the citizens were more in the habit of campaigning with one another, rather than shoulder to shoulder with Lydians, Phrygians, Syrians, and barbarians from all quarters of the world, who form the staple of our resident alien class. . . .

At this point I propose to offer some remarks in proof of the attractions and advantages of Athens as a centre of commercial enterprise. In the first place, it will hardly be denied that we possess the finest and safest harborage for shipping, where vessels of all sorts can come to moorings and be laid up in absolute security as far as stress of weather is concerned. But further than that, in most states the trader is under the necessity of lading his vessel with some merchandise or other in exchange for his cargo, since the current coin has no circulation beyond the frontier. But at Athens he has a choice: he can either in return for his wares export a variety of goods, such as human beings seek after, or, if he does not desire to take goods in exchange for goods, he has simply to export silver, and he cannot

have a more excellent freight to export, since wherever he likes to sell it he may look to realize a large percentage on his capital. . . .

Now the greater the number of people attracted to Athens either as visitors or as residents, clearly the greater the development of imports and exports. More goods will be sent out of the country, there will be more buying and selling, with a consequent increase in rents, dues, and customs.

C. The Periphery of the Greek World

1. THRACIAN COURT LIFE: A HEROIC SOCIETY

Xenophon,
Anabasis

The Greeks viewed the Thracians as the quintessential noncivilized "barbarians" from the Archaic period onward. In the fifth century B.C., however, one of the Thracian tribes, the Odrysians, succeeded in unifying the Thracians and creating a powerful state covering most of modern Bulgaria and European Turkey that played a major role in Balkan politics in the fourth century B.C. In this passage the Athenian historian Xenophon vividly describes the court life of the Odrysian king Seuthes I, highlighting the place of Greek immigrants in Thracian elite life and the role of ritual gift-giving in Thracian politics.[13]

After this the troops messed in their separate divisions, but the generals and officers were invited by Seuthes to dinner at a neighboring village which was in his possession. When they were at the doors, and on the point of stepping in to dinner, they were met by a certain Heracleides, of Maronea. He came up to each guest, addressing himself particularly to those who, as he conjectured, ought to be able to make a present to Seuthes. He addressed himself first to some Parians who were there to arrange a friendship with Medocus, the king of the Odrysians, and were bearers of presents to the king and to his wife. Heracleides reminded them, "Medocus is up country twelve days' journey from the sea; but Seuthes, now that he has got this army, will be lord on the sea-coast; as your neighbor, then, he is the man to do you good or do you ill. If you are wise, you will give him whatever he asks of you. On the whole, it will be laid out at better interest than if you gave it to Medocus, who lives so far off." That was his mode of persuasion in their case. Next he came to Timasion the Dardanian, who, some one had told him, was the happy possessor of certain goblets and oriental carpets. What he said to him was, "It is customary when people are invited to dinner by Seuthes for the guests to make him a present: now if he should become a great person in these parts, he will be able to restore you to your native land, or to make you a rich man here." Such were the solicitations which he applied to each man in turn whom he accosted. Presently he came to Xenophon and said, "You are at

---

[13] Xenophon, *Anabasis* 7.2–3. From Xenophon, *Anabasis*, trans. Henry G. Dakyns (London and New York, 1890).

once a citizen of no mean city, and with Seuthes also your own name is very great. Maybe you expect to obtain a fort or two in this country, just as others of your countrymen have done, and territory. It is only right and proper therefore that you should honor Seuthes in the most magnificent style. Be sure, I give this advice out of pure friendliness, for I know that the greater the gift that you are ready to bestow on him, the better the treatment you will receive at his hands." Xenophon, on hearing this, was in a sad dilemma, for he had brought with him, when he crossed from Parium, nothing but one boy and just enough to pay his traveling expenses.

As soon as the company, consisting of the most powerful Thracians there present, with the generals and captains of the Hellenes, and any embassy from a state which might be there, had arrived, they were seated in a circle, and the dinner was served. Thereupon three-legged stools were brought in and placed in front of the assembled guests. They were laden with pieces of meat, piled up, and there were huge leavened-loaves fastened on to the pieces of meat with long skewers. The tables, as a rule, were set beside the guests at intervals. That was the custom; and Seuthes set the fashion of the performance. He took up the loaves which lay by his side and broke them into little pieces, and then threw the fragments here to one and there to another as seemed him good; and so with the meat likewise, leaving for himself the merest taste. Then the rest fell to following the fashion set them, those that is who had tables placed beside them.

Now there was an Arcadian, Arystas by name, a huge eater; he soon got tired of throwing the pieces about, and seized a good three-quarter loaf in his two hands, placed some pieces of meat upon his knees, and proceeded to devour his dinner. Then beakers of wine were brought round, and every one partook in turn; but when the cupbearer came to Arystas and handed him the bowl, he looked up, and seeing that Xenophon had done eating, said, "Give it to him, he is more at leisure. I have something better to do at present." Seuthes, hearing a remark, asked the cupbearer what was said, and the cupbearer, who knew how to talk Greek, explained. Then followed a peal of laughter.

When the drinking had advanced somewhat, in came a Thracian with a white horse, who snatched the brimming bowl and said, "Here's a health to you, O Seuthes. Let me present you with this horse. Mounted on him, you shall capture whom you choose to pursue, or retiring from battle, you shall not dread the foe." He was followed by one who brought in a boy, and presented him in proper style with a health to Seuthes. A third had clothes for his wife. Timasion, the Dardanian, pledged Seuthes, and presented a silver bowl and a carpet worth ten minae. Gnesippus, an Athenian, got up and said, "It was a good old custom, and a fine one too, that those who had, should give to the king for honor's sake, but to those who had not, the king should give; whereby, my lord," he added, "I too may one day have the wherewithal to give you gifts and honor." Xenophon the while was racking his brains what he was to do; he was not the happier because he was seated in the seat next Seuthes as a mark of honor; and Heracleides bade the cupbearer hand him the bowl. He had already had a few drinks, as it happened; he rose, and manfully seized the cup, and spoke, "I also, Seuthes, have to present you with myself and these my dear comrades to be your trusty friends, and not one of them against his will. They are more ready, one and all, still more than I, to be your friends. Here they are; they ask nothing from you in return, rather they are forward to labor in your behalf; it will be their pleasure to bear the brunt of battle in voluntary service. With them, god willing, you will gain vast territory; you will recover what was once your forefathers'; you will win for yourself new lands; and not lands only, but horses many, and of men a multitude, and many fair women besides. You will not need to seize upon them in robber fashion; it is your friends here who, of their own accord, shall take and bring them to you, they shall lay them at your feet as gifts." Up got Seuthes and drained with him the cup, and with him sprinkled the last drops fraternally.

At this stage entered musicians blowing upon horns such as they use for signal calls, and trumpeting on trumpets, made of raw oxhide, tunes and airs, like the music of the harp. Seuthes himself got up and shouted forth a war song; then he sprang from his place and leaped about as though he would guard himself against a missile, in right nimble style. Then came in a set of clowns and jesters. But when the sun began to set, the Hellenes rose from their seats.

2. A GREEK TRADING POST IN THRACE

Odrysian
inscription of
rules protecting
foreign
merchants

Literary and spectacular archaeological discoveries in the royal cemetery of the Odrysian kings in Bulgaria document the wealth of the Thracian elite and the important place occupied by Greek imports in Thracian material culture. In this inscription an Odrysian official sets out the rules established by the Odrysian kings to protect foreign merchants from the cities of Maronea, Apollonia, and Thasos living in the trading post of Pistiros. It guarantees their right to judge disputes between themselves and protect their property and their persons against seizure or abuse.[14]

If a merchant brings suit against another merchant (*in Pistiros*), they shall be judged among their kinsmen and with regard to whatever is owed to the merchants by Thracians, there shall be no cancellation of these debts. All land and pasture owned by the merchants shall not be taken away from them. He shall not send holders of estates (?) to the merchants. He shall not install a garrison at Pistiros nor shall he transfer Pistiros to another. He shall not exchange the land lots of the Pistirians nor transfer them to another. Neither he nor members of his family shall seize the property of the merchants. He shall not levy road taxes on any goods exported by the merchants from Pistiros to Maronea or from Maronea to Pistiros or to the market place Belana of the Praseoi. The merchants shall open and close their wagons. Just as also in the time of Cotys [I swear this oath]: Neither I nor anyone of my family will bind or kill a citizen of Maronea; nor shall I or anyone of my family seize the property of a citizen of Maronea, whether he be alive or dead; nor shall I or a member of my family bind or kill or seize the property of

---

[14] Velizar Velkov and Lidia Domaradzk, "Kotys I (323/3–359) et L'Emporion de Pistiros en Thrace," *BCH* 118 (1994), pp. 2–4.

any citizen of Apollonia or Thasos, who is living in Pistiros, whether he be alive or dead. . . .

3. GREEKS AND NON-GREEKS IN THE BLACK SEA: AMAGE, QUEEN OF THE SARMATIANS, SAVES THE CITY OF CHERSONESUS

Relations between Greeks and non-Greeks are routinely described as hostile in fifth- and fourth-century B.C. literature. The reality was more complex. As this story about the Sarmatian queen Amage and the city of Chersonesus in the southwestern Crimea illustrates, Greek cities in the Black Sea survived by finding allies among their non-Greek neighbors and taking advantage of hostilities between them.[15]

> Polyaenus,
> *Strategemata*

Amage was the wife of Medosakkos, the king of the Sarmatians, whose territory extended to the shore of the Pontus. When she saw that her husband was sunk in luxury and drunkenness, she judged most matters, established guards for their land, repelled attacks of their enemies, and fought in alliance with those of their neighbors who had been wronged. Her fame was great among all the Scythians so that even the Chersonesians, who inhabited the Crimean Peninsula and were suffering ill treatment at the hands of the king of the nearby Scythians, asked to become her allies. At first she sent a message bidding the king to leave Chersonesus alone. But since the Scythian held her in contempt, she assembled a force of one hundred and twenty warriors who were among the bravest in spirit and body, assigned three horses to each man, raced over a distance of twelve hundred stades in a night and a day, and launched a sudden attack on the royal palace, and killed all the guards at the gates. While the Scythians had been thrown into confusion by the unexpected attack, thinking that the attackers were not as few as those they saw but were far greater in number, Amage burst into the palace with the force accompanying her, and killed the Scythian king, his kinsmen, and his friends. She returned their land to the Chersonesians and entrusted the kingdom to the son of the slain ruler, having exacted a promise from him that, having seen the end of his father, he would rule justly and refrain from attacking the neighboring Greeks and barbarians.

4. BOSPORUS: A MULTIETHNIC STATE IN THE BLACK SEA (347/6 B.C.)

The most remarkable response to threats from the Greeks' non-Greek neighbors was the creation of the multiethnic Bosporan state. Building on an alliance of Greek cities in the southestern Crimea, a dynasty probably of Thracian origin, brought under their control the Greek cities on both coasts of the Straits of Kerch as well as the non-Greek peoples eastward to the Caucasus Mountains. As their title, "Archon of Bosporus and Theodosia and King of the Sindoi and all the Maeotians," indicates, the rulers of Bosporus combined Greek and non-Greek political forms to govern their

> Athenian
> inscription
> regarding
> Bosporus' rulers

[15] From Polyaenus, *Strategemata* 8.56.

multiethnic subjects. Formation of the Bosporan state enhanced the security of the Crimean Greek cities. It also, however, gave Bosporus' rulers control of vast grain reserves, which, as this Athenian inscription reveals, they employed to gain political and military support from Greek states such as Athens, which increasingly depended on grain from the Black Sea to feed its population in the fourth century B.C.[16]

For Spartocus, Paerisades, Apollonius, the sons of Leucon.

In the archonship of Themistocles (347/6 B.C.), In the eighth prytany, that of Aegeis; in which Lysimachus, the son of Sosidemus, from Archanae, was secretary. Theophilus from Halimos, presided. Androtion, the son of Andron, from Gargettus, made the motion.

Concerning the message Spartocus and Paerisades (*i.e., rulers of Bosporus*) and the ambassadors, who came from them, brought, reply to them that the Athenian people praises Spartocus and Paerisades because they are good men and they informed the Athenian people that they care for the export of grain just as their father cared for it, and that they provide enthusiastically whatever the people may request of them. And inform the ambassadors that, if they do these things, they will meet with no misfortune from the Athenian people.

Also, since they have given to the Athenians the gifts which Satyrus and Leucon gave them, Spartocus and Paerisades shall receive the gifts which the people gave to Satyrus and Leucon; and the people will crown them with gold crowns worth one thousand drachmas each at the Great Panathenaea. The athlothetae shall have the crowns made in the year before the Great Panathenaea in accordance with the decree of the people which was previously voted for Leucon. It shall be proclaimed that the Athenian people crowns Spartocus and Paerisades, the sons of Leucon, on account of their excellence and their good will toward the Athenian people. Since they dedicated the crowns to Athena Polias, the athlothetae shall place the crowns in the temple after having inscribed them: Spartocus and Paerisades, having been crowned by the Athenian people, dedicated the crowns. The treasurer of the people shall allocate to the athlothetae the money for the crowns from the military fund. The secretary of the council shall inscribe the decree on a stone stele and place it near that of Spartocus and Leucon, and the treasurer of the people shall give thirty drachmas for the inscribing.

The people also praise Sosis and Theodosius, the ambassadors, because they look after people coming from Athens to Bosporus, and the people will invite them to dinner at the prytaneion tomorrow. And concerning the money owed to the sons of Leucon, in order that they shall be repaid, the presiders, who shall be allotted to preside in the people on the eighteenth day immediately after the sacred business, shall take action that they, being repaid, shall not bring suit against the Athenian people. The people shall also provide the ship's officers, which Spartocus and Paerisades requested. The ambassadors shall record the names of the officers which they receive from the secretary of the council. Those

---

[16] From *IG 2.², 212.*

whom they record shall fulfill their orders by doing whatever good they can for the sons of Leucon.

Polyeuctus, the son of Timocrates, from Crioa, moved. The other matters shall be just as Androtion proposed. The people shall also crown Apollonius, the son of Leucon. . . .

5. A HELLENIZED SATRAP: MAUSOLUS OF CARIA

Similar conditions existed elsewhere in the Greek world, particularly on the west coast of Anatolia,   Inscription
where Persian satraps ruled over mixed Greek and non-Greek populations. One such satrapy was   regarding
Caria, which was ruled by a hereditary dynasty of satraps called the Hecatomnids. The complex   politics of Caria
negotiation of ethnic and political differences is illustrated by this inscription, in which the Carian
city of Mylasa employs Greek political forms to ratify and enforce judicial decisions by the Persian
king and the satrap against personal enemies of Mausolus and his family.[17]

A. In the thirty ninth year of the reign of King Artaxerxes [II = 367/366 B.C.], when Mausolus was satrap. It was decided by the Mylasans in a main assembly. The three tribes ratified the decision. Since Arlissis, the son of Thyssollus, who had been sent by the Carians to the king, performed his ambassadorial role dishonestly and formed a plot against Mausolus, who is the benefactor of the city of the Mylasans—against him and his father Hecatomnus and their ancestors—and the king found that Arlissis had committed a criminal act and punished him with death; the city of the Mylasans also took action concerning his property in accordance with the ancestral laws. They added it to the property of Mausolus and they made a curse concerning these matters that no one should again propose anything contrary to these actions nor bring it to a vote. If anyone transgresses these decisions, let him and all his kin be destroyed utterly.

B. In the thirty fifth year of the reign of King Artaxerxes [II = 361/360 B.C.], when Mausolus was satrap. It was decided by the Mylasans in a major (?) assembly. The three tribes ratified the decision. That the sons of Peldemus, who had desecrated an image of Hecatomnus, who had done many good things for the city of the Mylasans both in word and deed, committed a wrong against the sacred dedications and the city and the benefactors of the city. Having decided that they had committed a wrong, they punished the sons of Peldemus by the confiscation of their property and they sold the possessions of the sons of Peldemus at public auction, with the right of secure possession to the purchasers. And they made a curse concerning these matters that no one should propose anything contrary to these actions nor bring it to a vote. If anyone transgresses these decisions, let him and all his kin be destroyed utterly.

[17] From P. J. Rhodes and Robin Osborne, ed., *Greek Historical Inscriptions 404–323 B.C.* (Oxford, 2003) No. 54.

C. In the fifth year of the reign of King Artaxerxes [III = 355/354 B.C.], when Mausolus was satrap. Manitas, the son of Pactyes, having plotted against Mausolus, the son of Hecatomnus, in the sanctuary of Zeus Lambraundos, at the time of the yearly sacrifice and festival, and Mausolus having been saved with the aid of Zeus, and Manitas having been condemned by a vote of hands, the Mylasans decided that, as the sanctuary had been violated and Mausolus, their benefactor, attacked, it would be investigated if any one else participated in or shared in the act. Thyssus, the son of Syscus, was convicted and judged to be a fellow conspirator with Manitas. It was decided by the Mylasans, and the three tribes ratified the decision. The property of Manitas, the son of Pactyes, and Thyssus, the son of Syscus, should be added to that of Mausolus, and the city sold their possessions at public auction, making a curse. The purchases shall be secure to the purchasers, and no one should propose anything contrary to these actions nor bring it to a vote. If anyone transgresses these decisions, let him and all his kin be destroyed utterly.

6. THE FUNERAL OF MAUSOLUS: A GREEK EXTRAVAGANZA (353 B.C.)

Aulus Gellius,
Attic Nights

The funeral of Mausolus was one of the most spectacular events of the fourth century B.C. and a remarkable testimony to the attraction of Greek culture for non-Greek aristocrats in Anatolia. Mausolus' sister and wife, Artemisia, invited the most famous Greek artists and orators to compete for prizes at her husband's funeral at Halicarnassus, the capital of the satrapy of Caria.[18]

Artemisia is said to have loved her husband Mausolus with a love supassing all the tales of passion and beyond one's conception of affection. Now Mausolus, as Marcus Tullius [Cicero] tells us, was king of the land of Caria; according to some Greek historians he was governor of a province, the official whom the Greeks termed a satrap. When this Mausolus had met his end amid the lamentations and in the arms of his wife, and had been buried with a magnificent funeral, Artemisia, inflamed with grief and with longing for her spouse, mingled his bones and ashes with spices, ground them into the form of a powder, put them in water, and drank them; and she is said to have given many other proofs of the violence of her passion. For perpetuating the memory of her husband, she also erected, with great expenditure of labor, that highly celebrated tomb, which has been deemed worthy of being numbered among the seven wonders of the world. When Artemisia dedicated this monument, consecrated to the deified shades of Mausolus, she instituted an *agon*, that *is* to say, a contest in celebrating his praises, offering magnificent prizes of money and other valuables. Three men distinguished for their eminent talent and eloquence are said to have come to contend in this eulogy, Theopompus, Theodectes and Naucrates; some have even written that Isocrates

---

[18] Aulus Gellius, *Attic Nights* 10.18. From Aulus Gellius, *Attic Nights*, trans. J. C. Rolfe (Cambridge, MA, 1927).

himself entered the lists with them. But Theopompus was adjudged the victor in that contest. He was a pupil of Isocrates.

7. A GREEK VIEW OF PERSIA: XENOPHON, *THE EDUCATION OF CYRUS*

Herodotus concluded his history of the Persian Wars with a passage in which he imagined Cyrus the Great, the founder of the Persian Empire, warning the Persians that enjoyment of the riches of the empire would sap their strength. Emboldened by events such as the successful retreat of the Greek mercenaries of the Persian rebel Cyrus the Younger at the beginning of the fourth century B.C. and chronic instability within the empire in succeeding decades, advocates of Philip's war insisted that Herodotus' prophecy had come true and that Persia was no longer the formidable military power that had built the empire. In this passage the historian Xenophon analyzes the current state of the Persian Empire from this perspective.[19]

Xenophon, *Cyropaedia*

1. That Cyrus's empire was the greatest and most glorious of all the kingdoms in Asia—of that it may be its own witness. For it was bounded on the east by the Indian Ocean, on the north by the Black Sea, on the west by Cyprus and Egypt, and on the south by Ethiopia. And although it was of such magnitude, it was governed by the single will of Cyrus; and he honored his subjects and cared for them as if they were his own children; and they, on their part, reverenced Cyrus as a father. 2. Still, as soon as Cyrus was dead, his children at once fell into dissension, states and nations began to revolt, and everything began to deteriorate. And that what I say is the truth, I will prove, beginning with the Persians' attitude toward religion.

I know, for example, that in early times the kings and their officers, in their dealings with even the worst offenders, would abide by an oath that they might have given, and be true to any pledge they might have made. 3. For had they not had such character for honor, and had they not been true to their reputation, not a man would have trusted them, just as not a single person any longer trusts them, now that their lack of character is notorious; and the generals of the Greeks who joined the expedition of Cyrus the Younger would not have had such confidence in them even on that occasion. But, as it was, trusting in the previous reputation of the Persian kings, they placed themselves in the king's power, were led into his presence, and had their heads cut off. And many also of the barbarians who joined that expedition went to their doom, some deluded by one promise, others by another.

4. But at the present time they are much worse, as the following will show: if, for example, any one in the olden times risked his life for the king, or if any one reduced a state or a nation to submission to him, or effected anything else of good or glory for him, such an one received honor and

[19] Xenophon, *Cyropaedia* 8.8.1–5, 13–15, 20, 26. From Xenophon, *Cyropaedia*, trans. Walter Miller (Cambridge, MA, 1914).

preferment; now, on the other hand, if any one seems to bring some advantage to the king by evil-doing, whether as Mithradates did, by betraying his own father Ariobarzanes, or as a certain Rheomithres did, in violating his most sacred oaths and leaving his wife and children and the children of his friends behind as hostages in the power of the king of Egypt—such are the ones who now have the highest honors heaped upon them.

5. Witnessing such a state of morality, all the inhabitants of Asia have been turned to wickedness and wrong-doing. For, whatever the character of the rulers is, such also that of the people under them for the most part becomes. In this respect they are now even more unprincipled than before. . . .

13. Again, it is still the custom for the boys to be educated at court; but instruction and practice in horsemanship have died out, because there are no occasions on which they may give an exhibition and win distinction for skill. And while anciently the boys used there to hear cases at law justly decided and so to learn justice, as they believed—that also has been entirely reversed; for now they see all too clearly that whichever party gives the larger bribe wins the case. 14. The boys of that time used also to learn the properties of the products of the earth, so as to avail themselves of the useful ones and keep away from those that were harmful. But now it looks as if they learned them only in order to do as much harm as possible; at any rate, there is no place where more people die or lose their lives from poisons than there.

15. Furthermore, they are much more effeminate now than they were in Cyrus's day. For at that time they still adhered to the old discipline and the old abstinence that they received from the Persians, but adopted the Median garb and Median luxury; now, on the contrary, they are allowing the rigor of the Persians to die out, while they keep up the effeminacy of the Medes. . . .

20. And so is it not to be expected that in military prowess they should be wholly inferior to what they used to be? In times past it was their national custom that those who held lands should furnish cavalrymen from their possessions and that these, in case of war, should also take the field, while those who performed outpost duty in defense of the country received pay for their services. But now the rulers make knights out of their porters, bakers, cooks, cup-bearers, bath-room attendants, butlers, waiters, chamberlains who assist them in retiring at night and in rising in the morning, and beauty-doctors who pencil their eyes and rouge their cheeks for them and otherwise beautify them; these are the sort that they make into knights to serve for pay for them. . . .

26. However, in as much as even they understand what sort of material for war they have, they abandon the effort; and no one ever goes to war any more without the help of Greek mercenaries, be it when they are at war with one another or when the Greeks make war upon them; but even against Greeks they recognize that they can conduct their wars only with the assistance of Greeks.

D. Philip II and the Emergence of Macedon

1. THE ACHIEVEMENTS OF PHILIP II: ALEXANDER THE GREAT'S SPEECH AT OPIS (324 B.C.)

In 324 B.C. Alexander the Great's army mutinied at Opis in Mesopotamia. According to the historian Arrian, Alexander defiantly faced his soldiers, delivering the following speech, in which he sought to shame them by detailing the contributions of his father Philip II and himself to Macedon. Although Arrian is the likely author of the speech in its present form, the content probably reflects ancient historians' views of the significance of Philip's reign.[20]

Arrian,
Anabasis

9. "The speech which I am about to deliver will not be for the purpose of checking your start homeward, for, so far as I am concerned, you may depart wherever you wish; but for the purpose of making you understand when you take yourselves off, what kind of men you have been to us who have conferred such benefits upon you. In the first place, as is reasonable, I shall begin my speech from my father Philip. For he found you vagabonds and destitute of means, most of you clad in hides, feeding a few sheep up the mountain sides, for the protection of which you had to fight with small success against Illyrians, Triballians, and the border Thracians. Instead of the hides he gave you cloaks to wear, and from the mountains he led you down into the plains, and made you capable of fighting the neighboring barbarians, so that you were no longer compelled to preserve yourselves by trusting rather to the inaccessible strongholds than to your own valor. He made you colonists of cities, which he adorned with useful laws and customs; and from being slaves and subjects, he made you rulers over those very barbarians by whom you yourselves, as well as your property, were previously liable to be carried off or ravaged. He also added the greater part of Thrace to Macedonia, and by seizing the most conveniently situated places on the sea-coast, he spread abundance over the land from commerce, and made the working of the mines a secure employment. He made you rulers over the Thessalians, of whom you had formerly been in mortal fear; and by humbling the nation of the Phocians, he rendered the avenue into Greece broad and easy for you, instead of being narrow and difficult. The Athenians and Thebans, who were always lying in wait to attack Macedonia, he humbled to such a degree, I also then rendering him my personal aid in the campaign, that instead of paying tribute to the former and being vassals to the latter, those states in their turn procure security to themselves by our assistance. He penetrated into the Peloponnese, and after regulating its affairs, was publicly declared commander-in-chief of all the rest of Greece in the expedition against the Persian, adding this

[20] Arrian, *Anabasis* 8.9. From Arrian, *Anabasis*, trans. Edward J. Chinnock (New York, 1893).

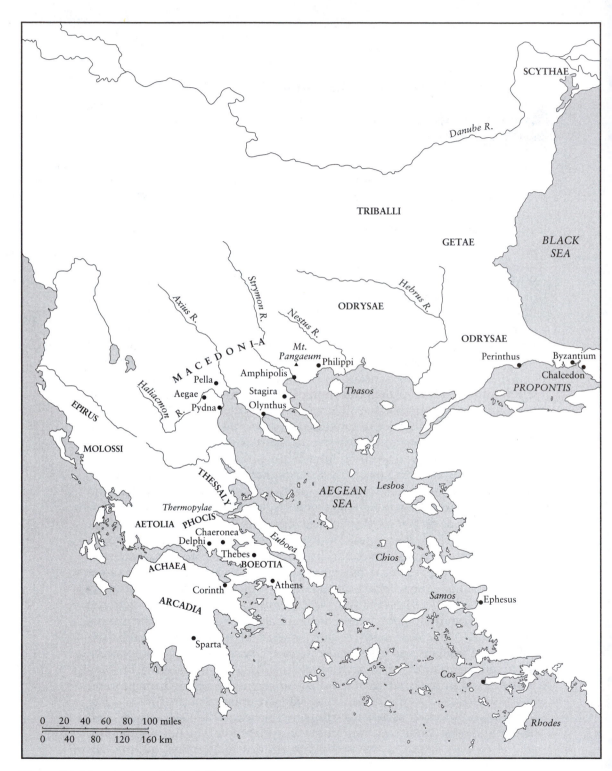

Figure 7.2 Macedonia and its neighbors.

glory not more to himself than to the commonwealth of the Macedonians. These were the advantages which accrued to you from my father Philip; great indeed if looked at by themselves, but small if compared with those you have obtained from me. For though I inherited from my father only a few gold and silver goblets, and there were not even sixty talents in the treasury, and though I found myself charged with a debt of 500 talents owing by Philip, and I was obliged myself to borrow 800 talents in addition to these, I started from the country which could not decently support you. . . . "

2. PHILIP II'S MILITARY REFORMS

Philip II's brother Perdiccas III, together with 4000 Macedonian nobles, was killed fighting the Illyrians in 359 B.C. Because Perdiccas' son was still a child, Philip assumed power as king in the same year. As part of his preparations for war against the Illyrians, Philip implemented the reforms described in the following passages, which transformed the Macedonian army from a loosely organized militia into the most powerful force the Balkans.

Diodorus (16.3.1–3)

Because of the disaster in the battle and the magnitude of the dangers threatening them, the Macedonians were placed in very great perplexity. Nevertheless, although such fears and dangers threatened, Philip was not terrified by the greatness of the impending risks, but he gathered together the Macedonians in a series of assemblies and, encouraging them by the forcefulness of his oratory, he built up their courage. He reorganized the military formations and equipped them suitably with weapons, and held continuous military reviews and competitive exercises. He devised also the close order and arrangement of the phalanx, imitating the battle order of the heroes at Troy, and he first organized the Macedonian phalanx. | Diodorus

Polyaenus (4.2.10)

Philip exercised the Macedonians before battles. Taking up their arms, they marched thirty stades, carrying at the same time their helmets, shields, grieves, sarisas, and in addition to their weapons, they also carried their rations and all the equipment for their daily needs. | Polyaenus

3. THE COMPANIONS OF PHILIP II

Perdiccas III's disastrous defeat opened great gaps in the Macedonian aristocracy and the royal companions, who provided the personal entourage of the king of Macedon and formed the core of the Macedonian army. Philip II responded to this crisis by recruiting new companions throughout the Balkans. These passages from the highly critical lost history of Philip II by the fourth-century B.C. | Theopompus' history of Philip II *historian Theopompus provides a vivid, if biased, impression of the diversity of Philip II's new companions.*[21]

"Licentious and Shameless" Companions

If there was any man in all Greece or among the Barbarians whose character was licentious and shameless, he was invariably attracted to Philip's court in Macedon, and got the title of the "King's companion." For it was Philip's constant habit to reject those who lived respectably and were careful of their property; but to honor and promote those who were extravagant, and passed their lives in drinking and dicing. His influence accordingly tended not only to confirm them in these vices, but to make them proficient in every kind of rascality and lewdness. What vice or infamy did they not possess? What was there virtuous or of good report that they did not lack? Some of them, men as they were, were ever clean-shaven and smoothskinned; and even bearded men did not shrink from mutual defilement. They took about with them two or three slaves of their lust, while submitting to the same shameful services themselves. The men whom they called "companions" deserved to be called "courtesans," and the title of soldier was but a cover to mercenary vice; for though blood-thirsty by nature, they were lascivious by habit. In a word, to make a long story short, especially as I have such a mass of matter to deal with, I believe that the so-called "friends" and "companions" of Philip were more bestial in nature and character than the Centaurs who lived on Pelion, or the Laestrygones who inhabited the Leontine plain, or in fact any other monsters whatever.

They Waged War "with Prodigality and Like Robbers, Not in an Orderly Fashion"

When Philip became master of great treasures, he did not spend them quickly, but threw them away and squandered them. Of all men that ever lived he was not only the worst manager himself, but all about him were so too. Absolutely not one of them had any idea of living properly or of managing his household with moderation. Of that condition he was himself the cause, being a most insatiable and extravagant man, doing everything in an off-hand manner, whether he was acquiring property or giving it away; for although he was a soldier, he was through pure laziness unable to count what he had coming in and what he spent. Then, too, his "companions" were men collected together from all quarters; some came from his own country, some from Thessaly, and some from other parts of Hellas, not selected for excellence; but if among either Greeks or Barbarians there was any licentious, impure, or avaricious man, he had almost every one of the same character assembled in Macedon, and they were all called friends of Philip. Even if any one came who was not entirely of that disposition, still under the influence of the life and manners of the Macedonians, he very soon became like the rest. The reason is that their wars and military expeditions and other great

---

[21] From G. W. Botsford and E. G. Sihler, *Hellenic Civilization* (New York, 1915), pp. 544–546.

expenses encouraged them to be bold and to live, not in an orderly fashion, but with prodigality and like robbers.

4. PHILIPPI: THE FIRST MACEDONIAN COLONY

In 356 B.C. Philip II took advantage of an appeal for help from the city of Crenides, which had been founded four years earlier by colonists from Thasos, to seize control of the city, refounding it as Macedonian colony with the name of "Philippi." In this way Philip gained an important foothold in Thrace and access to the nearby gold mines. The first passage translated here summarizes the advantages Philip gained by founding Philippi. The second is a fragmentary decree of Philippi reporting the results of an embassy to Alexander the Great seeking to clarify the property rights of the citizens of Philippi and their Thracian neighbors. Alexander's decision indicates that the Thracians occupied a subordinate position at Philippi because, first, whereas Philip granted full property rights to the citizens of Philippi, the Thracians gained only the right to work royal land, and, second, important natural resources such as timber remained under royal control.[22]

The Foundation of Philippi

After this Philip came to the city of Crenides. He increased it with a multitude of settlers and renamed it Philippi after himself. He expanded the gold mines in its territory, which had been very limited and insignificant, to the extent that they were able to bring him an income of more than a thousand talents. He quickly piled up from these mines wealth. With this wealth he steadily raised the kingdom of Macedon to great preeminence. For striking gold coins called "Philips" after himself, he put together a remarkable force of mercenaries and turned many Greeks with them into traitors to their cities.

Diodorus

A Decree from Philippi[23]

1. . . . the citizens of Philippi sent an embassy to Alexander; and Alexander determined the following: the citizens of Philippi shall work the fallow land and pay additional tax. The boundary shall be. . . . Philotas and Leonnatus . . . entered the land. . . . Philip gave to the citizens of Philippi . . . .

A Decree from Philippi

2. . . . as much as was given to the Thracians by Philip, the Thracians shall have the right to work just as Alexander has determined concerning these matters. And the citizens of Philippi shall have the land. . . . The hills on either side have. . . . [T]he citizens of Philippi shall cultivate the land around Seirake and Dainoros just as Philip granted, but no one shall sell the timber in Dysoros until the embassy returns again from Alexander. All the marshes as far as the bridge shall belong to the citizens of Philippi.

[22] From Diodorus 16.8.6–7.

[23] Translation based on the text in Lambros Missitzis, "A Royal Decree of Alexander the Great on the Lands of Philippi," *The Ancient World* 12 (1985), p. 5.

5. OATH OF MEMBERS OF THE LEAGUE OF CORINTH (338–337 B.C.)

Athenian inscription of the oaths sworn establishing the League of Corinth.

At the Battle of Chaeronea in 338 B.C., Philip II brought to a successful conclusion almost two decades of diplomatic and military activity aimed at establishing Macedonian hegemony in Greece. Philip followed up his victory by organizing a common peace similar to the King's Peace of the first half of the fourth century B.C. Called "The League of Corinth" by historians, it was intended to ensure secure Macedonian control of Greece by guaranteeing the security of pro-Macedonian governments in Greek cities and mobilize Greek support for Philip's projected war against Persia. This passage contains a fragment of an Athenian inscription recording the oaths sworn by the Athenians when they ratified the treaty establishing the League of Corinth.[24]

Oath. I swear by Zeus, Earth, Sun, Poseidon, Athena, Ares, and all the gods and goddesses. I will abide by the peace, and I will not break the agreements with Philip the Macedonian, nor will I take up arms with hostile intent against any one of those who abide by the oaths either by land or by sea. I will not seize in war by any device or stratagem any city or fort or harbor belonging to those who share the peace, nor will I suppress the kingdom of Philip or of his descendants or the constitutions in force among any of those [who share the peace], when they swore the oaths concerning the peace. I will not commit any act that contravenes the agreements nor will I permit any other to do so. If any one breaks the agreements, I will assist those who have been wronged in accordance with their requests and I will fight against those who break the common peace just as the common council and the leader decide. . . .

6. THE MARRIAGES OF PHILIP II

Satyrus quoted in Athenaeus

After almost two decades in which Alexander was Philip II's recognized heir and his mother, Olympias, was Philip's principal wife, this understanding and the stability of Macedon was disrupted by Philip's seventh marriage in 338 B.C. to a young Macedonian woman named Cleopatra. In this passage the third-century B.C. historian Satyrus discusses Philip's marriages and the role they played in his diplomacy and imperial policy.[25]

Philip always married in connection with war. So in the twenty-years in which he reigned, as Satyrus says in his *Life of Philip*, he married Audata, an Illyrian woman, and had by her a daughter Cyna. He married also Phila, the sister of Derdas and Machatas. Wishing also to establish kinship ties with the Thessalian people, he had children by two Thessalian women, one of whom was Nikesipolis from Pherae, who bore him Thessalonike and the other was Philinna from Larissa by whom he had Arrhidaeus. He also established connections with the

[24] From *IG* 2.236.

[25] Satyrus quoted in Athenaeus 12, p. 557 B.

kingdom of the Molossians by marrying Olympias by whom he had Alexander and Cleopatra. Also when he conquered Thrace, Cothelas, the king of the Thracians, came to him with his daughter Meda and many gifts. He married her and brought her into his home alongside Olympias. After all these women, he fell in love with and married Cleopatra, the sister of Hippostratus and the niece of Attalus. By bringing her into his home with Olympias, he threw his whole life into turmoil. For right away at the wedding Attalus said: "Now legitimate and not bastard kings will be born." Alexander on hearing this threw the goblet he was holding at Attalus, and Attalus threw a goblet at him. Afterwards, Olympias fled to the Molossians and Alexander to the Illyrians. Cleopatra bore Philip a daughter named Europa.

7. THE ASSASSINATION OF PHILIP II

Philip II was assassinated in the summer of 336 B.C. on the verge of launching his invasion of the Persian Empire. Historians have long debated whether Alexander and his mother Olympias were involved in the plot to kill Philip II. Aristotle (Politics 1311b2), however, claimed that the assassin Pausanias was motivated by a personal grievance, and his view is supported by the passage of Diodorus translated next, which provides a vivid picture of the intricate sexual politics of the Macedonian court and their political fallout.[26]

Diodorus

Finally, when the drinking was finished and the beginning of the contests determined for the next day, the people rushed toward the theater while it was still night. At dawn, the procession took place. Together with other richly outfitted equipment, Philip had carried in the procession images of the twelve gods which had been made with extraordinary skill and amazingly decorated with a brilliant show of wealth. Together with these a thirteenth image, one of Philip, which was suitable for a god, was also carried in the procession. In this way the king indicated that he was enthroned with the twelve gods.

93. The theater was filled and Philip came wearing a white himation. He had ordered his guards to follow him at a distance. For he would show to everyone that because he was protected by the common good will of the Greeks, he had no need of the protection of his guards. So great was his preeminence, and while everyone was simultaneously praising and congratulating him, a paradoxical and completely unexpected plot and death struck the king. In order that the account of his death may be clear, we shall set out the reasons for the plot.

Pausanias was a Macedonian from Orestis. He was a royal bodyguard and had become a friend of Philip because of his good looks. Observing, however, that another man also named Pausanias like him-

[26] From Diodorus 16.92.5–94.

self was beloved by the king, he spoke abusively to the other Pausanias, saying that he was a hermaphrodite and readily accepted the advances of any one who desired him. The other Pausanias did not endure the outrageous slander, but for the moment kept his peace. After, however, sharing with Attalus, one of his friends, what he intended to do, he willingly and remarkably brought about his own death. For a few days later, when Philip joined battle with Pleurias, the king of the Illyrians, he stood before the king, received all the blows aimed at him with his own body, and died.

His deed was widely acclaimed. Attalus, who was a member of the royal court and had great influence with the king, invited Pausanias to dinner and after plying him with unmixed wine, turned him over to the mule-drivers for outrage and drunken sex. When Pausanias awoke from his drunken stupor and became furious at the abuse of his body, he denounced Attalus in the presence of the king. Philip was furious at the criminality of the deed, but because Attalus was related to him and he needed his services at that time, Philip was unwilling to prosecute him. For Attalus was the nephew of Cleopatra, the woman that king had married and he had been selected to be general in the advance force that had been dispatched to Asia and he was a brave man in battle. For this reason, the king, wishing to calm Pausanias' righteous wrath over what he had suffered, gave him distinguished gifts and promoted him in rank among the bodyguards.

94. Pausanias, however, preserving his anger unchanged, looked to take vengeance not only from the man who had committed the deed, but also from the one who had not given him satisfaction. The sophist Hermocrates also particularly supported his decision. For Pausanias was his pupil and during a lesson inquired how a person might become famous. The sophist answered that he would if he killed the man who had done the greatest deeds. Pausanias connected his situation with the memory of this and his carrying out his plan. Subordinating his good sense to his rage and brooking no delay in his plan because of his anger, he made plans in the following way for his attack at the festival that was in progress. Stationing horses at the gates, he came to the entrance of the theater with a Celtic dagger hidden on his person. Philip ordered his friends who were accompanying him to enter the theater first and his guards to stand aside. Seeing the king alone, Pausanias rushed forward, stabbed Philip right through his side and stretched him out dead. Pausanias then ran toward the gates and the horses that were at the ready for his escape. Some of the bodyguards immediately hastened to the body of the king and others poured out in pursuit of the assassin. Among the latter were Leonatus, Perdiccas, and Attalus. Pausanias, who had the jump on their pursuit, would have mounted the horse and escaped, if his sandal hadn't caught on a vine and made him fall. As a result, Perdiccas and his men caught up with Pausanias as he was trying to rise from the ground, and speared him, killing him.

E. The Reign of Alexander the Great: Alexander and the Greeks

1. THE GREEKS IN EUROPE

In creating the League of Corinth, Philip II had ingeniously adapted the idea of Common Peace to the purposes of consolidating Macedonian suzerainty in Greece and support for his plan to invade the Persian Empire. Successful implementation, however, required the Macedonians to walk a narrow line between respecting Greek autonomy and intervening to support pro-Macedonian governments. In the following selection, an unknown orator urges the Athenians to resist Macedonian rule by cataloging examples of Macedonian violations of the League of Corinth charter.[27]

Ps. Demosthenes,
*On the Treaty
with Alexander*

Our hearty assent, men of Athens, is due to those who insist that we should abide by our oaths and covenants, provided that they do so from conviction. . . . But from the very terms of the compact and from the oaths which ratified the general peace, you may at once see who are its transgressors; and that those transgressions are serious, I will prove to you concisely. . . .

Therefore when Alexander, contrary to the oaths and the compacts as set forth in the general peace, restored those tyrants, the sons of Philiades, to Messene, had he any regard for justice? Did he not rather give play to his own tyrannical disposition, showing little regard for you and the joint agreement? . . . For it is further stipulated in the compact that anyone who acts as Alexander has acted shall be the enemy of all the other parties to the compact, and his country shall be hostile territory, and all the parties shall unite in a campaign against him. So if we carry out the agreement, we shall treat the restorer of the tyrants as an enemy. . . .

Again, the compact at the very beginning enjoins that the Greeks shall be free and independent. Is it not, then, the height of absurdity that the clause about freedom should stand first in the compact, and that one who has enslaved others should be supposed not to have acted contrary to the joint agreement? . . .

I come to another claim sanctioned by the compact. For the actual words are, "If any of the parties shall overthrow the constitution established in the several states at the date when they took the oaths to observe the peace, they shall be treated as enemies by all the parties to the peace." But just reflect, men of Athens, that the Achaeans in the Peloponnese enjoyed democratic government, and one of their democracies, that of Pellene, has now been overthrown by the Macedonian king, who has expelled the majority of the citizens, given their property to their slaves, and set up Chaeron, the wrestler, as their tyrant. . . .

Now for a still greater absurdity. For it is provided in the compact that it shall be the business of the delegates at the Congress and those responsible for

[27] Ps. Demosthenes 17: *On the Treaty with Alexander* (selections). From Demosthenes, *Orations*, trans. J. H. Vince (Cambridge, MA, 1930).

public safety to see that in the states that are parties to the peace there shall be no executions and banishments contrary to the laws established in those states, no confiscation of property, no partition of lands, no canceling of debts, and no emancipation of slaves for purposes of revolution. . . .

I will point out a further breach of the compact. For it is laid down that it shall not be lawful for exiles to set out, bearing arms, from the states which are parties to the peace, with hostile intent against any of the states included in the peace; but if they do, then that city from which they set out shall be excluded from the terms of the treaty. Now the Macedonian king has been so unscrupulous about bearing arms that he has never yet laid them down, but even now goes about bearing arms, as far as is in his power, and more so indeed now than ever, inasmuch as he has reinstated the professional trainer at Sicyon by an edict, and other exiles elsewhere. . . . But to prove to you still more clearly that no Greeks will accuse you of transgressing any of the terms of the joint agreement, but will even be grateful to you for exposing the real transgressors, I will just touch upon a few of the many points that might be mentioned. For the compact, of course, provides that all the parties to the peace may sail the seas, and that none may hinder them or force a ship of any of them to come to harbor, and that anyone who violates this shall be treated as an enemy by all the parties to the peace. Now, men of Athens, you have most distinctly seen this done by the Macedonians; for they have grown so arrogant that they forced all our ships coming from the Black Sea to put in at Tenedos, and under one pretence or another refused to release them until you passed a decree to man and launch a hundred war-galleys instantly, and you put Menestheus in command. . . .

2. THE GREEKS IN ASIA

Alexander's relationship to the Greeks in Asia differed significantly from his relationship to Greeks in Europe. Unlike the European Greeks, the Asian Greeks lived in territory Alexander claimed as his own by right of conquest. Freedom, therefore, was his to grant or withhold. The first selection is a letter from Alexander to the citizens of Chios setting out guidelines for the establishment of a democratic government to replace the pro-Persian oligarchy that had previously governed the city and defining Chios' role in his campaign. In the next selection Alexander asserts his authority over the territory of Priene, granting freedom and exemption from contributions to the war effort to the citizens and imposing tribute on the non-Greek inhabitants of Priene's hinterland. Alexander also could confer benefits on his subjects—both Greek and non-Greek—in Asia. The third selection records Alexander's construction and dedication of the temple of Athena in Priene.

Letter of Alexander to Chios[28]

Letter of Alexander to Chios

In the prytany of Deistheos, from King Alexander to the people.

All the exiles from Chios shall return, and the government in Chios shall be democratic. Law-writers shall be selected, who will draft and correct the laws,

---

[28] From *SIG*³ 283.

in order they should contain nothing opposed to the democracy or the return of the exiles. The laws which have been corrected or drafted shall be referred to Alexander. The Chians shall furnish twenty triremes manned at their expense, and these ships shall sail as long as the rest of the Greek fleet sails with us. As for the men who betrayed the city to the barbarians, all who may have escaped shall be exiled from all cities which share the peace, and they shall liable to seizure in accordance with the decree of the Greeks. All who have been captured are to be brought back and judged in the council of the Greeks. If there is any conflict between those who have returned from exile and the residents of the city, with regard to this they shall be judged before us. Until the Chians are reconciled, there shall be a garrison from Alexander that is as large as necessary in Chios, and the Chians shall maintain the garrison.

Alexander Settles Affairs at Priene[29]

From King Alexander

    As many of those living in Naulochon who are Prienians, they shall be autonomous and free, and they shall possess the land and all the houses in the city and the hinterland, just as the Prienians. . . . And the land of the Myrseloi and the Pedieis and the neighboring countryside I declare belongs to me, and those living in these villages shall pay tribute (*phoroi*). I release the city of Priene from the contribution (*syntaxis*) and the garrison. . . .

Dedication of the Temple of Athena at Priene[30]

King Alexander dedicated the temple to Athena Polias.

Cutting the Gordian Knot

Immediately before landing in Anatolia in 334 B.C., Alexander is reported to have thrown a spear into the land and claimed it as his own. During his visit to Gordium, the former capital of the kingdom of Phrygia, in 333 B.C., he claimed that he fulfilled an ancient prophecy that the person who released the knot attaching the drawpole to the wagon of the Phrygian king Gordius would rule Asia. Although "Asia" originally referred to the territory of Assuwa, a Hittite vassal state in western Anatolia, Alexander probably understood it in its fourth-century B.C. sense as referring to the Persian Empire.[31]

When Alexander arrived at Gordium, he was seized with an ardent desire to go up into the citadel, which contained the palace of Gordius and his son Midas. He was also desirous of seeing the wagon of Gordius and the cord of the yoke of his wagon. There was a great deal of talk about this wagon among the neighboring population. It was said that Gordius was a poor man among the ancient Phrygians, who had a small piece of land to till, and two yoke of oxen. He used one of these

Alexander Settles Affairs at Priene

Dedication of the Temple of Athena at Priene

Arrian, Anabasis

[29] *Inschr. Priene* No. 1.

[30] *Inschr. Priene* No. 156.

[31] Arrian, *Anabasis* 2.3. From Arrian, *Anabasis*, trans. Edward J. Chinnock (New York, 1893).

in ploughing and the other to draw the wagon. On one occasion, while he was plowing, an eagle settled upon the yoke, and remained sitting there until the time came for unyoking the oxen. Being alarmed at the sight; he went to the Telmessian soothsayers to consult them about the sign from the deity; for the Telmessians were skilful in interpreting the meaning of divine manifestations, and the power of divination has been bestowed not only upon the men, but also upon their wives and children from generation to generation. When Gordius was driving his wagon, near a certain village of the Telmessians, he met a maiden fetching water from the spring, and to her he related how the sign of the eagle had appeared to him. As she herself was of the prophetic race, she instructed him to return to the very spot and offer sacrifice to Zeus the king. Gordius requested her to accompany him and direct him how to perform the sacrifice. He offered the sacrifice in the way the girl suggested, and afterwards married her. A son was born to them named Midas. When Midas was grown to be a man, handsome and valiant, the Phrygians were harassed by civil discord, and consulting the oracle they were told that a wagon would bring them a king, who would put an end to their discord. While they were still deliberating about this very matter, Midas arrived with his father and mother, and stopped near the assembly, wagon and all. They, comparing the oracular response with this occurrence, decided that this was the person whom god told them the wagon would bring. They therefore appointed Midas king; and he, putting an end to their discord, dedicated his father's wagon in the citadel as a thank-offering to Zeus the king for sending the eagle. In addition to this the following saying was current concerning the wagon, that whosoever could loosen the cord of the yoke of this wagon, was destined to gain the rule of Asia. The cord was made of cornel bark, and neither end nor beginning to it could be seen. It is by said by some that when Alexander could find out no way to loosen the cord and yet was unwilling to allow it to remain unloosened, lest this should exercise some disturbing influence upon the multitude, he struck it with his sword and cutting it through, said that it had been loosened. Aristobulus says that he pulled out the pin of the wagon-pole, which was a wooden peg driven right through it, holding the cord together. Having done this, he drew out the yoke from the wagon-pole. How Alexander performed the feat in connection with this cord, I cannot affirm with confidence. At any rate both he and his troops departed from the wagon as if the oracular prediction confining the loosening of the cord had been fulfilled. Moreover, that very night, the thunder and lightning were signs of its fulfillment; and for this reason Alexander offered sacrifice on the following day to the gods who had revealed the signs and the way to loosen the cord.

F. Alexander and Egypt

Isolated from Persian support by Darius III's defeat in the Battle of Issus and facing a hostile Egyptian population, the satrap of Egypt surrendered to Alexander without putting up any resistance in the fall of 332 B.C. The first selection illustrates the tension between Alexander's efforts to appease the Egyptians by showing respect for their customs and his own Greek culture. The second section describes the foundation of Alexandria, highlighting the advantages of the site and the mixture of compulsion and incentives required to populate it. The third selection summarizes the story of Alexander's visit to the oracle of the Libyan god Zeus Ammon and his recognition as son of the god as told by Callisthenes, the official historian of the expedition. The fourth selection describes Alexander's reorganization of the government of Egypt, replacing the Persian satrapal system with one in which civil administration was to be shared by Egyptian and Greek officials while military authority remained under Macedonian control. The final selection illustrates fiscal devices used by Cleomenes of Naucratis, who made himself satrap after the collapse of Alexander's overly complex administrative system for Egypt.

1. SURRENDER OF EGYPT TO ALEXANDER[32]

1. Alexander now led his army into Egypt, whither he had set out at first from Tyre; and marching from Gaza, on the seventh day he arrived at Pelusium in Egypt. His fleet coasted along also from Phoenicia to Egypt; and he found the ships already moored at Pelusium. When Mazaces the Persian, whom Darius had appointed viceroy of Egypt, ascertained how the battle at Issus had resulted, that Darius had fled in disgraceful flight, and that Phoenicia, Syria, and most of Arabia were already in Alexander's possession, as he had no Persian force with which he could offer resistance, he admitted Alexander into the cities and the country in a friendly way. Alexander introduced a garrison into Pelusium, and ordering the men in the ships to sail up the river as far as the city of Memphis, he went in person towards Heliopolis, having the river Nile on his right. He reached that city through the desert, after getting possession of all the places on the march through the voluntary surrender of the inhabitants. Thence he crossed the stream and came to Memphis, where he offered sacrifice to Apis and the other gods, and celebrated a gymnastic and musical contest, the most distinguished artists in these matters coming to him from Greece. From Memphis he sailed down the river towards the sea, embarking the shield-bearing guards, the archers, the Agrianians, and of the cavalry the royal squadron of the Companions. Coming to Canopus, he sailed round the Lake Mareotis, and disembarked where now is situated the city of Alexandria, which takes its name from him.

Arrian, Anabasis

2. FOUNDATION OF ALEXANDRIA[33]

During his return trip from Ammon, Alexander came to the Mareotic Lake, which is located not far from the island of Pharos. Having considered the nature

Curtius Rufus

[32] Arrian, *Anabasis* 3.1. From Arrian, *Anabasis*, trans. Edward J. Chinnock (New York, 1892).

[33] From Curtius Rufus 4.8. 1–2, 5–6.

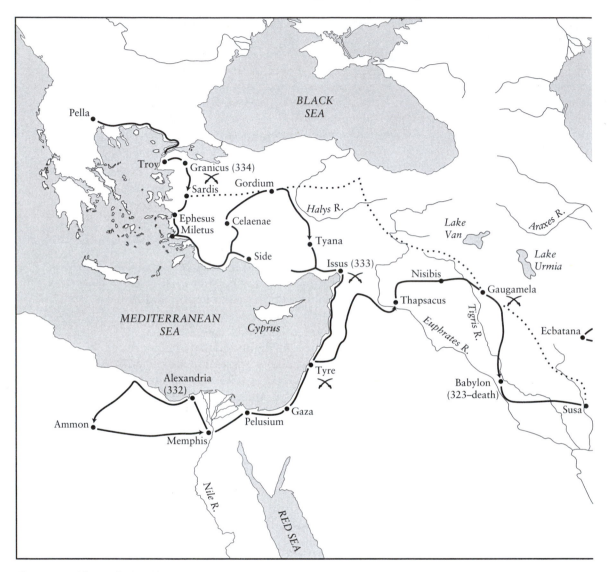

Figure 7.3 Alexander's campaign.

of the place, he first decided to establish a new city on the island itself. Then, as it appeared that the island was not large enough for a large settlement, he chose a place for the city, where Alexandria is now, drawing its name from that of its founder. Including whatever land there is between the lake and sea, he determined a circuit of eighty stades for the walls, and having left behind men who were to be in charge of building the city, he set off for Memphis. . . . Ordering

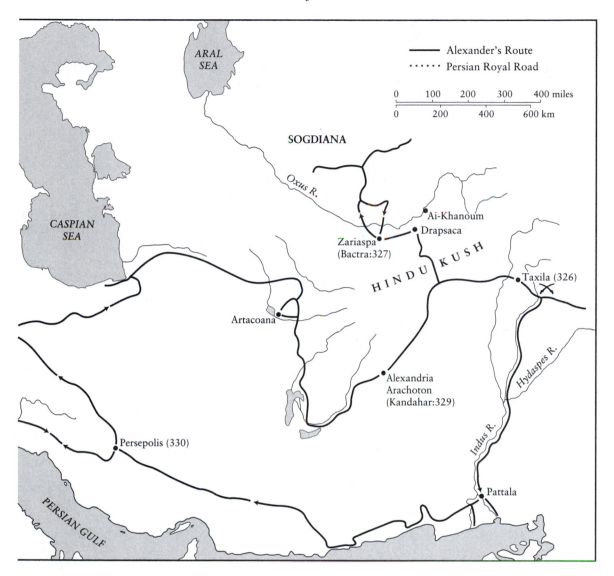

people to move to Alexandria, he filled the new city with a large population. There is a story that when the king marked out the circuit of the future wall with barley, as is Macedonian custom, flocks of birds flew in and ate the barley. Although this omen was considered hostile by many people, the seers explained that a crowd of immigrants would inhabit this city, and that it would provide food to many countries.

3. ALEXANDER'S VISIT TO SIWAH[34]

Strabo, *Geography*

At any rate, Callisthenes says that Alexander conceived a very great ambition to go inland to the oracle, since he had heard that Perseus, as also Heracles, had done so in earlier times; and that he started from Paraetonium, although the south winds had set in, and forced his way; and that when he lost his way because of the thick dust, he was saved by rainfalls and by the guidance of two crows. But this last assertion is flattery and *so* are the next: that the priest permitted the king alone to pass into the temple in his usual dress, but the rest changed their clothes; that all heard the oracles from outside except Alexander, but he inside; that the oracular responses were not, as at Delphi and among the Branchidae, given in words, but mostly by nods and tokens, as in Homer, "Cronion spoke and nodded assent with his dark brows"—the prophet having assumed the role of Zeus; that, however, the fellow expressly told the king that he, Alexander, was son of Zeus. And to this statement Callisthenes dramatically adds that, although the oracle of Apollo among the Branchidae had ceased to speak from the time the temple had been robbed by the Branchidae, who sided with the Persians in the time of Xerxes, and although the spring also had ceased to flow, yet at Alexander's arrival the spring began to flow again and that many oracles were carried by the Milesian ambassadors to Memphis concerning Alexander's descent from Zeus, his future victory in the neighbourhood of Arbela, the death of Dareius, and the revolutionary attempts in Lacedaemon. And he says that the Erythraean Athena also gave out an utterance concerning Alexander's high descent; for, he adds, this woman was like the ancient Erythraean Sibylla. Such, then, are the accounts of the historians.

4. ALEXANDER'S ORGANIZATION OF EGYPT[35]

Arrian, *Anabasis*

He then settled the affairs of Egypt, by appointing two Egyptians, Doloaspis and Petisis, governors of the country, dividing between them the whole land; but as Petisis declined his province, Doloaspis received the whole. He appointed two of the Companions to be commandants of garrisons: Pantaleon the Pydnaean in Memphis, and Polemo, son of Megacles, a Pellaean, in Pelusium. He also gave the command of the Greek auxiliaries to Lycidas, an Aetolian, and appointed Eugnostus, son of Xenophantes, one of the Companions, to be secretary over the same troops. As their overseers he placed Aeschylus and Ephippus the Chalcidean. The government of the neighboring country of Libya he granted to Apollonius, son of Charinus; and the part of Arabia near Heroopolis he put under Cleomenes, a man of Naucratis. This last was ordered to allow the governors to rule their respective districts according to the ancient custom; but to collect from them the tribute due to him. The native governors were also ordered to pay it

---

[34] Strabo, *Geography* 17.1. 43, C 813–814. From Strabo, *Geography*, trans. H. L. Jones (Cambridge, MA, 1932).

[35] Arrian, *Anabasis* 3.3. From Arrian, *Anabasis*, trans. Edward J. Chinnock (New York, 1893).

to Cleomenes. He appointed Peucestas, son of Macartatus, and Balacrus, son of Amyntas, generals of the army which he left behind in Egypt. . . .

5. THE ADMINISTRATION OF CLEOMENES OF NAUCRATIS[36]

When Cleomenes of Alexandria was satrap of Egypt and a great famine raged in other countries, but only a moderate one in Egypt, Cleomenes put a stop to the export of grain. The nomarchs [=*nome governors*] asserted that they were unable to pay the tribute because they could not export the grain. Cleomenes therefore gave them the right to export, but placed a high price upon the grain, so that he received a high revenue, although little grain was exported, and put an end to the excuses of the nomarchs.

Aristotle, *Oeconomica*

When Cleomenes was traveling by boat through the nome [=*one of 36 administrative districts in Egypt*] in which the crocodile is a god, one of his slaves was seized by a crocodile. Summoning the priests he stated that a wrong had been done him and that he wished to punish the crocodiles. So he gave orders to hunt them. In order that their god might not be subjected to insult the priests brought together all the money that they could collect and gave it to him, and so put an end to the affair.

When King Alexander bade Cleomenes build a city near Pharos and locate there the market which had formerly been at the Canopic mouth of the Nile, Cleomenes sailed down the river to Canopus and went to the priests and the wealthy citizens and said that he had come there in order to settle them elsewhere. The priests and inhabitants of Canopus brought money and gave it to him in order to induce him to leave the market in their district. He took the money and sailed away. Later, when he was quite ready to begin the building, he sailed down again and demanded an immense sum from them, saying that it was a great advantage to him to have the market at the other place rather than at Canopus. When they said that they could not possibly pay the money, he took them away as colonists.

When grain was selling in the country at ten drachmas he summoned those engaged in the grain business and asked them at what price they were willing to sell to him. They responded that they would sell it at a lower price than that at which they sold to the retailers. He ordered them to deliver it to him at the same price at which they sold to the others. He then fixed the price of grain at thirty-two drachmas and disposed of it at that price.

He called the priests to him and said that the expenditure upon the temples throughout the country was very great, and that the number of temples and priests must therefore be decreased. The priests individually and in common gave him the sacred treasures, thinking that Cleomenes was in truth about to decrease the number and each one wishing that his own temple should be left and he himself remain its priest.

[36] Ps. Aristotle, *Oeconomica* 33. From G. W. Botsford and E. G. Sihler, *Hellenic Civilization* (New York, 1915), pp. 584–585.

G. Alexander and the Non-Greeks

During the first years of the Asian campaign, Alexander's treatment of his new non-Greek subjects was opportunistic. Although he granted non-Greeks the right to live under their traditional laws provided they paid him the tribute they had paid the Persians, government was left sometimes to members of the previous ruling families, who swore loyalty to him and sometimes to Macedonian or Greek governors as circumstances dictated. The occupation of Babylon in 331 B.C. after his victory at Gaugemela marked a new direction in Alexander's treatment of non-Greeks. The first selection shows that, while continuing to court the support of local elites such as the Chaldaeans, Alexander sought Persian support by confirming in office the satrap Mazaeus. The second selection, which refers to conditions when Alexander returned to Babylon in 324 B.C., highlights the difficulties in his policies, revealing the existence of tension between Alexander and the Chaldaeans over the construction of a new temple to Belus (=Marduk), the principal god of Babylon.

1. ALEXANDER'S ORGANIZATION OF BABYLON[37]

Arrian,
Anabasis

He [sc. Darius III] fled towards Media for this reason, because he thought Alexander would take the road to Susa and Babylon immediately after the battle, inasmuch as the whole of that country was inhabited and the road was not difficult for the transit of baggage; and besides Babylon and Susa appeared to be the prizes of the war; whereas the road towards Media was by no means easy for the march of a large army. In this conjecture Darius was not mistaken; for when Alexander started from Arbela, he advanced straight towards Babylon; and when he was now not far from that city, he drew up his army in order of battle and marched forward. The Babylonians came out to meet him in mass, with their priests and rulers, each of whom individually brought gifts, and offered to surrender their city, citadel, and money. Entering the city, he commanded the Babylonians to rebuild all the temples which Xerxes had destroyed, and especially that of Belus, whom the Babylonians venerate more than any other god. He then appointed Mazaeus viceroy of the Babylonians, Apollodorus the Amphipolitan general of the soldiers who were left behind with Mazaeus, and Asclepiodorus, son of Philo, collector of the revenue. He also sent Mithrines, who had surrendered to him the citadel of Sardis, down into Armenia to be viceroy there. Here also he met with the Chaldaeans; and whatever they directed in regard to the religious rites of Babylon he performed, and in particular he offered sacrifice to Belus according to their instructions.

2. BABYLONIAN RESISTANCE TO ALEXANDER'S PLANS[38]

Arrian,
Anabasis

But he had a suspicion that the Chaldaeans were trying to prevent his march into Babylon at that time with reference rather to their own advantage than to

[37] Arrian, *Anabasis* 3.16. From Arrian, *Anabasis*, trans. Edward J. Chinnock (New York, 1893).

[38] Arrian, *Anabasis* 7.17. From Arrian, *Anabasis*, trans. Edward J. Chinnock (New York, 1893).

the declaration of the oracle. For in the middle of the city of the Babylonians was the temple of Belus, an edifice very great in size, constructed of baked bricks which were cemented together with bitumen. This temple had been razed to the ground by Xerxes, when he returned from Greece; as were also all the other sacred buildings of the Babylonians. Some say that Alexander had formed the resolution to rebuild it upon the former foundations; and for this reason he ordered the Babylonians to carry away the mound. Others say that he intended to build a still larger one than that which formerly existed. But after his departure, the men who had been entrusted with the work prosecuted it without any vigor, so that he determined now to employ the whole of his army in completing it. A great quantity of land as well as gold had been dedicated to the god Belus by the Assyrian kings; and from days of old the temple was kept in repair and sacrifices were offered to the god. But at that time the Chaldaeans were appropriating the property of the god, since nothing existed upon which the revenues could be expended. Alexander suspected that they did not wish him to enter Babylon for this reason, for fear that in a short time the completion of the temple would deprive them of the gains accruing from the money.

3. THE DESTRUCTION OF PERSEPOLIS

In the winter of 330 B.C., Alexander ordered the looting and destruction of Persepolis, the ceremonial capital of the Persian Empire. Alexander's reasons for this act of vandalism were debated by both ancient and modern historians. Whether the debate between Alexander and Parmenio reported by the historian Arrian in this selection actually happened cannot be determined, but the passage does highlight the tension between Alexander's need to attract the support of his new Persian subjects and the pressure to maintain the impression that he was continuing the Greek Crusade authorized by the League of Corinth.[39]

Arrian,
Anabasis

Alexander now marched back with all speed to the river, and finding the bridge already constructed over it, he easily crossed with his army. Thence he again continued his march to Persepolis, with such speed that he arrived before the guards of the city could pillage the treasury. He also captured the money which was at Pasargadae in the treasury of the first Cyrus, and appointed Phrasaortes, son of Rheomithres, viceroy over the Persians. He burned down the Persian palace, though Parmenio advised him to preserve it, for many reasons, and especially because it was not well to destroy what was now his own property, and because the men of Asia would not by this course of action be induced to come over to him, thinking that he himself had decided not to retain the rule of Asia, but only to conquer it and depart. But Alexander said that he wished to take vengeance on the Persians, in retaliation for their deeds in the invasion of Greece, when they razed Athens to the ground and burned down the temples. He also desired to punish the Persians for all the other injuries they had done the Greeks. But Alexander

[39] Arrian, *Anabasis* 3.18. From Arrian, *Anabasis*, trans. Edward J. Chinnock (New York, 1893).

does not seem to me to have acted on this occasion with prudence; nor do I think that this was any retributive penalty at all on the ancient Persians.

凹凹凹凹凹凹凹凹凹凹凹凹凹凹凹凹凹凹凹凹凹凹凹凹凹凹凹凹凹凹凹凹凹

H. The Challenges of Alexander

1. THE ATTEMPT TO INTRODUCE PROSKYNESIS

Arrian,
Anabasis

As part of Alexander's efforts to attract Persian support in Central Asia, he adopted parts of Persian royal regalia and court ceremonial. In this connection in 328 B.C. he attempted to require his Macedonian and Greek courtiers to offer him proskynesis—prostration—as his Persian courtiers already did. Historians agree that for the Persians proskynesis implied recognition of social superiority, not divinity. Greeks and Macedonians, however, viewed it as appropriate only for gods, as the reported debate between Callisthenes and Anaxarchus makes clear. Alexander must have been aware of this fact, so that his insistence on having them perform it suggests that he already had begun to think of himself not merely as a mortal who happened to be the son of Zeus Ammon, but as a god himself.[40]

How he [*i.e., Callisthenes*] resisted Alexander in regard to the ceremony of prostration, the following is the most received account. An arrangement was made between Alexander and the Sophists in conjunction with the most illustrious of the Persians and Medes who were in attendance upon him, that this topic should be mentioned at a wine-party. Anaxarchus commenced the discussion by saying that Alexander would much more justly be deemed a god than either Dionysus or Heracles, not only on account of the very numerous and mighty exploits which he had performed, but also because Dionysus was only a Theban, in no way related to Macedonians; and Heracles was an Argive, not at all related to them, except in regard to Alexander's pedigree; for he was a descendant of Heracles. He added that the Macedonians might with greater justice gratify their king with divine honors, for there was no doubt about this, that when he departed from men they would honor him as a god. How much more just then would it be to reward him while alive, than after his death, when it would be no advantage to him to be honored.

11. When Anaxarchus had uttered these remarks and others of a similar kind, those who were privy to the plan applauded his speech, and wished at once to begin the ceremony of prostration. Most of the Macedonians, however, were vexed at the speech and kept silence. But Callisthenes interposed and said, "O Anaxarchus, I openly declare that there is no honor

---

[40] Arrian, *Anabasis* 4.10–12. From Arrian, *Anabasis*, trans. Edward J. Chinnock (New York, 1893).

which Alexander is unworthy to receive, provided that it is consistent with his being human; but men have made distinctions between those honors which are due to men and those due to gods, in many different ways, as for instance by the building of temples and by the erection of statues. Moreover for the gods sacred enclosures are selected, to them sacrifice is offered, and to them libations are made. Hymns also are composed in honor of the gods, and eulogies for men. But the greatest distinction is made by the custom of prostration. For it is the practice that men should be kissed by those who salute them; but because the deity is located somewhere above, it is not lawful even to touch him, and this is the reason no doubt why he is honored by prostration. Bands of choral dancers are also appointed for the gods, and paeans are sung in their honor. And this is not at all wonderful, seeing that certain honors are specially assigned to some of the gods and certain others to other gods, and, by Zeus, quite different ones again are assigned to heroes, which are very distinct from those paid to the deity. It is not therefore reasonable to confound all these distinctions without discrimination, exalting men to a rank above their condition by extravagant accumulation of honors, and debasing the gods, as far as lies in human power, to an unseemly level, by paying them honors only equal to those paid to men."

He said that Alexander would not endure the affront, if some private individual were to be thrust into his royal honors by an unjust vote, either by show of hands or by ballot. Much more justly then would the gods be indignant at those mortals who usurp divine honors or suffer themselves to be thrust into them by others. "Alexander not only seems to be, but is in reality beyond any competition the bravest of brave men, of kings the most kingly, and of generals the most worthy to command an army. O Anaxarchus, it was your duty rather than any other man's to become the special advocate of these arguments now adduced by me, and the opponent of those contrary to them, seeing that you associate with him for the purpose of imparting philosophy and instruction. Therefore it was unseemly to begin this discussion, when you ought to have remembered that you are not associating with and giving advice to Cambyses or Xerxes, but to the son of Philip, who derives his origin from Heracles and Aeacus, whose ancestors came into Macedonia from Argos, and have continued to rule the Macedonians, not by force, but by law. Not even to Heracles himself while still alive were divine honors paid by the Greeks; and even after his death they were withheld until a decree had been published by the oracle of the god at Delphi that men should honor Heracles as a god. But if, because the discussion is held in the land of foreigners, we ought to adopt the sentiments of foreigners, I for my part demand, O Alexander, that you should think of Greece, for whose sake the whole of this expedition was undertaken by you, that you might join Asia to Greece. Therefore make up your mind whether you will return thither and compel the Greeks, who are men most devoted to freedom, to pay you the honor of prostration, or whether you will keep aloof from Greeks, and inflict this dishonor on the Macedonians alone, or thirdly whether you will make a difference altogether as to the honors to be paid you, so as to be honored by the Greeks and Macedonians as a human being and after the manner of the Greeks, and by foreigners alone after the foreign fashion. But if it is said that Cyrus, son of Cambyses, was the first man to whom the honor of prostration was paid and that afterwards this degrading ceremony continued in vogue among the Persians and Medes, we ought to bear in mind that the Scythians, men poor but independent, chastened that Cyrus; that other Scythians again chastened Darius, as the Athenians and Lacedaemonians did Xerxes, as Clearchus and Xenophon with their 10,000 followers did Artaxerxes; and finally, that Alexander, though not honored with prostration, has chastened this Darius."

12. By making these and other remarks of a similar kind, Callisthenes greatly annoyed Alexander, but spoke the exact sentiments of the Macedonians. When the king perceived this, he sent to prevent the Macedonians from making any further mention of the ceremony of prostration. But after the discussion silence ensued; and then the most honorable of the Persians arose in due order and prostrated their bodies before him. But when one of the Persians seemed to have performed the ceremony in an awkward way, Leonnatus, one of the Companions, laughed at his posture as mean. Alexander at the time was angry with him for this, but was afterwards reconciled to him. The following account has also been given: Alexander drank from a golden goblet the health of the circle of guests, and handed it first to those with whom he had concerted the ceremony of prostration. The first who drank from the goblet rose up and performed the act of prostration, and received a kiss from him. This ceremony proceeded from one to another in due order. But when the pledging of health came to the turn of Callisthenes, he rose up and drank from the goblet, and drew near, wishing to kiss the king without performing the act of prostration. Alexander happened then to be conversing with Hephaestion, and consequently did not observe whether Callisthenes performed the ceremony completely or not. But when Callisthenes was approaching to kiss him, Demetrius, son of Pythonax, one of the Companions, said that he was doing so without having prostrated himself. So the king would not permit him to kiss him; whereupon the philosopher said, "I am going away only with the loss of a kiss." I by no means approve any of these proceedings, which manifested both the insolence of Alexander on the present occasion and the churlish nature of Callisthenes. But I think that, so far as regards himself, it would have been quite sufficient if he had expressed himself discreetly, magnifying as much as possible the exploits of the king, with whom no one thought it a dishonor to associate.

2. THE PAGES' CONSPIRACY

Arrian,
Anabasis

Alexander's courting of Persian support and his insistence on his divine descent provoked increasing unrest among the older Macedonian officers. The murder of Cleitus the Black in 328 B.C. provided the most extreme example of the tension in Alexander's court over these issues, but the pages' conspiracy the following year illustrated the depth of the hostility to the king's plans in that it involved members of his personal bodyguard and most intimate companions.[41]

13. It was a custom introduced by Philip that the sons of those Macedonians who had enjoyed high office, should, as soon as they reached the age of puberty, be selected to attend the king's court. These youths were entrusted with the general attendance on the king's person and the protection of his body while he was asleep. Whenever the king rode out, some of them received the horses from the grooms, and brought them to him, and others assisted him to mount in the Persian fashion. They were also companions of the king in the emulation of the chase. Among these youths was Hermolaus, son of Sopolis, who seemed to be applying his mind to the study of philosophy, and to be cultivating the society of Callisthenes for this purpose. There is current a tale about this youth to the effect that, in the chase, a boar rushed at Alexander, and that Hermolaus anticipated him by casting a javelin at the beast, by which it was smitten and killed. But Alexander, having lost the opportunity of distinguishing himself by being too late in the assault, was indignant with Hermolaus, and in his wrath ordered him to receive a scourging in sight of the other pages, and also deprived him of his horse. This Hermolaus, being chagrined at the disgrace he had incurred, told Sostratus, son of Amyntas, who was his equal in age and his lover, that life would be insupportable to him unless he could take vengeance upon Alexander for the affront. He easily persuaded Sostratus to join in the enterprise, since he was fondly attached to him. They gained over to their plans Antipater, son of Asclepiodorus, who had been viceroy of Syria, Epimenes son of Arseas, Anticles son of Theocritus, and Philotas son of Carsis the Thracian. They therefore agreed to kill the king by attacking him in his sleep, on the night when the nocturnal watch came round to Antipater's turn. Some say that Alexander accidently happened to be drinking until day-break; but Aristobulus has given the following account: A Syrian woman, who was under the inspiration of the deity, used to follow Alexander about. At first she was a subject of mirth to Alexander and his courtiers; but when all that she said in her inspiration was seen to be true, he no longer treated her with neglect, but she was allowed to have free access to him both by night and day, and she often took her stand near him even when he was asleep. And indeed on that occasion, when he was withdrawing from the drinking party she met him, being under the inspiration of the deity at the time, and besought him to return and drink all night. Alexander, thinking that there was something divine in the warning, returned and went on drinking; and thus the enterprise of the pages fell through. The next day, Epimenes, son of Arseas, one of those who took part in the conspiracy, spoke of the undertaking to Charicles, son of Menander, who had become his lover; and Charicles

[41] Arrian, *Anabasis* 4.13–14. From Arrian, *Anabasis*, trans. Edward J. Chinnock (New York, 1893).

told it to Eurylochus, brother of Epimenes. Eurylochus went to Alexander's tent and related the whole affair to Ptolemy, son of Lagus, one of the confidential body-guards. He told Alexander, who ordered those whose names had been mentioned by Eurylochus to be arrested. These, being put on the rack, confessed their own conspiracy, and mentioned the names of certain others.

14. Aristobulus says that the youths asserted it was Callisthenes who instigated them to make the daring attempt; and Ptolemy says the same. Most writers, however, do not agree with this, but represent that Alexander readily believed the worst about Callisthenes, from the hatred which he already felt towards him, and because Hermolaus was known to be exceedingly intimate with him. Some authors have also recorded the following particulars: that Hermolaus was brought before the Macedonians, to whom he confessed that he had conspired against the king's life, because it was no longer possible for a free man to bear his insolent tyranny. He then recounted all his acts of despotism, the illegal execution of Philotas, the still more illegal one of his father Parmenio and of the others who were put to death at that time, the murder of Clitus in a fit of drunkenness, the assumption of the Median garb, the introduction of the ceremony of prostration, which had been planned and not yet relinquished, and the drinking-bouts and lethargic sleep arising from them. He said that, being no longer able to bear these things, he wished to free both himself and the other Macedonians. These same authors say that Hermolaus himself and those who had been arrested with him were stoned to death by those who were present. Aristobulus says that Callisthenes was carried about with the army bound with fetters, and afterwards died a natural death; but Ptolemy, son of Lagus, says that he was stretched upon the rack and then hanged.

3. ALEXANDER'S LAST PLANS

Diodorus | *The Roman Emperor Augustus remarked that he was surprised that "Alexander did not regard it as a greater task to set in order the empire which he had won than to win it." Since antiquity historians have wondered if Alexander planned to impose a new organization on the territory he conquered. It is known that Alexander was planning to invade Arabia at the time of his death in the summer of 323 B.C. The projects described in this document were supposed to have been discovered among Alexander's papers. After long debate historians have come to believe that they are authentic and suggest that Alexander was not planning to consolidate his empire at the time of his death but rather to undertake grandiose campaigns in the western Mediterranean that would have occupied him for many years.[42]*

The greatest and most worthy of memory of the memoranda were the following: to build a thousand warships larger than triremes in Phoenicia, Syria, Cilicia, and

---

[42] From Diodorus 18.4.4–5.

Cyprus for the campaign against the Carthaginians and the other peoples living along the coasts of Libya and Iberia and the neighboring coastal territory as far as Sicily; to build a road along the coast of Libya as far as the Pillars of Heracles; and to prepare harbors and shipyards at the most appropriate places that would be suitable for so great a fleet; to build six lavish temples, each one at cost of fifteen hundred talents; in addition there were to be foundations of cities and transfers of populations from Asia to Europe and in reverse from Europe to Asia, in order that he might bring the largest continents into unity of feeling and friendly kinship through intermarriage and family relationships. He intended to build the aforementioned temples on Delos and in Delphi and Dodona, and in Macedonia a temple of Zeus in Dion, a temple of Artemis Tauropolos in Amphipolis, and a temple of Athena at Cyrnus. Similarly there was also to be at Ilium a temple to the same goddess not inferior in size to any other; and a tomb for his father Philip equal in size to one of the largest pyramids in Egypt, which some people reckon among the seven greatest human works.

I. What Was Alexander: Saint or Demon?

Modern historians are divided in their assessments of Alexander, some seeing him as a farsighted statesman who hoped to improve the lives of the peoples he conquered while others view him only as another bloodthirsty conqueror, albeit one who was a military genius. This division of opinion already existed in antiquity. In the first selection the second-century A.D. Greek biographer and moralist Plutarch argues that Alexander was virtually a philosopher in action, striving to spread Greek culture to the barbarians and to realize the Stoic dream of universal harmony among men. In the second selection an unknown Zoroastrian author of approximately the ninth century A.D., drawing on earlier sources, offers a diametrically opposed view of Alexander, seeing him as a representative of the forces of evil who burned Persepolis and attempted to destroy the Zoroastrian holy books preserved there.

1. PLUTARCH: ALEXANDER A FORCE FOR THE SPREAD OF GREEK CULTURE[43]

2. And I think that he would speak in this way to Fortune, when she takes credit for his successes. "Do not slander my excellence, nor detract from my fame by diversion. Darius was your creation, whom you made master of the Persians from a servant and king's courier; and you also placed the royal diadem on Sardanapallus. As a result of my victory at Arbela, I went up to Susa. Cilicia opened to me broad Egypt; and the Granicus likewise Cilicia,

Plutarch, *On the Fortune of Alexander*

---

[43] Plutarch, *De Alexandri Magni Fortuna aut Virtute Oratio* 1.2–6. Adapted from *Plutarch's Essays and Miscellanies*, Vol. 1, trans. several scholars, corrected and revised by William W. Goodwin (Boston, 1909), pp. 475–482.

which I reached by trampling under foot the corpses of Mithridates and Spithridates. Adorn yourself, and boast of kings, who never felt a wound or shed blood. They were fortunate, your Ochuses and Artaxerxes, who immediately after birth were placed on the throne of Cyrus by you. But my body carries many marks of Fortune, who fought against me as an enemy instead of being my ally. First, among the Illyrians I was wounded in the head with a stone, and received a blow in the neck with a club. Near Granicus I was wounded in the head with a barbarian scimitar; and at Issus in the thigh with a sword. At Gaza I was shot in the ankle with an arrow; and I was whirled around and dislocated my shoulder. In the land of the Maracandani my leg was split with an arrow. There remain the wounds I received in India and the sufferings of famine. Among the Assacani I was shot through the shoulder with an arrow and among the Gandridae in the leg. Among the Malli I was wounded by a missile from a bow that pierced my breast and drove in its iron head. I was also struck a blow in my neck, when the scaling-ladders broke that had been placed against the walls, and Fortune closed me in alone, offering so great a deed not to a renowned enemy, but to worthless barbarians. If Ptolemy had not covered me with his shield, and Limnaeus had not fallen before me, struck by innumerable missiles; or if the Macedonians had not courageously and forcefully overthrown the wall, that barbarian and nameless village would have become Alexander's tomb.

3. As for the troubles of the whole expedition, there were storms and parching droughts, deep rivers, peaks not even birds could reach, amazing sights of wild beasts, harsh living, and revolts and betrayals of rulers. And as for what happened before the expedition, Greece lay prostrate from the effects of Philip's wars. But then the Thebans, rising from the defeat, shook from their arms the dust of Chaeronea; and Athens extended its hands to them and joined with them. All Macedon was secretly hostile, looking toward Amyntas and the sons of Aeropus. The Illyrians broke out into open war; and the Scythians were threatening their neighbors, who were in disorder; Persian gold, liberally scattered among the popular leaders of every city, was putting all Peloponnesus into commotion. King Philip's treasuries were empty of money, and there was, in addition, a debt, as Onesicritus records, of two hundred talents. In the midst of so much need and such menacing troubles, a youth, who was hardly past the age of childhood, dared hope for the conquest of Babylon and Susa, and, even to think of rule over all mankind; and all this, trusting only in his force of thirty thousand infantry and four thousand cavalry. For so many were his forces, according to Aristoboulus. Ptolemy, however, says that there were thirty thousand infantry and five thousand cavalry; and Anaximenes forty three thousand infantry, and five thousand five hundred cavalry. Now the glorious and magnificent campaign fund which Fortune had provided him was seventy talents, according to Aristobulus; or, as Duris reckons it, enough for only thirty days' provision.

4. Was Alexander, therefore, too ill advised and rash to set out upon so vast an undertaking with such limited resources? By no means. For whoever set out with greater or finer means than he: magnanimity, understanding,

selfcontrol, and courage, with which Philosophy supplied him for his expedition? Yes, he invaded Persia with greater assistance from Aristotle than from his father Philip. As for those who write how Alexander said that the *Iliad* and *Odyssey* accompanied him in his wars as his supplies, we believe them in honor to Homer. Should we object, however, if someone says that the *Iliad* and *Odyssey* accompanied him as relief from toil and a way of spending his leisure time; but that philosophical learning and works concerning fearlessness, courage, and, moreover, self-control and nobility of spirit, were his true equipment for the campaign? For, certainly, he never wrote about syllogisms or axioms; nor did he participate in walks in the Lyceum, or discuss theories in the Academy. For it is by such things that people define philosophy, who think it is a matter of talk, not of action. Yet Pythagoras, Socrates, Arcesilaus, and Carneades wrote nothing, although they were the most famous of the philosophers. Nor did they busy themselves in such great wars, civilize barbarian kings, found Greek cities among savage peoples, or teach laws to and establish peace among lawless and ignorant people. They, however, lived at ease, and surrendered the business of writing to the Sophists. On what basis, therefore, were they believed to be philosophers? It was either from their sayings, or from the lives they led, or from the precepts, which they taught. Upon these grounds, therefore, let Alexander also be judged; and he will be seen from what he said, what he did, and what he taught to have been a philosopher.

5. And first, if you wish, consider the most paradoxical matter, and compare the students of Alexander with those of Plato and Socrates. They taught people who were naturally intelligent and spoke the same tongue, understanding, if nothing else, the Greek language; and even then they didn't persuade many. Indeed, men like Critias, Alcibiades, and Cleitophon spit out their teaching like a bit, and turned aside to another path. If you examine the instruction imparted by Alexander, however, he taught the Hyrcanians to marry, instructed the Arachosians how to farm, persuaded the Sogdians to support and not to kill their parents, and the Persians to honor and not to marry their mothers. O amazing philosophy, which induced the Indians to worship the Greek Gods, and the Scythians to bury instead of eat their dead. We admire the power of Carneades, if, indeed, it made the Carthaginian Clitomacus, who was formerly called Hasdrubal, to follow a Greek way of life. We admire the character of Zeno, if, indeed, it persuaded the Babylonian Diogenes to become a philosopher. After Alexander civilized Asia, however, Homer was read, and the children of Persians, Susians, and Gedrosians chanted the tragedies of Euripides and Sophocles. Socrates lost his case to his Athenian accusers, who alleged that he introduced foreign deities, but because of Alexander, Bactria and Caucasus began to worship the Greek Gods. Plato, moreover, although he proposed one constitution, could not persuade any people to use it because of its harshness. Alexander, however, overcame uncivilized and savage ways of life by building more than seventy cities among barbarian nations, and sowing Asia with Greek offices. A few of us study *The Laws* of Plato, but innumerable people have made and still make use of those of Alexander. The peoples Alexander vanquished were

more blessed than they who escaped his conquests. For no one stopped them from living wretchedly, but those he conquered, he compelled to live happily. True, therefore, is the statement of Themistocles, when he became an exile, and he received great gifts from the king, and he acquired three tributary cities, one to supply him with bread, a second with wine, a third with relish: "O young men," he said, "we would have been undone, if we had not been undone." This, however, might even be more justly said of the peoples subdued by Alexander. Egypt would not have her Alexandria, nor Mesopotamia her Selcucia, nor Sogdiana her Propthasia, nor India her Bucephalia, nor Caucasus a Greek city nearby. For by founding these cities savagery was extinguished and the worse changed to the better through habit. If philosophers take greatest pride in taming and making harmonious harsh and foolish customs, then Alexander, who changed innumerable peoples and savage natures, should be thought to have been a very great philosopher.

6. And, indeed, the much admired *Republic* of Zeno, the founder of the Stoic sect, focuses on one central point: that we all should not live divided into cities or into villages with their own laws. We should consider, instead, all peoples to be our fellow demes-men and citizens, and there should be one way of life and order as is true of a herd that feeds together and lives in a common pasture. Zeno wrote this, as though he were giving shape to a dream or image of an orderly philosophy or constitution, but Alexander realized the idea. For he did not, as Aristotle advised him, rule the Greeks as a leader and the barbarians as supreme ruler, caring for the former as friends and kinsmen, and dealing with the latter as wild beasts or plants. If he had done so, he would have filled his empire with numerous wars and festering divisions. But thinking that he had come from god himself as the common moderator and arbiter of all peoples, he subdued by force those whom he could not unite by reason. He brought together from everywhere peoples, mixing together as in a loving cup their lives, customs, marriages and life styles. He ordered everyone to consider the inhabited world as their fatherland, the camp of his army as their stronghold and fortress, and good men as kin and evil men as foreigners. He would not have Hellenism and barbarism distinguished by Greek cloaks, shields, scimitars, or Median robes; but Hellenism was to be characterized by excellence and barbarism by evil. People were to consider their clothing and food and marriages and lifestyles common, having been mixed together through blood and offspring.

2. ALEXANDER THE ENEMY OF THE TRUE RELIGION: A ZOROASTRIAN VIEW[44]

The Book of Arda Wiraz

1: It is said that once the righteous Zoroaster propagated the religion that he had accepted in the world, 2: for three hundred years that religion was

[44] *The Book of Arda Wiraz* 1.1–7, trans. Dr. Mahmoud Omidsalar. From Philippe Gignoux, ed., *Le Livre D'Ardā Virāz*. Traduit en persan par Jaleh Amouzegar (Tehran: Institut Français de Recherche en Iran, 1993), pp. 39–40.

pure and the people were faithful. 3: Thereafter the accursed [and] deceitful Evil Spirit, in order to make the people doubtful about this religion, deceived the accursed Greek (lit: Roman) Alexander of Egyptian residence, so that he came to Iran with great oppressiveness, and warfare, and harm. 4: He slew the Iranian nobles (lit. Aryans) and destroyed the court and threw the administration (lit: lordship) into chaos. 5: And this religion, that is all of the *Avesta* and its commentary, was written upon fine parchment in golden ink, and was kept in the city of Estakhr of Pāpakān [= present-day Shiraz], in the archives. 6: And this evil, deceitful, abusive heretic, i.e., the Greek (lit: Roman) Alexander of Egyptian residence, took them all out and burned them. 7: And he slew many of the sages and judges and religious teachers, and the pious, and the artisans, and the learned of Iran, and cast discord among the nobles and lords of Iran, and thereafter died and went to hell.

8

THE HELLENISTIC AGE

A remarkable new era opened with the thirteen-year reign of Alexander the Great (336–323 B.C.). With his conquest of the Persian Empire, Alexander destroyed a state system that had regulated affairs in western Asia for over two centuries. His premature death at the age of 33 deprived Alexander of the opportunity to implement whatever plans he had for the organization of his empire. His chief generals warred for more than forty years before a new political system emerged in Asia. That new political system represented a major change from the recent past: The territory of the old Persian Empire was divided into several large kingdoms—most important were those of the Ptolemies in Egypt and the Seleucids in Asia—in which Greeks played a prominent role.

Until recently, historians have taken a "melting-pot" approach to understanding the Hellenistic Period (336–330 B.C.), viewing it as a time in which Greek and non-Greek cultures interacted to produce a new cosmopolitan civilization. Contemporary scholars hold a much less benign view of the nature of Hellenistic society. Far from blending to form a new culture, Greek and native societies tended to co-exist, with only limited contact between them in the new Macedonian-ruled kingdoms that were formed out of the wreckage of Alexander's empire. In other words, the Macedonian kingdoms in Egypt and Asia were essentially colonial regimes in which ethnicity was the principal determinant of social and political position. Whether or not Alexander intended his empire to be governed by a mixed elite of Macedonians, Greeks, and natives, in Ptolemaic Egypt and Seleucid Asia only Macedonians and Greeks belonged to the governing elites. The results of this situation were various and are explored in the following readings, but one of the most important was that the Hellenistic Period was a time of unprecedented opportunity for Greeks, who immigrated in substantial numbers in the third century B.C. to populate the new cities Alexander and his successors founded in Egypt and Asia and to staff the new bureaucratic governments that governed their kingdoms.

Although Greeks and Macedonians made up less than 10 percent of the total population of the Hellenistic kingdoms, they monopolized the higher levels of political and economic life in Egypt and Asia. Not surprisingly, the Greeks prospered in their new homes, some mightily, but most modestly, as is illustrated by the charming picture of middle-class life in Alexandria drawn by the third-century B.C. poet Theocritus in the selection entitled "Middle Class Life in Hellenistic Egypt." Entry into this privileged world required certification as a Greek, and because apartheid was not characteristic of ancient Greek culture, over time many of the citizen bodies of the Hellenistic cities came to include a significant number of individuals whose Greekness was not so much a matter of birth as of culture, that is, of education. All other inhabitants of the Hellenistic kingdoms, whatever the status of their ancestors, had rights that were significantly inferior to those of the Greeks and Macedonians and were subject to harsher laws and higher taxes. It is not surprising, therefore, that social conflict during this period tended to take the form of fierce revolts by the peoples who wanted to restore native rule to the various Macedonian kingdoms; some, like the Maccabees in Judaea, were even successful.

Still, whatever their shortcomings, and they were many, for almost three centuries until their remnants were absorbed into the expanding Roman and Parthian Empires, the Macedonian kingdoms provided the framework for a vibrant and complex social and cultural life. Their cities—Greek, Egyptian, and Asiatic—were not only centers in which art, literature, philosophy, and science flourished, but also places in which a wide variety of new social and economic roles developed for both men and women.

A. A New World

1. A GREEK PHILOSOPHER'S VIEW OF ALEXANDER'S CONQUESTS

Alexander the Great's conquest of the Persian Empire, which had been the one constant factor in the political world known to the Greeks for more than two hundred years, was as shocking and unexpected as would be the sudden collapse of the Soviet Union at the end of the 1980s. In this reading, Demetrius of Phaleron, peripatetic philosopher and tyrant of Athens from 317 to 307 B.C., reflects on the role of Tyche, "Fortune," in history and what it might portend for the new political order created by Alexander's conquests.[1]

Polybius, *The Histories*

For if you consider not countless years or many generations, but merely these last fifty years, you will read in them the cruelty of Fortune. I ask you, do you think that fifty years ago either the Persians and the Persian king or the Macedonians and the king of Macedon, if some god had foretold the future to them, would ever have believed that at the time when we live, the very name of the Persians would have perished utterly—the Persians who were masters of almost the whole

---

[1] Polybius 29.21.3–9, trans. W. R. Paton. From Polybius, *The Histories* (Cambridge, MA, 1927).

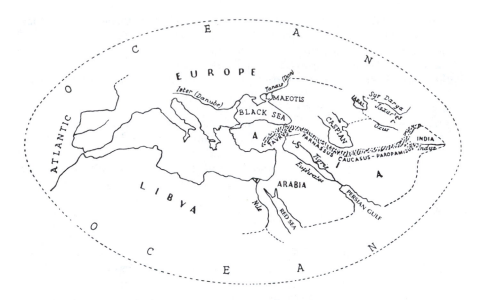

Figure 8.1 Greek view of the inhabited world in the Hellenistic Period. Reconstruction of the map of Eratosthenes. From E. H. Bunbury, *A History of Ancient Geography: Among the Greeks and the Romans From the Earliest Ages Till the Fall of the Roman Empire*, Second Edition (London: 1883), pp. 1, 661. Eratosthenes' map reflects the expansion of Greek geographical knowledge following the reign of Alexander. Particularly noteworthy is the new information concerning the upper Nile Valley, and Central and South Asia. On the other hand, the map reveals that some knowledge was lost. So, the Caspian Sea , which Herodotus knew was an inland sea, was treated as a Gulf of Ocean by Eratosthenes.

world—and that the Macedonians, whose name was formerly almost unknown, would now be the lords of it all? But nevertheless this Fortune, who never compacts with life, who always defeats our reckoning by some novel stroke; she who ever demonstrates her power by foiling our expectations, now also, as it seems to me, makes it clear to all men, by endowing the Macedonians with the whole wealth of Persia, that she has but lent them these blessings until she decides to deal differently with them.

2. THE BRUTAL STRUGGLE FOR ALEXANDER'S EMPIRE: THE HEIDELBERG EPITOME

The Heidelberg Epitome

The transition to this new world, however, was brutal. When Alexander the Great died in the summer of 323 B.C. at Babylon, he did not leave behind a mature and capable heir to his throne. The result was a bitter struggle for power between his generals that lasted until 281 B.C., in the course of which his family was wiped out and his empire divided up into several kingdoms. The following passage summarizes the principal phases of this struggle and clearly indicates the chaotic nature of the period.

When Alexander died [*323 B.C.*], he was survived by his wives and an unborn child, whom he had conceived by Roxane. When conflict about the kingship broke out, the brother of Alexander by Philip II, Arrhidaeus, who later was also named Philip, was designated to rule until the son of Alexander reached the appropriate age. Since Arrhidaeus was mentally retarded and also epileptic, Perdiccas was chosen to be his guardian and overseer of the royal affairs. Alexander, when he was dying, had given his own signet ring to Perdiccas because he was more trustworthy than the other generals.

Having considered the state of affairs, Perdiccas gave to each general a satrapy to govern, distributing all the satrapies, which were more than 24 in number. After going to their designated satrapies, they transgressed their authority to the extent each could. For this reason Perdiccas set out for Egypt with a large army to fight with Ptolemy. There he fell victim to a plot and was murdered by his own friends [*321 B.C.*]. Then Antipater succeeded to the oversight of royal affairs. After he also considered the state of affairs, he reassigned the satrapies granted by Perdiccas, giving them to other men, except for the satrapies of Ptolemy and Lysimachus, for he was unable to alter these. He gave the other satrapies to others, the satrapy of Susiana to Antigonus, and that of Babylonia to Seleucus; and he appointed his own son Cassander to the office of chiliarch [*prime minister*].

Shortly afterwards Antipater also died [*319 B.C.*], and Polyperchon succeeded to the position of the guardian [*of the kings*] and overseer of the royal affairs. During his administration Olympias [*the mother of Alexander the Great*] murdered Arrhidaeus and his wife Eurydice. After this happened, Cassander, bribing some of the royal servants, murdered Olympias, Roxane, and her son Alexander, the son of Alexander [*the Great*], who was about to succeed to rule of the whole empire [*317 B.C.*]. These things happened in Macedonia.

After this there was a great confusion of the satrapies, and the various satraps plotted against each other, the trickier of them added to their territories, gathered together larger forces, and killed the weaker satraps. Antigonus and his son Demetrius the Besieger became more powerful than many of his rivals. For this reason he also proclaimed himself king and began to wear a diadem [*305 B.C.*]. Those of the other satraps who were not inferior to him, also began to wear the diadem and proclaimed themselves kings: Ptolemy in Egypt and Syria, Lysimachus in Thrace, and Seleucus in Babylon, who, when Antigonus died [*301 B.C.*], ruled all Asia and his sons after him in succession.

B. Alexandria and the Colonial World of Hellenistic Egypt

Cultural and political life in the new Hellenistic kingdoms centered in the new cities established by Alexander and his successors. The first and greatest of these cities was Alexandria, which Alexander had founded during his stay in Egypt in 331 B.C. In the first of the following selections,

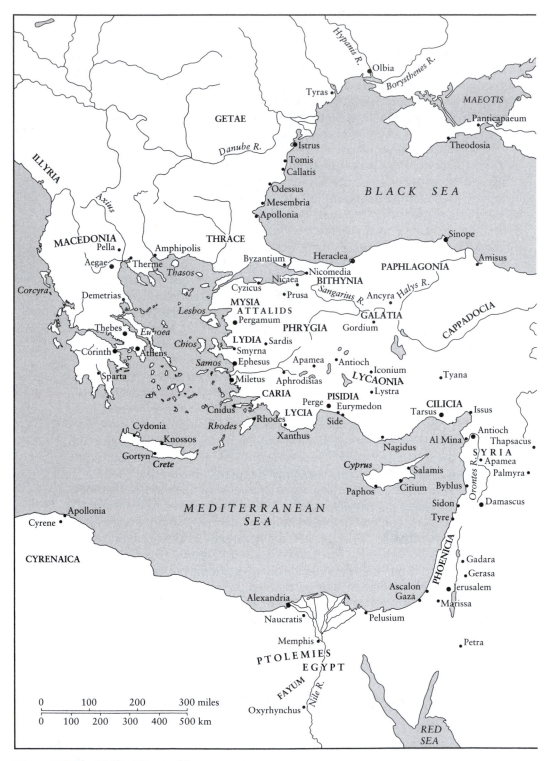

Figure 8.2 The Hellenistic world.

290

Figure 8.3 Some of the finest Greek coins date from the Hellenistic period. This gold octodrachm shows Ptolemy II of Egypt and his wife Arsinoe. Gold octodrachm showing Ptolemy II and Arsinoe. New York, American Numismatic Society 1977.158.112. Photo: Society.

the first-century B.C. geographer Strabo clearly indicates the factors—superb location and lavish royal patronage—that made Alexandria the principal commercial and cultural center of the Hellenistic world. Next, Theocritus, court poet of Ptolemy II (282–246 B.C.), gives a vivid picture of Alexandria's cosmopolitan cultural life and the multiethnic character of its population. In the last analysis, the prosperity of Alexandria and its Greek citizens depended on the efficient exploitation of the agricultural wealth of Egypt. The third selection, excerpts from a memorandum of instructions from a Ptolemaic financial official to one of his subordinates, illustrates the ideal of benevolent but firm administration that was the official policy of the Ptolemaic rulers of Egypt. That the reality was, unfortunately, different is clear from the excerpts in the next selection from a general amnesty decree issued in 118 B.C. that reveals the Ptolemaic government to have been corrupt and extortionate in its treatment of its Egyptian subjects.

1. A HELLENISTIC METROPOLIS: ALEXANDRIA IN EGYPT[2]

Strabo,
Geography

7. The site of Alexandria is advantageous for many reasons. For the city is bounded by two seas, on the north by the so-called Egyptian sea and on the south by Lake Mareia, which is also called Mareotis. The Nile fills Lake Mareia through many canals from both the south and the sides. Through these canals many more goods are brought to Alexandria than arrive from the sea, so that the lakeside harbor is richer than that on the sea, and by it more goods are exported from Alexandria than are imported into the city. . . .

8. The ground plan of the city is shaped like a military cloak. The long sides, which are both bounded by water, are thirty stades across. The short sides are formed by the isthmuses, which are each seven or eight stades in breadth and are hemmed in by the sea on one side and the lake on the other. The whole city is cut up by streets suitable for the riding of horses

[2] From Strabo, *Geography* 17.7–8 (selections).

and the driving of chariots. Two, which are especially broad—being more than a plethron wide—meet at right angles and bisect each other.

Alexandria has many fine public precincts and palaces, which occupy a fourth or even a third of the city's whole perimeter; for just as each of the kings added some adornment to its public monuments, so each added his own residence to those already existing so that, in the words of Homer, "one was on top of another." All the palaces are connected to each other and to the harbor, including those outside the harbor. The Museum forms one portion of the palaces. It has a walkway, an arcade with benches, and a large building in which is located the dining hall of the scholars who belong to the Museum. The faculty has both property in common and a priest, who is in charge of the Museum and was formerly appointed by the kings and is now by Caesar [*Augustus*]. Also part of the palace complex is the building called the Sema, which is a circular structure in which are the tombs of the kings and that of Alexander. Ptolemy, the son of Lagus, because of greed and the desire to seize control of Egypt, anticipated Perdiccas by stealing the body of Alexander when he was bringing it back from Babylon and was turning toward this country. . . . Having brought the body of Alexander to Egypt, Ptolemy buried it in Alexandria, where it now still lies, but not, however, in the same sarcophagus; for the present one is of glass, but Ptolemy buried it in one of gold.

2. A GIANT WARSHIP: THE FORTY OF PTOLEMY IV PHILOPATOR*

Significant technological developments occurred in the Hellenistic Period, particularly in the area of military technology. In the following passage the historian Callixeinus of Rhodes describes a giant warship built by the Egyptian king Ptolemy IV (222 BCE–205 BCE) and a form of dry dock invented for the purpose of launching such large vessels. The most likely reconstruction of this ship indicates that it was a giant catamaran moved by multiple rowers working large sweeps arranged in three banks. The Dionysiac aspects of its decoration—ivy leaves and thyrses (= a staff wrapped in vines and topped by a pine cone) —indicates that the ship was intended to celebrate both Ptolemy's power and his devotion to Dionysus.

Callixeinus of Rhodes' description of a warship and dry dock

Philapator built a ship, which was a forty. It was 420 feet long, 57 feet from side to side, and 72 feet in height to the top of the prow. Its height from the top of the sternpost to the keel was 79½ feet. It had four steering oars, each 45 feet in length, and the longest oars in the topmost bank were 57 feet long. Because they had lead in their handles and were very heavy inside the pivots, they moved smoothly in use. It was double-prowed and double-sterned and had seven rams. There was one main ram, several secondary rams, and several at the catheads. It required twelve undergirds, and they were 233 feet in length. It was extremely graceful.

* Callixeinus of Rhodes, *Die Fragmente der griechischen Historiker* 627 F 1.

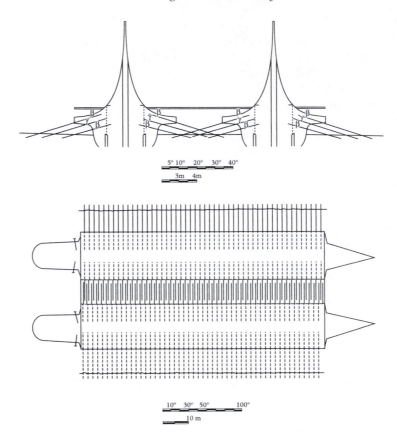

Figure 8.4 Reconstruction of Ptolemy IV's Forty. From Lionel Casson, *The Ancient Mariners: Seafarers and Sea Fighters of the Mediterranean in Ancient Times*, Second Edition (Princeton: 1991), p. 132. Used by permission.

The rest of the ship's design was remarkable. For it had figures that were not less than twelve cubits in height at the stern and the bow, and every place on it was decorated with painting; and whole side as far as the keel had ivy leaves and thyrses everywhere. There also was a great store of weapons and the various parts of the ship were filled with <everything> that was necessary. On a trial run, the ship had more than four thousand rowers, four hundred officers, and 2,850 marines on deck. There was another separate complement of men below deck, and a large store of provisions.

At first it was launched from a sort of cradle, which they say, was built with wood sufficient for fifty fifty-oared ships. A crowd of men dragged it into the water accompanied by shouting and the sound of horns. Later, however, a Phoenician devised a method of launching ships by digging a ditch equal in length to the ship near the harbor. In this he built a foundation with stone blocks of the same size that was about 7¼ feet square, and across these at right angles he laid rollers continuously across the breadth of the ditch, leaving a gap 5⅔ feet wide. Then after digging a channel from the sea, he flooded the whole excavated space, into which he easily brought the ship with the aid of a few men. <Then> after closing the open gates, and drawing off the seawater with pumps, the ship was seated safely on the aforementioned rollers.

3 . MIDDLE CLASS LIFE IN HELLENISTIC EGYPT[3]

GORGO: (*with her maid Eutychis at the door, as the maid Eunoa opens it*) Praxinoa at home?

PRAXINOA: (*running forward*) Dear Gorgo! At last! She is at home. I quite thought you'd forgotten me. (*to the maid*) Here, Eunoa, a chair for the lady, and a cushion in it.

GORGO: (*refusing the cushion*) No, thank you, really.

PRAXINOA: Do sit down.

GORGO: (*sitting*) O how helpless I am. What with the crowds and the horses, Praxinoa, I barely got here alive. It's all big boots and people in uniform. And the street was never-ending, and you can't think how far your house is along it.

PRAXINOA: That's my madman. Came and took one at the end of the world, and more an animal's den, too, than a fit place for a human being to live in. Just to prevent you and me being neighbors, out of sheer spite, the jealous old fool! He's always the same.

GORGO: My dear, don't call your husband Dinon such things in front of the child. See how he's staring at you. (*to the child*) It's all right Zopyrion, my dear. She's not talking about daddy.

PRAXINOA: By the Goddess, the child understands.

GORGO: Nice Daddy.

PRAXINOA: And yet that daddy of his the other day—the other day, now, I told him, "Daddy get mother some soap and rouge from the shop," and would you believe it? He came back with salt, the big fool!

GORGO: Mine's just the same. Diocleidas is a perfect spendthrift. Yesterday he gave seven drachmas apiece for mere bits of dog's hair, mere pluckings of old bags, five of them, all filth, all work to be done over again. But come, my dear, get your cloak and gown. Let's go to the palace of wealthy King Ptolemy to see the Adonis. I hear the Queen has put together something marvelous this year.

PRAXINOA: (*hesitating*) Fine folks, fine ways.

GORGO: Yes. But sightseers make good gossips, you know, if you've been and other people haven't. It's time we were on the move.

Theocritus,
Idyll 15

---

[3] Theocritus, *Idyll* 15, based on the trans. J. M. Edmonds. From J. M. Edmonds, *The Greek Bucolic Poets* (London, 1912).

PRAXINOA: (*still hesitating*) It's always holidays with people who've nothing to do. (*suddenly making up her mind*) Here, Eunoa, you scratch-face, take up the spinning and put it away with the rest. Cats always will lie soft. Come, wake up. Quick, some water! (*to Gorgo*) Water's wanted first, and she brings the soap. (*to Eunoa*) Never mind; give it to me. (*Eunoa pours out the soap*) Not all that, you wicked waste! Pour out the water. (*Eunoa washes her mistress's hands and face*) Oh, you wretch! What do you mean by wetting my bodice like that? That's enough. (*to Gorgo*) I've got myself washed somehow, thank goodness. (*to Eunoa*) Now where's the key of the big cupboard? Bring it here. (*takes out and puts on a gown*)

GORGO: (*referring to the style of the gown*) Praxinoa, that full gathering suits you really well. Do tell me what you paid for the material.

PRAXINOA :   Don't speak of it, Gorgo; it was more than two silver minas, and I can tell you I put my very soul into making it up.

GORGO: Well, all I can say is, it's most successful.

PRAXINOA: It's very good of you to say so. (*to Eunoa*) Come, put on my cloak and hat for me, and mind you, do it properly. (*Eunoa puts on her cloak and hat. She takes up the child*) No; I'm not going to take you, Baby. The bogey-horse bites little boys. (*the child cries*) You may cry as much as you like; I'm not going to have you lamed for life. (*to Gorgo, giving the child to the nurse*) Come along. Take Baby and amuse him, Phrygia, and call the dog indoors and lock the front-door. (*in the street*) Heavens, what a crowd! How we are to get through this mob and how long it's going to take us, I can't imagine. Talk of an antheap! I must say, you've done us many a good turn, Ptolemy, since your father went to heaven. Now no thief creeps up to mug us in the Egyptian way. They don't play those awful games now. They are all alike, all scum.

Gorgo dearest, what shall we do? The royal cavalry. Don't run me down, my good man. That bay's rearing. Look, what temper! Stand back, Eunoa, you reckless girl! He'll kill the man leading him. Thank goodness, my child remained at home.

GORGO: It's all right, Praxinoa. We've got well beyond them, you see. They're all where they ought to be now.

PRAXINOA: (*recovering*) And fortunately I can say the same of my poor wits. Ever since I was a girl, two things have frightened me more than anything else, a horrid slimy snake and a horse. Let's get on. Here's ever such a crowd pouring after us.

GORGO: (*to an old woman*) Have you come from the palace, mother?

OLD WOMAN: Yes, my dears.

GORGO: Then we can get there all right, can't we?

OLD WOMAN: Trying took Troy, my pretty ones; don't they say where there's a will there's a way?

GORGO :   That old lady gave us some oracles, didn't she?

PRAXINOA: My dear, women know everything. They even know all about Zeus marrying Hera.

GORGO: Look, Praxinoa, what a crowd there is at the door!

PRAXINOA: Marvelous. Give me your arm, Gorgo; and you take hold of Eutychis' arm, Eunoa; and you hold on tight, Eutychis, or you'll be separated. We'll all go in together. Mind you, keep hold of me, Eunoa. Oh dear, oh dear, Gorgo! My summer cloak is torn right in two. (*to a stranger*) For Heaven's sake, as you wish to be saved, mind my cloak, sir.

FIRST STRANGER: I really can't help what happens; but I'll do my best.

PRAXINOA: The crowd is simply enormous; they're pushing like a drove of pigs.

FIRST STRANGER: Don't be alarmed, madam; we're all right.

PRAXINOA: You deserve to be all right to the end of your days, my dear sir, for the care you've been taking of us. (*to Gorgo*) What a kind considerate man! Poor Eunoa is getting crushed. (*to Eunoa*) Push, you coward, can't you? (*they pass in*)

  That's all right. All inside, as the bridegroom said when he shut the door.

GORGO: (*referring, as they move forward toward the dais, to the draperies which hang between the pillars*) Praxinoa, come here. Before you do anything else, I insist that you look at the embroideries. How delicate they are and how beautiful! Clothes worthy of the Gods!

PRAXINOA: Mistress Athena! The weavers that made that material and the embroiderers who did that close detailed work are simply marvels. How realistic-ally the things all stand and move about in it! They're living! It is wonderful what people can do. And the young man, how wonderful he looks lying on his silver couch with the down of manhood just showing on his cheeks. Thrice beloved Adonis, who is beloved even in Acheron.

SECOND STRANGER: Ladies, stop that eternal cooing. Doves. They'll wear me out with their drawl.

PRAXINOA: My word! Where does that man come from? What business is it of yours if we coo? Buy your slaves before you order them about. You're giving orders to Syracusans. If you must know, we're Corinthians by descent, like Bellerophon himself. We talk Peloponnesian. I suppose Dorians may speak Doric! Persephone! Let's have no more masters than the one we have. I shall do just as I like, so don't waste your breath.

GORGO: Be quiet, Praxinoa. She's about to begin to sing the Adonis, the Argive person's daughter—the skilled singer, who sang the dirge last year. You may be sure she'll give us something good. She's beginning now.

  (*The Song*)

  Mistress, you who love Golgi, Idalion, and high Eryx, Goldenfaced Aphrodite, a year has passed and the Hours, who are not to be rushed, are bringing back to you Adonis from ever-flowing Acheron, dear Hours, longed-for Hours, tardiest of the immortals, who always come bearing gifts to all mortals. Cypris, daughter of Dione, you who, they say, made Bernice an immortal from a mortal, pouring ambrosia into her woman's breast. Blessed lady, goddess of many names and temples, Bernice's daughter, Arsinoe, who is like Helen, shows her affection for Adonis with all good things. . . . Beloved Adonis, dear Adonis, be gracious for another year. Joyous has been your coming this year and it will be joyous when you come again.

GORGO: O Praxinoa, how clever we women are! I do envy her knowing all
that, and still more her having such a lovely voice. But I must be getting back.
It's Diocleidas' dinner-time, and that man is all pepper. I wouldn't advise
anyone to come near him even when he's kept waiting for his food. Good-bye
Adonis darling; and I trust only that you may find us all thriving when you
come next year.

4 . GOVERNMENT IN PTOLEMAIC EGYPT: ADVICE TO A YOUNG OFFICIAL[4]

P. Tebtunis 703 ‖ During your tours of inspection, try, while making your rounds, to encourage
each individual and to make them bolder. Do this not only by word but also, if
some of them lay a complaint against the village scribes or headmen concerning
some matter pertaining to farming, look into it and, so far as you can, put an end
to such situations. And when the sowing has been completed, it would not be a
bad idea if you made a careful inspection; for, thus, you will accurately observe
the sprouting, and you will easily identify the fields that have been improperly
sown or not sown at all; and you will learn from this those who were careless and
you will know if some have employed the seeds for other purposes. In addition,
the sowing of the nome in accordance with the plan for planting is to be one of
your prime concerns. And if some are suffering because of their rents or even
have been completely ruined, do not allow this to be unexamined. Also, make
a list of the oxen involved in farming, both royal and private, and exercise due
care that the calves of the royal cattle, when they are ready to eat hay, are sent to
the calf-rearing barns.

It is your responsibility also that the designated provisions are transported
to Alexandria—of these we are sending you a list—on schedule, and not only in
the proper amount, but also tested and suitable for consumption. Go also to the
weaving sheds in which the linen is woven and take special care that as many
as possible of the looms are in operation and that the weavers are completing
the amount of fabric specified in the plan. If some are behind in their assigned
work, let them be fined for each category the scheduled price. Moreover, to the
end that the linen be usable and have the number of threads specified in the
regulation, pay careful attention. As for looms that are not in operation, have
all of them transported to the nome metropolis and stored in the storerooms
under seal. Conduct an audit also of the revenues, if it is possible, village by village, and this seems to be not impossible if you zealously apply yourself to the
task; but if not, then toparchy by toparchy, accepting in the audit with regard
to money taxes only what has been deposited at the bank; and with regard to
the grain taxes and oil produce what has been measured and received by the
sitologoi. If there is any deficiency in these, compel the toparchs and the tax

---

[4] *P. Tebtunis* 703 (selections). From Stanley M. Burstein, *The Hellenistic Age from the Battle of Ipsos
to the Death of Kleopatra VII* (Cambridge, 1985), pp. 128–129. Used by permission.

farmers to pay to the banks for arrears in the grain tax the price specified in the schedule and for arrears in the oil produce by wet measure according to each category. . . .

As the revenue from the pasture dues is among the most significant, it will be particularly increased if you conduct the census in the best way. The most suitable time for it is around the month of Mesore (June/July), for, at this time, because the whole land is covered by the flood waters, the herdsmen send their herds to the highest places, as they are unable to disperse them to other places. You should also take care that goods are not sold for more than the specified prices. As for those goods without set prices and for which the vendors may charge what they wish, examine this carefully and, having determined a moderate profit for the merchandise being sold, compel the [—] make the disposition. . . .

Make a list also of the royal houses and of the gardens associated with them and who is supposed to care for each, and inform us. Further, it should be your concern also that affairs regarding the machimoi be handled in accordance with the memorandum which we drafted concerning persons who had absconded from their tasks and [—] sailors in order that to [—] the prisoners be confined until their transportation to Alexandria. Take particular care that no fraud occur or any other wrongful act, for it ought to be clearly understood by everyone living in the countryside and believed that all such matters have been corrected and that they are free from the former evil conditions, since no one has the power to do what he wishes but everything is being managed in the best way. Thus you will create security in the countryside and (increase) the revenues significantly. . . .

The reasons I sent you to the nome, I told you, but I thought it would be good also to send you a written copy of them in this memorandum. Afterwards, you should behave well and be upright in your duties, not become involved with bad company, avoid any involvement in corruption, believe that if you are not accused of such things, you will merit promotion, have this memorandum at hand and write concerning each matter as required.

5 . GOVERNMENT CORRUPTION IN PTOLEMAIC EGYPT: THE AMNESTY OF 118 B.C.[5]

Col. I

King Ptolemaios and Queen Kleopatra, the sister, and Queen Kleopatra, the Wife, pardon those subject to their rule, all of them, for errors, wrongful acts, accusations, condemnations, charges of all sorts up to the 9th of Pharmouthi (April 28, 118 B.C.) of the 52nd year except those guilty of willful murder and sacrilege. They have given orders also that those who have fled because of being accused of theft and other charges shall return to their own homes and resume their former

P. Tebtunis 5

---

[5] *P. Tebtunis* 5 (selections). From Stanley M. Burstein, *The Hellenistic Age from the Battle of Ipsos to the Death of Kleopatra VII* (Cambridge, 1985), pp. 139–140. Used by permission.

occupations, and that they shall recover whatever of their property still remains unsold from that which had been seized as security because of these matters.

Col. II

They have given orders also that all those having land allotments and all those in possession of sacred land and other released land, who have intruded into royal land and others who possess more land than is proper, having withdrawn from all excess they possess and having declared themselves and paid a year's rent in kind, shall be forgiven for the period up to year 51—and they shall have full possession.

Col. III

No one is to take away anything consecrated to the gods by force nor to apply forceful persuasion to the managers of the sacred revenues, whether villages or land or other sacred revenues, nor are taxes on associations or crowns or grain-taxes to be collected by anyone from property consecrated to the gods nor are the sacred lands to be placed under patronage on any pretext, but they are to allow them to be managed by the priests themselves.

Col. IV

They have given orders that the costs for the burial of Apis and Mnevis are to be sought from the royal treasury as also in the case of those who have been deified. Likewise, also the costs of the other sacred animals.

Col. VIII

They have given orders that strategoi and other officials are not to seize any of those living in the countryside for their private purposes nor are their animals to be requisitioned for any of their personal needs nor are their cattle to be seized nor are they to be forced to raise sacred animals or geese or birds or pigs or to furnish grain at a low price or in return for renewals of their leases nor to compel tasks to be performed by them as a gift on any pretext.

Col. IX

They have given orders also concerning suits of Egyptians against Greeks and concerning suits of Greeks against Egyptians or of Egyptians against Greeks of all categories except those of persons farming royal land and of those bound to government tasks and of others connected with the revenues, that those Egyptians who have made contracts in the Greek manner with Greeks shall be sued and sue before the chrematistai [=*Greek judges*]. All Greeks who make contracts in the Egyptian manner shall be sued before the laokritai [=*Egyptian judges*] in accordance with the laws of the country. The cases of Egyptians against Egyptians are not to be usurped by the chrematistai, but they are to allow them to be settled before the laokritai in accordance with the laws of the country.

[decorative Greek key border]

C. Cultural Contact: Ptolemaic Egypt

Although a culturally and ethnically mixed civilization did not emerge in the Hellenistic Period, some interaction between Greek and non-Greek culture did occur in the various Hellenistic kingdoms, particularly in the area of religion. Being polytheists, Greeks, who settled in the new cities of Egypt and Asia, recognized and worshiped the gods of their new homes, as was only prudent. Egyptian and Asian deities attracted Greek followings, however, only when they were stripped of those aspects of traditional cults that conflicted with Greek religious ideas. Thus, in the first selection that follows, the early second-century A.D. Roman historian Tacitus tells how, during the reign of Ptolemy I, Greek and Egyptian theologians collaborated to create Sarapis, a Hellenized version of a Memphite form of the ancient Egyptian funerary god Osiris, who became the patron deity of Alexandria and whose cult was one of the most important rivals of early Christianity. Sarapis was not an isolated case. The Greek hymn in praise of Isis illustrates how the goddess Isis, traditionally the wife of Osiris and the divine mother of the Pharaonic rulers of Egypt, was worshiped by Hellenistic Greeks as a great mother goddess and the creator of civilization everywhere. The principal, but not the only, adherents of these new cults were Greeks. The next selection tells the story of three generations of an Egyptian priestly family who were responsible for bringing the cult of Sarapis to the Greek island of Delos in the central Aegean.

1. THE ORIGIN OF SARAPIS[6]

83. The origin of this God Serapis has not hitherto been made generally known by our writers. The Egyptian priests give this account. While Ptolemy, the first Macedonian king who consolidated the power of Egypt, was setting up in the newly built city of Alexandria fortifications, temples, and rites of worship, there appeared to him in his sleep a youth of singular beauty and more than human stature, who counselled the monarch to send his most trusty friends to Pontus, and fetch his effigy from that country. This, he said, would bring prosperity to the realm, and great and illustrious would be the city which gave it a reception. At the same moment he saw the youth ascend to heaven in a blaze of fire. Roused by so significant and strange an appearance, Ptolemy disclosed the vision of the night to the Egyptian priests, whose business it is to understand such matters. As they knew but little of Pontus or of foreign countries, he enquired of Timotheus,

Tacitus, Histories

---

[6] Tacitus, *Histories* 4.83–84. From *The Complete Works of Tacitus*, trans. John Church and William Jackson Brodribb (New York, 1942).

an Athenian, one of the family of the Eumolpids, whom he had invited from Eleusis to preside over the sacred rites, what this worship was, and who was the deity. Timotheus, questioning persons who had found their way to Pontus, learnt that there was there a city Sinope, and near it a temple, which, according to an old tradition of the neighborhood, was sacred to the infernal Jupiter, for there also stood close at hand a female figure, to which many gave the name of Proserpine. Ptolemy, however, with the true disposition of a despot, though prone to alarm, was, when the feeling of security returned, more intent on pleasures than on religious matters; and he began by degrees to neglect the affair, and to turn his thoughts to other concerns, till at length the same apparition, but now more terrible and peremptory, denounced ruin against the king and his realm, unless his bidding were performed. Ptolemy then gave directions that an embassy should be despatched with presents to king Scydrothemis, who at that time ruled the people of Sinope, and instructed them, when they were on the point of sailing, to consult the Pythian Apollo. Their voyage was prosperous, and the response of the oracle was clear. The God bade them go and carry back with them the image of his father, but leave that of his sister behind.

84. On their arrival at Sinope, they delivered to Scydrothemis the presents from their king, with his request and message. He wavered in purpose, dreading at one moment the anger of the God, terrified at another by the threats and opposition of the people. Often he was wrought upon by the gifts and promises of the ambassadors. And so three years passed away, while Ptolemy did not cease to urge his zealous solicitations. He continued to increase the dignity of his embassies, the number of his ships, and the weight of his gold. A terrible vision then appeared to Scydrothemis, warning him to thwart no longer the purposes of the God. As he yet hesitated, various disasters, pestilence, and the unmistakeable anger of heaven, which grew heavier from day to day, continued to harass him. He summoned an assembly, and explained to them the bidding of the God, the visions of Ptolemy and himself, and the miseries that were gathering about them. The people turned away angrily from their king, were jealous of Egypt, and, fearing for themselves, thronged around the temple. The story becomes at this point more marvellous, and relates that the God of his own will conveyed himself on board the fleet, which had been brought close to shore, and, wonderful to say, vast as was the extent of sea that they traversed, they arrived at Alexandria on the third day. A temple, proportioned to the grandeur of the city, was erected in a place called Rhacotis, where there had stood a chapel consecrated in old times to Serapis and Isis. Such is the most popular account of the origin and introduction of the God Serapis. I am aware indeed that there are some who say that he was brought from Seleucia, a city of Syria, in the reign of Ptolemy III, while others assert that it was the act of the same king, but that the place from which he was brought was Memphis, once a famous city and the strength of ancient Egypt. The God himself, because he heals the sick, many identified with Aesculapius; others with Osiris, the deity of the highest antiquity among these nations; not a

few with Jupiter, as being supreme ruler of all things; but most people with Pluto, arguing from the emblems which may be seen on his statues, or from conjectures of their own.

2. THE PRAISES OF ISIS[7]

Demetrios, the son of Artemidoros, who is also called Thraseas, a Magnesian from Magnesia on the Maeander, an offering in fulfillment of a vow to Isis. He transcribed the following from the stele in Memphis which stands by the temple of Hephaistos:

I am Isis, the tyrant of every land; and I was educated by Hermes, and together with Hermes I invented letters, both the hieroglyphic and the demotic, in order that the same script should not be used to write everything. I imposed laws on men, and the laws which I laid down no one may change. I am the eldest daughter of Kronos. I am the wife and sister of King Osiris. I am she who discovered the cultivation of grain for men. I am the mother of King Horos. I am she who rises in the Dog Star. I am she who is called goddess by women. By me the city of Bubastis was built. I separated earth from sky. I designated the paths of the stars. The sun and the moon's course I laid out. I invented navigation. I caused the just to be strong. Woman and man I brought together. For woman I determined that in the tenth month she shall deliver a baby into the light. I ordained that parents be cherished by their children. For parents who are cruelly treated I imposed retribution. Together with my brother Osiris I stopped cannibalism. I revealed initiations to men. I taught men to honor the images of the gods. I established precincts for the gods. The governments of tyrants I suppressed. I stopped murders. I compelled women to be loved by men. I caused the just to be stronger than gold and silver. I ordained that the true be considered beautiful. I invented marriage contracts. Languages I assigned to Greeks and barbarians. I caused the honorable and the shameful to be distinguished by Nature. I caused nothing to be more fearful than an oath. He who unjustly plotted against others I gave into the hands of his victim. On those who commit unjust acts I imposed retribution. I ordained that suppliants be pitied. I honor those who justly defend themselves. With me the just prevails. Of rivers and winds and the sea am I mistress. No one becomes famous without my knowledge. I am the mistress of war. Of the thunderbolt am I mistress. I calm and stir up the sea. I am in the rays of the sun. I sit beside the course of the sun. Whatever I decide, this also is accomplished. For me everything is right. I free those who are in bonds. I am the mistress of sailing. The navigable I make unnavigable whenever I choose. I established the boundaries of cities. I am she who is called Lawgiver. The island from the depths I brought up into the light. I conquer Fate. Fate heeds me. Hail Egypt who reared me.

[7] *Inscriptiones Graecae* 12.14. From Stanley M. Burstein, *The Hellenistic Age from the Battle of Ipsos to the Death of Kleopatra VII*, p. 147. Used by permission.

3. HOW SARAPIS CAME TO DELOS: THE FAMILY OF APOLLONIOS, PRIEST OF SARAPIS[8]

Delian Praises of Sarapis

The priest Apollonios recorded this in accordance with the command of Sarapis.

Apollonios, our grandfather, an Egyptian and a priest, came from Egypt with the god and continued serving him as was traditional. He is thought to have lived ninety-seven years. Demetrios, my father, succeeded him and also served the gods, and he was honored for his piety by the god with a bronze statue, which is set up in the temple of the god. He lived sixty-one years. After I took over the rites and attended scrupulously to the services, the god informed me in a dream that a Sarapieion of his own must be dedicated to him, and that it should not be in leased quarters as before. The god also told me that he would himself find the place where it was to be built and that he would indicate the place, and this happened. This place was full of dung. It was listed for sale on a little notice on the path through the market place; and as the god wished, the sale took place and the temple was built quickly in six months. Some men, however, conspired against us and the god and brought a public charge against the temple and myself about what penalty should be suffered or what fine should be paid. But the god promised me in a dream that we would win; and when the trial had been completed and we had won in a manner worthy of the god, we gave praise to the gods and rendered proper thanks.

D. Cultural Contact: Bactria and India

Greeks encountered another great ancient culture, that of India, at the other end of the Hellenistic world in Bactria (modern Afghanistan), where the descendants of Greek settlers left by Alexander created a kingdom that lasted until the late second century B.C., when it was overrun by Iranian nomads driven south by the Chinese. In the first selection the geographer Strabo describes the achievements of the Bactrian Greeks, emphasizing the extraordinary range of their contacts, extending from northern India to the borders of China. Maintaining Greek culture in this remote portion of the Hellenistic world was difficult. The second selection is a dedicatory inscription set up by a certain Clearchus—probably Aristotle's colleague Clearchus of Soli—commemorating his transportation from Delphi to Alexandria Eschate (modern Ai Khanum) of a brief summary of Greek ethics. In the third selection the Buddhist author of The Questions of King Milinda, *a dialog between Menander, a Greek king who converted to Buddhism, and an Indian wise man named Nagasena, describes the Greco-Indian city of Sagala as a multicultural trading center. As Menander's conversion indicates, Buddhist influence in Bactria was strong. The fourth selection is a Greek translation of one of the so-called Rock Edicts*

[8] *Sylloge Inscriptionum Graecarum*[3] 663. From Stanley M. Burstein, *The Hellenistic Age from the Battle of Ipsos to the Death of Kleopatra VII*, pp. 130–131. Used by permission.

Figure 8.5 In what is today Tajikistan/Uzbekistan, excellent Greek coins were minted to display the power of the kings who ruled that distant kingdom. Bactrian coin of Antimachus. New York, American Numismatic Society 8088.

of the Buddhist king Ashoka (268–232 B.C.). Greeks were attracted not only to Buddhism. The fifth selection is a Prakrit inscription commemorating the dedication to the Hindu god Vishnu of a sacred pillar by a Greek named Heliodorus. Some Indians, however, were attracted to Greek culture. The final selection in this section is a translation of a Greek poetic epitaph of a Greek-educated Indian named Sophytus, son of Naratus, who made a fortune as a merchant in Bactria in the second century B.C.

1. THE GREEKS IN BACTRIA AND INDIA[9]

The Greeks, who had revolted, grew in strength to such a degree because of the excellence of the country [=*Bactria*] that they conquered both Ariana and the Indians, as Apollodorus of Artemita records, and they subdued more nations than Alexander. Especially is this true of Menander—if, indeed, he crossed the Hypanis toward the east and advanced as far as the Isamos. Some were subdued by Menandros and some by Demetrios (I), the son of Euthydemos, the king of Bactria. Not only did they gain control of Patalene, but also of the whole coastal region which is called the kingdom of Saraostos and Sigerdis. And in general, he (*sc.* Apollodorus) says, Bactria is the jewel of all Ariana. And they even extended their realm as far as the Seres [=*China*] and the Phryni.

Strabo, Geography

2. GREEK WISDOM IN BACTRIA[10]

These wise (words) of ancient men are set up, utterances of famous men, in holy Pytho [=*Delphi*]. Whence Klearchos, having copied them carefully, set them up, shining from afar, in the sanctuary of Kineas: As a child be orderly. As a youth, be self-controlled. As an adult, be just. As an old man, be of good counsel. When dying, be without sorrow.

Greek wisdom in Bactria

[9] From Stanley M. Burstein, *The Hellenistic Age from the Battle of Ipsos to the Death of Kleopatra VII* (Cambridge, 1985), pp. 69–70. Used by permission.

[10] From Stanley M. Burstein, *The Hellenistic Age from the Battle of Ipsos to the Death of Kleopatra VII* (Cambridge, 1985), p. 67. Used by permission.

3. SAGALA: A GRECO-INDIAN METROPOLIS[11]

The Questions of King Milinda

Thus has it been handed down by tradition—There is in the country of the Yonakas [=*Greeks*] a great center of trade, a city that is called Sagala, situated in a delightful country well watered and hilly, abounding in parks and gardens and groves and lakes and tanks, a paradise of rivers and mountains and woods. Wise architects have laid it out, and its people know of no oppression, since all their enemies and adversaries have been put down. Its defenses are powerful, with many and various strong towers and ramparts, with superb gates and entrance archways; and with the royal citadel in its midst, white walled with a deep moat. Well laid out are its streets, squares, cross roads, and market places. Well displayed are the innumerable sorts of costly merchandise with which its shops are filled. It is richly adorned with hundreds of alms-halls of various kinds; and splendid with hundreds of thousands of magnificent mansions, which rise aloft like the mountain peaks of the Himalayas. Its streets are filled with elephants, horses, carriages, and foot-passengers, frequented by groups of handsome men and beautiful women, and crowded by men of all sorts and conditions, Brahmans, nobles, artificers, and servants. They resound with cries of welcome to the teachers of every creed, and the city is the resort of the leading men of each of the differing sects. Shops are there for the sale of Benares muslin, of Kotumbara stuffs, and of other cloths of various kinds; and sweet odors are exhaled from the bazaars, where all sorts of flowers and perfumes are tastefully set out. Jewels are there in plenty, such as men's hearts desire, and guilds of traders in all sorts of finery display their goods in the bazaars that face all quarters of the sky. So full is the city of money, and of gold and silver ware, of copper and stone ware, that it is a very mine of dazzling treasures. And there is laid up there much store of property and corn and things of value in warehouses—foods and drinks of every sort, syrups and sweetmeats of every kind. In wealth it rivals Uttara-kuru, and in glory it is as Alakamandâ, the city of the gods.

4. THE ROCK EDICT OF KING ASHOKA FROM KANDAHAR[12]

The Rock Edict of King Ashoka from Kandahar

Ten years *having been completed*, King Piodasses made piety known to men, and afterwards more pious he caused men to be and all things to flourish throughout the whole land; and abstinence the king practiced from animate (things), and also other men and all who were hunters or fishermen of the king have ceased hunting, and if there were some incontinent men, they have ceased from their incontinence to the extent possible, and they are obedient to their father and mother and the

---

[11] Adapted from *The Questions of King Milinda*, trans. T. W. Rhys Davids, vol. 1 (Oxford, 1890), pp. 2–3.

[12] From Stanley M. Burstein, *The Hellenistic Age from the Battle of Ipsos to the Death of Kleopatra VII* (Cambridge, 1985), p. 68. Used by permission.

elders in contrast to before, and in the future more profitably and better in every way will they live by doing these things.

5. DEDICATION TO VISHNU BY HELIODORUS (FIRST CENTURY B.C.)[13]

This Garuda pillar of the god of gods, Vasudeva (=*Vishnu*), was caused to be made by Heliodoros, the devotee, the son of Dion, from Taxila, who came as Greek ambassador from the court of the Great King Antialkidas to Bhagabhadra, the son of Kasi, the Savior, who was then in the fourteenth year of his prosperous reign. Three immortal precepts when practiced lead to heaven: self-restraint, charity, conscientiousness.

Dedication to Vishnu by Heliodorus

6. STELE OF SOPHYTOS, SON OF NARATOS[14]

Stele of Sophytos

The house of my ancestors had flourished for a long time, when the irresistible strength of the three Fates destroyed it. But I, Sophytos of the family of Naratos, while still a child, was deprived of the wealth of my ancestors. I cultivated the excellence of the Archer [=*Apollo*] and the Muses together with noble wisdom. Then I devised a plan to restore my ancestral house. Gathering from various places fruitful money, I left home, intending not to return before I had acquired great wealth. For this reason I went to many cities as a merchant and blamelessly gained great wealth. Full of praise, I returned to my fatherland after countless years and became a source of joy to my friends. At once my ancestral house which had decayed I restored to an even greater state. I also prepared a new tomb to replace the one that had fallen into ruin, and I placed a stele that would speak of my life by the road. The deeds I have done are worthy of emulation. May my sons and grandsons preserve my house.

Stele of Sophytos

E. Culture Clash: Jewish Resistance to Hellenism

Worshiping Hellenized deities was one way in which ambitious non-Greeks could attempt to bridge the gap between themselves and their Greek and Macedonian overlords, but it could also alienate them from the more traditional elements of their own society. The final selection of this section recounts the ill-fated attempt in the late 170s and early 160s B.C. by a faction of the Hellenistic Jewish

Second Maccabees

[13] From J. Puhvel and A. K. Narain, in Stanley M. Burstein, *The Hellenistic Age from the Battle of Ipsos to the Death of Kleopatra VII* (Cambridge, 1985), p. 72. Used by permission.

[14] From P. Bernand, G.-J. Pinault, and G. Rougemont, "Deux Novelles Inscriptions Grecques de l'Asie Centrale," *Journal des Savants* (July–December, 2004), p. 231.

elite to introduce the worship of a Hellenized form of Yahweh as part of a plan to convert Jerusalem into a Greek city. The result was unprecedented—the attempt by the Seleucid king Antiochus IV to overthrow Jewish law and custom in Judea and the outbreak of the first ideologically motivated guerilla war in history.[15]

1. JERUSALEM TRANSFORMED INTO A *POLIS* (ca. 175 B.C.)

But when Seleucus died, and Antiochus, who was called Epiphanes, succeeded to the kingdom, Jason the brother of Onias supplanted his brother in the high-priesthood, promising in a petition to the king 300 and threescore talents of silver, besides 80 talents from another fund, in addition to which he undertook to pay 150 more, if he was commissioned to set up a gymnasium and ephebeum and to register the Jerusalemites as citizens of Antioch. And when the king had given his assent, Jason at once exercised his influence in order to bring over his fellow-countrymen to Greek ways of life. Setting aside the royal ordinances of special favor to the Jews, obtained by John the father of Eupolemus who had gone as envoy to the Romans to secure their friendship and alliance, and seeking to overthrow the lawful modes of life, he introduced new customs forbidden by the law: he deliberately established a gymnasium under the citadel itself and made the noblest of the young men wear the Macedonian hat. And to such a height did the passion for Greek fashions rise, and the influx of foreign customs, thanks to the surpassing impiety of that godless Jason—no high-priest he!—that the priests were no longer interested in the services of the altar, but despising the sanctuary, and neglecting the sacrifices, they hurried to take part in the unlawful displays held in the palaestra after the discus-throwing had been announced—thus setting at naught what their fathers honored and esteeming the glories of the Greeks above all else. Hence sore distress befell them; the very men for whose customs they were so keen and whom they desired to be like in every detail became their foes and punished them. For it is no light matter to act impiously against the laws of God; time will show that.

Now games, held every five years, were being celebrated at Tyre, in the presence of the king, and the vile Jason sent sacred envoys who were citizens of Antioch to represent Jerusalem, with 300 drachmas of silver for the sacrifice of Heracles. The very bearers, however, judged that the money ought not to be spent on a sacrifice but devoted to some other purpose, and, thanks to them, it went to fit out the triremes.

---

[15] Second Maccabees 4:7–21, 5:21–6.11, 8:1–7, 9–10:8, trans. James Moffatt. From *The Apocrypha and Pseudepigrapha of the Old Testament in English*, Vol. 1, ed. R. H. Charles (Oxford, 1913), pp. 136–137, 139–140, 142–145.

2. ABOLITION OF JEWISH LAW (167 B.C.)

Antiochus, then, carried off from the temple 1,800 talents and hurried away to Antioch, thinking in his arrogance to make the land navigable and the sea passable by foot—so uplifted was he in heart. He also left governors behind him to ill-treat the Jewish people: at Jerusalem, Philip, a Phrygian by race, whose disposition was more barbarous than that of his master; at Gerizim, Andronicus; and, besides these, Menelaus, who lorded it worst of them all over the citizens. And in malice against the Jews he sent the Mysian commander Apollonius with an army of 22,000 under orders to slay all those that were of full age and to sell the women and the younger men. This fellow, on reaching Jerusalem, played the role of a man of peace, waiting till the holy day of the sabbath; then, finding the Jews at rest from work, he commanded his men to parade in arms, put to the sword all who came to see what was going on, and rushing into the city with the armed men killed great numbers. Judas Maccabaeus, however, with about nine others got away and kept himself and his companions alive in the mountains, as wild beasts do, feeding on herbs, in order that they might not be polluted like the rest.

6. Shortly after this the king sent an old Athenian to compel the Jews to depart from the laws of their fathers and to cease living by the laws of God; further, the sanctuary in Jerusalem was to be polluted and called after Zeus Olympius, while the sanctuary at Gerizim was also to be called after Zeus Xenius, in keeping with the hospitable character of the inhabitants. Now this proved a sore and altogether crushing visitation of evil. For the heathen filled the temple with riot and reveling, dallying with harlots and lying with women inside the sacred precincts, besides bringing in what was forbidden, while the altar was filled with abominable sacrifices which the law prohibited. And a man could neither keep the sabbath, nor celebrate the feasts of the fathers, nor so much as confess himself to be a Jew. On the king's birthday every month they were taken—bitter was the necessity—to share in the sacrifice, and when the festival of the Dionysia came round they were compelled to wear ivy wreaths for the procession in honor of Dionysus. On the suggestion of Ptolemy, an edict was also issued to the neighboring Greek cities ordering them to treat the Jews in the same way and force them to share in the sacrifices, slaying any who refused to adopt Greek ways. Thus any one could see the distressful state of affairs. Two women, for example, were brought up for having circumcised their children; they were paraded round the city, with their babies hanging at their breasts, and then flung from the top of the wall. Some others, who had taken refuge in the adjoining caves in order to keep the seventh day secretly, were betrayed to Philip and all burnt together, since they scrupled to defend themselves, out of regard to the honor of that most solemn day.

Second
Maccabees

3. ARMED JEWISH RESISTANCE BEGINS (167 B.C.)

Second
Maccabees

8. But Judas, who is also called Maccabaeus, together with his companions, went round the villages by stealth, summoning their kinsfolk and mustering those who had adhered to Judaism, till they collected as many as 6,000. And they invoked the Lord to look upon the people whom all men oppressed, to have compassion on the sanctuary which the godless had profaned, and also to pity the ruined city which was on the point of being levelled with the ground, to hearken to the blood that cried to him, to remember the impious massacre of the innocent babes and the blasphemies committed against his name, and to manifest his hatred of evil. Now as soon as Maccabaeus had got his company together, the heathen found him irresistible, for the Lord's anger was now turned into mercy. He would surprise and burn both towns and villages, gaining possession of strategic positions and routing large numbers of the enemy. He took special advantage of the night for such attacks. And the whole country echoed with the fame of his valour.

4. THE PURIFICATION OF THE TEMPLE AND THE RESTORATION OF JEWISH LAW (165 B.C.)

Second
Maccabees

9. Now about that time it happened that Antiochus had to beat a disorderly retreat from the region of Persia. He had entered the city called Persepolis and tried to rob temples and get hold of the city; whereupon the people flew to arms and routed him, with the result that Antiochus was put to flight by the people of the country and broke up his camp in disgrace. And while he was at Ecbatana, news reached him of what had happened to Nicanor and the forces of Timotheus. So, in a transport of rage, he determined to wreak vengeance on the Jews for the defeat which he had suffered at the hands of those who had forced him to fly, and ordered his charioteer to drive on without halting till the journey was ended. Verily the judgment of heaven upon him was imminent! For thus he spoke in his arrogance: When I reach Jerusalem, I will make it a common sepulchre of Jews. But the all-seeing Lord, the God of Israel, smote him with a fatal and unseen stroke; the words were no sooner out of his mouth than he was seized with an incurable pain in the bowels, and his internal organs gave him cruel torture—a right proper punishment for one who had tortured the bowels of other people with many an exquisite pang. He did not cease from his wild insolence, however, but waxed more arrogant than ever, breathing fire and fury against the Jews, and giving orders to hurry on with the journey. And it came to pass that he dropped from his chariot as it whirled along, so that the bad fall racked every limb of his body. Thus he who in his overweening haughtiness had supposed

the waves of the sea were at his bidding and imagined he could weigh the high mountains in his scales, was now prostrate, carried along in a litter—a manifest token to all men of the power of God. Worms actually swarmed from the impious creature's body; his flesh fell off, while he was still alive in pain and anguish; and the stench of his corruption turned the whole army from him with loathing. A man who shortly before had thought he could touch the stars of heaven, none could now endure to carry, such was his intolerable stench. Then it was that, broken in spirit, he began to abate his arrogance, for the most part, and to arrive at some knowledge of the truth. For, as he suffered more and more anguish under the scourge of God, unable even to bear his own stench, he said: Right is it that mortal man should be subject to God and not deem himself God's equal. The vile wretch also made a vow to the Lord (who would not now have pity on him), promising that he would proclaim the holy city free— the city which he was hurrying to lay level with the ground and to make a common sepulchre—that he would make all the Jews equal to citizens of Athens—the Jews whom he had determined to throw out with their children to the beasts, for the birds to devour, as unworthy even to be buried— that he would adorn with magnificent offerings the holy sanctuary which he had formerly rifled, restoring all the sacred vessels many times over, and defraying from his own revenue the expense of the sacrifices; furthermore, that he would even become a Jew and travel over the inhabited world to publish abroad the might of God. But when his sufferings did not cease by any means (for God's judgment had justly come upon him), he gave up all hope of himself and wrote the following letter, with its humble supplication, to the Jews:

To his citizens, the loyal Jews, Antiochus their king and general wisheth great joy and health and prosperity. If you and your children fare well and your affairs are to your mind, I give thanks to God, as my hope is in heaven. As for myself, I am sick. Your esteem and goodwill I bear in loving memory. On my way back from Persia I have fallen seriously ill, and I think it needful to take into consideration the common safety of all my subjects—not that I despair of myself (for, on the contrary, I have good hopes of recovery), but in view of the fact that when my father marched into the upper country, he appointed his successor, in order that, in the event of anything unexpected occurring or any unwelcome news arriving, the residents at home might know whom the State had been entrusted to, and so be spared any disturbance. Besides these considerations, as I have noticed how the princes on the borders and the neighbors of my kingdom are on the alert for any opportunity and anticipate the coming event, I have appointed my son Antiochus to be king. I have often committed and commended him to most of you, when I hurried to the upper provinces. I have also written to him what I have written below. I therefore exhort and implore you to remember the public and private benefits you have received and to preserve, each of you, your present goodwill toward me and my son. For I am convinced that with mildness and kindness he will adhere to my policy and continue on good terms with you.

So this murderer and blasphemer, after terrible suffering such as he had inflicted on other people, ended his life most miserably among the mountains in a foreign land. His bosom-friend Philip brought the corpse home; and then, fearing the son of Antiochus, he betook himself to Ptolemy Philometor in Egypt.

10. Now Maccabaeus and his followers, under the leadership of the Lord, recaptured the temple and the city and pulled down the altars erected by the aliens in the market-place, as well as the sacred enclosures. After cleansing the sanctuary, they erected another altar of sacrifice, and striking fire out of flints they offered sacrifices after a lapse of two years, with incense, lamps, and the presentation of the shew-bread. This done, they fell prostrate before the Lord with entreaties that they might never again incur such disasters, but that, if ever they should sin, he would chasten them with forbearance, instead of handing them over to blasphemous and barbarous pagans. Now it so happened that the cleansing of the sanctuary took place on the very day on which it had been profaned by aliens, on the twenty-fifth day of the same month, which is Chislev (November/December). And they celebrated it for eight days with gladness like a feast of tabernacles, remembering how, not long before, during the feast of tabernacles they had been wandering like wild beasts in the mountains and the caves. So, bearing wands wreathed with leaves and fair boughs and palms, they offered hymns of praise to him who had prospered the cleansing of his own place, and also passed a public order and decree that all the Jewish nation should keep these ten days every year.

F. Jewish Life in the Diaspora

Increasingly more Jews lived outside of Judea during the Hellenistic Period. Because the center of Jewish culture and worship remained the temple at Jerusalem, diaspora Jews had to create a new focus for Jewish religious and communal life in the various non-Jewish cities in which they lived. Their solution was the synagogue, a meeting house in which members of the Jewish community could meet for worship, education, and other communal functions. The following two passages illustrate the role of the synagogue in diaspora life. The first passage, from the Talmud, *describes the main synagogue in Alexandria, which contained the largest and most influential diaspora Jewish community in the eastern Mediterranean. In the second the Alexandrian Jewish philosopher Philo claims legitimacy for the Sabbath ritual as celebrated in the first century* A.D. *by ascribing its origin to Moses.*

1. THE SYNAGOGUE OF ALEXANDRIA[16]

It has been taught, R. Judah stated. He who not seen the double colonnade of Alexandria in Egypt has never seen the glory of Israel. It was said that it was like a huge basilica, one colonnade within the other, and it sometimes held twice the number of people that went forth from Egypt. There were in it seventy-one cathedra [sc. thrones] of gold, corresponding to the seventy-one members of the Great Sanhedrin, not one of them containing less than twenty-one talents of gold, and a wooden platform in the middle upon which the attendant of the Synagogue stood with a scarf in his hand. When the time came to answer Amen [sc. after the reader had finished a prayer] he waved his scarf and all the congregation duly responded. They moreover did not occupy their seats promiscuously, but goldsmiths sat separately, metalworkers separately and weavers separately, so that when a poor man entered the place he recognized the members of his craft and on applying to that quarter obtained a livelihood for himself and for the members of his family.

Tractate Sukkah

2. THE ORIGIN OF THE SABBATH RITUAL[17]

He [sc. Moses] required them to assemble at the same place on these seventh days, and sitting together in a respectful and orderly manner, hear the laws read so that none should be ignorant of them. And indeed they always assemble and sit together, most of them in silence except when it is the practice to add something to signify their approval of what is read. But some priest who is present or one of the elders reads the holy laws to them and expounds them point by point until about the late afternoon, when they depart, having gained expert knowledge of the holy laws and considerable advance in piety.

Philo in
Eusebius,
*Evangelical
Preparation* 8.7

G. Opportunities and Social Roles in the Hellenistic Period

Contemporary historians are increasingly aware that the life of the vast majority of people—both Greek and non-Greek—changed little in the Hellenistic Period. The low level of productivity of the ancient economy meant that the vast bulk of the population continued to live in rural areas as

---

[16] *Tractate Sukkah*, trans. Rev. Dr. Israel W. Slotki. From *The Babylonian Talmud: Seder Mo'ed in Four Volumes*, Vol. 3 (London, 1938), pp. 244–245.

[17] Philo in Eusebius, *Evangelical Preparation* 8.7. From F. E. Peters, *Judaism, Christianity, and Islam: The Classical Texts*, Vol. 3 (Princeton, 1990), p. 37.

subsistence farmers. Nevertheless, for the urban minority the Hellenistic Period saw a significant increase in economic opportunity and the variety of available social roles, particularly in the new cities of Egypt and the Near East. Not surprisingly, opportunities were greatest for the elite. The first selection describes the career of an important Greek official of Ptolemy I and Ptolemy II during the 280s and 270s B.C. and illustrates how such individuals served as spokesmen for their home cities at the courts of their royal masters. The opportunities available to most immigrants, however, were less glamorous. A selection from the playwright Menander vividly depicts the hopes as well as the risks that confronted those who joined the armies of the Macedonian monarchs in the hope of gaining quick wealth in the east, while the next selection provides insight into the more mundane world of the Hellenistic bureaucracies with their multitude of minor but potentially lucrative jobs and the means by which they were obtained.

New opportunities also appeared for women during the Hellenistic Period. Opportunities were clearly greatest for wealthy women, as can be seen from a selection illustrating the willingness of impoverished cities such as Priene in western Anatolia even to allow women who would use their wealth for public purposes to hold political office (Phyle, wife of Thessalos). Education also created opportunities for some women, not only upper-class intellectual women such as the Cynic philosopher Hipparchia, whose story is told in this section, but also women from less distinguished backgrounds such as the Athenian midwife Phanostrate, whose epitaph is translated here, and the professional harpist Polygnota of Thebes, whose generosity to Apollo of Delphi is recorded. There were also significant changes in the roles of men and women within the institution of marriage during the Hellenistic Period. Traditionally Greeks viewed marriage as a partnership of a man and a woman for the purpose of producing legitimate children to ensure the survival of the oikos *and* polis. *Although that view continued, Hellenistic thinkers increasingly emphasized the importance of the affective aspects of marriage, as can be seen from the observation of Stoic philosopher Antipater of Tarsus that "the man who has had no experience of a married woman and children has not tasted true and noble happiness" and from the popularity of stories of romantic love such as that of Antiochus and Stratonice, translated here. More important, the provision in the marriage contract of a wife's right to seek a divorce because of her husband's sexual misbehavior is clear evidence that such ideals found practical expression in the recognition of greater equality in relations between husband and wife than had been accepted in archaic and classical Greece.*

1. AN ATHENIAN IN PTOLEMAIC SERVICE: THE LIFE OF KALLIAS, PTOLEMAIC GOVERNOR OF HALICARNASSUS (ATHENS, 270–269 B.C.)[18]

Decree in Honor of Kallias, son Thymochares

The People (praises) Kallias, son of Thymochares, from Sphettos. In the archonship of Sosistratos (270/69), in the prytany of Pandionis which is the sixth, in which Athenodoros, son of Gorgippos, from Acharnai, was secretary, on the eighteenth day of Poseideon [=*December*], twenty-first day of the prytany; main assembly; of the proedroi the motion was put to the vote by the chairman, Epichares, son of Pheidostratos, from Erchia, and by his fellow proedroi. Resolved by the Boule [=*Council of 500*] and the People; Euchares, son of Euchares, from Konthyle, introduced the motion. Kallias, when the People rose against those occupying the city,

---

[18] *Supplementum Epigraphicum Graecum* 28 (1978) 60. From Stanley M. Burstein, *The Hellenistic Age from the Battle of Ipsos to the Death of Kleopatra VII*, pp. 74–76. Used by permission.

and it expelled the soldiers from the city, but the fort on the Museion hill was still occupied and the countryside was engaged in war by the soldiers from Peiraeus and Demetrios was marching from the Peloponnesos with an army against the city, Kallias, learning of the danger facing the city and having selected a thousand soldiers from those stationed with him on Andros and having distributed their salary to them and furnished their provisions, came quickly to the city to help the People, acting in accordance with the benevolent attitude of King Ptolemaios (I) toward the People. Marching out the soldiers who were with him into the countryside, he provided protection for the harvesting of the wheat, making every effort that as much wheat as possible into the city might be brought. And when Demetrios arrived, invested the city and laid siege to it, Kallias, fighting on behalf of the People and making sallies with his soldiers and being wounded, shrank from no risk on any occasion for the sake of saving the People. And King Ptolemaios, having sent Sostratos to accomplish what was advantageous for the city, and Sostratos inviting an embassy to meet him at Piraeus with which he would arrange terms of peace on behalf of the city with Demetrios, Kallias yielded in this to the strategoi and the Boule, undertook the embassy on behalf of the city and did everything that was advantageous for the city; and he remained in the city with the soldiers until the peace was completed. Then, having sailed to King Ptolemaios with the embassies sent by the People, he co-operated in every way and worked for the advantage of the city. After the succession to the throne of Ptolemaios (II), the younger king, Kallias, having visited the city and the strategoi having summoned him and informed him of the state in which the city's affairs were and urged him to hasten on behalf of the city to King Ptolemaios in order that as soon as possible there might be some help for the city in the form of grain and money, at his own expense Kallias sailed to Cyprus and, by there making a strong appeal to the king on behalf of the city, he obtained for the people fifty talents of silver and a gift of twenty thousand medimnoi of wheat, which was measured out at Delos to those sent by the People. When the king held for the first time the Ptolemaeia, the sacrifice and the games in honor of his father, the People, having voted to send a sacred embassy and having requested Kallias to agree to be the chief envoy and to lead on behalf of the People the [*sacred embassy*], K[al] lias agreed to this request with enthusiasm; and, having refused the fifty minas that had been voted to him by the People for the (expenses) of the office of chief envoy and having contributed them to the *People*, he led [*the sacred embassy*] at his own expense well and (in a manner) [*worthy*] of the People, and he took care of the sacrifice on behalf of the city and all the other things, which were appropriate, in association with the sacred ambassadors. At the time the People was first about to hold the Panathenaia in honor of the Foundress after the city had been recovered, Kallias, having spoken with the king about the tackle that had to be prepared for the peplos and the king having donated it to the city, took care that it be prepared as well as possible for the goddess; and the sacred ambassadors who with him had been elected immediately brought the tackle back here. And now, having been stationed in Halikarnassos by King Ptolemaios, Kallias continues zealously aiding both the embassies and the sacred embassies sent by the People to King Ptolemaios, and he privately on behalf of each citizen coming to him exerts every effort as well as for the soldiers there stationed with him, considering as most important [the advantage] and, in general, the well-being of the city; [—] with regard to the fatherland [—] Kallias not ever having endured [—] when the people had been suppressed, but his own property he allowed to be given as a contribution during the oligarchy so that he did nothing against either the laws or the democracy, which is that of all the Athenians. [*Since these things are so*], in order, therefore, that all may know who wish to exert themselves for the city that the people always remembers those conferring benefits on it and returns thanks to each; with good fortune, it has been resolved by the Boule that the proedroi, who shall be chosen by lot to preside at the Assembly according to the law, shall deliberate and refer the resolution of the Boule to the People that the Boule resolves to praise Kallias, son of Thymochares, from Sphettos, for his excellence and the good will which he continues to have for the Athenian People, and to crown him with a gold wreath in accordance with the law, and to proclaim the wreath at the contest for new tragedies at the Greater Dionysia.

2. THE DANGEROUS LIFE OF A SOLDIER OF FORTUNE[19]

Menander,
The Shield

DAVUS: (*addressing the master who, so far as he knows, is dead*) Cleostratus, at this moment I am living through the saddest day of my life. And my thoughts are far from the hopes I had the day I left. For I pictured you happily safe and sound after the campaign was over, and spending the rest of your days in a life of ease with an appointment as commanding officer or trusted counselor to someone. I pictured you returning home to those who missed you so and giving your sister in marriage—after all, it was for her sake that you went off—to a man like yourself. I pictured myself, as I entered old age, finding my devotion rewarded by rest after my never-ending hardships. But now you've gone off, you've been suddenly snatched away from us, and I, your servant since you were a boy, am the one who has come back—with your shield, which time and again you kept safe but which did not keep you safe. (*Sighing*) Ah, you were a man with a great heart, if ever there was one.

   (*While Davus is speaking, the door of Smicrines' house opens and Smicrines comes out. He is in his sixties, but looks even older. His clothes are cheap and ill-fitting, his figure is bent and gaunt, his face is a mirror of craftiness and avarice. As he listens intently, his eyes glisten. The minute Davus finishes, he goes over to him.*)

SMICRINES: (*rolling his eyes heavenward and speaking in sepulchral tones*) This is an unexpected blow, Davus.

DAVUS: A terrible one.

SMICRINES: How did it happen? How did he die?

[19] Menander, *The Shield*, trans. Lionel Casson. From *The Plays of Menander* (New York, 1971), pp. 83–85. Used by permission.

DAVUS: (*shrugging despondently*) What's hard for a soldier to find is the chance to stay alive; chances to die are all around.

SMICRINES: (*insistently*) Tell me what happened anyway, Davus.

DAVUS: There's a river in Lycia called the Xanthus. We fought a good number of battles there, and our side had done well: the enemy had left the plain and fled. (*ruefully*) But I guess not being a great success also has its useful side—the man who slips a bit is put on his guard. A devil-may-care attitude left us in total disorder for what was to come. A lot of the men, you see, left the camp and went off sacking villages, ravaging the fields, selling off booty; everyone came back with quite a haul.

SMICRINES: Not bad!

DAVUS: Cleostratus put together a shipment of some six hundred gold pieces, quite a lot of plate, and the batch of prisoners you see over there, and sends me off to Rhodes with instructions to leave it all with some friend and come right back.

SMICRINES: Well, what happened?

DAVUS: I set out at dawn. The day I left, the enemy, managing to sneak past the men we had on watch, was lying in wait, screened by a hill; they had learned from some deserters how disorganized our forces were. When it got dark, the men left the countryside with its rich pickings and all disappeared into the tents. Then, as will happen, most of them got good and drunk.

SMICRINES: (*shaking his head*) Bad, very bad.

DAVUS: Yes, since the enemy, I gather, made a sudden attack . . . [*About three and a half lines are lost here.*] Round about midnight I'm standing guard over the money and the captives, walking up and down in front of my tent, when I hear shouts, groans, wailing, running, men calling out to each other. And from them I heard what had happened. Luckily, where we were there was a small ridge that made a good strongpoint. We all gathered on top of it, and wounded men from the various units kept pouring in.

SMICRINES: Lucky thing for you Cleostratus had sent you off when he did.

DAVUS: At dawn we went about pitching a sort of camp there and stayed put, while the men who had gone off on the forays I told you about kept blaming themselves for our troubles. On the fourth day we found out that the enemy was off taking their prisoners to the villages inland, so we marched out.

SMICRINES: And he had fallen and you saw him among the dead?

DAVUS: I wasn't able to identify him for sure. After four days of lying there, the faces were all swollen.

SMICRINES: Then how do you know?

DAVUS: (*holding out the shield he has been clutching*) He was lying there with his shield. It was all bashed in—I suppose that's why none of the enemy bothered to take it. (*bitterly*) That fine commanding officer of ours didn't let us gather the bones and hold a funeral for each one, because he saw it would take too much time, but had us collect the corpses and hold a mass cremation. Then he had us carry out a quick burial and break camp right away. We first made it safely to Rhodes and, after staying there a few days, sailed here. (*shrugging despondently*) That's my whole story.

SMICRINES: (*being elaborately casual*) You say you have six hundred gold pieces?
DAVUS: That's right.
SMICRINES: And plate?
DAVUS: About forty pounds of it. (*noting Smicrines' face fall*) No more than that, Mr. Legal Heir.
SMICRINES: (*in a perish-the-thought tone*) What do you mean? You think that's the reason I'm asking? Good heavens! (*unable to restrain his curiosity*) The enemy get the rest?
DAVUS: (*nodding gloomily*) Just about the best part of it, except for what I got away with before the trouble started. (*pointing to the bundles some of the captives are carrying*) There are coats and cloaks in there. (*gesturing toward the whole group of captives*) And this bunch you see here is his property.

3. RECOMMENDATION FOR A GOVERNMENT JOB (EGYPT, 255 B.C.)[20]

P. Cairo Zen.
59192

Plato to Zenon, greetings. The father of Demetrius, who will give this letter to you, is living in the Arsinoite nome. The young man, therefore, also wishes to find some work there. On learning of your fairness, some of his friends asked me to write to you on his behalf in the hope that you might find a position for him in your office. Do us a favor, therefore, and see if there is something he can do which you think appropriate, and generally look after him, if, of course, you find him suitable. As a sign (of my feelings in this matter), I have sent to you from Sosus two bushels of chickpeas which I bought for five drachmas, and I will also try to buy an additional twenty bushels for you in Naucratis, if there are any available, and bring them to you. Farewell.

4. A POLITICAL WOMAN: PHYLE, WIFE OF THESSALOS
(PRIENE, FIRST CENTURY B.C.)[21]

Honors for
Phyle, daughter
of Apollonios

Phyle, daughter of Apollonios and wife of Thessalos, the son of Polydeukes, after having been the first woman to hold the office of crown bearer, paid for with her own money a cistern for water and the water pipes in the city.

5. A WOMAN PHILOSOPHER: THE LIFE OF HIPPARCHIA[22]

Diogenes
Laertius,
Lives of Eminent
Philosophers

Hipparchia, the sister of Metrocles, also fell in love with [*Crates'*] teachings. Both Hipparchia and Metrocles were from the city of Maroneia.

[20] From *P. Cairo Zen.* 59192.

[21] From *Inschriften von Priene* 208.

[22] From Diogenes Laertius, *Lives of Eminent Philosophers* 6.7.

She fell in love with the words of Crates and his life and ignored all her suitors and their wealth, noble birth and beauty. Crates became everything to her. She even went so far as to threaten to her parents that she would kill herself if they did not betroth her to Crates. Crates, therefore, who had been urged by her parents to discourage their daughter, tried everything. Finally, not having persuaded her, he stood up, stripped off his clothers in front of her, and said, "This is your bridegroom, this is his estate, make your choice from these facts." For she could not be his mate if she would not also share his manner of life.

The girl chose, and assuming the same dress as he, went around with her husband, lived with him in public, and accompanied him to dinners. And when she attended a drinking party hosted by [*King*] Lysimachus, she confounded Theodorus, the man known as the Atheist, by proposing the following sophism: Whatever would not be called wrong if done by Theodorus would also not be called wrong if done by Hipparchia. If Theodorus struck himself, he would not commit a wrong, nor, therefore, if Hipparchia struck Theodorus, would she commit a wrong. He did not reply to what she had said but tried instead to rip off her cloak. Hipparchia, however, was not frightened or upset as a woman would normally be. And when he said to her, "Is this the woman who abandoned the shuttle and the loom?" she replied, "I am that woman, Theodorus; but do I seem to you to have made a mistake if I devoted to education the time I would have spent on the loom?"

6. A PROFESSIONAL WOMAN: PHANOSTRATE, MIDWIFE AND DOCTOR (ATHENS, FOURTH CENTURY B.C.)[23]

Phanostrate . . . , the wife of Melitos, midwife and doctor, lies here. In life she caused no one pain, in death she is regretted by all.

Epitaph of Phanostrate

7. A PROFESSIONAL WOMAN: THE THEBAN HARPIST POLYGNOTA, DAUGHTER OF SOCRATES (DELPHI, 86 B.C.)[24]

Gods. Good Fortune. The archon being Habromachos, month Boukatios, the councillors for the first six-month period being Stratagos, Kleon, Antiphilos, Damon. Resolved by the city of the Delphians. Since Polygnota, daughter of Sokrates, a harpist from Thebes, was staying at Delphi at the time the Pythian games were to be held, but because of the present war, the games were not held, on that same day she performed without charge and contributed her services for the day; and, having been asked by the magistrates and the citizens, she played for three days and earned great distinction in a manner worthy of the

Decree in Honor of Polygnota, the Harpist

---

[23] From *Inscriptiones Graecae* 2.3² 6873.

[24] From *Sylloge Inscriptionum Graecarum*³ 738. From Stanley M. Burstein, *The Hellenistic Age from the Battle of Ipsos to the Death of Kleopatra VII*, pp. 105–106. Used by permission.

god and of the Theban people and of our city, and we rewarded her also with five hundred drachmas; with good fortune, the city shall praise Polygnota, daughter of Sokrates, a Theban, for her reverent attitude toward the god and her piety and her conduct with regard to her manner of life and art; and there shall be given by our city to her and to her descendants the status of a proxenos, priority in consulting the oracle, priority of trial, inviolability, exemption from taxes, a front seat at the contests which the city holds, and the right to own land and a house, and all other honors such as belong to the other proxenoi and benefactors of the city, and it shall invite her to the prytaneion to the public table; and it shall provide her with a sacrificial victim to offer to Apollo. God. Good Fortune. Resolved by the city of the Delphians. Since Lykinos, son of Dorotheos, a Theban, visited our city with his cousin Polygnota and behaved during his visit in a manner worthy of his own people and our city, it has been resolved by the city that it praise Lykinos, son of Dorotheos, a Theban, and that he have together with his descendants the status of a proxenos, priority in consulting the oracle, priority of trial, inviolability, exemption from taxes, a front seat at the contests which the city holds and other honors such as belong to the other proxenoi and benefactors of the city; and that it invite him also to the common table of the city. The archon being Habromachos, the son of Athambos, the councillors being Damon, Kleon, Stratagos, Antiphilos.

8. THE ROMANCE OF PRINCE ANTIOCHUS AND QUEEN STRATONICE[25]

Appian,
Syriaca

Seleucus, while still living, appointed his son, Antiochus, king of upper Asia in place of himself. If this seems noble and kingly on his part, even nobler and wiser was his behavior in reference to his son's falling in love, and the restraint which that son showed in regard to his passion; for Antiochus was in love with Stratonice, the wife of Seleucus, his own stepmother, who had already borne a child to Seleucus. Recognizing the wickedness of this passion, Antiochus did nothing wrong, nor did he show his feelings, but he fell sick, drooped, and strove his hardest to die. Nor could the celebrated physician, Erasistratus, who was serving Seleucus at a very high salary, form any diagnosis of his malady. At length, observing that his body was free from all the symptoms of disease, he conjectured that this was some condition of the mind, through which the body is often strengthened or weakened by sympathy; and he knew that, while grief, anger, and other passions disclose themselves, love alone is concealed by the modest. As even then Antiochus would confess nothing when the physician asked him earnestly and in confidence, he took a seat by his side and watched the changes of his body to see how he was affected by each person who entered his room. He found that when others came the

---

[25] Appian, *Syriaca*, trans. Horace White. From *The Roman History of Appian of Alexandria*, Vol. 1 (New York, 1899), pp. 317–320.

Fig. 8.6 This sculpture suggests the comfortable lifestyle available to the upper classes of the Hellenistic world. Hellenistic woman, fourth or third century B.C. Courtesy of the J. Paul Getty Museum, Malibu. Photo: D. B. Nagle.

patient was all the time weakening and wasting away at a uniform pace, but when Stratonice came to visit him his mind was greatly agitated by the struggles of modesty and conscience, and he remained silent. But his body in spite of himself became more vigorous and lively, and when she went away he became weaker again. So the physician told Seleucus that his son had an incurable disease. The king was overwhelmed with grief and cried aloud. Then the physician added, "His disease is love, love for a woman, but a hopeless love."

60. Seleucus was astonished that there could be any woman whom he, king of Asia, could not prevail upon to marry such a son as his, by entreaties, by gold, by gifts, by the whole of that great kingdom, the eventual inheritance of the sick prince, which the father would give to him even now, if he wished it, in order to save him. Desiring to learn only one thing more, he asked, "Who is this woman?" Erasistratus replied, "He is in love with my wife." "Well then, my good fellow," rejoined Seleucus, "since you are so

bound to us by friendship and favors, and have few equals in goodness and wisdom, will you not save this princely young man for me, the son of your friend and king, unfortunate in love but virtuous, who has concealed his sinful passion and prefers to die rather than confess it? Do you so despise Antiochus? Do you despise his father also?" Erasistratus resisted and said, as though putting forward an unanswerable argument, "Even you would not give Antiochus your wife if he were in love with her, although you are his father." Then Seleucus swore by all the gods of his royal house that he would willingly and cheerfully give her and make himself an illustrious example of the kindness of a good father to a chaste son who controlled his passion and did not deserve such suffering. Much more he added of the same sort and, finally, began to lament that he could not himself be physician to his unhappy boy but must needs depend on Erasistratus in this matter also.

61. When Erasistratus saw by the king's earnestness that he was not pretending, he told the whole truth. He related how he had discovered the nature of the malady and how he had detected the secret passion. Seleucus was overjoyed, but it was a difficult matter to persuade his son and not less so to persuade his wife; but he succeeded finally. Then he assembled his army, which perhaps by now suspected something, and told them of his exploits and of the extent of his empire, showing that it surpassed that of any of the other successors of Alexander, and saying that as he was now growing old it was hard for him to govern it on account of its size. "I wish," he said, "to divide it, in the interests of your future safety, and to give a part of it now to those who are dearest to me. It is fitting that all of you, who have advanced to such greatness of dominion and power under me since the time of Alexander, should cooperate with me in everything. The dearest to me, and well worthy to reign, are my grown-up son and my wife. As they are young, I pray they may soon have children to aid in guarding the empire. I join them in marriage in your presence and send them to be sovereigns of the upper provinces now. The law which I shall impose upon you is not the customs of the Persians and other nations, but the law which is common to all, that what the king ordains is always right." When he had thus spoken, the army shouted that he was the greatest king of all the successors of Alexander and the best father. Seleucus laid the same injunctions on Stratonice and his son, then joined them in marriage and sent them to their kingdom, showing himself even stronger in this famous act than in his deeds of arms.

9. THE MARRIAGE CONTRACT OF HERACLEIDES AND DEMETRIA (311 B.C.)[26]

P. Elephantine 1 ‖ Seventh year of the reign of Alexander, the son of Alexander, fourteenth year of the satrapy of Ptolemy, month of Dius. Marriage contract of Heracleides and Demetria. Heracleides, a freeman, takes as his lawful wife Demetria, a Coan

---

[26] From *P. Elephantine* 1, 2, lines 1–18.

and a freewoman, from her father, Leptines, a Coan, and from her mother, Philotis. Demetria will bring with her clothing and ornaments worth 1,000 drachmas. Heracleides will furnish to Demetria everything that is appropriate for a freewoman. We shall live together in whatever place seems best in the common opinion of Leptines and Heracleides.

If Demetria shall be detected devising something evil for the purpose of humiliating her husband Heracleides, she shall be deprived of everything she brought to the marriage. Heracleides shall declare whatever charge he brings against Demetria before three men who both approve. Heracleides may not introduce another woman into their home to insult Demetria nor have children from another woman nor devise any evil toward Demetria for any reason. If Heracleides shall be detected doing any of these things and Demetria declares this before three men who both approve, Heracleides shall return to Demetria the dowry of 1,000 drachmas which she brought and he shall pay to her in addition 1,000 silver Alexandrian drachmas. Demetria and those with Demetria shall be able to exact payment, just as though there were a legal judgment, from Heracleides himself and from all of Heracleides' property on both land and sea.

This contract shall be wholly valid in every way wherever Heracleides produces it against Demetria, or Demetria and those with Demetria produce it against Heracleides, in order to exact payment. Heracleides and Demetria each have the right to preserve their contracts and to produce the contracts against each other. Witnesses: Cleon, a Gelan; Anticrates, a Temnian; Lysis, a Temnian; Dionysius, a Temnian; Aristomachus, a Cyrenean; Aristodicus, a Coan.

H. The Coming of Rome

The Second Macedonian War (200–197 B.C.) was the first large-scale intervention of Rome in the affairs of Greece and resulted in the decisive expulsion of Macedon from territories in Greece that it had held since the reign of Philip II. In this passage Plutarch describes the dramatic scene at the Isthmian games in 196 B.C., when T. Quinctius Flamininus, the conqueror of King Philip V of Macedon, proclaimed to the Greeks that they were henceforth to be free and that Rome was going to withdraw completely from Greece.[27]

Plutarch,
Flamininus

1. T. QUINCTIUS FLAMININUS AND GREEK FREEDOM (196 B.C.)

And now the ten commissioners, who had been sent to Titus by the senate, advised him to give the rest of the Greeks their freedom, but to retain Corinth,

[27] Plutarch, *Flamininus* 10.1–5. From *Plutarch's Lives*, trans. Bernadotte Perrin (Cambridge, MA, 1921).

Chalcis, and Demetrias under garrisons, as a safeguard against Antiochus. Thereupon the Aetolians stirred up the cities with the most vociferous denunciations, ordering Titus to strike off the shackles of Greece (for that is what Philip was wont to call these three cities), and asking the Greeks whether they were glad to have a fetter now which was smoother than the one they had worn before, but heavier; and whether they admired Titus as a benefactor because he had unshackled the foot of Greece and put a collar round her neck. Titus was troubled and distressed at this, and by laboring with the commission finally persuaded it to free these cities also from their garrisons, in order that his gift to the Greeks might be whole and entire.

Accordingly, at the Isthmian games, where a great throng of people were sitting in the stadium and watching the athletic contests (since, indeed, after many years Greece had at last ceased from wars waged in hopes of freedom, and was now holding festival in time of assured peace), the trumpet signalled a general silence, and the herald, coming forward into the midst of the spectators, made proclamation that the Roman senate and Titus Quintius Flamininus, proconsular general, having conquered King Philip and the Macedonians, restored to freedom, without garrisons and without imposts, and to the enjoyment of their ancient laws, the Corinthians, the Locrians, the Phocians, the Euboeans, the Achaeans of Phtbiotis, the Magnesians, the Thessalians, and the Perrhaebians. At first, then, the proclamation was by no means generally or distinctly heard, but there was a confused and tumultuous movement in the stadium of people who wondered what had been said, and asked one another questions about it, and called out to have the proclamation made again; but when silence had been restored, and the herald in tones that were louder than before and reached the ears of all, had recited the proclamation, a shout of joy arose, so incredibly loud that it reached the sea. The whole audience rose to their feet, and no heed was paid to the contending athletes, but all were eager to spring forward and greet and hail the savior and champion of Greece.

2. THE REALITY OF ROMAN POWER: THE LETTER OF KING EUMENES II (156 B.C.)

Eumenes II's
letter to Cybele
at Pessinus

Although Rome did, in fact, withdraw its forces from Greece in the mid-190s B.C., Roman power and the possibility of Roman intervention dominated the politics of the Greek cities and the Macedonian kingdoms for the remainder of the second century B.C. The Pergamene king Eumenes II, one of Rome's closest allies in Anatolia, provides a vivid insight into this reality in this letter to the priest of the priest of Cybele at Pessinus, describing a meeting of the royal council in which the king and his advisors conclude that they can undertake no new initiative without taking into consideration the possible Roman reaction to it.[28]

[28] From C. Bradford Welles, *Royal Correspondence in the Hellenistic Period: A Study in Greek Epigraphy* (London, 1934), pp. 245–246.

[King Attalus to priest Attis, greeting. If you were well, it would be] as I wish; I myself also was in good health. When we came to Pergamum and I assembled not only Athenaeus and Sosander and Menogenes but many others also of my "relatives," and when I laid before them what we discussed in Apamea and told them our decision, there was a very long discussion, and at first all inclined to the same opinion with us, but Chlorus vehemently held forth the Roman power and counseled us in no way to do anything without them. In this at first few concurred, but afterwards, as day after day we kept considering, it appealed more and more, and to launch an undertaking without their participation began to seem fraught with great danger; if we were successful the attempt promised to bring us envy and detraction and baneful suspicion—that which they felt also toward my brother—while if we failed we should meet certain destruction. For they would not, it seemed to us, regard our disaster with sympathy but would rather be delighted to see it, because we had undertaken such projects without them. As things are now, however, if—which God forbid—we were worsted in any matters, having acted entirely with their approval we would receive help and might recover our losses, if the gods favored. I decided, therefore, to send to Rome on every occasion men to make constant report of cases where we are in doubt, while [we] ourselves make [thorough] preparation [so that if it is necessary] we may protect ourselves. . . .

3. GREEK REACTIONS TO THE DESTRUCTION OF CARTHAGE (POLYBIUS, *HISTORIES* 36.9–17)

In the following reading, the second century B.C. Greek historian of Roman imperialism, Polybius, reports on the state of Greek public opinion after the destruction of Carthage by the Romans in 146 B.C. Some of the opinions given may in fact reflect genuine Greek reaction to the event, but the third paragraph reveals the torturous, legalistic lengths Rome's supporters had to go to justify the annihilation of Carthage.

Polybius' report on public opinion after the destruction of Carthage

Some [Greeks] approved the Romans for their wise and statesmanlike actions in regard to protecting their own power. To have eliminated Carthage, a city which had been a perpetual threat to them and which had disputed with them for hegemony [of the western Mediterranean], was the act of intelligent and far sighted men. Indeed, if the Carthaginians still had the opportunity they would right now be contending with the Romans to obtain dominion for themselves. Others took the opposite view. They said that the Romans had no such policy in mind [i.e. self-defense] when they obtained their hegemony but that little by little had abandoned their own principles to embrace the lust for power that had possessed Athenians and Spartans before them . . . Indeed, originally they waged war only until their enemies were beaten and forced to obey them, but now they had given a foretaste of their new policy in their handling of Perseus and by their utter destruction of the kingdom of Macedonia [in 168 B.C.]. They fully revealed their new approach in their destruction of Carthage which had not committed any shocking offense against them but which they treated instead with deadly outrage . . . .

Others said that, generally speaking, the Romans possessed a civilized, constitutional form of government. They were proud of the fact that they conducted their wars simply and honorably, and that they used neither night attacks nor ambushes, disdaining any kind of deceit or fraud. In Roman eyes only facing danger openly and face-to-face was morally right. However, throughout their recent dealings with Carthage, they had, in fact, used both deceit and fraud . . . and engaged in a kind of behavior more characteristic of a despotic than a constitutional state. Their actions could rightly be described as impious and treacherous.

Others disagreed with these views. They said that had the Romans behaved that way *before* the Carthaginians had surrendered then they would indeed be guilty as charged. However, if the Carthaginians had voluntarily committed themselves to the good faith of the Romans and acknowledged the right of the Romans to treat them as they chose . . . then the subsequent actions of the Romans were neither impious nor treacherous. Some went so far as to say that what the Romans did was not even unjust. This was because there are three ways in which a crime may be defined and none of these could be attributed to the Romans. Impiety is a wrong committed against the gods, one's parents or against the dead; treachery is a violation of oaths or written agreements; an injustice is something done contrary to law or custom. In [the destruction of Carthage] the Romans could not be held guilty of any of these three violations. They did no wrong to the gods, their parents, the dead, their oaths or their treaties. . . . They broke no laws or customs, nor violated their own good faith. Having received the voluntary surrender of the Carthaginians they had full power to do what they pleased with them when the Carthaginians refused to obey their orders; only then did they resort to force (36.9–17).

4. ROME'S ROLE IN GREEK AFFAIRS: ARBITRATION OF DISPUTES

A characteristic feature of Greek life in the Hellenistic Period was the use of arbitration to peacefully settle disputes. As this inscription from Olympia reveals, Rome became an integral part of this process after the conversion of Greece into the province of Achaea in 146 B.C. This particular arbitration, which took place in 138 B.C., dealt with the long-standing dispute over the border between Sparta and Messene that originated with the liberation of Messenia from Spartan rule by Thebes in 371 B.C.

The inscription contains three documents. The first is a decree of Elis granting Messene the right to set up an inscription containing a record of the favorable judgment they had received at Olympia, where it would receive maximum publicity in the Greek world. The second is a cover letter from Miletus certifying the authenticity of the report of the judgment that was to be inscribed. The third and final document is the inscribed copy of the official report of the arbitration, describing the procedure used, identifying the speakers on both sides and the time allotted them as measured by a water clock—a device that measures time by the rate at which water drains at a predetermined rate from a container—and, finally, the decision.

Rome's role in the arbitration process was twofold. The Senate chose Miletus as the arbitrator and it defined how the issue was to be decided, namely, that the land should belong to whichever state possessed it during the consulship or proconsulship of Achaea of Lucius Mummius, the Roman commander in the Achaean War (149–146 B.C.) In fact, Sparta appealed the decision and the case was only definitively settled in Messene's favor by the Roman emperor Tiberius in A.D. 25.[29]

Judgment about territory between the Messenians and the Lacedaemonians

    A. Ambassadors arrived [at Elis] from the city of the Messenians—Menodorus, the son of Dionysius, Apollonidas, the son of Nicander, Charetidas, the son of Dorconidas—and handed over letters in which it was made clear that they had renewed the existing kinship and friendship of the cities [Messene and Elis] with each other. They proposed that the city grant that they inscribe at Olympia the judgment that was rendered to their city against the city of the Lacedaemonians concerning territory. The ambassadors also handed over the sealed letter from the Milesians which contained the written record of the judgment, and the ambassadors also spoke in accordance with their instructions.

    Resolved by the councilors that we reply that the kinship and friendship that had existed with the city of the Messenians be renewed and increased, and that, with regard to the permission to inscribe at Olympia the judgment that had been rendered to their city against the city of the Lacedaemonians concerning the territory by the people of the Milesians, it has been granted just as the city of the Messenians wrote and the ambassadors requested. The ambassadors also shall be praised for their visit and the conduct they displayed, and we shall grant them and Philonicus, the treasurer, the greatest awards allowed by the laws, and we shall invite them and the archons to the common hearth.

    B. The prytaneis of Milesians and the guardians to the archons and councilors of the Eleans, greetings. The ambassadors from the Messenians—Menodorus, the son of Dionysius, Philoitus, the son of Cratius—came to us and urged us to give to them for you [i.e., the Eleans] a copy of the decision that was rendered to the Messenians and the Lacedaemonians in accordance with the decree of the Senate. The council and assembly agreed to what had been proposed and instructed us to give the decision to them. After attaching it to this letter, we gave a copy to the ambassadors to bring to you sealed with the public seal.

    C. [Copy of the decree] In the year when Eirenius, the son of Asclepiades, was wreathbearer, on the second day of the month of Kalamaion (= June), and, as the Praetor Quintus Calpurnius, son of Gaius (138 B.C.), wrote, in the fourteenth month and on the eleventh day, according to the

Right margin notes:

A decree of Elis granting Messene the right to set up an inscription

A cover letter from Miletus certifying the authenticity of the information that was to be inscribed

The inscribed copy of the official report of the arbitration

---

[29] W. Dittenberger (ed.), *Sylloge Inscriptionum Graecarum*, 3rd ed. (Leipzig 1921–24) No. 683.

moon, after the day when the decree was passed, a sovereign assembly was held in the theater [at Miletus] on the aforementioned day, as the Lacedaemonians and the Messenians agreed, and a jury was drawn by lot from the whole people, the largest allowed by the law, namely, six hundred jurors.

The trial was held in accordance with the letter of the aforementioned Praetor and the decree of the Senate concerning the dispute between the Lacedaemonians and the Messenians as to which of them possessed the territory, when Lucius Mummius was Consul (146 B.C.) or Proconsul (143 B.C.) in that province, in order that that people should possess it. The water was divided between them by measure. For the first speech fifteen Milesian measures were assigned to each of them, and for the second speech five Milesian measures, just as they also had agreed. For the Lacedaemonians Eudamidas, the son of Euthycles, and for the Messenians Nicias, the son of Nicon, spoke in accordance with measure of the water. After the speeches were delivered by each speaker, it was decided that the territory was possessed by the Messenians when Lucius Mummius was Consul or Proconsul in that province, and that they should, therefore, possess it. The number of votes by which it was decided that the territory was possessed by the Messenians and that they should possess it were 584, and that it was possessed by the Lacedaemonians 16.

5. ROMAN EXPANSION IN THE EASTERN MEDITERRANEAN: A CYNICAL VIEW

Sallust, "Letter of Mithridates"

By the early first century B.C., Rome's dominance in the eastern Mediterranean basin was unchallengeable. The kingdoms of Macedon and Pergamum had both been annexed, the Achaean and Aetolian Leagues had been dismantled, and the Seleucid and Ptolemaic kingdoms had been rendered impotent. In this excerpt from a letter ascribed to Mithridates VI of Pontus (120–63 B.C.), Rome's last major enemy in the east, the first-century B.C. Roman historian Sallust imagines how these developments might appear to a hostile observer.[30]

In fact, the Romans have one inveterate motive for making war upon all nations, peoples and kings; namely, a deep-seated desire for dominion and for riches. Therefore they first began a war with Philip, king of Macedonia, having pretended to be his friends as long as they were hard pressed by the Carthaginians. When Antiochus came to his aid, they craftily diverted him from his purpose by the surrender of Asia, and then, after Philip's power had been broken, Antiochus was robbed of all the territory this side of Taurus, and of ten thousand talents. Next Perseus, the son of Philip, after many battles with varying results, was formally taken under their protection before the gods of Samothrace; and then

---

[30] Sallust, "Letter of Mithridates," 5–10. From *Sallust*, trans. J. C. Rolf (Cambridge, MA, 1921).

those masters of craft and artists in treachery caused his death from want of sleep, since they had made a compact not to kill him. Eumenes, whose friendship they boastfully parade, they first betrayed to Antiochus as the price of peace; later, having made him the guardian of a captured territory, they transformed him by means of imposts and insults from a king into the most wretched of slaves. Then, having forged an unnatural will, they led his son Aristonicus in triumph like an enemy, because he had tried to recover his father's realm. They took possession of Asia, and finally, on the death of Nicomedes, they seized upon all Bithynia, although Nysa, whom Nicomedes had called queen, unquestionably had a son.

GLOSSARY

Academy—The school founded by Plato at Athens during the 380s B.C. in the groves sacred to the hero Academus. Its most famous pupil was Aristotle. The Academy continued to function until the Christian emperor Justinian ordered it closed, along with other pagan schools, in 529 A.D.

acropolis—Literally, the "upper city," the citadel of a city or town. Many citadel hills had been the sites of Mycenaean palaces and remained as special places in *polis* life. The most famous is the Acropolis of Athens, the religious center of the city, which was magnificently adorned with temples in the fifth century.

agora—In Homer, the term for the "place of gathering," the assembly of the people. In the city-state period it denoted the public space of a city or town, being both the marketplace and civic center. Lingering in the agora was the best way to inform oneself about public affairs, make business contacts, and collect gossip.

Amphictyonic Council—The governing body of an ancient league of Delphi's neighbors, the Delphic Amphictyony, that administered the oracle. The Amphictyony also conducted the Pythian games and dealt with transgressions against the oracle and its territory. The members were *ethne*, of which the most important were the Thessalians, Phocians, Boeotians, Dorians, and Ionians. Votes were unequally divided among the members, so that Philip II's acquisition of the twelve Thessalian and two Phocian votes gave him a majority of the council's twenty-two votes and control of the Amphictyony.

archon—A common title (meaning "leader") for the highest ranking magistrate in the early city-states. During the Classical period, even when the *strategoi* had become the most important officials in Athens, nine archons continued to be chosen (by lot) to serve judicial and administrative functions. The archontate was used in larger contexts as well; for example, as the title of the civil and military head of the Thessalian League. This archon was elected by the League assembly and served for life.

330

aristocracy—The term *aristokratia* ("power in the hands of the best men") was coined, probably in the fifth century, as the word the elite used to describe their hold on power, in preference to the less noble-sounding *oligarchia*. (Plato defines aristocracy as the good form of oligarchy.) Aristocratic power and exclusiveness were strongest in the early Archaic period and gradually weakened as strong democratic sentiments emerged in the city-states.

Asia—The name of a small river valley in Anatolia (modern Turkey) near ancient Ephesus. Eventually the term was extended first to include all of Anatolia and then the whole region between Anatolia and the border of India.

Asia Minor—Corresponds to most of modern Turkey.

assembly—Along with the "council" (*boule, gerousia*), one of the two primary elements of Greek governance. From the Dark Age on, it was made up of the free adult males of the community, who met the minimum qualifications for citizenship, usually membership in a household and ability to perform military service. In the Dark Age, the assembly (called *agora* in Homer) had limited power vis-à-vis the chiefs, although its concurrence was crucial. Despite attempts by the oligarchical rulers of the Archaic period to curtail further the authority of the assembly, it eventually became the deciding body of state policy. In Athens, the assembly or *ekklesia* met in the open air on the hill called the Pnyx about forty times a year.

barbaros—The term used by the ancient Greeks for all people who were not Greek in language and culture. The contrast did not necessarily imply uncivilized crudity and savagery (the highly civilized and generally admired Egyptians and Persians were *barbaroi* to the Greeks), although increasingly from the fifth century on, *barbaroi* came to be stigmatized as the inferior "others."

basileus—The term for the legitimate single ruler, the "king." In Mycenaean society, the title *pasireu* denoted an official who had charge of a village or district; with the breakup of the Mycenaean kingdoms it became (in the form *basileus*) the title of the warrior-chiefs who ruled the villages and districts in the Dark Age. The hierarchy of *basileis* was replaced in the Archaic Age by landed aristocrats who ruled as an oligarchy.

boule—The most common term for the "council," which, along with the assembly, was one of the two primary governing institutions of the Greeks. Composed of the chiefs and other influential men in the Dark Age, it became the major organ of aristocratic power in the Archaic Age. In the democratizing city-states, the council became increasingly an organ of popular will. In Classical Athens, the *boule* consisted of five hundred men chosen by lot; it prepared business for the assembly. It could also try certain court cases.

city-state—See polis.

Common Peace—The term used to describe a number of fourth-century-B.C. treaties beginning with the King's Peace in 387 and ending with that sponsored by Philip II after the Battle of Chaeronea in 338. The characteristic feature of these treaties was that they guaranteed the autonomy of all subscribing states.

Corinthian League—The term used by modern scholars to designate the alliance organized to implement the Common Peace established by Philip II in 338 B.C. The League included the principal cities and *ethne* of Greece except Sparta and guaranteed its members freedom, autonomy, collective action against states who broke the peace, and protection against proposals to cancel debts and liberate slaves. The Corinthian League provided the framework for Macedonian domination of Greece until it was dissolved by Antipater in 322 B.C.

currency, Athenian—The basic nits of Athenian currency were the obol and the drachma (i.e. six obols). For accounting purposes, drachmas could also be collected into larger groups; so one hundred drachmas made a mina; and sixty minas (i.e., 6,000 drachmas) added up to a talent. A man who had a talent was rich. In fifth-century-B.C. Athens, a silver drachma coin was considered good pay for a day's labor by an unskilled worker and probably represented a living wage for a small family. A drachma was the standard pay for a rower in the fleet. Maintaining a trireme cost a talent a month.

Delian League—The modern name for the confederacy organized under Athenian leadership after the end of the Persian wars. Founded in 477 B.C., the League was slowly converted into an Athenian empire as Athens began forcing unwilling states to remain in the organization, or to join it if they were not already members.

demagogos—Literally, a "leader of the people." This was the term some Athenians used to categorize the politicians who arose in Athens after Pericles' death. Usually it had negative connotations and suggested that such a man was interested only in his own well-being, unlike a true statesman, who cared for the welfare of the state. Unlike the word "demagogue" today, however, it was occasionally used in a neutral way.

democracy—A form of government in Classical Greece that permitted all free men some degree of participation in politics, regardless of wealth or family background. Ideologies of equality were preached, although economic inequalities prevailed and generally brought political inequalities with them. Athens encouraged democratic governments in its allies. Like other forms of Greek government, democracies denied voting rights to women and assumed the appropriateness of slavery.

demos—A territory and the people who live in it; thus, "the land" and "the people." It occurs in the Linear B tablets in the form *damo*, meaning, apparently, a village community and its free inhabitants. Originally a neutral term, it came to be used by aristocrats (probably in the seventh century) as an exclusive term for the "commoners," or the "masses," although technically (as in legal inscriptions) it retained its inclusive meaning as "the (whole) people."

drachma—See currency, Athenian.

ekklesia—See assembly. The Athenian assembly (*ekklesia*) met about thirty to forty times a year on the hill known as the Pnyx. In its meetings it voted on business prepared by the *boule*.

ephor (*ephoros*)— "Overseer," an office found in Sparta and in other Dorian states. In Sparta a board of five ephors was elected annually by the assembly; the senior ephor gave his name to the year. The ephors had great power in the Spartan state, including general control over the king's conduct.

ethnos—The term used to describe a large group of people who shared a common identity and territory, but were not politically united, preferring local self-government. The story of the Greek *ethne* is their growing ability from the sixth century B.C. on to act as unified states by forming federations of local and regional segments of the *ethnos*. By the fourth century B.C., ethnic confederacies and leagues were playing a prominent, and even a dominant, role in the geopolitics of Greece.

Freedom of the Greeks—Propaganda slogan used by various Hellenistic kings and the Romans to attract the support of Greek cities. Although proclamations of "freedom" included guarantees that cities would be free, autonomous, and ungarrisoned, in practice kings did not hesitate to interfere in city affairs to achieve their goals.

genos—"Clan." A social group composed of families who claimed descent from a single male ancestor. A *genos* was led by its most prominent family and played a prominent part as a political group in the Archaic Age. The power and influence of the aristocratic *gene* (plural) waned in the Classical period, but continued to confer social prestige on the member families.

gerousia—The "council of elders" (from *geron*, "old man"). This was the term used at Sparta and in other *poleis* for the aristocratic council. The Spartan *gerousia* consisted of the two kings plus twenty-eight men over age sixty who served for life.

guest-friendship (*xenia*)— A form of ritual friendship, whereby a "stranger" (*xenos*) entered into a relationship of mutual friendship with a man from another *demos*, each obliged to offer hospitality and aid when they visited each other's community. The bond was perpetuated down through generations of the two families. A prominent feature of Homeric society, *xenia* continued throughout antiquity, evolving in the city-states into the more formal diplomatic relationship of proxeny (q.v.).

hegemon—A state or individual who headed an organization of states. Athens, for example, was the hegemon of the Delian League, Sparta of the Peloponnesian League. A hegemon was said to exercise hegemony; hence, the period of Theban ascendancy in the 360s B.C. is known as the Theban hegemony. Hegemon was also the title of the leader of the Corinthian League. This hegemon was officially elected by the League council and was its chief executive and commander-in-chief of the League's military forces with full authority to conduct its military and diplomatic activities.

hektemoroi—A term used in Solonian Athens meaning "sixth-parters," referring, presumably, to poor farmers who had fallen into debt to wealthy landowners and had to hand over to them a sixth of their produce under penalty of enslavement for their debt.

Hellenes—The name the Greeks called themselves (and still do). They had a myth of an eponymous ancestor, Hellen, who was the son of Deucalion, the Greek Noah, and the father of the eponymous ancestors of the Dorians, Ionians, and Aeolians. There is some reason to believe that the common name (and the supporting myth) arose relatively late, perhaps in the eighth century B.C.

helots—The term used to describe groups of conquered people in Greece who were forced by their conquerors to work as serfs on their former lands. The word is most commonly associated with Sparta, where helots probably outnumbered citizens by a ratio of seven to one. The Spartan way of life both depended on and was formed by the state's ownership of the labor of thousands of helots in Laconia and Messenia. Fear of helot uprisings often discouraged the Spartans from becoming engaged in campaigns far from home.

hetaira—Meaning literally "female companion," this was the term normally used for courtesans in Classical Athens. *Hetairai* usually came from the metic class. They were generally more cultivated than citizen women; they were trained (usually by older hetairai) to be entertaining and interesting rather than to be thrifty managers of households. Since Pericles' citizenship laws of 451–450 B.C. made it impossible for a man to marry a metic woman and still have his children enjoy citizenship rights, many Athenian men chose to have long-term associations with hetairai simultaneously with their legal marriages to Athenian women. Some hetairai functioned as entrenched mistresses or even common-law wives, but others less fortunate were essentially prostitutes.

hetaireiai—The military systems of some cities such as those in Crete grouped men in *hetaireiai* or "bands of companions," but the word is most commonly associated with Athens. There young men of the upper class frequently belonged to hetaireiai or social clubs with political overtones, often of an antidemocratic nature. The mutilation of the herms in 415 B.C. was rumored to be the work of such a *hetaireia*, and the subversive activity of *hetaireiai* probably played a part in the oligarchic revolutions of 411 and 404 B.C.

hetairos—"Companion" or "comrade." In the Dark Age, follower-bands of *hetairoi* formed the military and political support of the chiefs who recruited and rewarded them. Associations of *hetairoi* for political purposes continued to function in the city-states (see hetaireiai). In Macedonia, the *hetairoi* were an elite band of warriors and advisors who formed the retinue and personal bodyguard of the kings.

hippeis—See Solonic system.

hoplite—The heavily armored infantryman, named from his distinctive shield (*hoplon*). Hoplites were the dominant military arm from the seventh century on, gradually undergoing changes in weaponry and tactics. Because Greek governments did not issue arms to their soldiers, hoplites tended to come from the middle class, men able to afford armor and swords, unlike the rowers in the fleets, who were likely to be *thetes* (see thes).

King's Peace—The agreement that ended the Corinthian War in 387 B.C. A key role was played by Artaxerxes II of Persia, and Greeks were chagrined by the wording of the peace, which began, "I, King Artaxerxes, regard the following arrangements as just. . . ."

kleros—An allotment of farmland sufficient to support a citizen-family; it was passed on in perpetuity in the male line. In oligarchic states, full citizenship was frequently tied to the possession of a certain amount of land.

liturgies—An indirect system of taxation whereby the rich were required to spend their own money in the service of the state. Liturgies included financing the training of a chorus for dramatic performances or financing a delegation to a religious festival in another state. The most expensive liturgy was the trierarchy, which required a man to maintain a trireme for a year and to pay for the training of its crew.

Lyceum—The school founded by Aristotle in Athens in 335 B.C. It became a major center for scientific study, and Aristotle's pupils also collected the constitutions of 158 states.

megaron—A large rectangular building that served as the focal point of Mycenaean palaces. Its function as the "great hall" of the ruler continued in the reign of the Dark Age chiefs. In the city-states the ancient *megaron* achieved immortality as the basic plan of the Greek temple.

metics—Resident aliens in a Greek state. There were probably metics throughout Greece, but we know only about metics in Athens. Although they lacked citizenship, metics mingled comfortably in Athenian society and were often called on for help in wartime. The women known as *hetairai* were generally metics, although most metic women were housewives.

metropolis—"Mother-city," describing a *polis* that sent out a colony under its aegis. The relationship between the mother-city and the new *polis* was normally very close, combining economic, political, and spiritual ties.

myth—All cultures possess myths, traditional tales that treat aspects of life that are important to the collective group (e.g., marriage, initiation, food, cultural institutions, human–divine relations, etc.). The Greeks had an immensely rich storehouse of such orally transmitted stories going back to the second millennium B.C. and continually infused by additions from the mythologies of the Near East. The Greek historians depended on ancient myths to reconstruct the preliterate past. Modern researchers attempt to glean from them historical or psychological realities.

nomos—Custom or law. Sometimes it corresponds to the English word "mores," connoting a way of doing things that is deeply embedded in a value system. It can also be used, however, in a legal context; thus, for example, the rules laid down by Solon were called his *nomoi*.

nomothetai—A body of Athenian officials established after the restoration of the democracy in 403 B.C. The *nomothetai* reviewed and ratified proposed Athenian laws in a trial-like procedure. The number of *nomothetai* varied depending on the significance of the proposed law, but it could be as high as 1,001.

obol—See currency, Athenian.

oikos—"Household." The fundamental social and economic unit in Greek society, comprising the family group, its house, land, animals, and property, including slaves.

oligarchy—*Oligarchia* ("rule by a few men") was the standard form of government in the early city-states, having replaced the system of ranked chieftains. Opposition from below the narrow ruling circle caused most oligarchies to broaden inclusion in state affairs, while other states adopted democratic governments. Democratic *poleis* were subject to oligarchic revolutions, as in Athens in 411 B.C. and again in 404 B.C. Throughout the fifth and fourth centuries, tension between oligarchs and democrats—which often added up to tension between rich and poor, especially in the difficult economic times of the decades after the Peloponnesian War—was a constant factor in Greek political life and sometimes erupted in bloodshed.

Peloponnesian League—The modern name for a loosely organized group of states led by Sparta and formed some time in the sixth century B.C. Scholars have joked that it was neither Peloponnesian nor a league. It consisted of Sparta and less powerful allied states, who swore to have the same friends and enemies as the Spartans. Thus they were tied to Sparta but not really to each other, and some important members of the League, such as Thebes, were outside the Peloponnesus. The most important member after Sparta was Corinth, which provided naval power. After its victory over Athens in the Peloponnesian War (431–404 B.C.), Sparta increasingly interfered in domestic affairs in allied states, causing substantial friction. The League finally dissolved in the 360s B.C.

peltasts—Lightly armed Greek soldiers who carried light throwing spears and small, round shields. They functioned as skirmishers and could be deployed either alone or in concert with hoplites. Although they were utilized during the Peloponnesian War, they increased dramatically in importance in the fourth century B.C. The Athenian commander Iphicrates owed his successes to his well-trained peltasts.

pentakosiomedimnoi—See Solonic system.

perioikoi—"Those who dwell about," the term used to describe neighboring peoples who were in a subordinate relationship to a dominating *polis*. The most prominent example is Sparta, which treated the people of the perioecic communities of Laconia and Messenia as half-citizens, granting them local autonomy but obligating them to military service and allowing them no say in the conduct of policy.

phalanx—The tactical formation of a hoplite army, consisting in the Archaic and Classical periods of ranks of heavy infantry, usually eight deep. The phalanx underwent change and experiment in the fifth and fourth centuries B.C. The highly successful form of phalanx introduced by Philip II of Macedon consisted of six brigades of fifteen hundred men each, recruited on a regional basis. Macedonian "phalangites" were armed with a short sword, a small round shield, and a long pike (*sarissa*) up to 18 feet long, and they fought in rectangular formations sixteen men deep.

phratry—A subdivision of the tribe (*phyle*) and, at least theoretically, a kin grouping. In Classical times phratries were well-defined social groups concerned with defining descent and therefore citizenship. Every citizen family in Athens belonged to a phratry.

phylai—The term for the large, ancient descent groups into which a *demos* was divided. Ionian communities had four such "tribes," as modern scholars call them, Dorian communities three. The tribes functioned as organizational units in the city-states. In his reform of the Athenian government, Cleisthenes bypassed the four traditional tribes and divided Attica politically and militarily into ten new *phylai*.

polemarch—The office of *polemarchos* ("war leader") was common to many early city-states. As army commander for a specified term, usually a year, and subject to the policy of the aristocratic council, the polemarch was limited in his power. In 500 B.C. at Athens the polemarch was eclipsed by the board of ten *strategoi*, military commanders elected from the ten new *phylai*. After 487 B.C., when the polemarch became appointed by lot, his functions became mainly legal and ceremonial.

polis—"City," "town." Beginning in the eighth century, *polis* came to designate a political community, composed of a principal city or town and its surrounding countryside, which together formed a self-governing entity, the "city-state." The small polis was the principal form of Greek community throughout antiquity, numbering in the high hundreds by the fifth century B.C. *Poleis* were generally governed by some sort of republican government, whether oligarchic or democratic. Since the polis system implied some degree of political self-awareness, it was an open question whether a city ruled by a tyrant could be a polis.

proskynesis—Greek name for the Persian ritual greeting that social inferiors offered to their superiors and all Persians offered to the Persian king. In its simplest form, *proskynesis* involved merely blowing a kiss. Proskynesis to the Persian king, however, required full prostration before the ruler. Although Persians did not believe that their king was divine, Greeks and Macedonians considered the performance of proskynesis to be appropriate only to deities and resented attempts to make them perform it.

proxeny—The term used for a diplomatic arrangement whereby citizens in one state, called *proxenoi*, looked after the interests of other states in their communities. The *proxenos* was highly honored by the foreign state he represented. The system of proxeny (*proxenia*) developed from an earlier system of *xenia* or private "guest-friendship" (q.v.).

prytanis—One of the titles for the presiding magistrate (or a college of magistrates) in a city-state. In the reorganization of the Athenian *boule* (508 B.C.), ten boards of fifty *prytaneis* each, chosen by lot from the ten new "tribes" (*phylai*), took turns as the officials in charge of the daily business of the *boule* and *ekklesia* for a tenth of the year. Each group of fifty men comprised a prytany.

rhetores—The men who chose to involve themselves intensively in Athenian politics during the fourth century, proposing decrees and making speeches in the assembly. It is often translated "politicians," although the term referred to their skill as public speakers.

Royal Pages—The Royal Pages were a body of young men recruited, probably while still in their teens, from the Macedonian aristocracy. The pages lived at the royal court and were the king's personal attendants, guarding him while he slept, accompanying him on hunting expeditions, and performing whatever other tasks he might require of them. The institution was established by Philip II and served as the first step in the career of Macedonian aristocrats.

Sacred Band—Elite Theban infantry formed about 378 B.C. The Sacred Band consisted of 150 pairs of lovers. It played a major role in the Spartan defeat at Leuctra in 371 B.C. and later Theban military campaigns until it was totally destroyed at the Battle of Chaeronea in 338 B.C.

Satrap—Title of the governors of the principal territorial subdivisions of the Persian empire, then of Alexander III's empire, and later of the Seleucid kingdom. During the Peloponnesian War, the coastal satraps Tissaphernes and Pharnabazus enjoyed considerable independence from the king and entered freely into negotiations with the warring states.

satrapy—Originally a province of the Persian empire. Alexander III retained the satrapal system of the Persian empire as the administrative framework of his empire. After the division of Antigonus the One-Eyed's empire in 301 B.C., the term was used to designate the largest territorial subdivisions of the Seleucid kingdom.

Second Athenian Confederacy—A voluntary organization led by Athens which many Greek states joined, some at the inception in 377 B.C. and others later. Though member states sent delegates to a common deliberative body known as the *synedrion* and hence had far greater say in policy decisions than the helpless allies of the Delian League, disaffection nonetheless developed and the alliance began to disintegrate in the late 370s B.C. It suffered substantial defections in the 350s B.C. and was finally dissolved when the Corinthian League was established in 338 B.C.

Solonic system—According to the reforms made early in the sixth century B.C. by Solon, Athenian citizens were allotted political power in accord with the amount their land produced (a figure that correlated roughly with the amount of land they owned). Making use of property classes that had existed for some time, Solon divided citizens into four groups. To qualify for membership in the highest class, the *pentakosiomedimnoi* or "500-measure men," a man needed an estate that produced at least 500 *medimnoi* (bushels) of produce in any combination of oil, wine, or grain. Below these were the *hippeis* ("horsemen," since they were the men who could afford to keep a horse for the cavalry), whose income was more than 299 *medimnoi* but less than 500.

After them came the *zeugitai*, men who could afford to own a team of oxen, with 200 to 299 measures. The lowest class (above the slaves) consisted of the *thetes*, poor people whose land produced fewer than 200 measures; some had no land at all and so produced no measures.

sophists—The itinerant intellectuals who taught and gave speeches during the latter part of the fifth century B.C. Some were primarily teachers of oratory, while others engaged in thoughtful speculation about society that challenged entrenched conventions. Sophists were drawn to the climate of Athens, where response to them was mixed. Plato made the discrediting of the sophists an important part of his dialogues, accusing them of substituting showy rhetorical displays for real wisdom such as Socrates possessed.

stasis—The term first for a group of men who take the same "stand" in a political dispute—a faction—and then by extension the act itself of taking sides. In the city-states, *stasis* (civil strife) occurred between oligarchical factions and between the rich and the poor. At its worst, stasis entailed bloodshed; thus, containing it within nonviolent bounds was a principal objective of the city-states.

stele—A stone slab inscribed with a text, a decoration, or both. Stelae could be used to indicate graves, military victories, or property boundaries. Important texts such as legal decrees and treaties might also be inscribed on them.

strategos—The common term for a "military leader." In the city-states, this office was usually political as well as military. In Athens after 487 B.C., the ten *strategoi* were the only elected high officials (the others being selected by lot); thus most of the powerful politicians of the fifth century were strategoi. In the Hellenistic era, during the reigns of Alexander III, Philip III, and Alexander IV, *strategos* (general) was the title of the highest ranking Macedonian military commander in Europe and Asia.

symposion—In Archaic and later periods the after-dinner "drinking party," made up of a small number (between fourteen and thirty) of men, was a frequent event in adult male social life, primarily among the elite. The *symposion* was an important bonding ritual among young aristocrats and (like the *hetaireiai*, q.v.) was often the occasion of factional plotting. Meaning "drinking together," it is the origin of the English word "symposium."

synoecism (*synoikismos*)— The term used for the process whereby several separate communities were formed into a single political union. Synoecism also referred to the actual movement of people from several communities into a brand new composite settlement.

talent—See currency, Athenian.

thes—The term for a free man who was forced by his poverty to hire out as a laborer for wages. In Athens, according to the economic divisions attributed to Solon (ca. 600 B.C.), the *thetes* (plural) formed the lowest class of citizens.

Thirty Tyrants—The pro-Spartan puppet government installed in Athens by Lysander in 404 B.C. After murdering over a thousand citizens, as well as metics whose property they coveted, the Thirty were overthrown the following year.

trireme—The modern term for the standard form of Greek warship (*trieres*) in the Classical period. Propelled by three banks of oars and attaining speeds of nine knots, the trireme used its bronze ram to disable enemy ships. Athenian oarsmen were the best at this maneuver, and Athenian fleets dominated naval warfare during the fifth century.

tyranny (*tyrannis*)— The illegal seizure and control of governmental power in a *polis* by a single strong man, the "tyrant" (*tyrannos*). Tyranny occurred as a phase in many city-states during the seventh and sixth centuries and is often seen as an intermediate stage between narrow oligarchy and more democratic forms of polity. In the late fifth and the fourth century, a new kind of tyrant, the military dictator, arose, especially in Sicily.

wanax— "Lord," "master." The title of the monarchical ruler of a Mycenaean kingdom. In the form *anax* it appears as the title of gods and high-ranking chiefs in Homer.

xenia—See guest-friendship.

zeugitai—See Solonic system.